D1131528

Studies in Biblical Law

Studies in Biblical Law

BY

DAVID DAUBE

Regius Professor of Civil Law, Oxford University

Would'st thou read Riddles, and their Explanation?

KTAV PUBLISHING HOUSE, INC.

NEW YORK

1969

REPRINT BY PERMISSION OF CAMBRIDGE UNIVERSITY PRESS
FIRST PUBLISHED 1947

Dedicated to

PROFESSOR W. W. BUCKLAND

BS 639
D3
1969

NEW MATTER
© COPYRIGHT 1969
KTAV PUBLISHING HOUSE, INC.

LIBRARY OF CONGRESS CATALOG CARD NUMBER: 70-78503
MANUFACTURED IN THE UNITED STATES OF AMERICA

CONTENTS

PREFACE

The second study contained in this collection, 'Codes and Codas', appeared in *Juridical Review*, 1941, pp. 242 ff. (under the title 'Codes and Codas in the Pentateuch'); but it is here revised. The fourth is in print with the *Sociological Review* (under the title 'Two Notes on Communal Responsibility'), publication being held up during the war. Of the fifth study, 'Summum Ius—Summa Iniuria', the first section appeared in *Cambridge Law Journal*, 1942, pp. 70 ff. (under the title 'How Esau sold His Birthright') and is here revised, while the rest is based on an article in *Tijdschrift Voor Rechtsgeschiedenis*, 1936, pp. 48 ff. (entitled 'Some Comparative Law— Furtum Conceptum'), but is here thoroughly revised and considerably enlarged. I wish to express my thanks to the editors of these journals for allowing me to make use of the articles mentioned.

Otto Lenel, now dead, encouraged me to take up the study of legal history. He guided my first steps—and what an inspiring guide he was!—until at last, when I had to leave, he sent me to his friends in England. Professor W. Kunkel showed me much kindness when I worked under him at Göttingen, and Professor J. Hempel introduced me to Bible criticism. For many years I have been allowed to draw on my brother's, Dr B. Daube's, learning in ancient history and, particularly, Jewish history whenever I found myself in difficulties. Professor C. H. Dodd cannot fail to influence anyone coming into contact with him; he has taught me much about the way of dealing with problems of the New Testament. Professor S. A. Cook has read, and made valuable comments on, most of the typescript. I desire to express my gratitude to the Syndics of the Cambridge University Press for undertaking the publication of this book, and to Mr S. C. Roberts, the Secretary of the Syndics, for his helpful advice.

To two scholars the book is deeply indebted. Professor F. S. Marsh has followed its progress through all stages, with unfailing kindness if sometimes with a firm hand (or should I say, a pair of scissors?). He has made a large number of suggestions which now appear as integral parts of my book. His vast learning, his profound insight into the course of Jewish and early Christian history, and his mastery of the proper methods to be applied to any problem are all put at the disposal of his less fortunate colleagues; yet fortunate enough in being taught the meaning of great and self-effacing scholarship. What I owe to Professor W. W. Buckland is as much as any disciple can owe to his master. Not a line of this would have been written without him. To him, in love, this book is dedicated.

D. D.

CAMBRIDGE
2 *March* 1944

LAW IN THE NARRATIVES

M O S T writers nowadays share Maine's view[1] that law was not always distinguished from religion; and that, originally, all precepts were deemed to be of a religious character. It was God who told you to sacrifice the first-born child or animal, God who told you not to murder, and God who told you to pay your debts. If it be asked how such uncommon agreement is possible, the answer is not difficult to find. The oldest work that a European schoolboy gets to know is the Bible, portions of which go back to the second millennium B.C. Very often it remains the only work of that date he ever sets eyes on. In the Bible as we have it, the emphasis unmistakably lies on the religious side: every action is valued according as it may please or displease God. Small wonder, therefore, that our historians should be prejudiced in favour of the theory under notice, the theory that in the early life of nations all precepts were religious precepts, the separation of law and religion being achieved at a more advanced stage of civilization.

I shall express no opinion as to whether this scheme is tenable or not.[2] Suffice it to call attention to two points which ought to make us very cautious. In the first place, the Bible is the product of one small Eastern community. What is true of that particular community need not be true of others. Should it be correct (I do not say that it is) that the Hebrews did not mark off law from religion, this would not prove that the distinction was unknown to the ancient Egyptians or Babylonians or Chinese or Teutons. In the second place, the Bible, as we have it, is a collection of literature arranged by priests and prophets. Very naturally, they attached the greatest importance to religion; they subordinated law to religion; indeed, they represented legal rules as religious rules, destined to guide God's chosen people. But is it safe to argue that because the devout authors of the Bible saw law as part of religion, law must have formed part of religion in the Hebrew state?

Suppose we could persuade a bishop to write a history of leading English politicians, paying special regard to their merits and demerits as Christians, I doubt whether he would give us an exact account of the Statute of Frauds or the War Damage Act. If he dealt with them at all, he would depict them either as a gift from heaven or as the work of the devil, more probably as the latter. A future scholar who based his estimate of English law on this history and nothing else might reach some strange results: and so do we if we judge Hebrew law merely by what is said about it in the Bible.

It follows that one of the tasks of a legal historian interested in early law is to search, so to speak, beyond the Bible. He has to compare the law of the Bible with other ancient systems and decide, if possible, how far the familiar features of Biblical law are peculiar to the Bible, how far they must be regarded as typical of all ancient law. Proceeding in this way, he might discover that the Hittite code of 1300 B.C., or, say, the Icelandic Grágás of A.D. 1260, contains a fairly pure law, a law, that is, no more interwoven with religion than the Code Napoléon. But comparison is not enough. As pointed out, the Bible is an anthology compiled by priests and prophets, who were neither competent nor even desirous to furnish an accurate exposition of Hebrew law. Consequently, before we start comparing Hebrew law with other primitive systems, we ought to find out something about the true Hebrew law itself. We must separate Hebrew law from the dress in which priests and prophets have handed it down to us; we must, as in a jigsaw puzzle, assemble and combine the scattered fragments; we must supply the large gaps that are left, for example, by going into the non-legal portions of the Bible, into the legends and annals, and examining any legal ideas that may chance to occur there. The conclusion, if we use this method, would perhaps be that a good deal of what is commonly described as the religious character of Biblical law was not from the beginning inherent in that law, but is due to the very special theological tendencies of the authors of the Bible. Furthermore, we should probably find that the influence of religion on law was stronger at one time or in one of the various Hebrew tribes and weaker at another time or in another tribe.

In short, the maxim that law originally was not distinguished from religion, even if confined to the Hebrews, might well turn out to be something of a simplification. All this means, of course, giving much attention to details and putting less trust in general impressions.

Here a word may be said about an argument always stressed by those who would assume a religious origin of Hebrew law: it was the priests, they say, who in the earliest times were entrusted with the administration of justice, and the rest follows. In point of fact, however, the premise itself is quite uncertain. It may well be that, in some tribes at any rate, the 'Judges' were the earliest judges. Moreover, even if it proved true that justice originally was administered by the priests, this need signify no more than that the same superior class performed several important functions. The most daring conclusion to be drawn (a conclusion for which there is a great deal to be said on other grounds) would be that these functions were all considered as belonging to one province, were considered as one whole—let us call it, the defence of order. But why we should infer from it that law sprang from religion rather than that religion sprang from law, it is hard to see. I do not propose to penetrate any further into the labyrinth of this problem. All I intend to do is to submit a few illustrations: first, of how we may reconstruct ancient Hebrew law with the help of the sagas and annals preserved in the Bible; and secondly, of how legal ideas developed into religious ideas under the hands of priests and prophets.

I

First, then, two examples may be adduced of how Biblical tales can be exploited for the purposes of Hebrew legal history. Everybody remembers the story of Joseph, how his father gave him a coat of many colours, how his brothers hated him for it, and how one day they stripped him of his fine coat and sold him to the Ishmaelites. At this point the text continues:[3] 'And they took Joseph's coat, and killed a kid of the goats, and dipped the coat in the blood; and they sent the coat of many colours, and they brought it to their father and said, This have we found, know now whether it be thy son's coat or no. And he knew it and said, It is my son's coat; an evil beast hath devoured him; Joseph is without doubt rent in pieces.' A casual reader of this passage would perhaps assume that Joseph's brothers, when they brought his bloodstained coat to their father, were only choosing one of many possible ways of concealing their crime; and that they might have told any other lie to explain to Jacob the sudden disappearance of his son—except, indeed, for the special subtlety consisting in the use of the hated coat for doing away with the favourite. It can be shown, however, that they had good reasons for adopting precisely that remarkable course.

Candidates for Part I of the Law Tripos know that there were a number of cases in Roman law in which a man was liable for what was technically styled *custodia*. For instance, when you lent an object to a friend of yours, he was liable for *custodia*; that is to say, he had to pay you damages if he mislaid the object or if it was stolen from him—and, of course, if he made away with it—but not if he lost it by *vis maior*, through fire or an earthquake or the like. Hebrew law imposed this kind of liability on a shepherd.[4] A shepherd was responsible for an animal that strayed or was stolen from the herd by a third person. But he was not for an animal that he lost by *force majeure*: he was not compelled to replace an animal that died a natural death, and, above all, he was not compelled to replace one that fell victim to the wild beasts. With respect to the latter case, an old provision, Exodus xxii. 12 (13), runs: 'If it (the animal) be torn in pieces, then let him (the shepherd) bring it (the animal) for witness, and he shall not make good that which was torn.'[5] In other words, a shepherd who could prove, by producing the remnants of the unlucky animal, that it had been destroyed by a wild beast was free from any obligation: the accident was ascribed to *force majeure*, it was not in the power of an ordinary man to guard a herd against wolves and lions.[6] Clearly, from the story of Joseph it may be seen how this rule worked. For it was this rule which his brothers, by analogy, applied to their case, though, needless to mention, they abused it. Having sold Joseph to the Ishmaelites, they dyed his coat red and delivered it to Jacob as the only trace left of his child, just as a shepherd would submit to his master the last few scraps of an animal killed by a wild beast. In this manner they gave him to understand not only that they were innocent of deliberate treachery, but also that they were not to blame even for negligence: Joseph had perished, they suggested, by what the law recognized as an act of God. This by no means excludes the other element determining their action, the wish to make use of the coat that had been Joseph's distinction for his final overthrow. On the contrary, their subtlety in making this use of the coat becomes all the more striking when we consider how plausible everything must have appeared by being based on an idea that was sanctioned by the law.

The exact relation between the provision quoted and the story of Joseph need not concern us. Some such law, it should be recalled, is alluded to in Jacob's dispute with Laban, when Jacob says that throughout the time that he looked after Laban's cattle, he never advanced the excuse that an animal was destroyed by the wild beasts: 'That which was torn of beasts I brought not unto thee.'[7] Some such law obviously determines the procedure adopted by Joseph's brothers—this is all that matters. In point of fact, the law underlying their procedure appears to have been, if not identical with Exodus xxii. 12 (13), at least couched in remarkably similar language. For Jacob, when forced to admit to his sons that a wild beast has caused Joseph's death, uses the same emphatic form as we find in that provision. Literally translated, Exodus xxii. 12 (13) begins, 'If it (the animal) be tear, torn (surely torn) in pieces'; and literally translated, Jacob's words are, 'An evil beast hath devoured him; Joseph is tear, torn (surely torn) in pieces.'[8]

It may be worth adding, in support of the interpretation here attempted, that the narrative contains at least one more . term, and possibly two, the legal implications of which have not, as far as I am aware, hitherto been recognized. The word הכיר, 'to know', 'to discern', is twice used with reference to Jacob's verdict on the evidence submitted to him by the brothers: 'This (the coat) have we found, discern now whether it be thy son's coat or no. And he discerned it.'[9] There can be little doubt that this word was technical of the formal

finding out of, and making a statement to the other party
about, a fact of legal relevance;[10] be it one on which a claim
might be based, or one on account of which a claim must be
abandoned, or one on account of which the other party's
claim must be admitted. The nearest English analogy probably
is 'to find' as used of a jury or the like, 'to find' that an act
is theft, 'to find' that an object in dispute belongs to this or
that person. In the story of Judah and Tamar, the term is
employed in exactly the same way as in that of Joseph: there
is a submission of formal evidence with a request to acknowledge it, and the acknowledgement. Judah has promised Tamar
a kid and given her his signet, bracelets and staff as pledges.
She sends him the things: 'Discern, I pray thee, whose these
are, the signet, and bracelets, and staff. And Judah discerned
them.'[11] The word occurs also in the dispute between Jacob
and Laban, which I have already referred to as of legal
interest. To Laban, who accuses him of theft, Jacob replies
with the invitation, 'Before our brethren discern thou what
is thine with me.'[12] Again the technical meaning is noticeable:
Laban is asked to conduct a *quaestio*, to pick out his things
and declare, 'find', before witnesses what belongs to him.[13]
It is to be remarked that the word seems to have retained its
place in the domain of theft long after the Biblical era, though,
by this time, the formal *quaestio* had gone.[14] It denotes the
'discerning', the discovering and demanding back, of stolen
objects in the famous Mishnah Baba Kamma x. 3, which lays
down that he who 'discerns' things stolen from him with somebody not the thief may pay the price that the other paid for
them and take them. II Samuel iii. 36 should perhaps also
be adduced. David shows all the conventional signs of mourning on Abner's death, in order to demonstrate that he had
nothing to do with the murder: 'and all the people', the Bible
tells us, 'discerned and it pleased them'. It is not impossible
that here, too, 'to discern' has at least a semi-legal meaning.
The people accept David's fast as testimony of his friendship
with the dead man: we have to remember that the forms of
mourning were far stricter in ancient times than they are
now. A free rendering of the verse cited might run: 'And all
the people found according to the evidence and were satisfied.'

In several more passages the term, if it has not its full technical meaning, seems at least coloured by it. It denotes the 'acknowledging' of the firstborn son as entitled to two-thirds of the inheritance in Deuteronomy xxi. 17. This provision insists that if a man has two wives, one beloved and the other hated, and his firstborn son is of the hated, he must not attempt to disown him in favour of the son of the beloved: 'but he shall acknowledge the son of the hated for the firstborn, by giving him a double portion of all that he hath'. The 'acknowledgement' of a certain degree of relationship is referred to also in Deuteronomy xxxiii. 9, where the tribe of Levi is praised for taking sides against the worshippers of the golden calf uninfluenced by any consideration of family ties: 'who said unto his father and to his mother, I have not seen him; neither did he acknowledge his brethren,.nor knew his own children'.[15] In fact, it is possible that there is here a direct allusion to statutes otherwise lost to us. It is clear from Sumerian rules that the formula used to cut off a son was 'Thou art not my son'.[16] Again, severe penalties are imposed by some Sumerian provisions on a son who says to his father or mother, 'Thou art not my father' or 'Thou art not my mother',[17] and the Code of Hammurabi lays down[18] that if an adoptive son commits this offence, his tongue shall be cut out. If similar statutes existed in Hebrew law, Deuteronomy xxxiii. 9 may well have to be interpreted as referring to that formula and as indicating that the Levites disregarded the warnings enjoining loyalty to father and mother for the sake of the more important loyalty to God. (This view does not imply that the terms 'father', 'mother', 'brother' and 'child' may not be used in Deuteronomy xxxiii. 9 in a wider sense, denoting any kind of friendly relationship.) In Ruth ii. 10 and 19, הכיר signifies something like 'to acknowledge as ξένος, גר, as a person to be protected'. Boaz, who is as yet unaware of his special claim to Ruth, allows her to glean in his field and eat with his servants, and charges his young men not to touch her. 'Then she fell on her face. . .and said unto him, Why have I found grace in thine eyes, that thou shouldest acknowledge me, seeing that I am a stranger?. . .And her mother in law said unto her, Where hast thou gleaned today?. . .Blessed be he that did

acknowledge thee.' Even where it is a question of the relationship between God and His people, the legal force of the term
may be at the back of the writer's mind. Isaiah urges that
God is a stronger and more reliable father of the nation than
even the patriarchs.[19] 'Doubtless thou art our father, though
Abraham be ignorant of us, and Israel acknowledge us not:
thou, O Lord, art our father, our redeemer.' We have to
consider that the term 'redeemer' also is here of legal force:
it was the legal duty of a man to 'redeem' his relatives from
the worst situations of distress.[20] 'Thus saith the Lord',
Jeremiah exclaims, 'the God of Israel; like these good figs, so
will I acknowledge them that are carried away captive of
Judah.'[21] And the Psalmist says:[22] 'I looked on my right
hand, and beheld, but there was no man that would acknowledge me...I cried unto thee...Thou art my refuge.' 'To
acknowledge a man as entitled to the privileges of his rank'
would be a possible rendering of the term in those rules which
warn us not to 'acknowledge a face' when administering
justice, that is to say, not to consider wealth and distinction;[23]
as also in Job xxxiv. 19,[24] a passage dwelling on the futility
of quarrelling with God 'that accepteth not the faces of princes
nor acknowledgeth the rich more than the poor, for they all
are the work of his hands'.[25] The meaning 'to acknowledge
as a god' is to be found in Daniel xi. 39, in the course of the
account of the terrible king of the north and the 'strange god
whom he shall acknowledge'. Possibly, the noun מכר might
here be mentioned, if it is a derivative of the verb discussed.[26]
This noun occurs in II Kings xii. 6, 8 (5, 7) and is usually interpreted as signifying 'acquaintance'. The context renders it
probable, however, that it means something stronger; that is
to say, not just 'the acquaintance' of a priest, but 'a man
acknowledging' a priest. The priests concerned, it seems, each
had a group of men who would go to him and no other when
they wanted, or had, to bring an offering, perform any ceremony in the temple or get anything from there.[27]

　　Actually, we might, I feel, miss a subtlety in the narrative
of Joseph's disappearance if we do not do justice to the term
הכיר, 'to discern'. It signifies, as stated above, the formal
finding out of, and making a declaration about, a fact of legal

relevance. In the case of Jacob, it very much looks as if his 'discerning', his acceptance of the evidence presented by his sons, were nothing but formal. He has to accept it, he has to 'discern' it in the technical sense, but he does not really believe in it. 'If the animal be torn in pieces', the law says, 'then let the shepherd bring it for witness, and he shall not make good that which was torn.' Jacob's sons do bring for witness what can only be regarded as the remnants of Joseph, and Jacob must 'find' in their favour. Yet he does not trust them. This is strongly suggested by his reluctance, some time later, to let Benjamin, the only other son by Rachel who is left to him, go to Egypt with his brothers, for fear that he might vanish like Joseph. As we shall see, he allows him to go only after his brothers have unreservedly bound themselves to bring him back and not to invoke even *force majeure* should they fail to do so.[28] We have further to consider the highly ambiguous wording of the explanation that Jacob offers to his sons of his fear for Benjamin. As they later tell Joseph when he examines them, this is how Jacob expresses himself:[29] 'The one (Joseph) went out from me, and'—now we should expect 'he was torn in pieces', but he continues slightly differently—'I said, he is tear, torn in pieces.' This 'I said' can hardly mean anything else than 'I had to say', 'I had to admit'. Nor is this all. Jacob adds, 'and I saw him not since'. Of course not: Joseph is supposed to be dead. Why should he make this remark if he were not unconvinced at heart? The narrative goes back to an age when evidence was of a formalistic nature. It is in consequence of this that there may be a discrepancy between what a man has to admit, 'to find', and what he actually believes to be the true position. You have only to offer a certain prescribed proof to be acquitted, you have only to fail in furnishing the prescribed proof and you are deemed guilty: no further investigations as to the possibility of particular, exceptional circumstances are made. In the case under discussion, once you produce the remnants of the animal—or man—killed by the wild beasts, no charge can be brought against you.[30] But this does not mean that your antagonist may not have his suspicions. It is several times in the course of the story of Joseph that a com-

plicated and psychologically interesting situation arises as a
result of the prevalence of this formalistic principle.[31] It may
be well to mention at this stage that every narrative of the
Bible is not capable of such a minute exegesis. The story of
Joseph, however, is one of those highly refined pieces of literature in which clever devices, subtle allusions and the like may
be expected.

The other term that may perhaps be considered in this connection, as having a technical flavour about it, is אָסוֹן, 'mischief', 'disaster'. It comes no less than three times in the
story of Joseph, always denoting the 'disaster' that Jacob
is afraid will overtake Benjamin should he accompany his
brothers to Egypt.[32] Jastrow's Dictionary suggests a genetic connection with אוֹנֶס , which, in Rabbinic legal literature, is the
technical term for a disaster brought about by *force majeure*,
through events beyond anybody's control. It is frequent precisely in the discussions of the rule that a shepherd need not
replace an animal lost through such a disaster; the very rule of
which, as we have seen, Joseph's brothers treacherously avail
themselves for getting him out of the way unpunished.
Mishnah Baba Metzia vii. 9 f., for example, says: 'If one wolf
attacks a flock, it does not count as אוֹנֶס , as *force majeure,*
but two wolves count as *force majeure....* A brigand counts
as *force majeure....* If an animal dies a natural death, this
counts as *force majeure*, but not if it dies of cruel treatment.'[33]
Evidently, if we hold that this technical meaning is hinted at
in the three passages from the story of Joseph which contain
אָסוֹן , they gain not a little in significance. The first of them,
for instance, would have to be rendered thus:[34] 'But Benjamin,
Joseph's brother, Jacob sent not with his brethren; for he
said, Lest peradventure אָסוֹן, "mischief by *force majeure*",
"another disaster such as happened to Joseph, which can be
considered nobody's fault", befall him.' Jacob (on the basis
of this interpretation) of course has in mind, though he carefully refrains from saying, 'another *force majeure* engineered'.
On the other hand, it must be noted that the noun אָסוֹן, in
the only chapter outside the story of Joseph where it occurs
in the Old Testament, is not used in a technical sense, though,
curiously, the context is again legal.[35] Nor is it used as a
technical legal term in Sirach.[36] Despite the solid Rabbinic

testimony, therefore, it remains doubtful whether it is technical in the story of Joseph.[37] If we assume that אונס did not
become a term of law until the Rabbinic period, the question
arises whether the Rabbis, in giving it the sense of *force
majeure*, were perhaps influenced by the Roman legal term
casus. *Casus,* it may be noted, may mean 'accident' either in the
sense of 'disaster' or in the sense of 'unpredictable and unprevent-
able occurrence'. However, though it is tempting to suppose a
connection between the Hebrew term and the Roman, an independent development of the former is more plausible.

To return to the plan thought out by Joseph's brothers,
possibly (but this I put forward with all reserve) we may go
a step further than I have done so far. Joseph's brothers based
themselves on the law regulating, and limiting, the liability
of a shepherd. There are indications that their analogy, the
analogy between an elder brother and a shepherd, was more
than just an ingenious notion hit upon on the spur of the
moment; and that at some period an elder brother was definitely bound, if not by law at any rate by custom, to answer
for his younger brother to very much the same extent as a
shepherd had to answer for his herd. In the epoch of polygamy,
when brothers might differ widely in age and strength and not
even have the same family connections, the advantages of a
rule establishing some kind of responsibility must be considerable. Indirect evidence for such a system can perhaps
be derived from institutions like the guardianship of brothers
over their sisters. This, as is well known, was very common
in the old Orient and no doubt implied duties, and above all
a duty to protect, as well as rights.[38] It might perhaps be
argued that this evidence is not too strong. For the guardianship of brothers over their sisters in all probability originated
in certain rights of the former to the property or persons of
the latter, possibly even in the right of the former to marry
the latter. But, then, we do not know whether the guardianship of elder brothers over the younger does not also go back
to economic rights.[39] Another institution that might be worth
investigating for traces of a guardianship of elder brothers
over the younger is artificial brotherhood, in particular blood

brotherhood. Blood brothers not infrequently made themselves responsible one for the other's life, a practice conceivably modelled, to some extent, on a law governing the relations between ordinary brothers. It is true that the practice may well have been introduced simply in imitation, and elevation, of the love and care that ordinary brothers would naturally show for one another while on good terms. Maybe one should here also adduce, as a remote offshoot of the system postulated, the religious idea that the members of a community are brothers and as such answerable for one another to God. It must be admitted that, in its polished literary form at least, this idea appears remarkably late—not, as far as I can see, before the Rabbinic age.[40] This does not prove, however, that it cannot have existed in substance long before, and, indeed, its rudiments may be discovered in earlier literature.[41]

Some less vague evidence, however, is not lacking. To take the story of Joseph itself, it contains several incidents besides the one discussed (the production of Joseph's bloodstained coat after the manner of shepherds) in which it may be right to see vestiges of a rule that elder brothers are responsible for the younger. We are told how Reuben, not present when the other brothers sold Joseph, on noticing that Joseph had gone, 'rent his clothes; and he returned unto his brethren, and said, The child is not (is no longer there); and I, whither shall I go?'[42] This behaviour and language seem to have sprung from a definite feeling of special responsibility. In the other passages to be cited—they relate to Reuben's and Judah's responsibility for Benjamin[43]—the position, it is true, is not quite the same: the responsibility of Reuben and Judah for Benjamin, in contradistinction to that for Joseph, rested on an express undertaking, an express promise given by them to Jacob. One might perhaps argue, therefore, that it cannot be considered as reflecting any established practice. This conclusion, however, is not absolutely decisive. For, first of all, in ancient times, the express undertaking of a responsibility does not necessarily imply that no responsibility would exist even without this undertaking. We have dozens of documents, Babylonian, Roman and others, with clauses by which the parties appear simply to agree to observe the law or custom of the land. Secondly, in the case under notice, the case of the negotiations between Jacob and his sons as to whether Benjamin was to go with them to Egypt, obviously there were reasons of a particular kind why the obligation of the sons should be confirmed once again even if it was laid down by the law itself: they had proved none too reliable when in charge of Joseph. Thirdly, it must not be overlooked that the responsibility undertaken by Reuben and Judah for Benjamin was of an exceptionally strict character. It was what lawyers usually call an 'absolute' responsibility, including even *vis maior*. Reuben and Judah, that is, declared that if they did not bring Benjamin back safe and sound, whatever the cause of their failure, they were willing to be held liable; they were not, for example, to be entitled even to plead an attack by a wild beast. This 'absolute' responsibility, indeed, would not be imposed on them by law or custom. It far exceeded the responsibility of a shepherd, and this alone would explain the necessity of its being expressly assumed. Why Jacob wished his sons to be accountable for Benjamin without the normal limitations has been shown above.[44] He knew, at heart, that they had abused these limitations in the affair of Joseph, and for that matter, they knew that he knew: it was not he who first required, but they who first offered him, that 'absolute', extraordinary guarantee about Benjamin.[45]

Be this as it may, if the suggestion here tentatively advanced is correct, if there existed a practice of holding an elder brother responsible for the younger, a well-known text acquires a more pregnant meaning than it has hitherto been credited with. When Cain, after murdering Abel, was asked by God, 'Where is Abel, thy brother?', he answered, 'I know not: am I my brother's keeper?'[46] It is not inconceivable that Cain here disclaimed an obligation under which the law or custom of the time put him. The Hebrew word for 'keeper', שֹׁמֵר, is used in legal language of a person entrusted with the custody and care of an object, and, accordingly, of a shepherd who has to 'keep' his flock. The *locus classicus* is the old provisions Exodus xxii. 6 (7) ff. It is under the influence of this section that the term שֹׁמֵר has become quite technical of a bailee in Talmudic law, more precisely, of one to whom goods

14   *Law in the Narratives*

are confided under a contract of *depositum, commodatum* or
locatio conductio.[47] But even in Biblical language it is technical
at least of the task of a shepherd. Jacob, undertaking to look
after Laban's herds for another seven years, said, 'I will again
feed thy flock and keep.'[48] The addition 'and keep' may well be
more than a pure pleonasm.[49] It may well be, seeing that the
whole narrative is permeated with legal thought, an expression
of Jacob's consent to be liable under the laws concerning the
'keeping', the guarding of sheep. Again, when David left his
father's flock to join the army of King Saul, he 'rose up early
in the morning, and left the sheep with a keeper'. Nor was
it superfluous for him to make proper arrangements with a
trustworthy shepherd, for the first question that his angry
brother asked him when he arrived in the camp was, 'And
with whom hast thou left those few sheep?'[50] Hosea, alluding
to Jacob's service with Laban, says: 'And Israel served for
a wife, and for a wife he kept (Laban's sheep). And by a
prophet the Lord brought Israel out of Egypt, and by a
prophet was he kept.'[51] This passage not only gives us another
example of 'to keep' in the technical sense here discussed (the
verb means 'to keep a herd' though no object—'sheep' or
'herd'—is stated); it also shows that when God 'keeps' Israel,
the relationship referred to may be that between a shepherd
and his sheep. This is confirmed by other texts, for instance,
Jeremiah xxxi. 9 (10), 'He that scattered Israel will gather him,
and keep him, as a shepherd doth his flock.' The word occurs
in other contracts by which a man is entrusted with an object,
but none of them is mentioned as frequently as that of the
shepherd and there is not always enough evidence to make it
certain that we have before us really technical usage. An
interesting case where it is certain is I Kings xx. 39.[52] Here
the prophet, in a parable, tells the king how he was in the
midst of the battle when another soldier came up to him,
charging him with a prisoner: 'Keep this man; if by any means
he be missing, then shall thy life be for his life.' This is legal
language, and that 'to keep' has technical force in arrangements of this kind is clear from the fact that משמר, derived
from שמר, 'to keep', signifies 'prison'.[53] In the domain of what
to-day would be described as public law or administration,

the word is technical of a number of offices such as that of the watchman who has to 'keep, guard' the city[54] or him who has to look after an army's baggage, the 'keeper of the carriage',[55] or the guard 'keeping, guarding' the palace and person of the king.[56] In the numerous passages calling God or His prophets 'keepers' of the people, the metaphor, while it often has regard to the activities and attitude of a shepherd (this is the case in the two texts from Hosea and Jeremiah just quoted), may also have regard to other kinds of 'keeper', the guard of a king, for example, or even the watchman of a city.[57] In view of these uses of the term 'to keep', it does look as if the frightful thing about Cain's reply had been that he bluntly repudiated the normal duties of an elder brother. Whether these duties are here thought of as analogous to a shepherd's, as they seem to be in the story of Joseph, or, say, to a military bodyguard's, we have no means of knowing. The point is that the existence of a special responsibility of some sort or other appears implied.

It would lead too far afield here to examine precisely under what conditions the responsibility of an elder brother arose: of what age he had to be, of what age his younger brother; whether they had to be of different mothers, as they were in the case of Joseph; what their respective positions as to the inheritance had to be, and so on. I am afraid, even if I did go into these questions, I should not get far beyond the stage of conjecture. Nor shall I deal with the problem of what were the normal penalties if an elder brother neglected his duty. That at least wilful murder of one brother by another was avenged in the usual way, without regard to the double loss thus caused to the family, may be gathered from several texts;[58] and Reuben, when he assumed 'absolute' responsibility for Benjamin's safety, offered Jacob the heads of his two boys should Benjamin not return—'Slay my two sons if I bring him not to thee.'[59] Apparently Jacob was supposed, if he lost his son Benjamin, to seek compensation by putting to death his two grandsons by Reuben. In any case, there can be no question as to the principal fact: the scheme by which Joseph's brothers established their innocence was carefully designed so as to satisfy the law of *custodia*.

II

This has been a case of a narrative showing how a certain
provision that we find in the Bible operated in practice. There
is preserved in Exodus an old law respecting the liability of a
shepherd, and from the story of Joseph, where the law is
applied to an analogous situation, we may see the way in
which it was handled. Let us next consider a case where a
narrative is our only source of information, where the Bible
has no express law on the matter whatever.

Once more I may proceed from Roman law, as being familiar
to many lawyers, though close parallels might be adduced
from several other systems.[60] In Roman law there was an
agreement called *locatio conductio rei*, the letting and hiring,
at a price, of an object to be used and enjoyed. (It must be
at a price, for if I lent you an object free of charge, the contract
was *commodatum*, with different rules.) It was *locatio conductio rei*, for instance, if I hired your house or ship for two
years at a yearly rent of 10 *sestertia*; or if I hired your mule
for half a day's journey at the price of 5 *denarii*; or if I hired
your slave to recite Homer to my guests and paid you
2 *sestertia*.[61] In the Bible not a single provision is left concerning this kind of agreement. According to Rabbinic interpretation, it is true, there is one, namely, the brief and difficult
clause Exodus xxii. 14*b* (15*b*); and it is Rabbinic interpretation, ultimately, which underlies our English version, 'If it be
an hired thing, it came for his hire.' But the original meaning
of שכיר (as opposed to that laid down for this passage by the
Rabbis and consequently accepted in the orthodox Jewish
system), here as everywhere else, seems to be 'paid labourer',
'hired man', not 'hired': the word is a noun denoting the
member of a certain profession, not an adjective referring to
a piece of property.[62] Accordingly, the last word of the clause
in question, שכרו, must be translated as 'the wages of a
labourer', not as 'the rent for a hired thing'.[63] It follows that,
taken in its original sense, that is to say, severed from Rabbinic
interpretation, the provision in Exodus has regard to *locatio
conductio operarum*, not *rei*, the letting and hiring of services,
not of an object: the difference will be illustrated presently.

A possible rendering would be: 'If he (the borrower of the cattle that has suffered damage or died) be a labourer (employed and paid by the owner of the cattle), it shall be set against his hire (he shall make amends up to the amount of his wages).'[64]

We have, then, to put up with the fact that the Bible does not explicitly regulate *locatio conductio rei*. The priests and prophets who composed the Bible were not deeply interested in private law, they did not bother to create a *Corpus Juris Civilis*. It is none the less possible to demonstrate that this kind of agreement did exist in Biblical times. We might perhaps have guessed it, on the basis of comparative law[65] and in view of the fact that *locatio conductio rei* appears as a well-established form of hire in the earliest post-Biblical Rabbinic documents on matters legal.[66] But we have more direct evidence than that. The Bible itself contains, though no express provision, yet a tale—and, be it noted, one tale only—in which allusion is made to *locatio conductio rei*, the letting and hiring of an object. It is the tale of Reuben's mandrakes.[67]

Before going any further, however, it may not be out of place briefly to discuss another variety of *locatio conductio*, to wit, the agreement that the Romans named *locatio conductio operarum*, the letting and hiring, at a price, of services. (It must be at a price, for if I undertook a service for you free of charge, the contract was *mandatum*, with different rules.) It is necessary here to distinguish it from the type of agreement described above, since *locatio conductio operarum*, indeed, occurs very frequently in the Bible. There are a number of rules about it in the Pentateuch, and examples of it may be found in many parts of the Old Testament, the best known probably being Jacob's seven years' service with Laban undertaken for Rachel's sake.[68] The difference between *locatio conductio rei* and *locatio conductio operarum*, as may be gathered from the terms themselves, was that whereas the former meant the letting by *A* to *B* of an object (a house, a mule, a slave), the latter meant the letting by *A* to *B* of his own services (for instance, a man's becoming another man's secretary or gardener). To make this quite clear, if you let me your slave to help me in the harvest, the contract was *locatio conductio rei*;[69] if you, a free man, took service with me yourself during the harvest, the contract was *locatio conductio operarum*. As I said, *locatio conductio operarum* is often to be met with in the Bible. I have already adduced the case of Jacob in the employ of Laban, and also Exodus xxii. 14*b* (15*b*), a provision concerning the liability of a labourer who works with his employer's cattle. Injunctions in favour of the hireling are numerous and well known: I need mention only those condemning oppression of the hired labourer and insisting that his wages should be paid to him at the appointed time.[70] There is legislation setting limits to the participation of alien labourers in religious ceremonies, and so on.[71] In fact, how common an agreement *locatio conductio operarum* was is manifest from the way in which certain transactions of the public law, or international law, were brought under this heading. We come across quite a few references to the 'hiring' of mercenaries, native or foreign,[72] and even to one king's 'hiring' of another king, which means the purchase of an alliance.[73] Religion also borrowed a term from the agreement under notice: the reward that the faithful receive from God is called 'hire', 'wages'— the faithful are God's labourers.[74] One text dominated by this idea will be discussed at some length below.[75] Again, to pay someone in order to gain him as an accomplice in a mischievous design, to bribe someone and the like, can be 'to hire' in Biblical language.[76] All these references are to *locatio conductio operarum*, the letting and hiring of services. It is *locatio conductio rei*, the letting and hiring of an object, which, by some freak of history, has left its trace only in a single narrative.

One result which immediately follows once we realize that this narrative alludes to *locatio conductio rei* may here be anticipated. It is the discovery that Biblical law, like Roman, had the same term for both types of letting and hiring. The same term שׂכר, that is, like *locare conducere*, was applied to both *locatio conductio operarum* and *locatio conductio rei*: and, incidentally, this use of שׂכר as the common appellation continues in the Talmud.[77] It is merely saying this in other words to claim that the Hebrews, like the Romans, made no fundamental distinction between *locatio conductio rei* and *locatio conductio operarum*. The letting and hiring of an object, a

house, a horse or a slave, and the letting and hiring of services,
a man becoming another man's gardener or secretary, in their
eyes were essentially the same kind of agreement. Actually,
in view of this result, it may be slightly ambiguous if I assert
that the story of Reuben's mandrakes proves the existence in
Biblical law of two types of agreement, that is to say, of
locatio conductio rei (referred to only here) as well as *locatio
conductio operarum*. To avoid any misunderstandings one ought
perhaps to say rather that this story proves the wide scope
in Biblical law of the agreement of שכר, of *locatio conductio*: it
embraced what we call *locatio conductio rei* as well as what we
call *locatio conductio operarum*. That, in physical reality, the
letting and hiring of an object was something different from
the letting and hiring of services was, of course, seen by both
Hebrews and Romans.[78] Here may be the place to point out
that the old Babylonian law also subsumed under the same
notion of letting and hiring, and used the same term for, both
the letting and hiring of an object and the letting and hiring
of services, welcome confirmation of the conclusion here advocated. (Greek law also had one term covering all types of
hire, μίσθωσις.[79]) In fact, there is some evidence that, in old
Babylonian law at least, the letting and hiring of services was
evolved from the letting and hiring of an object. More precisely, on the letting by *A* to *B* of *A*'s slave, a case of *locatio
conductio rei*, seems to have been modelled the letting by *A*
to *B* of himself, the case of *locatio conductio operarum*.[80]
Whether or not this was also the evolution of the Hebrew law
of *locatio conductio* need not here be examined. Very possibly
it was, though I am not in favour of postulating a certain
development in one system merely because we find it in
another related system.

If we now turn to the episode of Reuben's mandrakes,
Jacob had two wives, Leah and Rachel, of whom he loved
Rachel best. One day, Leah's son Reuben presented his
mother with fresh mandrakes, a fruit that was, and up to
this day is, supposed by the Orientals to make anyone
partaking of it love the giver. Rachel, eager to have some of
them, asked Leah to share them with her. Here the text goes
on:[81] 'And she (Leah) said unto her (Rachel), Is it a small

matter that thou hast taken my husband? and wouldest
thou take away my son's mandrakes also? And Rachel said,
Therefore he (Jacob) shall lie with thee tonight for thy son's
mandrakes. And Jacob came out of the field in the evening,
and Leah went out to meet him and said, Thou must come
in unto me; for surely I have hired thee with my son's mandrakes. And he lay with her that night. And God hearkened
unto Leah, and she conceived.' Obviously, Leah, in her
speech, used a legal metaphor; and she referred to nothing
else than *locatio conductio rei*. If we analyse her comparison,
Jacob was the *res*, the object of the compact: Rachel was his
owner, she owned him as one might own a slave: and Leah,
if she wanted to spend the night with him, had to hire that
slave from his mistress, had to hire him at the price of her
mandrakes. I have outlined above[82] the difference between
locatio conductio rei and *locatio conductio operarum*. The bargain
in question is concluded between Rachel and Leah, Jacob
being merely its passive object. This corresponds to the letting
by *A* to *B* of a thing, in this case, a slave—*locatio conductio rei*.
If, for instance, Leah had extracted a promise to be with her
from Jacob himself, then it would have been analogous to
the letting by *A* to *B* of his own services, *locatio conductio
operarum*.[83]

In the latest edition of Gesenius's standard dictionary, we
get a somewhat misleading translation of the decisive clause
of the passage quoted. The dictionary, while rendering the
verb שׂכר by 'to hire' in all other texts,[84] in this one text,
for reasons unknown to me, renders it by *kaufen*, 'to buy'
(adding that it is here used figuratively). In other words, as
translation of the final clause of Leah's speech it proposes,
'for surely I have bought thee with my son's mandrakes',
not 'I have hired thee'. Possibly, this translation was chosen
under the influence of Luther's version, *ich habe dich erkauft*.
Yet there is much less to be said against Luther's translation
than that of the *Handwörterbuch*. The former uses the verb
erkaufen, the latter *kaufen*, and the difference, though slight,
is by no means negligible. Luther's *erkaufen* differs from
Gesenius's *kaufen* in that it is no legal term. It does not mean
'to buy' in the proper sense and is employed only in more or

less poetical language; with reference, for instance, to the gaining of a man's friendship by doing him a good turn, or the attaining of one's object through heavy sacrifices. Luther's translation, therefore, as compared with that of the *Hand-wörterbuch*, has at least the negative advantage that it does not suggest a direct analogy between the bargain of the two women and the legal contract of buying and selling. I do not think, however, that Gesenius means what he appears to mean, namely, that the metaphor introduced by Leah was not based on the ordinary sense of שכר, on the sense of 'to hire': and if he does mean this, his view cannot be accepted. Leah did not 'buy' Jacob, not even metaphorically—though no doubt she might have chosen this metaphor had she wished to, but in that case the whole sense of what she said would be different; she did not acquire him for good. She only 'hired' him: the right that she obtained for her mandrakes was of a subordinate and temporary nature. Rachel still remained Jacob's owner, and Leah got him for a short while only. To put *kaufen*, 'to buy', instead of *mieten*, 'to hire', is to obscure an element in Leah's speech which, in a subtle way, is pathetic at once and sarcastic.[85] The A.V.'s use of 'to hire' ('for surely I have hired thee'), therefore, is far preferable even to Luther's rendering. 'To hire' accurately represents the Hebrew שכר: as the Hebrew text suggests a direct analogy between the bargain of the two women and the legal contract of letting and hiring, a translation ought to do the same.[86] I do not mean to say that there is any highly technical point in this story, as there certainly is in that of Joseph's coat discussed above. What I do think may be maintained is that Leah would hardly have described herself as hiring Jacob from Rachel, however natural such a figure of speech may sound to us, unless the agreement of *locatio conductio rei* had been known from actual law. We must remember that it was Issachar who was conceived in that night. The second half of the name 'Issachar' comes from שכר, 'hire' (in the sense of 'hiring' or that of 'wages'). If whoever recorded the incident of the mandrakes did so with this name in mind—and modern commentators are agreed on the point—some moderately legal features are only to be expected.

Such features, at any rate, are present also in the narrative of Issachar's naming,[87] where we find the Bible's main and direct explanation of the name. Only, there, the reference is to *locatio conductio operarum*, not *rei*. It may perhaps be useful, for the sake of contrast, to give a short account of that other story. Issachar, the Bible says, obtained his name in the following way. Leah, having given birth to four sons, bore no more children for some time. She therefore lent her husband Zilpah, her maid, to have children from. After a while, however, she herself had another son. 'And Leah', thus the narrative continues,[88] 'said, God hath given me my hire, because I have given my maiden to my husband: and she called his name Issachar.' I have observed above[89] that the reward that a man receives from God for his good works is often called 'hire' in the Bible, almost as if there existed a contract of *locatio conductio operarum* between them. It is this notion that governs the story of Issachar's naming. Leah, in offering Zilpah to Jacob, did her duty like a good servant of God: God, her master, she concluded, gave her her pay, her 'hire', in the form of a son of her own. A far later piece of literature, Psalm cxxvii. 3, says, quite generally, that children are God's reward, God's 'hire', for his favourites. I should like to remark, however, that while for the sake of clarity I emphasize here the legal background of these metaphors, I am not suggesting that the Psalmist, for instance, may not have used the term 'hire' in a very spiritual sense and have been almost unaware, on this occasion, of its worldly connections.

From a rough comparison of the two episodes of the mandrakes and the naming, these points seem to emerge. (1) In both episodes the idea of letting and hiring is prominent. This similarity is inevitable if both are intended to account for Issachar's name, which is derived from שכר, 'hire' (be it 'to hire' or 'wages'). (2) In both episodes the transaction construed by Leah as letting and hiring has regard to her married life: the arrangement with Rachel about Jacob in the one, the lending Zilpah to her husband in the other. This similarity also is not surprising. Nearly all Biblical tales about the wives of the patriarchs relate to their doings and sufferings as wives, their experiences with husbands and children. (What a difference between the lives of Sarah, Rebekah, Leah and Rachel on the one hand and those of, say, Bathsheba and Jezebel on the other!) In the tales of Leah and Rachel this tendency is perhaps most strongly noticeable. It would naturally dominate a narrative concerning the birth of a child. (3) Wherever the two stories can differ, they do. They differ in the particular transaction interpreted as *locatio conductio*. In the first story, Rachel temporarily hands Jacob over to Leah in order to get her mandrakes. In the second Leah does her duty which she owes to God, bestows her maid on Jacob, and is requited by God with a son. (4) Further, the interpretation as *locatio conductio* of the first transaction strikes one as quite unique, of the second as rather more ordinary. Leah's description of Jacob, ceded to her for one night, as 'hired' seems a most remarkable *jeu d'esprit*. Her description of Issachar as the 'hire' paid to her by God for a good deed is only the application to her particular case of an idea that was no doubt common from a fairly early date. (5) Leah's description of Jacob as hired is founded on the verbal sense of שכר, 'to hire': 'for surely I have hired thee'. Her description of Issachar as her hire from God is founded on שכר *qua* noun, 'hire', 'wages': 'God hath given me my hire'. (6) Finally, the point of difference concerning us most is the appearance in the two stories of two different varieties of letting and hiring. In the story of Issachar's naming (to begin with the second), Leah likens the position to *locatio conductio operarum*. If we pursue her analogy, she has let her services to God; by giving Zilpah to Jacob, she has acted in accordance with her contract, has performed her part of it, has done a deed pleasing to God: and now she receives Issachar as her wages, as the price paid to her by her employer. In the story of Reuben's mandrakes, she likens the position to *locatio conductio rei*. She here speaks of Rachel as Jacob's owner, as letting this object, this servant, to her; of herself as hiring him; and of the mandrakes as the price she has to pay for the privilege.

As has been stated above, it is in this episode of Reuben's mandrakes that we come across the only Biblical trace of *locatio conductio rei*, the letting and hiring of an object. Thus, to sum up, the episode of the mandrakes, besides allowing us an insight into the tragi-comic dealings that took place in a harem between the favourite and the neglected, fills a gap in ancient Hebrew law which, without it, would remain a matter for conjecture. Conversely, it should be noted that unless we realize what was the basis for Leah's metaphor— 'for surely I have hired thee with my son's mandrakes'— namely, *locatio conductio rei*, we shall not be able to appreciate her speech and all the irony that it implied. For that matter, it is not unimportant to see the legal background to the story of Issachar's naming and to bear in mind that Leah, on that occasion, introduced the concept of *locatio conductio operarum*. She referred, that is, to her lending of Zilpah to Jacob as to a service done for God, for which she expected her 'hire'. Why? Was it not perfectly usual for a wife, once she could bear children no longer, to allow her husband to have children from her maid? Were not the children thus borne by the maid to some extent even regarded as children of the wife herself? And yet, Leah looked upon Issachar as her special reward, 'because I have given my maiden to my husband'. This little story is as good as a psychological tractate. That custom of providing the husband with a younger companion could not but cause bitter pain to the wife who complied with it. Indeed, she must feel that she was conducting herself with great unselfishness and piety: and she would hope to be blessed for it by God. Modern commentators sometimes incline to deny any tenderness of feeling in ancient nomads. But if an early narrative confines itself to listing external events, this must not be taken as an indication that the people concerned were less affected by them than the characters in a novel of Stendhal. The narrative of Issachar's naming, properly interpreted, furnishes good evidence to the contrary.

III

I now go on to the second class of examples which I mentioned in the beginning. It may be well briefly to recall where we stand. I started by saying that if the Bible we have before us makes law form part of religion, this proves little as far

as the ancient Hebrew state is concerned. The authors of the
Bible were theologians, and it is not surprising that they
treated the law somewhat cavalierly. So far, I have attempted
to show how, by casting our nets in the non-legal narrative
sections of the Bible, we can, to a certain degree, recover the
law. I shall now submit two cases from which it may be seen
how priests and prophets, with their theology, obscured the
legal substance of history and legend, or even entirely transferred legal concepts into the religious sphere. Of the latter
process, I have indeed offered an illustration already: the
notion of *locatio conductio operarum*, of letting and hiring
services, found its way, we have seen, into religion and was
there applied to the relationship between man, God's labourer,
and God, the employer who will pay him his reward. (The
notion of God as 'keeper', 'guardian', of His people also has
some at least of its roots in the law, as pointed out above.)
It is commonly maintained that religion came first and law
followed. In the two cases that I am going to investigate one
might say that law came first and religion followed.

Moses died, we learn from the Bible, before Palestine, the
promised land, was reached. Surely, this fact must have
excited the imagination of many a Hebrew poet: what a
terrible thing that the man who delivered his people from
Egyptian slavery and led them through all the perils of the
desert should not have marched with them into their country!
In the Bible, indeed, the death of Moses, at the threshold of
Palestine, is mentioned and commented upon in no fewer than
nine or ten different places,[90] and the relevant passages in the
Talmud and Midrash are far more numerous still. Now what
view did the authors of the Bible take of that event? It is
clear that they regarded it under a chiefly theological aspect.
According to the Bible, in its present form, it was for a sin
which he had committed that Moses died prematurely, before
reaching his goal.[91] He was allowed to behold the land from
afar, but, having offended God on an important occasion, he
was not allowed to go there. The final scene, when the great
general, alone on the summit of a mountain, looks down on
Palestine, well knowing that he will never enter it, is splendid
tragedy. Some of the text may be quoted:[92] 'And Moses went

up from the plains of Moab unto the mountain of Nebo.... And
the Lord showed him all the land.... And the Lord said unto
him, This is the land which I sware unto Abraham, unto Isaac
and unto Jacob, saying, I will give it unto thy seed: I have
caused thee to see it with thine eyes but thou shalt not go over
thither. So Moses the servant of the Lord died there in the
land of Moab.'

It will be asked where the law comes in. It does come in
if only we look below the theological surface of the story (and
I should like to mention that I am indebted to my brother,
Dr B. Daube, for the discovery of an older version). In Roman
law there was a mode of transfer of ownership called *traditio*.
If you wished to make over a thing to me, you 'tradited' the
thing to me, that is to say, you put me in possession, in control, of the thing, and the moment you had done this it became
mine. As is to be expected, the Roman jurists had a great deal
to say about what amounted to control, about what exactly
was needed in various circumstances for control, and with it
ownership, to pass from one party to the other. Everything
would be clear, for example, if in order to pay you I took a
coin and handed it over to you. You would now have command of the coin, *traditio* would manifestly be completed, the
coin would therefore belong to you and my debt would be
paid. But what if I handed over the coin, not to yourself,
but to your friend or to your agent, asking him to give it to
you for me? Who, while the commission was not yet executed,
would be its owner? Did I retain control, or did it pass to
your friend or agent, or, maybe, immediately to yourself?
Would the debt be considered as paid or not? Again, if I
wanted to transfer to you a herd of sheep, had I to hand over
to you each single animal, or only one as representing all,
or what else might I do to 'tradit' the herd, *i.e.* to put you
in control?

Special problems arose in the case of land and buildings.
Evidently, these cannot be delivered as simply as movables;
they cannot be physically handed over by the former owner
to the new like a horse or a sack of corn. In this dilemma,
the Romans appear to have recognized a way of transferring
control without a literal 'handing over'. More precisely, there

appears to have been an ancient rule concerning land and buildings, to the effect that, provided you took me to the spot and pointed out the property to me, this counted as *traditio*: I acquired control and the transfer was good. It was not even necessary for me to step on the land or touch it with my hands: I might seize it, it was held, with my eyes. Actually, this form of *traditio*, pointing out the property to the transferee, may well have been quite frequent. The expression *fines demonstrare* occurs in early and late references to transfer of land, and is used in a manner suggesting that this was the ordinary way of 'traditing' land.[93] In order to prevent misunderstandings, however, I have to emphasize that I am not maintaining that the mere pointing out by the former owner as such and the mere seeing by the new owner as such had any legal effects. The former owner must have the intention of transferring the property (an intention that might be explicitly declared or understood)—otherwise there was no conveyance. If you pointed out to me your estate simply to show me its beauties, I did not acquire; just as, in the case of a moveable, say, a ring, I did not acquire if you handed it to me simply to enable me the better to appreciate its setting. In the following discussion, when I speak of conveyance by pointing out, and looking at, an object, I am always implying the transferor's intent to convey the object. The mere looking at an object might, indeed, be of far-reaching consequences in the magical sphere. Moreover, we shall see that there is a close connection between those magical notions and the law; and that Thor, the god of lightning, acquires the world by flinging his hammer across it, without any previous owner's consent. But in the domain of legal conveyance, Roman or Hebrew, things are somewhat more rational and *traditio* involves a certain attitude of the parties.

If we proceed now with the Roman rules on transfer by pointing out and seeing, in the *Digest* we are told:[94] 'It is unnecessary to take possession by physical contact but it can be done by sight and intention, and this is proved by those things which owing to their great weight cannot be moved (and therefore cannot be actually handed over) such as columns.' It should be noted that what the author of this fragment is trying to make out is the possibility of acquiring 'by sight and intention' any object, even light things such as a coin or a book. He takes for granted and, indeed, bases his thesis upon, the possibility of acquiring in this fashion heavy things like columns. It follows that, though it may still have been doubtful in his time whether the method 'by sight and intention' was to be generally applied to any movables, yet this method must have been well established in the case of movables difficult to handle and, *a fortiori*, in that of land and buildings. Another fragment of the *Digest* rather reminds one of the story of Moses standing on the mountain and being shown the promised land.[95] 'If my vendor from my tower points out neighbouring land to me who have bought it, and says that he delivers vacant possession, I begin to possess no less than if I had set foot within its boundary.'

To leave Roman law and return to the main topic, it seems to me that there once existed an account of Moses' end widely different from that which we find in the Bible. The compilers of the Bible, priests and prophets, explained his failure to reach Palestine by saying that God had to punish him for a sin; and, as for his seeing the land, this was nothing, in their interpretation, but a last favour which he had wrung from God. It is very conceivable, I submit, that there existed an earlier version which did not explain his failure at all but, in a sense, denied it. Instead of Moses' tragedy, that earlier version set out to depict Moses' triumph. True, he did not really cross into Palestine at the head of his army, yet he did take possession of it. When God led him to the top of a mountain and from there showed him Palestine, he was not merely granting him a last personal wish, but was performing an act with a definite legal effect. God, the owner, pointed out the land to him, *fines demonstrabat*, indicated to him the boundaries of the territory, and thereby made him its sovereign.

Some of the passages in the Bible dealing with the end of Moses record in a remarkably elaborate manner that God let Moses see, not part of, but all Palestine. These portions, we may suppose, go back to the earlier version in which it was essential that Moses should have surveyed, and thus acquired possession of, the whole. According to Deuteronomy iii. 27, for instance, God said to Moses: 'Get thee up into the top of (the mountain) Pisgah, and lift up thine eyes westward and northward and southward and eastward, and behold it (the land) with thine eyes.' This precise formulation, this command to look around in all four directions, seems slightly out of place in the Biblical narrative, which tells us that Moses just desired to have a glance at the land before he died. The words, however, become perfectly intelligible if we assume that they derive from the older account which represented God as 'traditing', as conveying the land to Moses. In fact, there is a curious little difficulty in the text which may perhaps be got rid of on the basis of this explanation. Moses had to look not only to the west, north and south, but also to the east, though the east, obviously, was not Palestine. Possibly, this may be claimed to be a sign of how stereotyped a procedure that kind of *traditio*, that *fines demonstrare*, was, or at least how stereotyped the words or gestures of the vendor.[96] However, the difficulty is perhaps non-existent, namely, if by 'and lift up thine eyes westward and northward and southward and eastward' is meant 'regard the western, northern, southern and eastern parts of Palestine', not 'look to the west, north, south and east of where thou art': for this can be done even by a man looking down on Palestine from outside.[97] Another text in which some emphasis seems to be laid on Moses being shown all is Deuteronomy xxxiv. 1 ff., though the wording is here far less formal. An exact and most valuable parallel, however, of the formal request to look in all four directions is furnished by Genesis xiii. 14, the promise of Palestine to Abraham, also a quasi-legal act, to which I shall have to come back. In this case, incidentally, no problem arises about the east, since Abraham is thought of as being within Palestine, not like Moses without. There is Palestine all around him, therefore.[98]

Here I have to state some reservations. When I oppose to the Biblical account in its present form, which makes Moses' failure result from a sin, an older one denying his failure, I am restricting myself to what appears to me the most likely development. There are, however, several other possibilities. In fact, the question of the growth of the story under dis-

cussion is highly complicated. One thing we may be certain
of: the great liberator of the nation did actually die before the
final conquest of Palestine, or at least was regarded as having
so died in the entire tradition underlying the versions that
we can trace. I can think of no reason why, had there ever
existed a different view, this should have been ousted by one
far less pleasing to the mind. On the other hand, given the
fixed tradition that Moses had died prematurely, it was the
most natural thing for Hebrew bards and historiographers to
seek for a cause or even to attempt as far as possible to reverse
this tradition. In other words, given the tradition of his
premature death, it was the most natural thing to say that
he must have committed a sin, or to make him yet acquire
the country by seeing it. So far, then, we are on safe ground.

As soon, however, as we examine the various comments on
Moses' end to be found in the Bible, there arise difficulties
of interpretation and, above all, difficulties in determining
their relative chronology. A brief survey of the relevant
passages may help to show the nature of the problem. If
taken singly, a number of passages merely speak of Moses'
premature death, sent as a punishment, without mentioning
his seeing the land at all.[99] In one pericope his seeing the
land is mentioned but not made much of: it is Deuteronomy
iii. 23 ff. Verse 27, it is true, contains the formal request,
cited above, to look in all four directions; nevertheless, as
part of the whole narrative, verses 23–8, this occupies no
central position. Other texts give much prominence to Moses'
seeing the land, as a great privilege granted him in mitigation of the punishment;[100] and one pericope, finally, Deuteronomy xxxiv. 1 ff., is very brief on the point of punishment,
laying all stress on the positive side, on Moses' being shown
the land of promise. If we had to stop here, the conclusion
would be that the 'legal' version, the version of Moses'
triumph, is not strongly represented. However, for one thing,
it is worth noting that in some cases the reference to Moses'
death as premature and resulting from a sin could be eliminated
quite easily, when we should still be left with a fairly complete
narrative describing his acquisition of the land by seeing it.[101]
In Deuteronomy xxxiv. 1 ff., indeed, it is only the second half

of verse 4 which brings in the notion of punishment. For another thing (and this is a more fundamental consideration), we do not know how far it is correct to interpret these passages singly, each by itself. The mere fact that a text is silent on a point occurring in others surely does not prove that this point is not implied. For instance, though Psalms xcv and cvi do not say that Moses saw Palestine, the authors most probably knew, and accepted, this tradition. On the other hand, the narrative Deuteronomy xxxiv. 1 ff., with little emphasis on the punishment, yet strikes us as deeply tragic because of what we remember from other chapters of the Pentateuch— God's refusal to let Moses go into Palestine, the latter's wish to look at it at least from afar; and it is possible that the author wrote for just such a public as we are and thought it superfluous to dwell on circumstances that must be familiar to his readers.

On the whole, the development that I have outlined above seems to me nearest the truth. Originally the episode of Moses' seeing the land was introduced as of real importance, indeed, as fully explaining, since it explained away, that terrible fact in Hebrew history, his death before the final conquest. Later a more theological version appeared in which his end was related to the supreme principle of just reward, a principle so often to be met with as governing the Biblical presentation of events. His seeing the land now lost most of its original force and became a last favour that God, moved by sentiments of pity, did not wish to refuse him. Besides general considerations, there are quite a few details indicating that the accounts arose in this order, the most conclusive perhaps being that peculiar vagueness of the Bible about Moses' sin. Up to our day commentators have been puzzled what exactly was the crime perpetrated by Moses: it is no exaggeration to say that the matter has been controversial for thousands of years, since even the Rabbis of the Talmudic era differ from one another. In fact, in Deuteronomy i. 37, iii. 23 ff., iv. 21 f., Psalms xcv. 8 ff. and cvi. 32, it is not even a sin of his own but a sin of the people for which Moses had to die in Moab. All this becomes explicable on the assumption that the version of Moses' sin and punishment was superimposed on the original, 'legal' version of Moses' acquisition of the land. It would none the less be rash to declare the reverse development—from the theological account to that insisting on the acquisition of the land—entirely impossible. Nor would I reject the possibility of the two accounts having existed side by side, or rather as a whole, from the outset. For the one does not absolutely exclude the other. It is just conceivable that the idea of Moses acquiring the land legally, by seeing it, and the idea of his expiating a sin, in not entering it physically, together formed the basis of one explanation, only that they meant two different aspects of the story; and that, in the various passages quoted above, it was simply the requirements of the context that led to the emphasizing of this idea here and that idea there.[102] Moreover, it may not be superfluous to add that, even on the basis of the view that I have adopted as the most likely, to a certain extent, both accounts are of a religious character. For even the older one, which makes Moses acquire the land, is an attempt to vindicate the justice of God and the 'sense' of history. The difference is that the way in which this is done in the older account seems less schematically theological than that in which it is done in the later, which speaks of sin and punishment. Another point that it is well to bear in mind is that it was by no means in order to do away with the legal elements as such that the later version was substituted for the earlier. The legal element of the earlier version was watered down merely because it was no longer needed, or even troublesome, in the later version, according to which Moses had to be chastised. Precisely this, however, renders the case particularly interesting for us: we may see from it how the theological tendencies of the Bible might produce a suppression or falsification of legal points even where no direct attack on, or change of, the law was intended.

There remains one question. I am claiming that in a pre-Biblical legend Moses most probably was given the promised land. The question arises: Was it possible in ancient Hebrew law, or at least ancient Hebrew legal thought, as it was in Roman, to obtain possession 'by sight and intention', to seize land by looking at it? So far I have given examples only from

Roman law. Was the same possible in Hebrew law? No doubt
it was possible. We have ample evidence that the ancient
Hebrews, like the Romans, attributed to the eye a great deal
of power. You might harm things or persons by looking at
them; you might do them good; you might also lay hold of
and rule them. To cite a case where, as in the story of Moses'
death, a man is made to look down from a mountain: when
Balak led Balaam 'into the high places of Baal',[103] 'to the
top of Pisgah'[104] and 'to the top of Peor',[105] one of the reasons
no doubt was that the prophet's power over Israel would be
greater if he saw them well and from above. It is worth
noting in this connection that the Hebrew ראה, 'to see', is
used in all those senses in which its English equivalent is,
and possibly in some more. It may mean 'to understand',
'to enjoy', 'to suffer', and so on. Some curious instances of
this free use of the word may be found precisely in passages
dealing with Moses' end. For example, according to Deuteronomy iii. 23 ff., Moses asked God to let him 'go over and see
the good land': here 'to see' means 'to enjoy', 'happily to
dwell in'. God, however, answered that He would allow him
'to see it with his eyes', but not 'to go over this Jordan':
here 'to see' means 'merely to behold from afar', or, if we
go back to the original version postulated in this study, 'to
seize by seeing'. All this goes to show how powerful an organ
the eye was in the view of the ancient Hebrews. Clearly, the
basis was there for making the look a symbol of acquisition.

A word may be said here about a theory of Ihering's[106]
which, though its author had in mind Roman law only, yet
must be considered also in discussing Hebrew law. In Ihering's
opinion, the Roman lawyers originally treated the problem
of possession from a purely materialistic standpoint. Consequently, he says, *traditio* by pointing out and seeing the object
cannot, at an early period, have been sufficient. If this theory
were true, it might perhaps be used as an argument against
what I have suggested—though even then there would be good
enough evidence, as we shall see presently, in ancient Hebrew
sources to prove that the theory could not be applied to the
Bible. The proposition, however, is extremely doubtful. In
the first place, one hesitates to accept the premiss, a purely

materialistic attitude in this question of the early Roman lawyers. (This is not subscribing to the modern Swedish school, according to which even the classical Roman law was a mere system of magic.[107]) In the second place, even if we accept the premiss, it is highly probable that, for the early lawyers, to see an object was an act almost as 'materialistic' as to take up an object in one's hand. Ihering seems quite to overlook the very concrete role assigned to the eye in ancient thought, a role, moreover, which has some basis in rational reality.[108] In the case of land, in particular, being pointed out and seeing the property must have been a most convenient symbol of taking control. I fail to see that this procedure is any more spiritual than others dating from early times, and admitted by Ihering, such as taking up a clod of earth or stepping on the property.

There are two texts at least which can be regarded as direct confirmation that the idea of transferring land by pointing it out to the new owner was current from the beginning of the Biblical era right down to the end. The one, to which I have already referred, is the solemn promise to Abraham of Palestine: 'And the Lord said unto Abraham...Lift up now thine eyes, and look from the place where thou art northward, and southward, and eastward, and westward. For all the land which thou seest, to thee I will give it, and to thy seed for ever.'[109] The form of the gift here recorded is exactly parallel to that of the gift to Moses: and there is nothing in this case to obscure the legal nature of the proceedings. Readers coming from Roman law may wonder whether there ought not to be a difference between the form used for the promise to Abraham and that used for the transfer to Moses. For, in Roman law, the mere promise of an estate and the actual transfer of an estate are two transactions clearly distinguished in form and result. In the case of Abraham, where God merely gives a promise, a Roman lawyer would expect something like a *stipulatio*; it is only in the case of Moses, where God actually transfers the land, that a *traditio* seems the proper thing. However, no such clear distinction between promise and transfer is made in Oriental law, and still less, of course, in Oriental sagas.[110] To put it roughly, in Oriental law, the

promise of an estate is already a kind of transfer: yet, as it is
not a real, physical transfer, it may well be followed by a
second ceremony giving actual effect to it. To a Roman
lawyer, used to the strict notions of the classical system, this
must appear very confusing, I am afraid. But it would be
wrong to make Oriental law more precise than it is. Legally
and morally, the land belonged to Abraham as soon as the
promise was made and the ceremony of looking round performed—none the less, it was only a promise that he received,
he was not made actual owner of the land. This discrepancy
between the legal and the real position of a promisee—closely
connected with the discrepancy between Abraham's position
as ancestor and representative of the whole people, to whom
Palestine belongs, and his position as individual, who lives
before its conquest and therefore possesses nothing—explains
why Abraham is described as the true owner of Palestine in
some texts and as a landless wanderer in others. In Genesis
xv. 7, he appears as the true owner of Palestine: 'I am the
Lord that brought thee out of Ur of the Chaldees, to give thee
this land to inherit it'; in Acts vii. 5, he appears as beggar:
'And he (God) gave him none inheritance in it, no, not so
much as to set his foot on.' Again, this discrepancy between
the legal and actual position of a promisee explains why God
might say to Jacob in one breath that the land had already
been disposed of—legally, in favour of Abraham and Isaac—
was now being disposed of—legally, in favour of Jacob—and
would be disposed of in future—legally and physically, finally,
in favour of Israel. As we are told in Genesis xxxv. 12, God
addressed Jacob thus: 'And the land which I gave to Abraham
and Isaac, to thee will I give it, and to thy seed after thee will
I give the land.' In view of these texts, obviously, there is
nothing surprising in the fact that the promise of Palestine
to Abraham and the transfer of Palestine to Moses should
be made in the same form.

The other narrative containing the idea of transfer of land
by pointing it out and seeing it, many centuries later than
that of Abraham, is the narrative of the temptation of Jesus,
with Satan's offer of all the kingdoms of the world:[111] 'Again,
the devil taketh him up into an exceeding high mountain,

and sheweth him all the kingdoms of the world, and the glory of them; and saith unto him, All these things will I give thee, if thou wilt fall down and worship me.' There is no need to go into the parallels of this episode in other religions. I am not suggesting that there is any emphasis on the legal points; all that I mean to say is that the notion of transfer of ownership by one party offering and pointing out the object and the other accepting and seeing it is here noticeable in the background. Indeed, it is no mere coincidence that the property to be transferred is here offered from a high place, as in the case of Moses and in that from the *Digest* where 'my vendor from my tower points out neighbouring land to me'. It would be easier thus to overlook the land, *fines demonstrare*. Satan was a good lawyer, and, incidentally, aware how attractive the glory of the world must look when you are so placed that you can take it all in at one glance: the transaction that he contemplated failed only through non-acceptance by the other party.[112]

Perhaps it will be useful here to insert a somewhat more general consideration bearing on the problem of legal elements in sagas and legends. In tracing these elements, one has to distinguish between law and what might be called legal thought. It is not always easy to decide whether a narrative reflects the one or the other, but the distinction must be borne in mind. When a modern author writes a detective story about a gang of thieves, future historians will be justified in presuming that the crime described was punishable as theft under the present law of England (needless to say, even so the presumption may turn out wrong, if, for example, this particular author is careless about his law[113]). In contradistinction, when a modern left wing politician calls the capitalists thieves, future historians would be rash if they drew any direct conclusions from this statement as to the actual law of the time. What they might do would be to say that, according to the legal thought of the time, that is to say, according to popular feelings influenced by legal ideas, unjust profits were comparable to theft. As for the actual law, all that could be inferred would be that there must have existed a crime termed theft, an essential feature of which was the robbing of one

man by another: but any further details would have to
remain conjecture. Supposing no other source were left mentioning theft, even that vague conclusion would be of value.

If we draw the moral for the case under notice, this will
be the result. In several narratives, one of them concerning
Abraham, one concerning Moses and one concerning Jesus,
we find the notion of transfer of ownership of land by one
party pointing out the property and the other seeing it. Yet
the presence of this notion does not prove that land could
ever be transferred in this way in actual Hebrew law. Very
probably there was a time when it could: but if we are to
avoid anything hypothetical, we ought to be satisfied with
the result that the notion was current in Hebrew legal
thought, or, one might say, in legal folklore. Similarly,
we find in the Bible the ideas—which, like the one just mentioned, recur in many ancient systems—of a man acquiring
land by stepping or lying on it, and of a man acquiring land
by walking through the whole of it. According to Genesis
xxviii. 13, God spoke to Jacob when he had his vision of the
ladder thus: 'I am the Lord...the land whereon thou liest, to
thee will I give it, and to thy seed.' Again, in Genesis xiii. 17
(a few verses only after the one discussed before, in which the
notion of acquisition by seeing is predominant) we are told
how God said to Abraham: 'Arise, walk through the land in
the length of it and in the breadth of it, for I will give it unto
thee.' Whether Hebrew law actually recognized all these forms
of acquisition, or whether it recognized only some of them,
or even none, is quite uncertain. But it is also irrelevant as
far as our investigation is concerned. What is relevant is that
these forms existed in popular legal thought; that they would
therefore be practised or at least be spoken of in everyday
life; and that, above all, they would be introduced, as having
legal effect, in saga and legend. Moreover, it is clear that all
these variations of *traditio* have one fundamental point in
common, and this point, we may safely conclude, did play
a part in actual Hebrew law: what they all have in common
is the formally giving and taking control of the land to be
acquired. This must have been the basis of transfer of ownership in the actual law of the time, whatever the exact form

prescribed may have been. There is a Nordic myth in which
we get this element of taking control; yet the particular form
of acquisition depicted in that myth cannot possibly have
been the form prescribed in actual law. Thor, the god of
lightning and thunder, declares that his realm is to extend
as far as he can fling his hammer. He flings it and it touches
the very ends of the universe; thus his domination over the
whole world is established. It is hardly likely that flinging
one's hammer was ever a symbol of acquisition in actual law.
On the other hand, it does follow even from this myth that
the actual law must have had some symbolic act of taking
control in the case of transfer of land. It is noteworthy that
the three Biblical symbols of taking control of land, which
may or may not have existed in actual Hebrew law, can all
be paralleled from Roman legal sources proper. I have already
quoted the texts referring to the acquisition of property by
seeing: in one of them, *Digest* 41.2.18.2, the land is pointed
out to the transferee from a tower much as Palestine is shown
to Moses from the top of Pisgah. In *Digest* 41.2.3.1 the question is discussed whether you have to walk through the whole
land that you want to acquire, as Abraham has to according
to Genesis xiii. 17, or whether entering a part of it is sufficient,
as is presupposed in the case of Jacob lying on the land
according to Genesis xxviii. 13. 'The statement that we have
made...must not of course be taken to mean that one who
wishes to take possession of an estate must visit every parcel
of it' (like Abraham who walks in the length and in the breadth
of Palestine); 'it is enough to enter any part of the estate,
provided one has the purpose and intention to take possession
of the whole estate up to its boundary' (like Jacob, to whom
the land whereon he lies is given). The reference in the *Digest*
to acquisition by walking through the whole of the land is
not any the less interesting because this form is declared unnecessary and only a mere stepping on the land (or a seizing
with the eyes) prescribed: it is sufficient for my purpose to
show that at least in Roman legal discussion concerning *traditio*
the idea of walking through the whole of the land did come up.

From the narratives here considered, accounts like that of
Jeremiah's acquisition of land in Jeremiah xxxii. 6 ff. are

fundamentally different: they contain, or at any rate are meant to contain, the true law of the time, and so, of course, do Talmudic tractates concerned with the matter. It would obviously lead too far afield to examine these here.

If the view here advanced is accepted, one of the last few verses of the Pentateuch may be somewhat more significant than it looks. The Bible tells us that 'Moses was an hundred and twenty years old when he died: his eye was not dim, nor his natural force abated'. It is tempting to assume (this again I have from my brother) that this little note, too, was at first connected with the earlier version in which God made Moses owner of Palestine. 'His eye was not dim': by this the author of the note may have intended to indicate that Moses saw the land full well, that in spite of his age he was capable of controlling and validly taking it with his eyes.

IV

The last point that I propose to discuss is the history of the religious idea of redemption, more precisely, of redemption in the narrower sense, 'red-emption', the buying back. I am not concerned, that is, with redemption in the wide, indefinite sense of help and rescue. Hebrew has many words to denote this general concept, פדה, גאל, עזר, הציל, הושיע, and so on. Here I have in mind chiefly the term גאל (with גאלה etc.), though the meaning of פדה (with פדות etc.) is very similar. The main difference seems to be (I am considering Hebrew only, not the cognate tongues) that whereas גאל signifies the buying back of a man or thing that had once belonged to one or one's family but had got lost, פדה signifies the ransoming of a man or thing whose fate otherwise would be destruction, consecration or slavery.[114] Thus גאל primarily suggests the return of men or things into their old legitimate place, פדה the saving of men or things from their doom. In illustration, and confirmation, of this it may be pointed out that whereas men, animate things and inanimate things may be the object of גאל, since, given certain conditions, any of these may be the object of 'red-emption',[115] there appears to be no case of an inanimate thing being the object of פדה: this most probably is the result, not of chance, but of the fact that only men or beasts can properly be regarded as objects of 'ransoming from a doom', of 'saving'.[116] It is only to be expected that, in figurative speech, the two groups of גאל, גאלה and פדה, פדות should often be employed side by side, almost as if they were interchangeable. Indeed, occasionally, this happens even in legal language. To take the latter case first, if the owner of a firstborn animal, which is God's, offers to pay its value instead, the transaction may be called a 'buying back' or a 'ransoming';[117] and as regards metaphorical use, a prophet who speaks of Israel's deliverance by God may express this idea equally well by saying that God 'buys back' Israel or that He 'ransoms' Israel.[118] What is rather surprising, at first sight, is that the notion of גאל, 'to buy back', on the whole occupies a more prominent position in passages concerning the final deliverance of Israel than that of פדה, 'to ransom'. Surely, if we consider the two terms as such, forgetting for a moment what roles they played in ancient Hebrew history, we must admit the metaphor פדה, 'to ransom Israel', 'to save Israel from utter doom', to be far simpler and stronger than גאל, 'to buy back Israel'. The predominance of גאל, where Israel's final deliverance is concerned, is, I believe, due to the very point which it is the purpose of the following remarks to bring out, and, in fact, may itself be considered as not a little supporting the thesis advanced: namely, the descent of גאל in its metaphorical, religious application from גאל as occurring in the social legislation of the Pentateuch.

It may be well to state at the outset that 'to buy back' is not a perfectly accurate translation of גאל. It would be safer to translate 'to take back', seeing that the word is as often as not employed where he who recovers makes no payment. The word simply denotes the rightful getting back of a person or object that had once belonged to one or one's family but had been lost. When a man marries the childless widow of a near relative, for example, or kills the murderer of a near relative, he is acting as גאל:[119] obviously, these are instances of recovering lost persons or goods without paying for them. Again, the release of a slave in the seventh year or the jubilee and the reversion of land to its original owner in the jubilee seem to be subsumed under the heading of גאלה, 'redemption', though they take place automatically, no payment being required.[120] Further, in many, perhaps in the majority of, passages where גאל is used metaphorically, there is nothing to suggest the idea of payment: we must not overlook this under the influence of what became the dominant concept of redemption in Christianity. References to redemption like Exodus vi. 6, 'I will bring you out from under the burdens of the Egyptians, and I will rid you out of their bondage, and I will redeem you with a stretched out arm and with great judgments', mean only that God takes back His Israel from its oppressors, but not that He offers them any compensation.

On the other hand, it so happens that those legal cases in which גאלה, recovery, depends on payment, such as redemption of a debtor who had to sell himself or of the property which he had to sell,[121] by reason of their social and ethical implications, were of particular importance in the eyes of the prophets. It is these cases, therefore, which, as will emerge more clearly in the following discussion, formed the basis of most of the prophetic metaphors about Israel's redemption—even while the idea of payment dropped out. In the passage just quoted relating to the redemption from Egypt, Exodus vi. 6, the idea of payment is quite absent. Yet there can be no doubt that the basis for this metaphor of redemption was the laws arranging for the redemption of slaves. The prophets proceeded from these laws, neglecting the point of payment which was not so essential for their purposes. There are, however, a few texts in which the metaphor corresponds very closely to the original laws underlying it and where the idea of payment is introduced. One of them is Isaiah lii. 3: 'For thus saith the Lord, Ye have sold yourselves for nought; and ye shall be redeemed without money.' Here the allusion is distinctly to the redemption of an enslaved debtor by satisfying his creditor—even though the prophet declares that no satisfaction will be necessary in the special case of Israel. What an enormous part redemption by satisfaction plays in Christian teaching is well known. In the following study I shall use the somewhat inexact translation 'to buy back', 'to redeem', for גאל whenever it is convenient. But it may be stressed once more that גאל as such means 'to recover', 'to take back to its old legitimate place what was lost', whether by means of payment or no.

After these philological considerations, I may go on to the main topic, the history of the religious idea of גאל. This idea, of fundamental importance in the Old Testament and Talmud, in the gospels and all Christian doctrine, has its root in early law. It is, one might justly say, an outstanding example of a legal notion being taken up and made into a religious notion by priests and prophets. Exactly how this was achieved it is impossible to say; I shall attempt no more here than to suggest what seems a plausible evolution, and even this I shall sketch very summarily since it would not be safe to pronounce upon details. Briefly, early Hebrew law had the institution of גאלה, of redemption, in cases like enslavement of debtors or murder: the enslaved debtor or murdered man was to be 'redeemed', was to be taken back into his old family.[122] Gradually, the concept arose of God as redeemer of the nation, a development that received its main impetus from the fact that Israel's deliverance from Egypt by God was construed as an application, on a higher plane, of the ordinary laws regarding redemption. In the end, the notion of redemption was even more spiritualized, and God thought of as redeeming His people not only from physical slavery but also from the fetters of sin and death.

In attempting to substantiate this thesis, we come up against a certain difficulty: it is by no means to be taken for granted that the laws on redemption to be found in the Pentateuch are the oldest version of Hebrew legislation in this matter. In fact, it is very hard to reconcile with one another the various Biblical pronouncements themselves; the authors of the Talmud had to face knotty problems in demonstrating, for instance, that the laws respecting slavery in Exodus, Leviticus and Deuteronomy constituted one homogeneous whole. Accordingly, there is a strong possibility of the metaphorical use of 'redemption' having sprung from a version somewhat different from the one (or those) preserved; and even if this is disregarded, the question remains which of the various Biblical sections dealing with the law of redemption shows that state of the law, or is nearest that state of the law, in which the religious concept of redemption originated.

I shall try to overcome the difficulty outlined, not by a frontal attack, but by evading it as best I can. Certainly, if I were to write a minute, critical account of the history of the Hebrew laws of redemption, the questions to which I have referred would have to be tackled. But my present task consists in showing, in a general way, how the legal concept of redemption was turned into a religious concept. This can be done by starting from the Biblical legislation in the form in which we have it before us. The main features of the Biblical laws are undoubtedly the same as those of the laws that may have preceded them; and the main features of the Biblical laws are the same whether we consult Exodus, Leviticus or Deuteronomy. In other words, we are safe in assuming that it was at least this kind of legislation—no matter how far we have to reckon with divergencies in detail—that is at the bottom of the metaphorical application of the notion of 'buying back'. As far as detail is concerned, it would be wrong indeed to rely on what we find in the Pentateuch; and in one or two cases I shall have to make suggestions regarding the pre-Biblical stage of the law. One such point, rather more important than the others, is implied in what I have already said. I think that there existed social legislation of the type to be found in the Bible long before the exodus from Egypt was made the general basis of such statutes: actually, the exodus itself was construed, I think, on the model of that legislation—but I shall have to discuss this later on.

To proceed, then, from the Pentateuch, Hebrew law provided that if poverty forced you to sell yourself to your creditor, into slavery, your relations were entitled and bound to redeem you, that is to say, to satisfy your creditor in order to secure your freedom. In case you had no relatives, or in case they did not act, you yourself might demand your release as soon as you had acquired the means wherewith to pay your master.[123] (It would seem, however, that this right of redemption was confined to the case where the creditor was a foreigner dwelling in Palestine, not a Hebrew.[124]) Similarly, if you were forced by poverty to give away your land, the land, that is, which you had inherited from your father, your relatives had the right and duty to buy it back for you, to redeem it for you from the new owner. In case you found no relatives to redeem it, you yourself retained the right to buy it back when things improved and you could afford to do so.[125]

It is evident that these rules were intended to keep as intact as possible any free family and the family property: it is also clear that they must from the outset have been considered as strongly favouring the socially inferior groups and limiting the rights of the wealthier. Yet there was a serious flaw in the machinery. Once you were ruined to such an extent that you had to sell your land or even your liberty, the chances of recovery by your own, unassisted exertions were, it is to be supposed, slender. Normally, therefore, your only hope was that your relatives would restore you to your former state. It is significant that both in the paragraphs about redemption of a man who has had to sell himself[126] and in those about redemption of property that a man has had to sell,[127] the provision allowing redemption by the impoverished person himself follows, and is introduced as subsidiary to, the provision allowing redemption by his relatives. In the former section, we are told that 'one of his brethren may redeem him: either his uncle, or his uncle's son...or any that is nigh unto him...; or if he is able, he may redeem himself'. The arrangement is the same in the latter section: 'One of his kin may come to redeem it (the property)...: and if the man have none to redeem it, and himself be able to redeem it; then let him count....' (It looks as if the rules allowing the impoverished man himself to buy back his freedom or property were a Biblical innovation and had not existed in pre-Biblical legislation. But as the question is irrelevant to my main argument, I shall not here go into it.) Now if you belonged to a powerful and generous family, you were safe: they would be able and willing to deal with the matter. But it was different if you belonged to a small family with no wealth or influence, or to a family like Marco Polo's, incapable of recognizing a man whose attire is changed from decent to mean. Nobody would stand up for you in this case, which no doubt was by far the most frequent. The problem must have been all the more urgent as you had to rely on your relatives, *qua* redeemers, not only when you had lost your freedom or property, but also on a number of other occasions no less serious. Two of them only may be mentioned. When a man was killed, it was the task of his nearest relative to 'redeem', to get back, his blood;[128] and when a man died leaving a wife but no children, his nearest relative had to 'take back' the widow—who otherwise would be lost to the family and, mostly, destitute herself—by marrying her.[129] Obviously, the position of the member of a weak family was far from enviable. Indeed, it is hardly going too far to say that all those commands, which would have had an enormous stabilizing effect and led to the alleviation of much distress if carried into practice, during the greater part at least of the life of the nation were a social programme rather than actually functioning law. This appears to be true also of the provisions designed to make the preservation of freedom and family property independent of chance and the individual position. The seventh year and the jubilee seem to have been of little use to those who lacked the backing of a mighty house. The episode recorded in Nehemiah v, a general 'disburdenment' taking place in highly exceptional circumstances, only serves to confirm this impression. There can be no doubt whatever that, say, the Roman regime, under which an insolvent debtor, given certain conditions, either had to find a *vindex*, a guarantor, or was imprisoned, was, in reality, equally hard on the poor and friendless.

It seems to have been at this point that the transformation of the concept of גאלה, 'redemption', from a legal concept into a religious one started. The sources show that the moral leaders of the Hebrew people were fully awake to the inadequacy and iniquity of the system of redemption described. At some period, it appears, they demanded that where a man had no relatives who could protect him from oppression, the state should intervene in his behalf. One Psalm contains a description of the ideal king, and it is said of him that he undertakes to redeem you if you are without relatives able to do it:[130] 'He shall redeem their (the needy's) soul from deceit and violence, and precious shall their blood be in his

sight.' This is a cry for legal reform, utopian though it may
be. The state ought to see to it that the laws concerning
redemption be really carried out; and it may be observed that,
as in many other texts which will be considered below and in
which God is represented as redeemer, the reference is at once
to redemption of the poor who are enslaved, redemption of
the property of the poor, and redemption of the blood of the
poor who are murdered. I need hardly add that this, too,
remained mere wishful thinking. No Hebrew government was
high-minded and strong enough to put poor people with no
connections in the position enjoyed by the members of wealthy
clans. It is perhaps more than accidental that, as far as I
can see, the Psalm just quoted is the only instance of the king
being urged to exercise the function of a redeemer. Probably
it was hopeless to make a demand of this kind. I wish to
repeat, however, that I am only tracing here what looks a
plausible evolution, with no pretence to exactitude in details.
The reason why Psalm lxxii. 14 stands alone may well be
quite different; but it would lead too far afield to examine all
possibilities.

At any rate, in consequence of the failure of the law on the
matter, the social reformers pinned their faith on God, as men
will do when their own measures prove fruitless. They now
declared that a man whose relatives were incapable of redeeming him, his land or his blood, would be helped by God
Himself. There are many passages in the Bible representing
God as redeeming the poor. In Proverbs, for example, we get
the injunction: 'Remove not the old landmark; and enter not
into the fields of the fatherless; for their redeemer (God) is
mighty; He shall plead their cause with thee.'[131] Here, manifestly, we are no longer in the province of law, actual or
utopian. We are in the province of religion. But it should be
observed how closely at this stage the religious concept corresponds to the original legal concept. God, the loyal relative
of the poor, redeems for them their property which the unjust
thinks he can withhold from them for ever, just as, under the
ordinary rules, a rich man would redeem what a kinsman of
his has been deprived of. Even the concluding threat, 'He
shall plead their cause with thee', is in keeping with this

description of God as maintaining the rights, at law, of a patron relative. While the meaning of this text clearly is that, in the case of the friendless, God will enforce the laws concerning the redemption of a man's property, passages like Jeremiah xx. 11 ff. and Psalms ix. 13 (12) and cxix. 154, about the similar case of the persecuted pious, ought perhaps to be interpreted as implying that He will also enforce the laws concerning the redemption of a murdered man's blood. In Psalm cxix. 154 the legal terminology is unmistakable: 'Plead my cause, and redeem me.' In the other two passages, it is true, the term גאל, 'to redeem', itself does not occur. But this is not decisive. Psalm ix. 13 (12), in particular, speaks of God as 'claiming the blood', דרש דמים, of murdered men, a phrase that may well come from the sphere of blood feud in which 'redemption', the 'taking back', of the victim's blood plays a prominent part.[132] We shall presently see that, at any rate, the idea of God as redeemer of the blood of Israel is quite common in the writings of the Old Testament.

For it was not only the poor whom God was supposed to save as redeemer. In the eyes of the great Hebrew writers, God was the owner and relative of the whole people. Therefore, they believed, whenever the nation had to submit to the yoke of a conqueror, He, God, could assert His claim. God redeems Israel as father in Exodus iv. 22 f.[133] and Isaiah lxiii. 16—which latter text, as I have shown above,[134] uses the semi-legal term הכיר of God who, more reliable than the patriarchs, will 'acknowledge' His sons as entitled to redemption—as owner in Isaiah xliii. 1, as owner or friend in Jeremiah xxxi. 10 (11). Very naturally, in most cases it is not clear exactly on what basis God redeems Israel: He becomes Israel's redeemer without any further explanation. Isaiah makes God promise, 'Ye have sold yourselves for nought, and ye shall be redeemed without money.'[135] Jeremiah says, 'Their (the children of Israel's) redeemer is strong.... He shall thoroughly plead their cause';[136] and the Psalmist exclaims, 'O give thanks unto the Lord.... Let the redeemed of the Lord say so, whom he hath redeemed from the hand of the enemy.'[137] In none of these passages are we told precisely in what capacity God buys back His people, whether as owner

or as relative; and whereas in the first two the wording is still
taken from procedure in court—'ye shall be redeemed without
money', 'He shall plead their cause'—the third, like the
majority of texts concerning redemption, contains no such
reference.

However, even this notion of God as Israel's redeemer from
the enemy, though very theological, still clearly reflects the
original legal provisions about redemption. The argument of
those Hebrew writers was that when their ancestors had
actually been slaves to the Egyptians, slaves in the ordinary
meaning of the word, and when neither relatives nor previous
owners with a stronger right had redeemed them, God had
stepped in, thus assuming the place of relative and owner.
He would again and again, they concluded, exercise His right
as relative and owner and deliver them from their tyrants.
When we hear, about the first redemption from actual slavery,
that 'I will bring you out from under the burdens of the
Egyptians, and I will rid you out of their bondage, and I will
redeem you with a stretched out arm, and with great judgments, and I will take you to me for a people',[138] this is the
immediate basis for prophecies like Isaiah's,[139] 'Art thou
(O arm of the Lord) not it...that hath made the depths of
the sea a way for the ransomed to pass over? Therefore the
redeemed of the Lord shall return, and come with singing
unto Zion.' There is ample evidence—and it is all the more
surprising that it does not seem to have been recognized—that
the great deliverance from Egypt was construed as a proper
act of redemption, on the model of the ordinary social laws
regarding the deliverance of slaves. The whole tone of the
narrative bears testimony to this, even apart from texts using
the term גאל. Needless to say, the various methods by which
an ordinary slave could be freed are not scrupulously distinguished in the description of the exodus. There was no
need to be over-careful in the metaphorical application of the
social laws to that event, and it would be rash to expect that
the authors of the narrative must have made up their minds
as between the possibilities of God enforcing the freedom of
His people as relative, or His enforcing it as owner, or His
enforcing it in accordance with the provisions on the seventh

year or the jubilee. All these ideas are present: it is merely
the requirements of the context that determine which of them
is to be in the foreground in any particular passage. I have
already adverted to a passage where God demands the release
of Israel as of His son:[140] 'Israel is my son....Let my son go,
that he may serve me.' But how closely the exodus was
modelled on the ordinary laws regarding the release of slaves
is perhaps best seen from two other points not hitherto sufficiently considered.

We are told that God, when He first announced to Moses
His intention of delivering the people from Egypt, promised
him, 'And it shall come to pass, that, when ye go, ye shall
not go empty.'[141] This means that God will induce the
Egyptians to release their Hebrew slaves in precisely that
fashion in which a Hebrew slave must be released, after seven
years, according to Deuteronomy xv. 13. There we find the
rule: 'And when thou sendest him out free from thee, thou
shalt not send him out empty.' It is clear from the identical
structure of the two sentences that a deliberate allusion is
made in the one to the other: 'when ye go—ye shall not go
empty' is the promise of God to Moses; 'when thou sendest
him out free from thee—thou shalt not send him out empty'
is the law concerning the seventh year. It must be observed
that, when the promise made to Moses is being fulfilled, even
the liberality and generosity required in Deuteronomy of the
releaser are shown by the Egyptians—from the formalistic
point of view at least. According to Deuteronomy xv. 14, the
releasing master has to 'furnish the slave liberally out of his
flock' and so on. So, according to the story of the exodus,
the Egyptians are not really robbed or otherwise deprived of
their valuables against their will; but they are so inclined by
God as to part with them readily, like a friendly master.[142]
God, we are told, 'gave the people favour in the sight of the
Egyptians and they made them presents'.[143] The English
version, it is true, takes שאל in the sense of 'to borrow', and
represents the Egyptians as 'lending' to the Israelites what
these are later not to return. But this is a mistranslation. שאל,
to be sure, may mean 'to borrow', since its primary meaning is
'to ask'.[144] But, since its primary meaning is 'to ask', it may

also mean 'to ask as a gift'; it occurs in this sense in old and late documents.[145] In Exodus, the meaning is undoubtedly 'to ask as a gift'. The Israelites are to ask their masters for gifts, just as, under the social legislation, any Hebrew slave may when he is being released. God makes the Egyptians follow the social commandments of Deuteronomy (or some rules prior but similar)—the redemption from Egypt was assimilated to ordinary redemption even in a detail like this.[146] The reason why the English version substitutes a loan for the gifts is not difficult to find: it has adopted the interpretation of the Vulgate, which uses *commodare* in Exodus xii. 36. As for the Vulgate, its authors found it as difficult as modern (and ancient) commentators to understand why the Egyptians should let the Israelites have any of their valuables, be it as a gift or as a loan; but a gift, of course, was even more unintelligible than a loan. In fact, the whole episode makes sense only when we connect it with the laws relating to the release of a slave: and once this is recognized, the nature of the transaction as a gift becomes obvious.

It might perhaps be asked why I assume that Exodus iii. 21 is an allusion to Deuteronomy (or some rule like it) rather than that the latter is modelled on the former. My main argument, besides general considerations, is precisely the fact that Exodus iii. 21 has little meaning unless intended as an application of the provisions from Deuteronomy or some similar provision. In favour of the other alternative, one might say that Deuteronomy xv. 15 gives the deliverance from Egypt as the motive why the social legislation of xv. 12–18 ought to be observed: it follows, one might argue, that this legislation cannot have been prior to the deliverance from Egypt. It will presently be shown, however, that this argument is not conclusive. There is nothing unusual in the Bible making the exodus the basis of laws which themselves influenced the description of, and indeed the whole way of looking at, that event.

The other detail in regard to which a close parallel seems to have been attempted between the deliverance from Egypt and the legislation concerning redemption is the notion that, through the liberation from Egypt, the Hebrews have become the people of God or the slaves of God. We are so used to this idea that it seems quite natural to us. But an explanation is called for when we find passages like 'And I will take you to me for a people, and I will be to you a God, and ye shall know that I am the Lord your God, which bringeth you out from under the burdens of the Egyptians';[147] or 'They shall be as still as a stone, till thy people pass over, O Lord...which thou hast purchased';[148] or again, 'For unto me the children of Israel are servants, they are my servants whom I brought forth out of the land of Egypt.'[149] The explanation lies in the laws of redemption. Let us take first the case of a man redeeming what was his property once before. Here, when he buys back his property, it becomes his again—so the Israelites become again the property of God. But even when we proceed from the case of a man redeeming, not his own property, but a relative's property or freedom, the explanation holds. Under the legislation to be found in the Bible, it is true, property redeemed by a relative or a slave redeemed by a relative does not belong to the redeeming relative: the former goes to its previous owner, the latter becomes free. But at least both return to the old family and into the protection of the mighty relative; and similarly, the nation redeemed becomes the people and servants of God. Maybe, however, we are justified in going a step further. It is quite possible that, in a legislation earlier than that which we find in Leviticus, when a relative redeemed property or a slave, that property or man, up to the final year of release at any rate, fell to the redeemer. The famous gesture of Jeremiah,[150] who bought his cousin's estate while Jerusalem was besieged by Nebuchadrezzar, may be adduced in support of this suggestion. As the Bible records, Jeremiah was offered the field as the nearest relative, as redeemer: 'and I bought the field of Hanameel my uncle's son...and weighed him the money'. Evidently, it is not as if Jeremiah had paid his cousin's debts and left him the field. The 'redemption' in this case consisted in Jeremiah's buying the estate and keeping it himself.[151] If there was legislation of the kind suggested, and if it was on the basis of that earlier stage that the exodus was construed, then we have a precise analogy even where God is thought of as relative of the nation: the Israelites, by being freed through God, necessarily become His property or His slaves.

The part played in Hebrew thought by the deliverance from thraldom in Egypt, construed as a proper act of redemption, can hardly be overrated. For one thing, if the laws concerning redemption had been the main element in the interpretation of the exodus (a thesis which I hope I have made probable), the exodus thus interpreted in turn influenced social legislation to a very high degree. Egypt is mentioned in connection with a large number of laws, most of them of a social character, in favour of slaves and the poor, either as a particularly cogent reason why a law should be faithfully observed [152] or even as the reason why a law has been laid down.[153] In the majority of cases, the law in question, or some similar law at least, is far older than the idea of founding it on the deliverance from Egypt: but, once that event was construed as in accordance, on a higher plane, with the legislation concerning redemption, it must have been a tremendously strong argument. For instance, we know that at some early stage of Mediterranean civilization usury was not practised. (Remember that even in classical Roman law *mutuum* was, formally at least, free of interest.) When usury appeared, it was soon fought; and in Hebrew law it was no doubt prohibited long before Leviticus xxv. 35 ff.[154] But in this text the prohibition is founded on the argument that God redeemed Israel from Egypt. In Exodus xxii. 24 (25) and Deuteronomy xxiii. 20 (19) f. usury is forbidden with no reference to Egypt—which clearly confirms my thesis. Similarly, the fourth of the ten commandments, the law of the Sabbath, is said to have been laid down because of the deliverance from Egypt only in one version, Deuteronomy v. 15. The reason given for the law in Exodus xx. 11 is very different. It is that God created the world in six days, resting on the seventh. Evidently, the law as such existed before it was based on either of the two reasons.

What is particularly striking is the fact that the deliverance by God of the Israelites, and their becoming God's slaves as a result, are advanced in Leviticus and Deuteronomy in support of precisely those laws concerning redemption

of enslaved relatives, jubilee and so on which themselves
gave rise to the metaphors of God as the nation's redeemer
from Egyptian slavery.[155] It is easy to show that the
actual laws concerning redemption, or some such laws, go
back to a time before they were rested on the motive of
the exodus. We need only look at the way in which, in
Leviticus for instance, the motive is introduced to notice that
it is secondary. In the last section of chapter xxv we find the
provisions, fairly elaborate, regarding the possibility of redeeming a debtor who has had to sell himself into slavery.[156]
The final rule, verse 54, says that, if no redemption takes
place before the jubilee, in that year at the latest a slave must
become free. Then, in verse 55, follows the reason for the
legislation: 'For unto me the children of Israel are servants;
they are my servants whom I brought forth out of the land
of Egypt.' This is manifestly added, if not at a period after
this specific legislation in Leviticus was established, at all
events considerably after the '*Ur*'-legislation was. Again,
section xxv. 39–42, laying down the duty of a Hebrew master
to release his slave in the jubilee, is indeed shorter and less
intricate. Yet here, too, the reference to Egypt looks like an
appendix. It follows that we have a development in three
stages. There is the ancient Hebrew social legislation on redemption; there is its application to the case of Egypt; and
there is the exploitation of this case, thus construed, to provide
the basis for the social legislation. This is a most interesting
and, it seems, fairly typical development. A parallel case
would be, for example, that of secular kingship or chieftainship
influencing the interpretation of the rule of God; and the
latter, in turn, being made the basis for the former. It is clear,
however, that the case of Egypt and the social legislation is
in some respects *sui generis*. Law here determined the interpretation of what was not merely a religious institution but
also the decisive event at the opening of the history of the
people of Israel. It should be added that, in all probability,
when the case of Egypt was made the basis of the social
legislation, it also affected the substance of that legislation;
I do not propose to examine how far it did so.

There was another consequence, however, of regarding the

exodus as a proper act of redemption; a consequence of greater
importance in this connection where we are concerned with
the notion of God as the reliable, constant redeemer of His
people. It is the fact that, as a result of this interpretation
of the exodus, one could be quite confident of final salvation:
and, surely, here lies one of the reasons—though, true enough,
one of many—why the first redemption so constantly and
dominantly appears in prophecies announcing the last. Final
salvation was not a mere myth based, say, on nature's bringing
spring after winter. Nor was it a vague hope, of the kind:
'God helped us in Egypt, why should He not help us again?'
It was a certainty: 'God acted the part of redeemer in Egypt;
therefore, though He may forsake us temporarily, eventually
He must intervene again.' In fact, there is traceable in this
a tendency that seems characteristic of several branches of
Old Testament religion: the tendency to 'legalize', to put on
a firm, reliable basis so that you can draw practical conclusions
from day to day, the relation between man and God. I shall
have to come back to this feature.

Certain minor points become explicable on the basis of what
I have said. The deliverance from Egypt, I have said, as the
great historical precedent, formed the main starting-point for
the further development of the religious idea of redemption.
I think that it is largely due to this that, in the visions of final
salvation, God acts as redeemer of the enslaved and wrongfully
withheld faithful more frequently than as redeemer, by inflicting vengeance, of the murdered faithful's blood: it had
been a case of slavery in Egypt. No doubt there are additional
reasons. One of them may be that, whilst redemption of
freedom and redemption of property remained possible and,
in theory at least, important throughout all periods of Hebrew
history, the role of the גאל הדם, the redeemer of a murdered
relative's blood, became less and less essential in proportion
to the taking over by the state of the punishment of criminals.
Similarly, the chief reason why God is never, as far as I can
see, compared to the redeemer, by marriage, of the childless
widow of a relative most probably is the simple fact that
that custom gradually fell into disuse and, in the case of the
widow of one's brother, was even directly prohibited.

It should here be added, however, that the concept of God the redeemer of His nation's blood is far from uncommon. Isaiah says,[157] 'I will take vengeance (on Babylon)....As for our redeemer, the Lord of hosts is His name....' Maybe a considerable number of texts representing God as avenging Israel—נקם, etc.—such as Deuteronomy xxxii. 43, are intended to suggest the idea of redemption of blood even though they do not actually use the term 'to redeem'. Of the possible influence of the concept of redemption of blood on the metaphors of the redemption by God from spiritual destruction, something will have to be said presently. Quite often a passage alludes to both redemption of slaves and property and redemption of blood at the same time. It must be remembered that when God takes back captive Israel, He does it, in nearly all prophecies, not in a mild, quiet manner, but at the same time destroying the cruel oppressors; and for this, too, the exodus from Egypt furnished the precedent, when He redeemed the slaves 'with a stretched out arm, and with great judgments'.[158] An example may be found in Isaiah lxiii. 4, 'For the day of vengeance is in mine heart and the year of my redeemed is come.' The first half of this sentence alludes rather to redemption, by vengeance, of blood, the second half to the liberation of enslaved debtors and of property in the seventh year or the jubilee.[159] In the vast majority of texts, however, God appears simply as redeemer, no particular kind of redemption being specified. For instance, Isaiah comforts the people by saying,[160] 'Fear not, thou worm Jacob..., I will help thee, saith the Lord, and thy redeemer, the Holy one of Israel.'

So far we have seen God as the redeemer of men from slavery, oppression and murder. We have seen Him saving the poor and pious from the hands of hard creditors, restoring them to their property and inflicting retribution on those who slay them; and we have also seen Him freeing and avenging the nation under the heel of its enemies. With the next and final step they took, priests and prophets moved even farther from the original legal starting-point. They now developed the idea of redemption quite independently in their own theological domain. They maintained that God would redeem the faithful, not only from actual physical misfortunes, not only when it was a question of getting back the person from slavery, the property from the wealthy and ruthless stranger or the blood from the murderer; but He would redeem them also from the clutches of error, evil and death. To some extent, even this final step was a result of the dominant part played by the exodus in Hebrew *Weltanschauung*. The exodus, while it was a deliverance from physical slavery, yet did lead to a new and higher religious life: in the Hebrew historiographer's view, the exodus included mount Sinai. No wonder, therefore, that once that event was considered the historical model of what would happen in the last days, there was produced the concept of God as redeemer from guilt as well as that of God as redeemer from material suffering. At any rate, Hosea makes God say of Ephraim's children,[161] 'I will ransom them from the power of the grave, I will redeem them from death; O death, I will be thy plagues, O grave, I will be thy destruction....' This idea of redemption from evil is more frequent than a superficial glance through the Old Testament might lead one to believe. For in many visions of the final redemption of the nation, though the material rise may be in the foreground, it is no doubt thought of as combined with a spiritual rise. This is evident, for example, in Isaiah xxxv. 9 f.: 'No lion shall be there...but the redeemed shall walk there; and the ransomed of the Lord shall return, and come to Zion with songs...they shall obtain joy and gladness.' It is highly improbable that the prophet has here in mind nothing but good food and plenty of wine. Similarly, both material and spiritual elevation are often prayed for by the persecuted pious. In their case, indeed, there is a special reason for the linking of the two. Material misfortunes are regarded, by the unthinking mass at least, as a sign of God's anger, as the reward of sin.[162] Consequently, when the persecuted pious prays for redemption from sin, this more or less implies praying for redemption from material misery which can be deemed proof of his wickedness; and when he prays for redemption from material misery, he does so partly because material misery can be deemed proof of his wickedness and he wishes to be free from sin and the appearance of sin. Job xix. 25, 'For I know that my redeemer liveth, and that he shall stand up at the latter day upon the earth', and Lamentations iii. 58, 'O Lord, thou hast pleaded the causes of my soul; thou hast redeemed my life', are examples of such passages referring to both redemption from material sufferings and redemption from sin and the mark of sin.

It is interesting to observe, by the way, how distinctly the two texts just quoted connect the metaphor of redemption by God with its legal basis. In Job xix. 25, God is invoked as redeemer clearly because those who would be the natural, ordinary redeemers, brothers, relatives and friends, have failed: 'He hath put my brethren far from me...my kinsfolk have failed, and my familiar friends have forgotten me; they that dwell in mine house, and my maids, count me for a stranger.'[163] Moreover, the phrase 'he shall stand' refers to the standing up as claimant and witness in a law-suit. In Lamentations iii. 58 also we get a term of procedure, 'thou hast pleaded the causes of my soul'.[164] This is not a mere linguistic curiosity, though it is true that language frequently reflects an earlier stratum which is no longer present in the mind of him who speaks. In this case, a good deal of the legal setting of ordinary redemption was taken over and adapted by priests and prophets even when they worked out redemption of the purely religious kind. We have also to consider that, while priests and prophets evolved the religious notion of redemption, the social laws with the legal notion continued all the time. Thus there remained a constant opportunity of relating the religious notion to its secular ancestor and again and again rejuvenating it in this way.

I have remarked before that in the prophecies of final salvation God is more commonly represented as redeemer of the people enslaved and wrongfully withheld than as redeemer of the murdered people's blood. It must now be added that of those texts which emphasize the spiritual side of salvation the majority seem primarily to allude to redemption of a murdered man's blood. The reason for this may be that in the case of spiritual salvation, salvation from sin, the destruction of the opposing party, of sin, is even more requisite than in the case of salvation from human enemies. The passage quoted above from Hosea[165] is typical: 'O death, I will be thy plagues, O grave, I will be thy destruction.' As death and grave are to be utterly destroyed, the parallel with the redemption of a murdered man's blood, carried out by killing the murderer, is particularly appropriate. It is possible to think of a second reason, partly terminological but partly more than that. When God redeems man from sin, He redeems not so much his body or property as his נפש, his soul (this translation is, of course, inexact but will do for our purposes). Just so it is the soul which, in the case of murder, has to be redeemed by the גאל הדם, the redeemer of blood. It may be recalled that the old law of retaliation begins, נפש תחת נפש, soul for soul.[166] It follows that the same term is central in the provinces of murder and its punishment and of sin and its extirpation. But there is more than just a terminological link. The redeemer of blood 'redeems', 'takes back', the blood; that is to say, according to early notions, he frees the blood from evil masters, from the fetters in which the murderer has bound it, and thereby enables the soul to find its proper resting-place.[167] Surely, these notions did not soon completely die out, however much in the course of time they may have been refined and reinterpreted. Now God, when redeeming the soul from sin, in a higher sense does the same as the redeemer of blood. Once again, Hosea xiii. 14 may be quoted as typical: there God promises, 'I will ransom them from the power of the grave, I will redeem them from death.' It is easily understandable, therefore, why spiritual redemption, redemption from sin, was likened by the prophets to redemption of a murdered man's blood rather more readily than to redemption of slaves or property. The curious point about this is that that form of redemption which to us looks by far the most archaic, the redemption undertaken by the גאל הדם, the 'taker back of blood', should thus survive as the principal basis for the most advanced of all metaphorical references to redemption, for the metaphor of the spiritual redemption by God.

This idea of spiritual redemption is the idea of redemption in its noblest form. What you are delivered from is not material sufferings, loss of land or liberty or blood, but moral sufferings —it might be better to say, religious sufferings—iniquity, wickedness, despair. In this noblest form, the idea of redemption was first proclaimed in the Old Testament, and worked out and given a new significance in the gospels. Jesus, according to the gospels, reclaimed the world, not from material sufferings, but from the worse dangers of moral evil: though, it is true, we have to remember that amongst those who heard him were not a few who supposed his aims to be secular, material, revolutionary and who, when they found that his aims were not what they supposed, left him. The precise mode in which he reclaimed the world and paid for it, namely, by offering himself as ransom, by vicarious sacrifice, need not concern us. (Even here, however, it may be remarked, the legal substratum is far stronger than one might be inclined to think. When considering the history of vicarious sacrifice, it is important not to forget ancient legal institutions like that of עָרֵב, 'surety', or the Roman *vindex* and *sponsor*, and ancient legal customs like that of taking hostages. It has never been properly investigated how far they may have influenced the religious development.) The result that I wish to stress is that the idea of God or Jesus redeeming mankind from sin and damnation, apparently a purely religious idea, derives from those ancient rules on insolvent debtors and victims of murder, on the preservation of the existing clans and the patrimony of clans. To dwell at length on those passages of the New Testament in which the redemption by Jesus is still consciously connected with the original legal kind of redemption would be beyond the scope of this study. Nor is it possible to trace here the manifold elaborations, in the various writings of the New Testament, of the idea of redemption.[168] Best known and most momentous of all is perhaps Paul's doctrine of the redemption from the curse of the Law.[169] But it may well be that precisely some of the more complicated versions would become clearer by taking account of the legal history behind them. The teaching, for instance, that those who are redeemed from sin are slaves of righteousness[170] is strongly reminiscent of the notion, discussed above, that the Israelites, in consequence of their redemption from Egypt, have become slaves of God; a notion in its turn reflecting the ordinary law, under which a powerful man might redeem, and thus bring again under his protection and control, any property or relative that has been lost to another family. That, possibly, at some early stage, a man who was redeemed by a relative or the property of a man which was redeemed by a relative actually became the redeemer's slave or property has been argued above.[171]

It may be noted, incidentally, that the concept of redemption by vicarious sacrifice probably played a much greater part in the tradition underlying the synoptics than would appear if we relied merely on the wording of the text, on the vocabulary. In Mark x. 45[172] we are told that the Son of man 'gives his life a ransom for many'. There are only very few passages in the synoptics stating this concept so explicitly. But, then, we have to consider that the concept does not as such constitute the main point of the pericope. The concept as such seems to be presupposed as well known: it is used as illustration of the warning that the disciples ought to be prepared to serve, instead of to govern, like their master. In other words, it is not this concept, but the inference to be drawn from it, the conclusion that he who wishes to follow and imitate Jesus must prefer to minister rather than be ministered to, which is new, which constitutes the teaching, and to which the narrative is intended to lead up. The author assumes that his readers are quite familiar with the premiss.

In conclusion, let me say that to be clear about the legal source of the religious notion seems of greater importance in the case of the idea of redemption than in the case of many other religious ideas which also have a legal past. For it appears that one or two far-reaching conclusions can be drawn. The concept of salvation, in one form or another, is to be found in a large number of religions. Judaism and Christianity are not unique in this respect. In the Hellenistic age, especially, there were hopes and speculation about deliverance in every corner of the civilized world. Inevitably, Judaism and Christianity were much influenced by all kinds of pagan ideas in this matter; so much so that it is not always easy to say whether a certain idea is genuinely Hebrew or of foreign origin. Yet that peculiar element from the legal-social sphere, the idea of salvation by means of 'red-emption', as far as I know, occurs in no other system. It is a distinctive mark of the Jewish-Christian edifice. (There is nothing legal, in this sense, for example, about the Hellenistic σωτήρ.) It is there, as we have seen, from very early times. It may be more or less accentuated in different periods and writings. But, even up to our day, it has never quite been lost sight of.

Such a unique feature is remarkable enough in itself, and particularly welcome when enabling us to distinguish between what is native growth and what is alien. But here it is of more than academic significance, since it throws light on some of the most striking characteristics of Jewish and Christian religion. In the first place, the prominent part played in the visions of final deliverance by this legal-social element, redemption, by the idea of God reclaiming His own as relative or master, may well be one of the causes, and effects, of a great feeling of confidence that we come across time and again. Salvation is not a vague myth: there is absolute certainty, as within a good family and one the head of which is very powerful, that God will and can and must act. In the second place, the prominent part played by this legal-social element, redemption, no doubt is one of the causes, and effects, of that constant stressing, in the leading religious literature of Judaism and Christianity, of the tremendous importance attaching to our practical work, here and now, by being merciful to the weak, for the final deliverance of the world. In Judaism and Christianity more than in other religions that I can think of is the idea of salvation combined with that of social justice and charity on earth. Salvation is the triumph of love, but it is not dim, sentimental love, but serious love, on which you can rely because it acts in a definite way. If this might seem overrating the influence of the early history of the idea of redemption, surely the very least that one can say is: it must be the result of something specific in the ·spirit of Jewish-Christian religion that one of the main terms for salvation, גאלה, redemption, should have its origin in that province of the protection of the weak, in the province of social legislation.

In the Middle Ages, the legal element in the idea of redemption by God, and in allied ideas, was very much emphasized. At times perhaps it was over-emphasized: salvation, with some theologians, became almost a business transaction. There were, however, great results too, and an outstanding example is Calderón. He was no expert in history of law, and I doubt whether he knew a great deal about the ancient provisions which I have discussed and their role in the evolution of Hebrew doctrine. But in the *Nave del Mercader*, one of his allegorical plays, man is represented as a bankrupt debtor, imprisoned by his creditors, and Jesus as the bankrupt's wealthy brother who, in order that the other may be free, goes to prison himself, willingly suffers all tortures and in the end pays the debt from his immense fund of treasures.[173] Thus the poet retranslates the doctrine of redemption from the religious into exactly that legal sphere from which, some three thousand years before, it had sprung.

NOTES

CHAPTER I

1 *Ancient Law*, first published 1861, new edition, with introduction and notes by Pollock, 1930; *Early Law and Custom*, 1883.

2 We do not know nearly enough. Professor S. A. Cook, to whom I submitted some results of this study, kindly draws my attention to *Primitive Law* by A. S. Diamond, 1935. Dr Diamond says about Maine's system, somewhat harshly though not a great deal too harshly, that 'there is no substance in any of these conclusions' (p. 4). He himself, however, is on ground no firmer when he goes on: 'indeed the contrary can be clearly demonstrated by evidence'. I am afraid it cannot. It is, for instance, pure conjecture, and of the most hazardous kind, to maintain (p. 124) that 'almost until the close of Biblical history, rules of the law, on the one hand, and rules of morality and religion, on the other, were separate conceptions among the Hebrews and were to be found in separate documents'; or that 'so far from the Hebrew law being derived from rules of religion or morality, it can hardly be doubted that the relative order in which they appear is, firstly rules of law...secondly rules of morality...and lastly rules of religious ritual'. One of Dr Diamond's arguments from Greek history is that the notion of pollution of land by homicide is to be met with in Aeschylus but not in Homer, who is earlier (pp. 150 f.). Here he seems to forget about the very remark with which he opens his book (p. 1, see also p. 175), namely, that the same point in the evolution of law may be reached at an earlier date here and a later date there: which surely implies that before assuming a development between Homer and Aeschylus, we have to make quite certain that Homer is representative not only of an earlier period but also of an earlier stage of civilization. The *leges regiae*, not suiting Dr Diamond's theory at all, are, he says, 'of no great age and have no connection with the Roman law' (p. 134). Of the XII Tables, equally inconvenient, Dr Diamond asserts (p. 139): 'The great bulk of the clauses belong to the date of approximately 190 B.C....A few of the clauses may be later, and a few are spurious, and there is evidence that one or two of the rules were earlier than 194 B.C. and had ceased to be in force.' This is his example of spurious law (pp. 141 f.): 'Finally an example of spurious law may be given. There is a

group of clauses defining details of the process whereby personal execution is levied on a judgment debtor—Tab. III—culminating at the point where he is cut up and divided equally among the creditors. It is even provided that no creditor who cuts more or less than his share shall be guilty of fraud. This is nonsense.' It is superfluous to show that history is here made to comply with a theory. I fail to see why rules to govern the relations between man and God, or nature, should not have been worked out by some tribes as early as rules to govern the relations between man and man. Nor is it clear to me why rules of law, morality and religion (as far as they were consciously distinguished at all) should not have interacted on one another from the outset, at least in this or that community. May not a few of the lowest First Hunters have felt, rightly or wrongly, that cohabitation, for example, was a phenomenon not of a purely practical, 'legal' nature, but somehow connected with and directed by a superhuman power; that homicide was more than a private affair between the parties concerned; and even that there was something morally (not only practically or religiously) wrong about killing a trusting fellow with malice aforethought or breaking one's word? It is apparently a popular procedure among modern writers to combine numerous little scraps of evidence taken from every quarter of the earth, as if the whole world must be the same. But it may fairly be questioned whether the praise bestowed by an Icelandic saga on 'a great manslayer' (Diamond, p. 148) argues the absence of moral and religious qualms about homicide at any period in, say, the Far East. Actually, it does not even prove that these qualms were unknown to the author of the saga himself (not to mention the less heroic classes of the society of his age). The fact is that at present we have no more than a smattering of any of the ancient systems of law, not excepting ancient (I mean, pre-Republican and early Republican) Roman law. It is useless to try to derive from these half-known quantities fundamental results, or rather (for this is what is being sought) support for preconceived fundamental opinions, as to the genesis of civilization. To adduce in confirmation of such theories evidence from contemporary primitive tribes, as is amply done both by the advocates of a religious origin of civilization and by the materialists, only makes matters worse. For even if our information about the aboriginals were less scanty and insecure than it is, the assumption that these tribes in all essential features are like our, or their own, remote ancestors, though, as it seems, enjoying universal acceptance, has yet to be proved. Nothing is easier, once the methods of accurate research are dropped, than so to date, arrange and revise early sources that they agree with whatever one's ideas of evolution may be. Of the countless rivalling schemes built up in this way, one is as good as the other.

3 Genesis xxxvii. 31 ff.

4 See F. Schulz, *Zeitschrift für vergleichende Rechtswissenschaft*, xxvii, 1912, pp. 150 f., with no reference, however, to the story of Joseph.

5 Ehrlich, *Randglossen zur hebräischen Bibel*, cited in Gesenius's *Handwörterbuch*, 16th ed., by F. Buhl, 1915, s.v. עד (not in the *Hebrew and English Lexicon*, hereafter cited as *Lexicon*, by Brown, Driver and Briggs, 1906), substitutes יביא העֹר, 'let him bring the skin', for יבאהו עד, an emendation as ingenious as rash. I can think of two points in the existing text which one might at first sight find strange, but neither of them actually is. First, the shepherd has to bring the remnants of the animal 'as witness': can an inanimate thing be called 'a witness'? It can, as may be seen from many passages, *e.g.* Genesis xxxi. 52, 'This heap be witness, and this pillar be witness', or Deuteronomy xxxi. 26, 'It (the book of law) may be there for a witness, against thee'. How far the expression is a metaphor, how far inanimate objects were really looked upon as animate, need not here be decided. Secondly, is this use of the double accusative, 'to bring something (the animal) as something (as witness)', normal Hebrew? It is: see, *e.g.* Genesis xxxi. 45, 'And Jacob...set it (the stone) up for a pillar', Exodus xxxi. 16, 'The children of Israel shall keep the Sabbath...for a perpetual covenant', or Numbers xv. 25, 'They shall bring their offering, a sacrifice made by fire unto the Lord'; cp. also constructions like Judges v. 7 ('double nominative' one might term them), 'I arose a mother in Israel'. One positive factor speaks strongly in favour of the traditional text. According to the traditional text, the shepherd must bring for witness 'it', that is to say, the animal that is torn. In Genesis xxxi. 39 Jacob reminds Laban, 'That which was torn I brought not unto thee.' In the face of this close similarity to emend Exodus xxii. 12 (13) seems quite unjustifiable. I may add that the question does not affect the main argument submitted.

6 According to Schulz, *loc. cit.*, a shepherd had to produce the remnants as evidence not only that the loss was in fact due to a wild beast but also that he had valiantly fought the assailant. The question has no bearing on the main argument of the text. It may be observed, however, that Schulz's theory rests on I Samuel xvii. 34 ff. and Amos iii. 12, a very slender basis. In the former passage, David describes how he saved a sheep from a lion and bear. His purpose is to convince Saul that he is a match for Goliath. This impression would be conveyed by his story whether there was a rule that a shepherd must fight or not: one might even hold that it would be conveyed with greater force if such a rule did not exist, his resistance having been spontaneous. In Amos iii. 12, the prophet announces, not that God will fight, but on the contrary that He will not fight for Israel: 'As the shepherd taketh out of the mouth of the lion two legs (*i.e.* only two legs) or a piece of an ear (*i.e.* just a last bit of an ear); so shall the children of Israel be taken out that dwell in Samaria in the corner of a bed, and in Damascus in a couch.' The warning means that there will be a disaster after which the nation will look like the scraps saved out of a lion's mouth by the shepherd: it is impossible to say whether the prophet has in mind a shepherd acting with a view to a rule that he must fight, or only a rule that he must show how the sheep was killed, or, for that matter, no rule whatever.

7 Genesis xxxi. 39. See above, this page, n. 5, towards the end.

8 Genesis xxxvii. 33. It is relevant to note that the emphatic form recurs again in xliv. 28, where the brothers tell Joseph how their father reminded them of the affair on a later occasion: 'And the one went out from me, and I said, He is tear, torn (surely torn) in pieces.'

9 Genesis xxxvii. 32 f.

10 This does not imply that it was not used in non-technical senses. See Gesenius's *Handwörterbuch* and the *Lexicon* for references; and also for literature on the original meaning of the root נכר, and the connection between נכר as underlying forms meaning 'to know' and נכר as underlying forms meaning 'not to know'.

11 Genesis xxxviii. 25 f.   **12** Genesis xxxi. 32.

13 On the legal background of the search of Jacob's tents, the *quaestio*, see below, in the fifth study, pp. 205 ff.

14 See below, pp. 206, 256.   **15** Cp. Exodus xxxii. 27 ff.

16 Sumerian Laws 5; Sumerian Family Laws 3 f.

17 Sumerian Laws 4; Sumerian Family Laws 1 f.

18 Par. 192.

19 Isaiah lxiii. 16. See also p. 47.   **20** For details, see pp. 39 ff.

21 Jeremiah xxiv. 5.   **22** Psalm cxlii. 5 (4) f.

23 Deuteronomy i. 17, xvi. 19, Proverbs xxiv. 23, xxviii. 21.

24 The verb here appears in the Piel, נכר.

25 Possibly, I Kings xviii. 7 belongs here: 'And as Obadjah was in the way, behold, Elijah met him: and he discerned him, and fell on his face.' 'To discern' might mean not just 'to realize the identity of the other person', but 'to realize the identity and acknowledge as prophet'. In I Kings xx. 41, however, the word probably means no more than 'to realize': 'And he (the prophet)...took the ashes away from his face; and the king of Israel discerned him that he was one of the prophets.' Similarly, in Lamentations iv. 8 (where the verb appears in the Niphal, נִכַּר), the translation 'to realize the identity' is quite sufficient, though 'to acknowledge' is not impossible: 'Their visage (the visage of the Nazarites of fallen Zion) is blacker than a coal; they are not discerned in the streets.' It is to be noted that in Job ii. 12, where the situation is not unlike that of Lamentations iv. 8, הִכִּיר cannot mean more than 'to realize the identity'. Job's friends do acknowledge him, but find it difficult to recognize the former Job in the figure sitting among the ashes: 'And when they lifted up their eyes afar off, and discerned him not, they...wept.' In Isaiah lxi. 9, the prophet promises that 'their seed shall be known among the Gentiles...all that see them shall discern them, that they are the seed which the Lord hath blessed'. Here again, we have probably to translate 'to realize the identity', for the redeemed will be so happy and exalted that nobody can be mistaken about them. But the idea of 'acknowledgement' may conceivably play some part also.

26 See Gesenius's *Handwörterbuch* and the *Lexicon*, *s.v.* מַכָּר.

27 Five passages from Talmudic, medieval, Renaissance and modern writings may be compared. (1) Mishnah Baba Kamma x. 3 has been mentioned above. (2) הִכִּיר was used by Rabbi Judah the Prince when he told Bar Kappara that he did not recognize him as worthy of having intercourse with scholars, or that he did not recognize him as an ordained scholar: Babylonian Moed Katan 16a, Palestinian Moed Katan 81c. (In view of these passages, it seems possible that the verb הִכִּיר is behind utterances like Matthew vii. 23, xxv. 12, II Timothy ii. 19.) (3) According to Abraham Ibn-Daud (*Seder Ha-Kabbalah*, last chapter), Anan, founder of the Caraites, was not made leader of the Jews because הכירו בו שמץ פסול, 'they discerned in him the stain (the defamation) of unfitness'. (4) When Fiesco's conspiracy had ended by his being drowned, a rumour, it seems, arose among the populace that he had escaped and was still alive. Andreas Doria decided to stop this and, as Joseph Ha-Cohen tells us (*Dibhre Ha-Yamim Le-Malkhe Tzarphat* 2), שנית ויכירוהו להכיר ויעלוהו היו, 'They fetched him up that he might be discerned and threw him back once again into the sea.' (5) *Beur* (Joel Löwe), commenting on Psalm xci. 14, remarks that the knowledge of the name of God is meant to lead to 'the discernment, the recognition, of His greatness'.

28 Genesis xlii. 4, 36 ff., xliii. 3 ff., xliv. 27 ff. (see also p. 13). By this time, indeed, they had temporarily lost Simeon also: see Genesis xlii. 18 ff.

29 Genesis xliv. 28.

30 This might be regarded as an illustration of what has been said of early English law, namely, that we must not speak of the burden of proof but of the benefit of proof. 'Proof was a benefit, not a burden' (Holdsworth, *History of English Law*, 3rd ed., vol. II, 1923, p. 107). I should agree with the maxim if it were not for the fact, just mentioned, that if you cannot furnish the prescribed proof, the decision will inevitably be against you.

31 Two other instances will be pointed out below, pp. 248 ff.

32 Genesis xlii. 4, 38, xliv. 29.

33 It may be noticed that, under Talmudic law, it was not sufficient to prove the mere fact that the animal had been killed by the wild beasts: in addition to this, it had to be shown what and how many wild beasts had done it. A much freer method of collecting and valuing evidence than had prevailed at an earlier age made it possible to take into consideration these fine points.

34 Genesis xlii. 4.   **35** Exodus xxi. 22 f.

36 For references, see Gesenius's *Handwörterbuch*. (Sirach is not yet considered in the *Lexicon*.)

37 The point against its being technical is far from decisive. I have said before, in dealing with the verb הכיר, that a term may have a technical meaning in one text and a non-technical in another (see above, p. 64, n. 10). In the case of אסון as in that of הכיר is involved the whole problem of 'hibernation', of the survival in post-Biblical literature of words, or special meanings of words, to be found in very early sources, conspicuously absent from later, and suddenly reappearing in Rabbinic writings. Needless to say, the absence of a word or meaning from the sources of a certain period does not prove that the word or meaning was not, in reality, used during that time. From this point of view, the expression 'hibernation' is dangerous.

38 Incidentally, in Solomon's Song viii. 8–10, I do not think that the brothers speak as mere guardians of their little sister (if indeed the terms 'brother' and 'sister' are used in the narrow, literal sense and not simply as terms of endearment or as denoting a more distant relationship). They speak, at least poetically, as pretenders to her hand: one of them will be her husband. The reference to marriage between brother and sister is perfectly clear in viii. 1 f. (it may again be purely poetical, of course), though the translations tend to obscure it. Cp. below, p. 99, n. 9.

39 Quite possibly, the guardianship was confined to the case where the brothers were of different mothers and the younger had no claim to the inheritance; see p. 15.

40 Siphra on Leviticus xxvi. 37.

41 See, *e.g.*, Ezekiel iii. 16 ff. and xxxiii. 1 ff. (referred to below, n. 45). In the early Christian community, incidentally, with its intense consciousness of a very special vocation, the idea under notice played a great part: see I Thessalonians v. 14 and II Thessalonians iii. 6–15.

42 Genesis xxxvii. 29 f.

43 Genesis xlii. 37, xliii. 9 and xliv. 32.   **44** See p. 9.

45 It may be worth noting that, whilst a shepherd's responsibility, according to Exodus xxii. 9 (10) ff., does not extend to *force majeure*, that of a man who borrows cattle, according to xxii. 13 (14) f., in certain circumstances does. Two cases where the wording seems to suggest 'absolute' responsibility may be found in I Kings xx. 38 ff. and II Kings x. 24; both times it is a guard who is 'absolutely' responsible for prisoners entrusted to him. On the former case, something will be said presently, in discussing the term שמר; and more will be said about it and the latter case below, pp. 116 ff. An instance of limited responsibility of one man for another occurs in Ezekiel iii. 16 ff., and xxxiii. 1 ff. (see this page, n. 41): the prophet is compared to a watchman who sees the enemy and, if he warns those in his charge of the approach of danger, is free from liability, but, if he fails to warn them, will have to answer for the consequences.

46 Genesis iv. 9.

47 See, *e.g.*, Mishnah Baba Metzia vii. 8. It may be added that שמר remains frequent also in non-technical senses (cp. above, p. 64, n. 10, and this page, n. 37).

48 Genesis xxx. 31.

49 Gesenius's *Handwörterbuch*, *s.v.* I שמר, makes it a mere *nähere Bestimmung* *zu* רעה. The *Lexicon* lists the passage as one of many where the verb means 'to tend a flock'.

50 I Samuel xvii. 20, 28.

51 Hosea xii. 13 (12) f. It seems to me that the parallel structure of the two clauses requires the translation: 'And for a prophet (for the sake of Moses) the Lord brought Israel out of Egypt, and for a prophet was he (Israel) kept.' The question does not, however, affect the argument of the text.

52 See above, p. 66, n. 45, and below, pp. 116 f.

53 For references, see Gesenius's *Handwörterbuch* and the *Lexicon*.

54 Solomon's Song iii. 3.   **55** I Samuel xvii. 22.

56 I Samuel xxvi. 15 f., II Kings xi. 5 ff. (here שׁמר משׁמרת, literally translated, 'to guard the guard' of the palace, for 'to guard' the palace).

57 The latter is the case in Isaiah xxi. 11 f., lxii. 6. In texts like Genesis xxviii. 15 or Psalm cxxi. 3 f., it is impossible to determine exactly which specific application of שׁמר underlies the metaphor—probably it is more than one.

58 II Samuel xiv. 1 ff., referring to xiii. 28 f. Cp. Genesis iv. 8 ff. and, possibly, xxvii. 45.

59 Genesis xlii. 37. As for Judah, he declares that he will 'bear the blame for ever' if he does not restore Benjamin: Genesis xliii. 9 and xliv. 32.

60 See this page, n. 65, and p. 19.

61 See, however, this page, n. 69, on *locatio conductio operarum* as an alternative description of this latter case.

62 Gesenius's *Handwörterbuch* and the *Lexicon* accept the Rabbinic interpretation, adducing Isaiah vii. 20 as a second text where שׂכיר is employed as an adjective. It will soon be seen, however, that in Isaiah, too, the term signifies 'hired man': the best translation there would be 'hired ally'—see below, pp. 68 f., n. 73, under (3).

63 Gesenius's *Handwörterbuch*, *s.v.* I שׂכר, quotes the verse under discussion as the only passage in the Bible where the noun שׂכר denotes, not 'the hire paid for a man's services', but 'the hire paid for a hired thing'. I have no doubt that שׂכר could be used in this sense even in the Biblical period. Yet, as it happens, it is not so used in any text preserved to us, and Exodus xxii. 14*b* (15*b*) forms no exception. Once we recognize that the שׂכיר, to whom this rule relates, is a labourer, the שׂכר obviously must be the hire, the wages, paid for his services. In the *Lexicon*, *s.v.* I שָׂכָר, Exodus xxii. 14 (15) and Zechariah viii. 10 are said to use the noun in the sense of 'wages of a beast'. As far as Exodus xxii. 14 (15) is concerned, this is obviously wrong: it is not the beast that is paid, whatever interpretation of the verse as a whole we adopt, but either its owner or the labourer. The translation is correct for Zechariah viii. 10. Here beasts are spoken of as deserving reward for their labours like men: 'For before these days there was no hire (wages) for man, nor any hire (wages) for beast.'

64 See also Geiger, *Urschrift und Übersetzungen der Bibel*, 2nd ed., 1928, pp. 190 ff. There are other conceivable interpretations, but all of them, if to be persuasive at all, must be based on the translation of שׂכיר by 'labourer', not 'hired thing'.

65 I have mentioned Roman law. As for Babylonian law (and Greek law), see p. 19.

66 *E.g.* the Mekhiltha on Exodus xxii. 6 (7) ff. and Mishnah Baba Metzia vii. 8. Cp. Daube, *Tulane Law Review*, xviii, 1944, p. 384.

67 Genesis xxx. 14 ff.   **68** Genesis xxix. 15 ff.

69 Occasionally, however, the lawyers called this contract also *locatio conductio operarum* (see this page, n. 61). My whole account of the Roman *locatio conductio* is somewhat simplified, my purpose being to elucidate the Biblical position.

70 Leviticus xix. 13, Deuteronomy xxiv. 14 f. Some provisions speaking of the 'paid labourer', the 'hireling', may well have regard to the poorer type of workmen only.

71 Exodus xii. 45, Leviticus xxii. 10.

72 Judges ix. 4, Jeremiah xlvi. 21, II Samuel x. 6, I Chronicles xix. 6 f. (on this passage see also the following note), II Chronicles xxv. 6. In Ezekiel xxix. 18 f. there seems to be a metaphorical reference to the noun שֶׂכֶר in the sense of 'the hire of mercenaries', 'the payment of mercenaries'.

73 Three texts are to be adduced, though Gesenius's *Handwörterbuch* and the *Lexicon* do not list this meaning at all. (1) II Kings vii. 6: 'And they (the Syrians) said to one another, Lo, the king of Israel hath hired against us the kings of the Hittites, and the kings of the Egyptians, to come upon us.' According to Gesenius's *Handwörterbuch*, *s.v.* שָׂכַר, 'to hire' is here used in an unpleasant sense, as in some other texts (they will be quoted in note 76) where it refers to dealings like the bribing of an official. I can detect no trace of this nuance in the passage under notice. 'To hire' in this sentence signifies 'to purchase an ally': the Syrians believed that the hard-pressed king of Israel, by making a good enough offer of reward, had gained the Hittite and Egyptian kings as allies. The *Lexicon*, *s.v.* שָׂכַר, classes the text not among those where the verb is used in an unpleasant sense but among those where it signifies 'to hire soldiers etc.' This, indeed, is correct as far as it goes; only my point is that the meaning 'to hire a king' deserves special attention. (2) I Chronicles xix. 6 f.: 'Hanun (king of Ammon) and the children of Ammon sent a thousand talents of silver to hire them chariots and horsemen out of Mesopotamia, and out of Syria-maachah, and out of Zobah. So they hired thirty and two thousand chariots, and the king of Maachah and his people.' Gesenius's *Handwörterbuch* and the *Lexicon* quote this text as one in which 'to hire' is used of the engaging of mercenary soldiers, and the *Lexicon* says that the meaning is exactly the same as in II Samuel x. 6 ('II Samuel x. 6 = I Chronicles xix. 6 f.'). Like the *Lexicon*'s treatment of II Kings vii. 6 discussed under (1) in this note, this is in order as far as it goes (see the preceding note); only it is not exhaustive. In II Samuel x. 6, it is merely the employment of mercenary troops that is mentioned. According to I Chronicles xix. 6 f., however, King Hanun and the Ammonites 'hired' not only troops but also the king of Maachah and his people. Obviously, at least as far as this king and his people are concerned, we have once more to interpret שָׂכַר as denoting the securing by payment of an ally. Needless to say, the line between this and the recruiting by payment of mercenaries must often be difficult to draw. (3) Isaiah vii. 20: 'In the same day shall the Lord shave with a razor, with the one that is a hireling, namely, by them beyond the river, by the king of Assyria, the head and the hair of the feet: and it shall also consume the beard.' The meaning of this prophecy is that God will punish King Ahaz of Judah through the very Assyrians on whom, despite the prophet's warning, he relies for help against Syria. The Assyrians are called 'a razor' because, by robbing, slaying and taking captive, they will destroy the pride—the hair and the beard—of Judah. They are called a razor that is a 'hireling' because they are being 'hired', paid for their services against Syria, by King Ahaz. This we know from II Kings xvi. 7 ff. (cp. II Chronicles xxviii. 16 ff.), where it is recorded how Ahaz 'sent messengers to Tiglath-pileser...saying... Come up and save me out of the hand of the king of Syria....And Ahaz took the silver and gold that was found in the house of the Lord, and in the treasures of the king's house, and sent it for a present to the king of Assyria. And the king of Assyria hearkened unto him...and went up against Damascus, and took it.' It is clear that Isaiah uses the phrase 'a razor, the hireling' in the sense of 'Assyria, the ally whom you are gaining by payment, purchasing'. (This remains true even if we interpret Isaiah's prophecy as a promise to

Ahaz, not a threat—an interpretation just possible; namely, as meaning that God will defeat the Syrians who are menacing Ahaz, will have consumed their hair and beard, through the Assyrians, the 'hireling', the ally of Ahaz.) Gesenius's *Handwörterbuch* and the *Lexicon*, *s.v.* שָׂכִיר, offer what I am afraid is a wrong translation. They say that in two passages out of twenty, of which this is the one and Exodus xxii. 14*b* (15*b*) the other, the word שָׂכִיר does not signify 'a labourer', 'a hireling', but is used as an adjective signifying 'hired'. But as for Exodus xxii. 14*b* (15*b*), small support anyhow since it is so obscure, I have already pointed out that the word there seems to have its normal meaning, that is to say, the meaning of 'labourer' (see above, p. 16); and the same, it must now be added, is true of Isaiah vii. 20. Here, too, the word means 'hireling'. For, although the first member of the apposition, 'a razor, the hireling', or 'a razor, the one that is a hireling', is apparently an inanimate thing, for which the description as 'hireling' does not seem suitable, yet this is not the whole truth (it is, indeed, this half-truth which must have led to the slip in Gesenius's *Handwörterbuch* and the *Lexicon*). The word 'razor' is employed metaphorically, and stands for the very animate Assyrians and their king: it is really they whom the prophet calls 'hirelings'. It follows that, in Gesenius's *Handwörterbuch*, *s.v.* שָׂכִיר, the first division, with שָׂכִיר as *adj. pass.*, 'hired', ought to go. Exodus xxii. 14*b* (15*b*) ought to be taken under what is now 2*a*, 'paid labourer'; and Isaiah vii. 20 either under what is now 2*b*, 'mercenary troops', or even under a separate, fresh class, 'purchased ally'. In the *Lexicon*, similarly, the first, adjectival meaning ascribed to שָׂכִיר should be dropped. Exodus xxii. 14*b* (15*b*) should be given as an instance of the meaning 'hireling, hired labourer', Isaiah vii. 20 as one of the meaning 'mercenaries'—though it might be worth indicating that in the latter passage we find the nuance 'purchased ally'.

74 *E.g.* Genesis xv. 1, Isaiah xl. 10. In course of time, there arose the danger of people's really thinking of the reward expected from God for their good works in terms of a legal or quasi-legal claim. This is not the place to pursue the various manifestations of, and reactions against, this idea.

75 Genesis xxx. 18, the naming of Issachar.

76 Deuteronomy xxiii. 5 (4), Nehemiah xiii. 2, vi. 12 f., סָכַר in Ezra iv. 5 (on this passage see also below, p. 70, n. 86). That II Kings vii. 6 does not, as Gesenius's *Handwörterbuch* (but not the *Lexicon*) asserts, belong to this group has been pointed out in note 73, at the beginning.

77 See, *e.g.*, Mishnah Baba Metzia vi. 1–5, with the Gemara attached. As it is only in the episode of the mandrakes that the Bible applies שׂכר to *locatio conductio rei*, there being no further references to this kind of agreement in the whole of the Old Testament, and as the word is again used of *locatio conductio rei* in the Talmud, this may be regarded as another instance of 'hibernation', like the case of הכיר (and, possibly, that of אסון): see above, p. 66, n. 37. There can be no doubt, however, that though our sources happen to be silent throughout the period between the story of the mandrakes and the Talmud, the agreement did exist and the word שׂכר was used to denote it all the time.

78 Indeed, as for the Romans, the mere fact that the phrases *locare conducere rem* and *locare conducere operas* became more and more stereotyped as time went on argues a tendency towards making a stronger distinction between the two; though the express classification into two types is probably medieval. It should be noted, by the way, that the further Roman subdivision of *locatio conductio operis* does not seem to have existed in ancient Hebrew law, though it is adumbrated in some Talmudic provisions. The Romans, as we have seen, described as *locatio conductio operarum* the letting and hiring of services, the becoming and engaging a gardener or secretary. But it may now be recalled that they described as *locatio conductio operis* the letting out by the employer, and hiring by the employee, of a definite piece of work to be performed, such as the painting of a portrait or the building of a house.

79 The word belongs to the same family as the German *Miete*, which is a legal term signifying 'hire', and the English 'meed', which nowadays is confined to poetical style.

80 See J. G. Lautner, *Altbabylonische Personenmiete und Erntearbeiterverträge*, 1936.

81 Genesis xxx. 15 ff.   **82** See pp. 17 f.

83 In Plautus, *Asinaria* 1. 3. 172, the procuress who negotiates about the fee for her daughter compares their undertaking to *locatio conductio operarum*.

84 They number seventeen, and in addition there are many in which the notion of 'hire' is expressed by derivatives of שכר. On Gesenius's rendering of סכר in Ezra iv. 5, see this page, n. 86.

85 Curiously, while the *Handwörterbuch* is too strong, making the transaction a sale, the *Lexicon* is slightly too weak. The latter, *s.v.* שכר, translates Genesis xxx. 16 by 'to hire a husband's favour'. But Leah does not hire Jacob's favour: she hires himself, though, of course, the term is used figuratively. The temptation to tone down a metaphor like this must be resisted.

86 Gesenius is similarly, though not quite so, loose when he translates סכר in Ezra iv. 5 by *erkaufen*, this time even without the support of Luther, who very correctly says, *und dingten Ratgeber*. As I have just pointed out, *erkaufen* is a less objectionable rendering of שכר than *kaufen*, 'to buy', and exactly the same applies, of course, to the case of סכר, the only difference between שכר and סכר being one of spelling. None the less the precise translation of סכר, as of שכר, is *mieten, dingen*, 'to hire'. The meaning of Ezra iv. 5 is that the enemies of Zerubabel bribed some Persian ministers, secured their services by paying them, 'hired' them as one might hire people under *locatio conductio operarum*. (Cp. above, p. 69, n. 76, for the whole group of texts in which שכר, 'to hire', is used in this or a similar sense.) The A.V., here as in the story of the mandrakes (see pp. 20 f.), has the accurate 'to hire': 'and hired counsellors against them, to frustrate their purpose'. The *Lexicon*, *s.v.* II סכר, translates correctly, 'to hire'.

87 Genesis xxx. 9 and 17 f.   **88** Genesis xxx. 18.

89 See p. 18.

90 Numbers xx. 7 ff., xx. 23 ff., xxvii. 12 ff., Deuteronomy i. 37, iii. 23 ff., iv. 21 f., xxxii. 48 ff., xxxiv. 1 ff., Psalm xcv. 8 ff. (?), cvi. 32 f.

91 More precisely, for a sin that he and Aaron had committed according to Numbers xx. 7 ff., xx. 23 ff., xxvii. 12 ff. and Deuteronomy xxxii. 48 ff., and for a sin that the people had committed according to Deuteronomy i. 37, iii. 23 ff., iv. 21 f., Psalm xcv. 8 ff. and cvi. 32. See also p. 31.

92 Deuteronomy xxxiv. 1 ff.

93 Cicero, *Pro Tullio* 7. 17; *Digest* 18. 1. 18. 1, 21. 2. 45.

94 41. 2. 1. 21.   **95** 41. 2. 18. 2.

96 Or is the east added? This would account for the otherwise somewhat puzzling sequence of directions: west (looking straight ahead), north (looking to the right), south (to the left)—and east added.

97 The question does not affect the main argument as to the original, legal significance of the last event in Moses' life.

98 The sequence of directions, north, south, east, west, is quite plausible.

99 Numbers xx. 7 ff., xx. 23 ff. (chiefly about Aaron), Deuteronomy i. 37, iv. 21 f., Psalm xcv. 8 ff. (if referring to Moses), cvi. 32 f.

100 Numbers xxvii. 12 ff., Deuteronomy xxxii. 48 ff.

101 Numbers xxvii. 12 ff., Deuteronomy iii. 23 ff., xxxii. 48 ff.

102 It may be remarked that, especially when we assume this co-existence of the two ideas from the outset, the analysis here attempted of the story of Moses' death is not, as far as I can see, in conflict with the axioms of orthodox Judaism.

103 Numbers xxii. 41.   104 Numbers xxiii. 14.

105 Numbers xxiii. 28.

106 See *Geist des Römischen Rechts*, vol. II, part II, 6th/7th ed., 1923, p. 429.

107 See, *e.g.*, A. Hägerström, *Der Römische Obligationsbegriff*, 1927.

108 When the author of *Digest* 41. 2. 1. 21, cited above, p. 27, contrasts 'sight and intention' with 'physical contact', this is the view of the lawyer of the Principate or Dominate. I doubt whether it would have been that of the lawyer in the time of the Kings or the early Republic.

109 Genesis xiii. 14 f.

110 For that matter, I know of no other Western system, independent of Roman law, with the clear Roman distinction, though few are as hazy as Oriental law.

111 Matthew iv. 8 f.; cp. Luke iv. 5 ff.

112 There are a large number of texts showing that the notion of the eye as exercising great power had not disappeared by the time of the New Testament, at least not from language. When Jesus says (Matthew v. 28), 'That whosoever looketh on a woman to lust after her hath committed adultery with her already in his heart', or when the Rabbis say (Leviticus Rabba on xviii. 3, towards the end) that 'Not only he who commits adultery with his body is called adulterer, but also he who commits adultery with his eyes is called adulterer', it is not without significance that the evil intention, which is equated with the deed, finds expression in 'looking', 'the eyes'. An interesting parallel outside Rabbinic literature is furnished by the story of Gellius (*Noctes Atticae* 7. 8. 2), which he says he takes from Apion, and according to which Alexander, having heard of the beauty of the wife of Darius, gave orders not to bring her before him when she had been captured, *ut eam ne oculis quidem suis contingeret.*

113 Stevenson, in *The Treasure of Franchard*, disarmingly says of his French law of treasure trove: 'Let it be so, for my tale!'

114 The passages with גאל will be discussed in the course of this inquiry. For פדה, see Exodus xxi. 30, a homicide ransoming himself, cp. Psalm xlix. 8 (7) f., ransoming a man from the verdict of God; Numbers iii. 46 ff., ransoming a number of firstborn children; Exodus xxi. 8, Leviticus xix. 20, ransoming a bondwoman, cp. Isaiah l. 1 f., God ransoming Israel who had to sell themselves.

115 גאל with a person as object occurs, *e.g.*, in Leviticus xxv. 48, with a beast in xxvii. 27, with a field in xxv. 25; and from Numbers v. 8 it looks as if even movables might be the object (the text implies that in some cases a man who defrauds another man must make restitution not to the defrauded himself but to the גאל, 'the redeemer'; whether it would be correct Hebrew—on the basis of this text—to say that the latter person 'redeems' the object or money which was withheld is not quite certain, but in all probability it would).

116 פדה with a person as object occurs, *e.g.*, in Leviticus xxvii. 29, with a beast in Leviticus xxvii. 27.

117 Leviticus xxvii. 27.

118 See גאל, Exodus vi. 6, and פדה, Deuteronomy vii. 8, with reference to God delivering Israel from the slavery of Egypt; both גאל and פדה in Isaiah xxxv. 9 f. and Jeremiah xxxi. 10 (11), of God's final deliverance of Israel; both גאל and פדה in Hosea xiii. 14, of God delivering Israel from grave and death; and גאל, Psalm ciii. 4, and פדה, Job xxxiii. 28, with reference to God delivering the pious from spiritual destruction.

119 Ruth iii. 13, Numbers xxxv. 16 ff.

120 Isaiah lxiii. 4; see Gesenius's *Handwörterbuch, s.v.* גאולים, and the *Lexicon, s.v.* גאולי.

121 Leviticus xxv. 47 ff., xxv. 25 ff.

122 On the origin of the idea that by killing the murderer you 'redeem', 'get back', the blood of the murdered, see some tentative remarks below, pp. 123 f., 128.

123 Leviticus xxv. 47 ff.   **124** Leviticus xxv. 47.

125 Leviticus xxv. 25 ff., Ruth iv. 3 ff. There are many special rules about special cases, *e.g.* about redemption of a house in a walled town, Leviticus xxv. 29 f.

126 Leviticus xxv. 47 ff.   **127** Leviticus xxv. 25 ff.

128 Numbers xxxv. 16 ff. See below, pp. 123 f., 128.

129 Ruth iii. 13.   **130** Psalm lxxii. 14.

131 Proverbs xxiii. 10 f.; cp. pp. 47 f. on Jeremiah l. 34 and p. 57 on Lamentations iii. 58.

132 The phrase דרש דם (on which something will have to be said in a different connection below, p. 123) occurs in the same sense in Genesis ix. 5, where God says that He will require man's blood from man and beast, in Genesis xlii. 22, where Reuben thinks that God is requiring Joseph's blood from him and his brothers, and Ezekiel xxxiii. 6, where God says that He will require the blood of the murdered from the faithless watchman. This is not the place to examine why the phrase דרש דם or דרש דמים is employed only where God avenges an injury, but never where a man does it.

133 Though this particular passage does not contain the term גאל, it forms part of the story of the deliverance from Egypt in which, as will be shown, the idea of redemption occupies a specially prominent place.

134 See p. 8.   **135** Isaiah lii. 3.

136 Jeremiah l. 34.   **137** Psalm cvii. 1 f.

138 Exodus vi. 6 f.   **139** Isaiah li. 10 f.

140 Exodus iv. 22 f.   **141** Exodus iii. 21.

142 Exodus iii. 21 f., xi. 2 f., xii. 35 f. Of course, the actual result is, as the Bible says, a despoliation of the Egyptians.

143 Exodus xii. 36. Whether these laws about release were ever, in fact, applicable to Hebrew slaves in the hands of foreigners is a question that need not here be examined. The writers composing the narrative of the exodus surely considered themselves free to represent God as acting on Hebrew laws in any situation.

144 The verb refers to *commodatum* in Exodus xxii. 13 (14), for example, and II Kings iv. 3, vi. 5.

145 See *e.g.* Joshua xv. 18, Judges i. 14, I Kings iii. 5, 10 f., Psalm ii. 8, xxi. 5 (4), Proverbs xxx. 7, II Kings ii. 9 f., iv. 28, Psalm cix. 10, Proverbs xx. 4 ('to beg'). Luther translates correctly: in Exodus iii. 22, xi. 2, xii. 35, he has *fordern* (though the humbler *bitten* would be better of slaves saying good-bye) and in xii. 36 *willfährig sein*. Similarly, in I Samuel i. 17, 27, 28, ii. 20, a gift is certainly meant, and Luther translates *bitten* and *geben*, while the English version again refers to a loan.

146 This is not pronouncing on the actual events behind the narrative. In particular, I do not mean to suggest that the orthodox Jewish view must be wrong. In maintaining that the description of a certain event is influenced by a certain law, I am not maintaining that the facts may not have been precisely as recorded.

147 Exodus vi. 7. **148** Exodus xv. 16.

149 Leviticus xxv. 55. **150** Jeremiah xxxii. 6 ff.

151 Under Roman law, when a Roman captured by the enemy was redeemed by payment, his redeemer had a lien over him for the money and he was not restored to his rights till this was discharged. Some authorities even hold that, in classical law, the redeemer became owner of the former prisoner. The history of redemption of a captured slave is obscure but we know that, in later law, he belonged to a redeemer but could be reclaimed by his old owner on payment. According to the Code of Hammurabi 280 f., if a man buys abroad the Babylonian slave of a Babylonian master, and, on his return, the master recognizes his slave, he becomes free; while if a man buys abroad the foreign slave of a Babylonian master, his master can claim him only on offering the price paid by the buyer.

152 Leviticus xxv. 38, Exodus xxiii. 9.

153 Leviticus xxv. 42, 55, Deuteronomy xv. 15.

154 This view is not, as far as I can see, in conflict with the principles of Jewish orthodoxy. I am not denying that, for the Bible and those who obey it, it is chiefly the memory of the deliverance from Egypt which must make usury abhorrent.

155 Leviticus xxv. 55; cp. xxv. 42. Deuteronomy xv. 15 has already been considered from this point of view above, p. 50.

156 Leviticus xxv. 47 ff.

157 Isaiah xlvii. 3 f. Cp. also Isaiah lix. 17–20.

158 See Exodus vi. 6, cited above, pp. 41 and 48.

159 Similar examples are Jeremiah l. 33 f., Micah iv. 10.

160 Isaiah xli. 14. **161** Hosea xiii. 14.

162 It is unintelligible to me how a man so rational and religious as C. Montefiore can say (*Outlines of Liberal Judaism*, 2nd ed., 1923, p. 138): 'For, in spite of many exceptions, and with due regard paid to what constitutes true happiness and misery even of the external type, it is surely true to say that, *on the whole*, righteousness produces prosperity and happiness, and that wickedness produces calamity and woe.' This is far from put right by the qualification which he adds: 'Only it does not follow that the sin of one man will cause *him* calamity. It may cause calamity to *another*.'

163 Job xix. 13 ff.

164 Cp. the wording of Proverbs xxiii. 10 f., to which attention was called above, pp. 46 f., and Jeremiah l. 34, pp. 47 f.

165 Hosea xiii. 14. **166** Exodus xxi. 23.

167 See below, pp. 123 f., 128.

168 See, for instance, I Corinthians vi. 20, I Peter i. 18 f., I Timothy ii. 6, Titus ii. 14.

169 Galatians iii. 13, iv. 5 and so on.

170 Romans vi. 14 ff., Galatians iv. 8 f. Cp. I Corinthians vii. 23.

171 See p. 51. **172** Matthew xx. 28.

173 Cp. Calderón's *Los Alimentos del Hombre*.

CHAPTER II

CODES AND CODAS

THE purpose of the following remarks is to examine a certain
method not infrequently used in ancient times when new
provisions were to be added to an existing code. This method,
of which some particularly clear examples are to be found
in the Pentateuch, may be described as follows. There is a
code dealing with various matters. Some day it is decided
to add another rule on one of these matters. Now a strictly
logical mind would insert the new rule, in accordance with
its contents, between these or those two of the old provisions.
As a matter of fact, however, it is not inserted in this manner.
The existing code is left undisturbed, and the new rule simply
tacked on at the end.

I was first struck by this peculiar method while analysing
an ancient Roman statute, the *lex Aquilia*. In its present
form, that statute contains three chapters. Chapter I deals
with killing another man's slave or beast. Chapter II deals
with some sort of fraud. Chapter III, if we accept the interpretation of the Roman classical lawyers, covers any damage
to property not coming under chapter I; though I have
attempted to show that, originally, it was of a much narrower
scope, referring exclusively to injuring (without killing) another
man's slave or beast.[1] It is an old puzzle why chapter III,
on injuring a slave or beast (or, according to the classical
interpretation, on this and all remaining damage to property
save killing a slave or beast), is separated from chapter I,
on killing a slave or beast, by chapter II regulating an entirely
different matter. Surely the most primitive law-giver—and
the *lex Aquilia* is by no means primitive—must have seen that
killing someone else's slave or beast and wounding someone
else's slave or beast (or smashing someone else's door or
tearing his clothes) belong to the same category of offences.
To say, as is frequently said, that the author of the statute
put together the killing of a slave (chapter I) and the fraudulent release by an agent of the debt due to his principal

(chapter II)[2] because both delicts are cases of destruction, the one of a being, the other of an obligation, is ascribing to the law-giver a concept of destruction so wide, so sophisticated and, *sit venia verbo*, so stupid that he is hardly likely to have been capable of it. Certainly, primitive codes are often arranged on the basis of a cruder association of ideas than we expect at a more advanced stage of civilization. But the *lex Aquilia* simply does not show that primitive kind of association of ideas. It is interesting to note that the explanation here combated is not unlike that adopted by the Romans themselves when they set out to make sense of even the less intelligible features of their traditional material and when, unacquainted with the historical method of treating that material, they had to assume particular subtlety where, in fact, there was some accident. For the problem of the arrangement of the *lex Aquilia* goes back at least to the period of Gaius. He, in *Institutes* 3. 216, assures us that everything is in order. Chapter II, he says, like I and III, relates to a case of *damnum* in the wider sense, that is to say, a case in which a person has incurred some loss somehow: *qua et ipsa parte legis damni nomine actionem introduci manifestum est.* But it is anything but manifest: his solution is artificial.

I hope I have solved the puzzle.[3] There are indications that at some date the statute in question, or rather its predecessor, consisted of two chapters only; the one dealt with killing another man's slave or beast, the other with a case of fraud. Later it was considered necessary to add a chapter about the case where I injured your slave or beast without killing him or it (or, on the basis of the classical interpretation, about all damage outside chapter I). This new chapter was not, as strict logic would have required, intercalated between the two original chapters. It was simply affixed right at the end of the original text: with the result that we now have before us a quite unsystematic arrangement—first the rules on killing a slave or beast, next those on fraud, and finally those of later origin, on injuring a slave or beast (or in the view of the classics, on any damage not contemplated by chapter I). Of the points suggesting a later origin of chapter III independently of its position, it will be sufficient to mention three. For one thing, the case of killing another man's slave or beast seems to have been regulated earlier than that of wounding in many legislations, for obvious reasons. In Exodus xxi. 28 ff., for example, we are given elaborate rules about the liability of the owner of an ox or a pit that causes the death of a man or beast, but nothing is said about what is to happen if the victim is merely hurt but not killed.[4] For another thing, it is only in chapter iii that the fairly advanced legal notion of *damnum*, 'loss', is introduced. While chapter i simply speaks of the case where 'a man kills another man's slave or beast', chapter iii subsumes all kinds of wounding under the heading of *damnum* and speaks of the case where 'a man causes another man a loss by *urere, frangere* or *rumpere* his property'. Again, the assessment of the damage caused is far more progressive in chapter iii than in i. Under chapter i, the highest value that the slave killed had in the previous year is to be paid, a not very satisfactory mode of assessment. Above all, there is in this a penal element not really justifiable in a statute that embraces damage by accident as well as intentional wrong-doing. Under chapter iii, in its original meaning, the person responsible has to pay only *quanti ea res erit*, only the actual sum lost at the time that amends are made. It was only in classical law, when chapter iii was assimilated to i, that here, too, the highest value was made the basis of assessment.[5]

I can think of five reasons why ancient codes were treated in the fashion outlined. First of all, mere laziness, or to use a more respectable term, the force of inertia, may have contributed, though it was hardly decisive. If one has a code and wishes to add another paragraph, the least troublesome thing to do is not what we do when we amend our College Statutes ('The following section to be inserted after section vii, the first two words of section viii to be deleted', and so on), but just to make a postscript of it ('N.B.—The College Council may postpone until the end of the war the election to the Mastership'). Secondly, we must remember that a much more advanced legal technique is required for really amalgamating new and old law than for simply adding a new rule after all the old ones. Any writer knows how difficult it is, when an idea occurs to him after he has finished his work, to fit in this idea in its proper place—unless, indeed, he is prepared to put up with a few jumps in the argument—and how great the temptation to choose the line of least resistance and tack it on at the end. Thirdly, ancient codes were often written on stone, bronze or the like. Now admittedly, even on stone it is possible to make insertions, or erase one chapter and put two chapters instead, or take a new block and write the whole revised code afresh. The method of insertion, however, cannot usually be applied when a great deal is to be inserted; and the other methods are somewhat uneconomical. Frequently enough, therefore, if a new chapter was to be introduced, it must have seemed best not to touch the old inscription and, no matter what the topic of the new chapter was, to add it as an appendix, on the same stone that contained the main text or on a second one.[6] Fourthly, we have to consider that statutes were not always put in writing, and even those that were did not necessarily circulate as written literature. A good many were promulgated and handed down to succeeding generations orally; they were recited at the meetings of the people; the wise men knew them by heart. Obviously, speakers and audience would be less upset by a mere addition to the familiar sequence of rules than by a disturbance of that sequence itself.[7] Lastly (and this may well have been the most important factor), tradition was a great power in ancient times. Lawyers then, as to-day, were particularly conservative, and most so when dealing with a statute, with formally enacted law. It is only to be expected that they preferred to leave an existing code intact and to add an appendix rather than squeeze the fresh provisions anywhere into the established, almost holy, text.

The five factors I have mentioned, laziness, undeveloped legal technique, writing on stone or the like, oral transmission of the law, and regard for tradition, no doubt played much the same part in the history of Hebrew law as in that of Roman law. Hence it is not surprising to find several examples in the Pentateuch of the method under notice, that is to say, of new provisions being joined to an existing code as an appendix instead of being worked in properly. A good illustration is furnished by the code relating to sexual commerce, in Leviticus xx. If we take the code as a whole, the various rules appear to be arranged without any system. The arrangement, however, becomes intelligible as soon as it is recognized that there are at least three sections dating from different periods, none of them having been really combined with the other, but the oldest coming first, next appendix I, and last appendix II.

In the first section, from verse 10 to verse 16, we find the rules prohibiting intercourse with another man's wife, intercourse with the wife of one's father, intercourse with one's daughter-in-law, intercourse between man and man, intercourse between man and beast and intercourse between woman and beast. (I am leaving aside, for the moment, verse 14, the prohibition of taking a woman and her mother.) So far this is a sensible order: adultery (another man's wife), incest (one's father's wife, one's daughter-in-law) and unnatural unions (pederasty, bestiality). But if we read on, we get in verse 17 the prohibition to marry one's sister. Clearly, this rule should come earlier in the code, among the cases of incest, not after the unnatural unions. The explanation why it does come after the unnatural unions—which evidently cannot be sought in any kind of primitive association of ideas—is that the code originally ended with these: which implies that the original, first section, verses 10–16, goes back to a time when marriage with one's sister, or at least with the sister from the same father, was not yet forbidden. At some later date, it was held necessary to declare this union a crime. A provision to that effect was drawn up and added to the old code. But, instead of being inserted where, logically, it belonged, namely, among the cases of incest, it was attached at the end; possibly together with the following rule, verse 18, condemning intercourse with a woman in the menses. The result was the queer arrangement we have before us to-day: adultery, incest, unnatural unions, now again incest (the sister) and then intercourse with a woman in the menses. That the arrangement is to be accounted for in this way, namely, by assuming various sections artlessly joined to one another, is confirmed by a number of facts, two of which I may specify. First, the evolution from a regime under which marriage with the sister from the same father is allowed to one under which it is forbidden is an almost universal phenomenon. As for Hebrew law in particular, we know from parts of the Old Testament other than the code under notice that to marry the sister from the same father was quite admissible in the earlier periods. Abraham and Sarah had one father,[8] and Amnon's offence seems to have consisted, not in casting his eyes on his half-sister, but in violating her without having contracted a marriage and in contracting no marriage after having violated her.[9] It is Ezekiel, in xxii. 10 f., who regards as monstrous this association as well as that with a woman in the menses. Secondly, the older section, Leviticus xx. 10–16, and the appendix, verses 17 and 18, differ in more than one respect. I need only mention that whereas the former imposes on the offender capital punishment (יומת מות), the latter imposes the punishment of excommunication (נכרת).[10]

I have not dealt so far with one rule disturbing the order within the older section itself, verse 14, the prohibition of taking a woman and her mother. This rule comes in a curious place, namely, between verses 13 against homosexuality and 15 f. against intercourse with a beast. It speaks of marriage, לקח, whilst the other provisions in this first section, for example, verse 12 against taking one's daughter-in-law, speak of copulation, שכב. (Verses 13 and the like, against unnatural unions, do not, of course, count in this connection; they must inevitably use שכב or a similar expression.) There is also a different penalty, death by fire. It is just conceivable that somebody clumsily interpolated verse 14 after the whole section, 10–16, was completed. But I think it far more likely that we have the same relation between 10–13 and 14, and again between 10–14 and 15–16, that exists, as has just been shown, between 10–16 and the following section. Briefly, verses 10–13 were the earliest part of the code: adultery, incest with the father's wife, incest with the daughter-in-law, homosexuality. Later the prohibition of taking a woman and her mother was added, verse 14; tacked on, instead of being fitted in before the rule against homosexuality. Still later, verses 15 and 16 were added, directed against intercourse with beasts, a crime probably less frequent and dangerous than

homosexuality.[11]   These verses also were simply appended:
logically they ought to follow 13, on homosexuality, not 14,
on marriage with a woman and her mother.

   Whichever of the two possible solutions we prefer in dealing
with the position of verse 14, the main argument remains
unaffected: verses 10–16 once stood by themselves, verses
17–18 are an appendix. But even marriage with the half-
sister was not the last union to be pronounced incestuous.
As it stands, Leviticus xx contains, after the rules forbidding
this marriage and intercourse during the menses, some more
provisions, directed against marriage with the sister of one's
mother, the sister of one's father, the wife of one's uncle and
the wife of one's brother. This group, verses 19–21, evidently
forms a third section, still later than the second, and again
pieced on to the earlier statutes, not really amalgamated with
them. Had it been systematically amalgamated with the
earlier statutes, it would have been inserted either among the
oldest cases of incest (intercourse with the wife of one's
father, etc.) or at any rate immediately after the case of the
sister, but not after the prohibition to cohabit with a woman
in the menses. In support of the view that this is a further
appendix, I would point out that the punishment again differs
from that in the preceding verses: this time the wrongdoer is
to be childless (עֲרִירִי). It may also be noted that none of
the unions condemned in this last section (marriage with one
of the various aunts, marriage with one's brother's wife)
appears in the above-quoted passage from Ezekiel. In fact,
the union condemned in verse 19 was contracted by no less
important a person than the father of Moses and Aaron;[12]
and as for marriage with the widow of one's brother, this,
we know, for a long time was compulsory in certain circumstances, and Deuteronomy xxv. 5 ff. subjects to a rather
unpleasant ceremony a man who refuses to marry the childless
widow of his brother.

   Of verse 19, however, prohibiting marriage with the sister
of one's mother or father, it must be remarked that it may
well be an interpolation which came into the text later (or
even, though this is less likely, earlier) than 20–21. Its form
strikingly differs from that of all other rules in this code,

Leviticus xx, and is like that used in Leviticus xviii. It is
'Thou shalt not do so and so' instead of 'If a man do so and
so, he shall be punished in this or that way'. True, the last
clause in the verse, 'they shall bear their iniquity', is a
substitute for a penalty, but it is very loosely attached to
the main injunction. Indeed, it looks as if the interpolator
had concocted verse 19 from xviii. 12 and 13.

It would lead too far afield to compare chapter xx of
Leviticus with chapter xviii or with the analogous statutes
in Deuteronomy xxvii. I should only like to remark that
whilst in Leviticus xviii the order is far more rational, the
products of different periods far better mixed, in Deuteronomy
xxvii, just as in the code that I have discussed, the prohibition
to marry the sister clearly marks the beginning of a fresh
section: the curse in verse 20 is against intercourse with the
father's wife, 21 is against intercourse with a beast; then,
in 22 and 23, come two other cases of incest, namely, intercourse with the sister and intercourse with the mother-in-
law. But a closer analysis would detect traces of this development even in Leviticus xviii. Verse 7 forbids intercourse with
father or mother, 8 with the father's wife, 9 with the sister
from the same father or mother, 10 with the granddaughter,
11 with the sister from the same father, 12 with the father's
sister and so on. It is clear that 11 forbids what is already
forbidden by 9, and no harmonizing explanation can get rid
of this fact. The most probable solution is that this code also
came into existence bit by bit. The original part extended as
far as verse 10, and, while this part stood by itself, verse 9
referred only to the sister from the same mother.[13] Then a
second series of prohibitions was introduced, opening with
verse 11, the prohibition of the sister from the same father.
This second series was simply appended to the first: had it
been properly worked in, verse 11 would have been put
after 9, the prohibition of the sister from the same mother,
not after 10, the prohibition of the granddaughter. The mention, in verse 9 as it stands to-day, of the sister from the same
father is best accounted for by assuming that this clause was
interpolated at a date later still than the addition of the
second series of prohibitions. It was in consequence of this

interpolation that verse 11 became, strictly speaking, super-fluous.[14]

Before going any further, I must say a word of warning. I have cited a few cases, and shall soon adduce some more, where the illogical arrangement of a code is due to a peculiar ancient method of amendment; a method by which, roughly speaking, additions to an existing law (such as the chapter on injuring a slave or beast without killing him or it in the *lex Aquilia*, or the prohibition to marry one's sister in Leviticus xx) were put right at the end, after part II of the code (after the chapter on fraud in the *lex Aquilia*, the rules against unnatural intercourse in Leviticus xx), even if according to strict logic they ought to have been inserted after part I (the chapter on killing a slave or beast, the prohibition of intercourse with the stepmother or daughter-in-law). Now this is the warning. When we come across an instance of that method, we may indeed conclude that the addition is later than the general framework of parts I and II; more precisely, that the general framework of parts I and II existed at a time when the addition did not yet exist or at least not yet in connection with this code. But we must not without specific proof conclude that the actual present text of the addition is later than the actual present text of parts I and II. We must not, for example, conclude, unless there are good reasons for doing so, that the third chapter of the *lex Aquilia* in its present form is later than the first two chapters in their present form; or that the actual present text of the prohibition to marry one's sister (Leviticus xx. 17) is later than the actual present text of the rules against intercourse with one's father's wife, pederasty and so on (xx. 10–16). Certainly, in what may be called the ideal case, and no doubt is a very frequent case, of the method under discussion, the addition is not only later than the general framework of the original parts, but also later than their final present text. In this 'ideal' case, a code consisting of two chapters was some day found inadequate; a supplementary chapter was added and, though logically allied to chapter I, added at the end, after the second chapter; nothing more happened. There are, however, other, more complicated cases. For example, everything may have gone as in the 'ideal' case; a code some day was found inadequate, a supplementary chapter was added and, though allied to chapter I, added after II. But now something more did happen: at an even later period all three parts, chapter I, chapter II and appendix, were overhauled, modernized and promulgated as an entirely new statute. This new statute might still preserve the traditional order, or better disorder, chapter I, chapter II, appendix, thus bearing the traces of its gradual growth. Yet the actual text of the three parts would all have been fixed at one and the same time, namely, in the course of the last, complete modernization of the code, and of the original wording of the first two chapters very little or nothing need be left. The addition of an appendix, by the method that I am examining, in this case took place prior to the final redaction which we have before us to-day. Again, the reformer may have revised parts I and II precisely when he added part III, in order to avoid inconsistencies. Here, too, the present version of the former clearly is no earlier than that of the latter: and to decide just how much survives of the older, superseded text of parts I and II, a separate detailed investigation is required.

In point of fact, there exists even the extreme possibility of the addition's showing a text of greater antiquity than the basic, first two sections of the law. This strange situation results, for instance, where for some exceptional reason a revision of the code, though undertaken after the appendix had been introduced, remained confined to the first two parts. But it also results where the appendix was not newly created when given its place after the original two chapters, but had been in existence already, and been in existence, either independently or as part of another code, even before those original chapters themselves were composed. The following example is from the ritual law but may serve to illustrate the sort of complication that I have in mind. In Deuteronomy xiv. 3–21*a* we find a large list of what things are fit to be eaten and what are not. A concluding phrase follows in verse 21*b*: 'For thou art an holy people unto the Lord thy God.' After this, in verse 21*c*, comes the rule: 'Thou shalt not seethe a kid in his mother's milk.' If we had to produce a rational arrangement, we should certainly transpose this command-

ment and fit it in before the concluding sentence. The reason
for its actual position is that it did not belong to the original
catalogue of food allowed and prohibited; it is an appendix
to that catalogue, put right at the end, even after the final
admonition. At the same time, however, it can be shown
that it existed long before it was here appended. True, its
meaning at that earlier stage probably was rather different
from that which it has in Deuteronomy; the fact that it
appears in Exodus xxiii. 19 and xxxiv. 26 suggests that it
was then directed against a certain type of sacrifice.[15] But in
this connection, as a precept referring to sacrifice, it may well
be older than the whole list of clean and unclean animals
(Deuteronomy xiv) to which it was subsequently joined.

The upshot of all this, if I may be forgiven for some repeti-
tion, can perhaps be summarized thus. To find a break between
the first two sections of a statute and the third, the first two
forming a complete whole and the third coming as a surprise,
is not sufficient evidence that the first two sections and the
third section in their present form date from different periods.
The only safe thing to say is concerning the outlines of the
code: the general framework of the first two sections goes
back to a time when section III was not yet in being or, at
any rate, not yet included in this statute. On the other hand,
it must always be borne in mind that even if we know the
three sections of a statute to have received their present form
at the same time from the same author, section III may yet
have to be regarded as later than the others from the point
of view of structure; the first two sections, or rather their
predecessors, may yet have stood by themselves before it
came to the ultimate edition of the whole. The history of the
framework and arrangement of a code and the history of its
text and substance, however closely interwoven, must not be
mixed up with one another.[16] The number of combinations
possible is unlimited. As regards the *lex Aquilia*, most likely
the three chapters as they are to-day all date from 287 B.C.
It was some earlier statute that had confined itself to the
first two cases, killing a slave or beast and fraud; and it seems
that of the actual wording and regulations contained in that
earlier statute a small fraction only was taken into the *lex*

Aquilia.[17] In contradistinction, the material discrepancies between Leviticus xx. 10–16 and 17–18, and between 10–18 and 19–21, are considerable: the different kinds of penalty seem to be especially significant. I am inclined to assume, therefore, that not only the framework but most even of the actual text of 10–16 is older than 17–18, and these verses again are older than 19–21.

I may now submit two further illustrations of the method in question, both from the *Mishpatim,* the Judgments, Exodus xxi and xxii. Towards the end of xxi, in verses 28–36, we find provisions about the liability first of a man whose ox kills another man; next of the owner of a pit who, by failing to set a protection, becomes responsible for the death of another man's animal; and last of a man whose ox kills another man's ox. Once again, the various offences appear to be arrayed in the strangest fashion: your ox kills a person, an animal falls into a pit that you have dug, your ox kills an ox. Obviously, the first case and the third should stand side by side—your ox kills a person, your ox kills an ox—and the case of the pit should follow them. Once again, the disorder we have before us is due to the fact that there is an older part and a supplement, and that the supplement has never been combined with the older part but has simply been put at the end.[18] The example actually is not unlike that of the *lex Aquilia* which I mentioned in the beginning. Originally, two offences only were dealt with: the case where your ox killed a person and the case where your pit caused the death of an animal. The former case was important because it involved the loss of human life; and it is worth mentioning that the Code of Hammurabi, whilst it has some rules on the case where an ox kills a man,[19] has none on the case where an ox kills an ox. The other case, of the pit, was important because it must have been fairly frequent at a time when people got their water from wells. It was not until a later period that a paragraph was appended on the less urgent case (not appearing in the Code of Hammurabi) where your ox killed an ox. It was appended: but it was not introduced where we should introduce it, between the two original paragraphs.

There is strong internal evidence, too, both formal and

material, that the verses about this less urgent case are an
addition. A formal sign of addition may be seen in the fact
that whereas ordinarily the provisions in the *Mishpatim* begin
with כי or אם, 'if' (the former introducing fresh sections, the
latter detailed cases within a section), the section about an
ox that kills another ox uses או, 'or', to open a special case:
'Or it be known that the ox hath used to push in time past.'
There is one other rule only in the *Mishpatim* beginning with
או, 'or', Exodus xxi. 31, and this also, as we shall see below,[20]
is an addition to the original stock of the *Mishpatim*.

Of greater importance, however, is the evidence from the
substance of the rules concerned. The older, first paragraph, on
the case where an ox kills a person, speaks of נגח only, of
'goring', 'pushing with the horn': 'If an ox gore a man or a
woman, that they die.' The supplement, on the case where
an ox kills an ox, speaks of נגף, of 'pushing, hurting, in any
manner whatsoever': 'If one man's ox hurt another's, that
he die.' Clearly, the older paragraph was made in an age
when a charge could be established only through the strictest,
most formal proofs: no condemnation would take place unless,
for example, the marks of a horn were visible on the body
of the victim. By the time the supplement was added, the
rules of evidence had become looser. Provided I was able to
show that your ox had killed mine, it no longer mattered
whether he had done it by goring him or in a less usual mode
such as crushing him with his body: you had to pay.[21] The
analysis that I am putting forward is confirmed by a second
difference between the older paragraph and the supplement,
which points the same way. According to the older paragraph,
on an ox killing a person, the owner is to be punished more
severely if the animal was always particularly wild, והועד,
and this fact 'had been solemnly announced to him'. According to the supplement, on an ox killing an ox, the owner
is to be punished more severely if נודע, if 'it is known' that
the animal was always particularly wild. The main idea is the
same in the two provisions: a man who makes no scruple to
keep a dangerous beast has to take the consequences. But
there is a significant disagreement in detail. The older paragraph says that the risk is yours from the moment a formal

announcement is made to you concerning the ferocious character of the beast. This means that the judge need not examine whether or not you were really clear on the point— which might be difficult for him to discover. He need only examine whether or not the necessary announcement was made to you—a very easy thing to find out. If the announcement was made, you are responsible for everything that has happened since; and it would be no excuse to say that you personally had not believed that the ox was so savage. If no announcement was made, you are not responsible even if you yourself had seen all the time how dangerous the ox was. To use some technical language, the decision of the judge as to whether you are guilty or not is based on a strict, archaic, 'objective' kind of proof: Was it or was it not formally announced to you that the ox was of an unruly nature? The judge does not raise the freer, more advanced, 'subjective' question: Did you or did you not know about the nature of the ox? Now in the other, later paragraph, on the case where your ox kills an ox, we do get this 'subjective' element. No mention is here made of the necessity of a formal announcement: the responsibility is yours from the moment you are aware, or should be aware, that your ox is not to be trusted. At this more advanced stage of the law, the judge must investigate the affair much more closely; he must, above all, search men's hearts. If he reaches the conclusion that you knew the beast was dangerous, he will find you guilty even though no announcement was ever made to you in the matter.

This argument is not, in the main, affected if the change introduced by the supplement was slightly less radical than I have assumed so far. For it is very conceivable that it was slightly less radical. What seems certain is that whereas under the older paragraph the judge was restricted to one single 'objective' question—Did the owner of the ox receive the prescribed warning as to the danger?—under the supplement he was not. What seems not so certain, however, is that he now had complete liberty, might admit any kind of evidence and directly attack the 'subjective' question: Did the owner of the ox know or guess the danger? Quite possibly, the interpreters even of the supplement fixed a number of more or less 'objective' proofs which alone were to form the basis for the judge's decision. They may have laid down, for example, that the owner should be treated as guilty, as having disregarded what was common knowledge, 'if the wild nature of his ox had been spoken of in the market-place, or if the ox had assaulted a person or beast in the same village twice before'.[22] In any case, whatever the exact implications of the change may have been, its tendency is perfectly clear: the supplement, on the case where an ox killed an ox, meant some advance on the road from archaic rigid evidence to a modern flexible system. We shall soon find a similar advance in the case of another supplement to the older *Mishpatim*.

Before proceeding to that other example, however, I have to call attention to a detail of some interest if we wish to understand the growth of the code under notice. As we have seen, the later rule, on an ox which kills an ox, is introduced as an appendix, not properly amalgamated with the older rules. It must be observed, however, that it is an appendix only in the sense that it was added after all earlier rules on indirect damage, so as to follow the verses about an open pit, instead of being inserted after the rules on an ox which kills a man. But it was not added as appendix to the whole of the *Mishpatim*, so as to follow the verses about the enticing of a maid, Exodus xxii. 15 (16) f., or those about festivals and sacrifices, xxiii. 10 ff. I have suggested above[23] that the method of appending new rules at the end of a code instead of inserting them in the middle may have been chosen so frequently because the reformers did not want to upset the traditional sequence of the older part; and it doubtless was for this reason that the later rule here in question was not inserted exactly where, from the systematic point of view, it should have been. But, naturally enough, the method was not carried to extremes. If this later rule had been relegated to a place after the whole of the *Mishpatim*, a large collection of law, it would have been completely in the air, far removed from the other rules concerning this kind of delict. In fact, though the traditional order of the code would have been diligently preserved in a pedantic sense, the abrupt disconnected piece at the end would have spoilt the whole structure. Moreover, for the people reading the code or hearing it read, it would have been most perplexing if, in the section *ex professo* dealing with indirect damage, they had found the old law only, and had had to wait for the amendment until they were through all remaining chapters of the *Mishpatim*. The authors of the later rule did the sensible thing in introducing it immediately after that section to which it belonged, the section on indirect damage. They thus treated this section as a separate independent unit—a remarkable fact which throws not a little light on the history of the interpretation of Hebrew codes. Within this section, the old traditional sequence of rules was not interrupted (ox killing a person, pit); the new rule was put at the end (ox killing a person, pit, ox killing an ox). But that the new rule came to stand in the middle of the *Mishpatim* as a whole was not regarded as objectionable. It will be seen below[24] that the argument here advanced applies equally to a supplement added to the older rules on theft.

The other example from the *Mishpatim*, the Judgments, that I wish to adduce as illustrating the method of putting amendments at the end is the statute on theft, Exodus xxi. 37–xxii. 3 (xxii. 1–4). This statute speaks first about the damages payable by a man who steals an animal and either kills or sells it; next about the questions when it is permissible to slay a thief and what is to happen if a thief cannot pay (a break that can be discerned even within this paragraph will be discussed below); and last about the damages payable by a man who steals an animal but does not kill or sell it, or at any rate, has not killed or sold it when detected. Surely, the natural order would be: first, compensation from a thief who has killed or sold the animal; next, compensation from a thief who has not, or not yet, killed or sold the animal; and last, the questions when I may slay a thief and what I am to do if the thief cannot pay. The reason why the rules do not appear in this natural order is that one of them is later than the rest. Originally, there existed two paragraphs only: the first about the damages payable by a thief who had killed or sold the animal, the second about the questions when to slay a thief and what to do to a thief who could not pay. It was not until a later date that a third paragraph was added, about the damages payable by a thief who had not, or not yet, killed or sold the animal: and, precisely as in the cases that I have already reviewed, the new rule was not inserted where, according to strict logic, it should have been, but the older, traditional sequence of rules was left intact and the new rule simply tailed on to them. But why, it will be asked, did the code in its original form speak only of the thief who had killed or sold the animal?

One of the most ancient problems in the domain of theft is the problem at what moment a man can with certainty be said to have stolen a thing. Is theft committed as soon as the thing has been touched? Or only when it has been taken away from its place? Or only when it has been brought into the thief's house? Or only when it has been actually used by the thief? Clearly, so long as it has not been used, a thief might say that he never intended to appropriate it. If the stolen thing is an animal, he might say that it mixed with his herd of its own will and that he was returning it the next day. When we consider the gravity in ancient times of the crime of theft and the severity of its punishment, we cannot be surprised that no one should be treated as a thief unless he could really be shown to be one. I submit that, when the statute on theft was first enacted, the view prevailed that theft was not proved until the stolen thing had been used. A thief who had killed or sold the animal was liable to a heavy penalty: killing and selling were the normal modes of disposing of an animal, for in a small community a thief would not ordinarily use the stolen beast for drawing a cart or plough but try to get rid of it as quickly as possible.[25] But a thief who had not, or not yet, killed or sold the animal was, at this period, not punishable at all: he was not treated as a thief. In other words, the judge, at this period, was not required to examine all the details of the case; not required to find out what had been the 'subjective' intentions of the accused. He was given one 'objective' criterion to go by. If the animal had been killed or sold, he was to regard the charge as established; if the animal were still there, he was to regard the charge as not proven.

Later lawyers, however, took a more progressive view. They

laid down that even if the animal were still there, the thief—provided he was a thief—should pay a penalty, though a comparatively slight one. Once this rule was added, the judge could no longer rely on one simple 'objective' test: Has the animal been killed or sold or has it not? He now must collect all evidence available, go into the 'subjective' intentions of the accused and by some means or other discover whether he was a thief, having attempted to secure the animal, or no. The picture of this evolution remains the same, on the whole, even if we interpret the new regime set up by the supplement as not quite so progressive. There is, indeed, a good deal to be said for the assumption that it was not quite so advanced; and that even now the lawyers agreed on certain 'objective' proofs as the only evidence admissible. They may, for example, have agreed that the defendant was to be acquitted unless he had shown his bad faith by 'killing the animal or selling it or riding it or putting it to the cart or plough or shutting it up in his stable'. From the wording of the new rule, which extends punishment to the thief 'in whose hand the theft is found alive', it seems fairly certain that at least *contrectatio*, touching the object, if not *ablatio*, the taking away of the animal from its place, was deemed an essential element of theft, in the absence of which no condemnation would take place. This would mean that no condemnation would take place, say, where a man had approached a herd of sheep in suspicious circumstances but not yet actually handled any of the animals. Anyhow, whatever the precise range of the innovation may have been, the fact remains that the rigid criterion of killing or selling was no longer considered the only safe one. Some other, freer criteria at any rate were admitted. It was an advance of much the same kind as in the domain of damage caused by an ox, of which development I have treated above.

It may be important, at this point, to dissociate myself from a certain line of thought which, in modern writings, is often to be met with in connection with phenomena of the sort described. When I say that, under the original statute on theft, a man was not punished unless he had killed or sold the animal, I do not mean that the authors of this regulation were unaware of the possibility of a man stealing a beast and not killing or selling it. I only mean that in order to prevent unjust verdicts, they required what was in that epoch the safest proof practicable. Modern writers frequently make the mistake, where a particular rule for a particular reason refers to 'objective' evidence, to assume that the 'subjective' aspect of the matter was entirely neglected, was simply not seen, by the lawyers of the time. In the case under notice at least it is quite obvious that it was seen. The provision permitting a thief to be slain if he is caught breaking into the enclosure belongs to the same stratum as the provision confining ordinary punishment to the thief who has killed or sold the beast; it is part of the original statute. Yet it can never have been the law that the person surprising a burglar has to wait for the 'objective' criterion, and let some beast be taken and killed or sold, before proceeding to self-help. That criterion is very appropriate in the regular, calm proceedings of the court, but not at all in the heated scene when the thief is detected in the act. Here the 'subjective' evidence, the criminal intention proved by breaking in, is sufficient.[26] Similarly, in Rome, in the classical period, there was a rule that a man, to be condemned as a thief, must have been guilty of *contrectatio*, that is to say, must have handled the object; and in the period of the XII Tables, no doubt even more than plain *contrectatio* was required. But there was also a rule in the XII Tables that a thief who came by night might be killed on the spot, and under this rule, clearly, a man was considered a thief even if he had not come anywhere near the object that he intended to take. Surely it cannot be held that the person visited by a thief at night had to ask him to touch some object before availing himself of the right to slay him. On the other hand, it should constantly be remembered that a large measure of 'objective' evidence is indispensable even in the most progressive system; and that no human being can grasp the 'subjective' basis of a case without the help of external signs. For example, where the animal said to be stolen has entirely disappeared and no traces of the crime whatever are to be discovered, only *cadi* justice would inflict punishment on anybody. Again, there has been no secular code so far imposing punishment on him who 'covets his neighbour's ox or ass' or on him who 'looketh on a woman to lust after her': and, in fact, the latter phrase itself contains an 'objective', physical element, the look.[27]

So far I have attempted to distinguish two stages in the growth of the statute on theft: the older paragraphs speaking about him who steals an animal and kills or sells it, about the slaying of a thief and about a thief who cannot pay, and the appendix speaking about him who steals an animal but is detected before killing or selling it. As a matter of fact, however, even within the older paragraphs themselves, there seem to be distinguishable an original part and an appendix added by the method here discussed. We should expect the law to speak first about what a thief who has killed or sold the animal has to pay, next about a thief who cannot pay, and finally about self-help, slaying a burglar. The order we have before us (first, damages from a thief who has killed or sold the animal, next, self-help, and finally, a thief who cannot pay) becomes intelligible by assuming that the law at first contained merely the provisions about what a thief who has killed or sold the animal has to pay and self-help; and that the provision about a thief who cannot pay was tacked on at a later date. Before this provision was added, an insolvent thief, we may suppose, was entirely left to the tender mercies of the other party: the new provision laid down that he might be sold—but nothing worse must be done to him. If this assumption is correct, the statute on theft was created, not in two, but in three stages. The earliest rules stated what a thief who had killed or sold the animal must pay and under what conditions a thief might be slain. Then an appendix was added, concerning the case where a thief could not pay. Still later, a further supplement followed, stating what a thief who had not killed or sold the animal must pay.

Be this as it may, there can be no doubt as to the principal break in the statute, a break between the older portion which imposes punishment on him who steals an animal and kills or sells it and deals with self-help and insolvency of a thief, and the later portion which imposes punishment on the thief who has not killed or sold the animal. It is not only the position of the later portion as an appendix that proves it to be later; nor is it only the progress represented by it in the matter of evidence. There are quite a few additional points to confirm the suggestion here made. First of all, the statute in its present enlarged form sets up a contrast between a man who has killed or sold the stolen animal and one who has not. This contrast at first sight looks simply absurd and the explanations that have been tried in the course of the centuries are most of them amusing rather than helpful. In fact, it has never hitherto been satisfactorily explained. Yet as appears from what I have said, it is not impossible to understand it: it is the result of the gradual growth of the statute. There is an earlier rule and a later rule, and between them lies an advance from a system of formal and narrow evidence towards freedom and adaptability. The earlier rule regarded theft as proved only if the accused had used, that is to say, killed or sold, the beast: the later allows a verdict of theft even if the thief has not yet used the beast. That this old crux, this queer contrast, can be accounted for on the basis of my thesis seems to me strong confirmation. Secondly, we have to observe that the older rule, confined to the thief who has killed or sold the animal, lays down a heavier penalty than the later rule, referring to the thief who has not, or not yet, killed or sold the animal. This also supports the assumption of two strata, for the difference is significant. It reflects a change in the general view taken of theft, which in Hebrew law, as in many other systems, began by being treated as a serious crime and gradually descended to the rank of a petty offence. There are traces in the Old Testament indicating that at least certain kinds of theft—theft of sacred objects from a temple or palace[28] and theft of free persons[29]—but more probably all kinds[30] were at some time punishable by death. By the time that the later portion was appended to the statute under discussion, a twofold penalty was all that was deemed called for. The evolution in Roman law was very similar indeed. Thirdly, the older rule makes a rather primitive distinction between theft of an ox and theft of a sheep: for one ox you have to give five, but for one sheep only four. No such distinction occurs in the later rule. Whatever kind of animal you steal, you have to restore two for one. Indeed, it looks as if the later rule rather meant to emphasize the abandonment of that primitive distinction: 'Whether it be ox, or ass, or sheep, he shall restore double.'

The most interesting confirmation, however, comes from a point itself of some importance: it seems that the law relating to theft of persons developed in much the same way as I am postulating for the law relating to theft of animals. In its original form, Exodus xxi. 16, on theft of persons, applied only to the case where a man was stolen and sold by another man. The words ונמצא בידו, making the rule cover the case where a man is stolen but not, or not yet, sold, are a manifest interpolation. For one thing, if they are translated literally, the whole rule makes no sense: 'And he that stealeth a man and selleth him and he be found in his hand, shall surely be put to death.' Clearly, the kidnapped man cannot be sold by the thief and be found in his hand at the same time. What the interpolator meant to say (and what the A.V. has) is, of course: 'And he that stealeth a man and selleth him, or if he be found in his hand, shall surely be put to death.' For another thing, it is in consequence of the interpolation that the rhythm of the rule differs from that of the otherwise parallel rules, verses 12, 15 and 17. It should be noted that a provision as late as Deuteronomy xxiv. 7 is confined to the case where a man steals another and, treating him as an article of trade, sells him, והתעמר בו ומכרו; the case where he does not sell him does not appear here even in an interpolation. Thus the law regarding theft of persons went through the same stages as that regarding theft of animals. There was a time when the theft of a person was deemed to be proved only if the person had been sold by the thief. (Killing, though a normal way of using a stolen animal, is not a normal way of using a stolen person: therefore the only evidence specified in the rules on theft of persons is selling.) The later stage, when even a thief who had not sold the person stolen might be convicted is represented in the Pentateuch, not by a special rule added to the older one, but by an interpolation in Exodus xxi. 16.

The analysis here attempted of two amendments to be found in the *Mishpatim*, the Judgments, the one in the section on indirect damage, the other in that on theft, has a bearing on the history of the *Mishpatim* as a whole. One inference was drawn above, in discussing the appendix on damage by an ox: the inference that the various sections within the *Mishpatim* were treated by those who amended the code as complete units. This result is supported by the appendix to the section on theft. For here also the new rule has been appended, not at the end of all the *Mishpatim*, but at the end of the provisions concerning theft. The old portion of this section was indeed left undisturbed, and the new portion was tacked on to it instead of being inserted in the middle. But no harm was seen, sensibly enough, in the new portion thus coming to stand in the middle of the *Mishpatim* as a whole: it was not put right at the close, after Exodus xxii. 16 (17) or xxiii. 19. Another result may here be added. It is highly probable that both the appendix on damage by an ox and that on theft represent one reform. For their tendency is exactly the same. Both of them replace formalistic and rigid principles of evidence by freer and more flexible ones. Just as the supplement on damage by an ox (added after the provision concerning open pits) entitles the judge to consider the charge proved even if the ox has not caused the damage in the 'correct' manner, with his horn, provided he has undoubtedly caused it somehow; just as the same supplement entitles the judge to find the owner of an ox guilty even if no formal announcement has been made to him about the dangerous character of the beast, provided he undoubtedly knew of the danger; so the supplement on compensation from a thief (added after the provisions concerning self-help and insolvency of the thief) entitles the judge to convict the accused even if he has not, so to speak, satisfied the form by killing or selling the animal, provided he undoubtedly seized it in bad faith, with the intention of appropriating it. The two appendices, on damage by an ox and on theft, are governed by the same *leit-motiv*, and from this and the fact that they were introduced by the same method it seems right to infer that they are products of one reform. They were put in the code of *Mishpatim*, Judgments, at the same time and by the same hand.

In conclusion, one or two more general remarks may be made suggesting some of the implications and limitations of the thesis advanced in this study. First, I would draw attention to one of the minor results to be gained by working out this thesis. When a code contains rules going back to different periods, it is not always easy to decide whether the later part has been added by some private glossator or whether it has been added officially, by the usual organs of legislation. Now I suggest that as regards the four chief cases I have presented (*lex Aquilia*, Leviticus xx, damage by an ox in the *Mishpatim* and theft in the *Mishpatim*), we can answer the question with some confidence. In general, a private reader will insert his comments wherever the text appears to him obscure or otherwise unsatisfactory. Take, for example, a code enumerating first the various relatives one must not marry and then several kinds of unnatural unions. A private reader, if he holds that the part concerning the relatives is not complete, will insert any additional rules in that part. Consequently, when we find additions that are not inserted in this ruthless fashion, when we find that they are introduced by the careful method that I have discussed, the older part of the code left intact and the fresh rules put right at the end, the presumption is (of course, it is no more than a presumption) that these rules have been added authoritatively, by the official guardians of the law. It is they who will think twice before interfering with the traditional text. As regards the cases I have presented, therefore, it is probable that the supplementary provisions were at some time laid down by the ordinary law-giver.

Secondly, it may be useful to emphasize that great care should be exercised in applying the thesis here submitted. I have tried to demonstrate that when we find a code, or a section within a larger code, where the topics are arranged in the sequence 1a (cases of incest, for example), 2 (unnatural unions), 1b (further cases of incest), this may be the result of 1b being a later addition,[31] appended instead of being worked in. Far be it from me, however, to suggest that there can be only this cause and no other; and that 1a and 2 must necessarily have been combined before 1b came in. Actually, I should never regard a case of this kind as established unless,

in addition to the formal criterion, two further conditions were
satisfied (I hope I have satisfied them in dealing with my four
illustrations). In the first place, there must be weighty
material arguments, arguments regarding the substance of 1*b*,
not merely its position as an appendix, if the case is to be
convincing. In other words, 1*b* is to be considered an addition
only if strong indications, independent of its position in the
code, point that way; if, for example, its contents are incompatible with 1*a* or if we know from other sources that its
contents date from a different period or province. (The
prohibition of marriage with the sister in Leviticus xx has
a different punishment from the earlier prohibitions, and other
parts of the Old Testament show that this union was not
deemed sinful until a fairly late date.) In the second place,
the sequence 1*a*, 2, 1*b* ought to give rise to suspicion only if
it occurs either in a 'good' code, that is to say, in a disciplined,
cultivated, generally well-arranged code (such as the *Mishpatim* or the *lex Aquilia*) or in a catalogue so simple that even
an inferior legislator would hit upon the proper order (such
as the catalogue of prohibited marriages in Leviticus xx).
If, however, it occurs in a 'bad' code, it seems safer, as a rule,
to ascribe the queer arrangement to the inefficiency or indifference of the author.[32]

The results here submitted as to the growth of codes in
the Pentateuch have no direct bearing on the question in
what year or years these codes were finally completed; and
are not, therefore, as far as I can see, essentially incompatible
with the orthodox Jewish conception of the Torah. In the
orthodox view, the Pentateuch was indeed complete at the
moment of its revelation, and has undergone no changes ever
since. But it is not part of this doctrine to say that the various
codes may not have grown up in a gradual manner even before
the revelation.[33] It might perhaps be argued that on the basis
of orthodox doctrine, as the Torah is perfect, we must not
say that transitions from one stage to the other are discernible:
for this would mean, it might be argued, that there exist
unnecessary breaks and irregularities in the Torah, owing to
historical accidents, and would one not thus admit some
blemish? But this objection loses much of its force when

we consider that the very retention in the Torah of the traces of a long historical development perhaps constitutes a point to be admired and to be taken to heart. It is by recognizing this development that the most valuable lessons can be learnt. Moreover, to take one of the examples discussed in this study, when the prohibition of marriage with the sister was introduced, a prohibition not found in all ancient systems, it certainly acquired a good deal of emphasis by coming after the primeval portion of the code instead of being enumerated together with the earlier and long familiar cases of incest. The new demands made by God and the difference between the duties of His people and those of neighbouring tribes could be stressed no better than in this way, by appending innovations rather than working them into the old pattern.

NOTES

CHAPTER II

1 *Law Quarterly Review*, LII, 1936, pp. 253 ff.; see also *Cambridge Law Journal*, VI, 1938, pp. 400 f., and VII, 1939, pp. 40 ff. Cp. A. Bernard's summary and criticism of the article from the *Law Quarterly Review* in *Revue Historique de Droit Français et Étranger*, ser. iv, XVI, 1937, pp. 450 ff.

2 More precisely, I ought to say: the release by the *adstipulator* of the debt due technically to him or the main *stipulator* but in reality to the latter only.

3 *Law Quarterly Review*, LII, 1936, pp. 267 f.

4 On the question why the XII Tables mention only the *os fractum* of a slave but neither the *membrum ruptum* nor killing, see *Law Quarterly Review*, loc. cit.

5 See *Law Quarterly Review*, LII, 1936, p. 262.

6 I once stayed in a hotel which had two dining-rooms in different wings: one of them was fairly recent, having been added when the other no longer sufficed. A far-seeing architect would have built a large enough dining-room at the outset; if the owner, when the first dining-room became too small, had had a great deal of money to spare, he might have built an entirely new hotel. As it was, his place reminded me of the lex *Aquilia*.

7 Some songs, children's songs especially, get one verse after the other added to them; but the additions are nearly always tacked on at the end, even at the expense of strict logic, and only rarely inserted in the middle. The latter course would not be tolerated by the youngsters.

8 Genesis xx. 12.

9 II Samuel xiii. Cp. the affair of Dinah, Genesis xxxiv. On some probable allusions to marriage with the sister in Solomon's Song viii, see above, p. 66, n. 38.

10 On the history and meaning of this kind of punishment, see Daube, *Symbolae Friburgenses in honorem Ottonis Lenel*, 1931, pp. 249 ff.

11 It is very prominent, however, in the Hittite Code.

12 Exodus vi. 20: 'And Amram took him Jochebed his father's sister to wife.'

13 This is also the most satisfactory explanation of the 'whether she be born at home or abroad'. The point of verse 9 in its original form was to prohibit the sister from the same mother even if she was born 'abroad', that is to say, to a different father. But the sister from the same father and a different mother was not yet forbidden at this period.

14 It might perhaps be argued that, on the basis of my view, the prohibition of the daughter-in-law belongs to the later portion of Leviticus xviii—it appears as far down as xviii. 15—and that this cannot be. (In chapter xx, we have seen, it belongs to the oldest part of the law, appearing as it does in xx. 12, before homosexuality.) To this it could be replied, however, that intercourse with one's daughter-in-law does not seem to have been universally condemned from the earliest times. The story of Judah and Tamar, Genesis xxxviii, where Tamar at least knows who the other party is, may be recalled.

15 For further details, see Daube, *Journal of Theological Studies*, XXXVII, 1936, pp. 289 ff.

16 Two examples from very different provinces may illustrate this. (1) Our College Chapel was completed in 1375, provided with a new entrance by Dr Caius, enlarged and provided with a new ceiling in 1637, given a stone facing and deprived of the sacred turret in 1716–18, provided with an apse, organ-gallery and decorations by Waterhouse, and with an entirely new roof four years ago. Is the Chapel earlier or later than the three Gates? (2) Before Beethoven, a sonata normally had three movements. He introduced a fourth, a minuet or scherzo. When a modern musician composes a sonata with four movements, is his minuet of the same age as the other three parts or is it later? As minuet in a sonata, as a nowadays usual part of the structure, it is later, namely, nineteenth century. As far as its actual substance is concerned, it is of the same age as the rest, and may even be older if he has lifted it from Haydn.

17 The minute enumeration at the opening of the first chapter, however, *si quis servum servamve alienum alienamve quadrupedemve pecudem*, may go back to the earlier statute which, it is to be supposed, laid down fixed money penalties for various cases of killing, distinguishing in a crude way between slave and beast and between male and female.

18 It might perhaps be argued that the point of the present arrangement is to bring first the case where a man is killed and then the two cases where an animal is killed. This may be admitted: but even so the case where an ox kills an ox should come immediately after that where an ox kills a man, these two cases being so much more closely parallel to one another, both in substance and language, than either of them is to the case of the pit.

19 Paragraphs 250 ff.   **20** See pp. 105 f., 166 f.

21 As is only natural, the technical term for an exceptionally wild ox, שׁוֹר נַגָּח, though literally signifying 'an ox accustomed to push with the horn', was adopted without change from the older paragraph into the supplement. The author of the latter was not pedantic enough to think of substituting some new, more comprehensive phrase, which might conceivably have been more exact (now that all manners of hurting were included) but would inevitably have been less brief and familiar.

22 Some Talmudic provisions strongly suggest an evolution of this kind.

23 See p. 77.   **24** See p. 96.

25 Remember what happens in *La Farce de Maître Pathelin*.

26 There are, of course, more reasons for the difference in the evidence required in the two cases. For one thing, seeing a thief break into the enclosure is, in a sense, good, 'objective' evidence. Once he has carried the animal home undetected, this evidence is no longer possible and another equally good one has to take its place. But, be this as it may, it remains true to say that the permission to slay a thief breaking into the enclosure shows that even the older law-giver was aware of the possibility of a man being a thief without killing or selling the stolen beast.

27 Cp. also above, p. 71, n. 112.

28 See Genesis xxxi. 32, 'With whomsoever thou findest thy gods, let him not live', and xliv. 9, 'With whomsoever of thy servants it (the cup used for divining the future) be found, let him die'. In both these cases, however, the crime is aggravated not only by the fact that it concerns holy objects but also by being *manifestum*: the thief is pursued very soon after he has committed the crime and the pursuer searches his home. See below, pp. 201 ff. The story of Achan who took some of the booty of Jericho, Joshua vii, may also be mentioned in this connection; see below, pp. 203, 207. Theft of sacred objects is considered an especially grave offence also in other Oriental systems: see below, pp. 203, 207 and 307 n. 31.

29 This remained a capital offence throughout the Biblical era: see Exodus xxi. 16 and Deuteronomy xxiv. 7.

30 In Exodus xx. 15 and Deuteronomy v. 17 (19), 'Thou shalt not steal' is paired off with 'Thou shalt not kill' and 'Thou shalt not commit adultery'. Moreover, in II Samuel xii. 5, where theft of a sheep is concerned (with some aggravating points, it is true), the verdict is 'The man that hath done this thing shall surely die.' (On xii. 6, adding a monetary penalty, see below, p. 153 n. 93.) Last but not least the very passage referred to above, pp. 92 f., Exodus xxii. 1 (2), must be adduced: 'If a thief be found breaking up, and be smitten that he die, there shall be no blood shed for him.' This provision, indeed, does not allow you to kill a thief unless he is caught in the act, a *fur manifestus*. But the very fact that you are allowed to kill a *fur manifestus* appears to be a remnant of an era when the crime of theft was capital. Cp. below, p. 241.

31 I have stated above, pp. 82 ff., what I mean by 'later addition' in this connection, namely, a portion of the code later than an earlier portion as far as the structure of the code is concerned. The text of the addition itself may be as old as or even older than the text of the original section.

32 In a way, admittedly, this means a vicious circle. We may draw conclusions as to various strata only if a code in general shows a rational order; and a code may be considered as showing a rational order if deviations can be proved to be due to the existence of various strata. This mode of arguing, however, is inevitable, and not only in the particular case here under discussion. The assumption of an interpolation on the ground of a disturbance in rhythm or metre is justified only if the Psalm in question shows strict regularity; and a Psalm may be considered as showing this if deviations can be proved to be due to interpolation. Perhaps it is possible to put the matter in general terms: only where there is form, can we notice breaks—only where breaks strike us as such, can we speak of form.

33 Curiously, though paying lip-service to the possibility of a gradual growth before the revelation, orthodoxy is averse to any detailed inquiry into this question and prefers the most improbable explanations to a critical, historical account. With regard to Leviticus xx, for example, it is said that this is not a catalogue of crimes but one of penalties. Consequently (so the argument goes) we have to get first the crimes punishable by death (verses 10–13, 15–16), next those punishable by excommunication (17–18) and then the others (19–21), even though the subject of incest thus comes in three different places. (How the position of verse 14 can be accounted for on the basis of this explanation, I do not know.) But to mention only the most obvious fallacy of this doctrine, the very fact that there are different punishments in, say, the cases of intercourse between father-in-law and daughter-in-law and marriage between brother and sister proves the two regulations to date from different periods; cp. above, pp. 79 f.

CHAPTER III

LEX TALIONIS

THE following remarks are intended to show that the principle of compensation, in Hebrew law, goes back to the earliest period of legal history open to inquiry. It is often pointed out that a good many notions which in modern law are connected only with crime, above all, the notion of punishment, in ancient times played a greater or lesser part in what to-day would be pure civil law transactions, say, in the matter of damages where a man accidentally destroys another man's property. It was mentioned above[1] that under the *lex Aquilia*, for example, a man who kills another man's slave or beast—whether intentionally or not—has to pay the highest value that the victim had in the previous year. There is clearly a penal element in this rule, not merely the principle of compensation. What does not seem to have been much noticed is the opposite phenomenon, the presence in ancient times of civil law notions in what to-day would be pure criminal law affairs.

There are several reasons why the one fact is seen whereas the other is not. In the first place, criminal law features are more arresting than civil law features. When an ancient law introduces a criminal law feature (punishment) in a civil law context, few historians will fail to observe it; whereas when a civil law feature (compensation) comes in a criminal law context, it does not strike us with the same force. Here is an obvious source of mistakes in judging the character and evolution of legal systems. In the second place, there seems to be universal agreement that civil law is of a subtler nature than criminal law and, therefore, must have come into existence at a more advanced stage: it was not known to, we are asked to believe, or at least not developed by, the primitive lawyers, who confined themselves to criminal law. This, however, appears to be a prejudice rather than a reasoned and well-evidenced view. An impartial analysis of the sources suggests a somewhat different conclusion, though there is too little material to be absolutely certain about anything. The most probable inference is that criminal law notions and civil law notions, the principle of punishment and that of compensation, are of equal age. In the absence of decisive proof to the contrary, I do not see why this should surprise us. Is it surprising that the notion of having to give back what you have unlawfully taken away (compensation) should have arisen as early as the notion of hitting again if you have been hit (punishment)? Both seem the most natural reactions. The difference between the primitive stage and the present lies chiefly in this, that the two, criminal law and civil law, were not always so strictly distinguished as they are nowadays. Any given case was considered from both the criminal law standpoint and the civil law standpoint at the same time, or better, from one standpoint that embraced everything. Naturally enough, this or that aspect might be preponderant according to the particular circumstances involved: but there was not the clear-cut separation of the two domains. It is as a result of this unity of the law that, in ancient rules, the principle of compensation is frequently concealed behind criminal law elements, even though the matter regulated would come entirely under civil law in a modern system. On the other hand, I submit, civil law notions intrude where a modern lawyer would see nothing but crime and punishment. I propose to illustrate my thesis mainly by calling attention to the part played by the principle of compensation in that law which, at first sight, belongs as exclusively as any to the province of criminal law, the law of retaliation.

The law of retaliation occurs three times in the Pentateuch, for the first time, and in its fullest form, in the *Mishpatim*, the Judgments, Exodus xxi. 23 ff.: 'Thou shalt give life for life, eye for eye, tooth for tooth, hand for hand, foot for foot, burning for burning, wound for wound, stripe for stripe.' The Hebrew word translated by 'for' (in 'life for life', etc.) is תחת, with the basic meaning of 'under'. Its value is somewhat similar to that of the Greek ὑπό or the Latin *sub*. Like these, it frequently refers to one thing's taking the place of another[2] and, in legal language, to one thing's being given in the place

of another by way of compensation. In fact, a precise rendering
of the formula quoted would have to take account of this;
and we ought to translate, 'Thou shalt give life in the place
of life, eye in the place of eye' and so on. It is true that
תחת occasionally approaches the meaning of 'because of'.[3] But,
for one thing, even where it does, the idea of substitution
usually plays some minor part at least. For another thing,
though it may be that 'because of' also was in the mind
of the author of Exodus xxi. 23 ff. ('Thou shalt give life
because thou hast destroyed life' and so on), yet he did think
chiefly of compensation: the phrase 'thou shalt give' makes
this quite clear. 'To give something תחת something' simply
signifies 'to give something in the place of something'; any
other interpretation would be artificial from the strict, linguistic point of view. This conclusion is supported by the
use of תחת in the remaining rules of the *Mishpatim*. We
find תחת in Exodus xxi. 26 f., 36 and 37 (xxii. 1). According
to xxi. 26 f., a master who deprives his slave of an eye or tooth
has to 'let him go free in the place of his eye, in the place of
his tooth'. The A.V.'s translation 'for the sake of his eye, his
tooth' is better English but less exact. The slave is to be
granted freedom in compensation for his eye or tooth: instead
of the organ that he has lost he gets his freedom. Again,
xxi. 36 provides that if as a result of the owner's negligence
an ox kills another ox, the owner 'shall surely pay an ox in
the place of an ox'. Evidently, this is a case of compensation.
The third provision to use the word תחת is Exodus xxi. 37
(xxii. 1) which says that a thief shall pay 'five oxen in the place
of an ox, and four sheep in the place of a sheep'. Here also the
main idea expressed by תחת is restitution, though, as will be
discussed at greater length below,[4] the rule also includes a
penal element: a thief has to do more than just replace what he
has stolen. It follows that we have to recognize that the law of
retaliation as worded in Exodus xxi. 23 ff. contains this תחת,
'in the place of'. It means, primarily, 'Thou shalt give life in
the place of life, eye in the place of eye....' But what has
restitution to do with retaliation? What does the law mean
by making the life, the eye or the wound of the wrongdoer
take the place of the life, the eye or the wound of his victim?

It has been suggested, for a reason not connected with this problem, that the law of retaliation in Exodus is interpolated and does not belong to the actual *Mishpatim*.[5] The reason that has been given for this opinion is of a formal character: whereas ordinarily the provisions belonging to the *Mishpatim* speak of the wrongdoer in the third person, 'if a man does this or that, he is to be punished in this or that way', the law of retaliation addresses him directly: 'thou shalt give'. Moreover, this direct address not only differs from the usual form of the *Mishpatim*; it also constitutes a break within the very section in which it comes. The section begins by employing the third person: 'If men strive, and hurt a woman with child, so that her fruit depart from her, and yet no mischief follow (the woman herself neither dying nor suffering any permanent damage[6]), he shall be surely fined, according as the woman's husband will lay upon him; and he shall pay as the judges determine.' It is only in the second half that all of a sudden the second person is introduced: 'And if any mischief follow, then thou shalt give life in the place of life' and so on. Clearly, this looks like interpolation.

The impression thus gained becomes even stronger when we consider that the formal argument need not remain the only one. It looks as if the rule in question, which prescribes retaliation to be inflicted on the criminal himself, had replaced one, belonging to the original stock of the *Mishpatim*, according to which if *A* had killed or wounded *B*'s wife, it was *A*'s wife or daughter, not *A* himself, who was to be killed or wounded by way of punishment. Such practices were not uncommon in the ancient Orient.[7] In the Code of Hammurabi, it is laid down that 'if a man has struck a gentleman's daughter and caused her to drop what is in her womb, he shall pay ten shekels of silver for what was in her womb; if that woman has died, one shall put to death his daughter'.[8] It is quite likely that the original *Mishpatim* dealt with the matter in a similar fashion and that the interpolation was made with a view to doing away with this ruthless kind of retaliation: from now only the wrongdoer himself was to be killed or wounded for his deed. If this is correct, we have before us a development parallel to that underlying

Exodus xxi. 31. Here it is ordained that if your ox kills another man's son or daughter, the same rules are to apply as when a *paterfamilias* has been killed; which means—as was shown years ago[9]—that in no case is the punishment to affect your son or daughter. The Code of Hammurabi brings an instance of indirect damage, though it is not damage by animals but damage by a house that you have erected, with exactly the type of punishment combated by Exodus xxi. 31: paragraphs 229 f. say that if a house collapses and the owner's son is killed, the builder's son, not the builder himself, is to be put to death. Exodus xxi. 31 is directed against this kind of practice, and it seems to me that, like the law of retaliation, it did not form part of the oldest collection of *Mishpatim* but was introduced at a later stage. It begins with אוֹ, 'or', not like most provisions belonging to the *Mishpatim* with כִּי or אִם, 'if': 'or he have gored a son or he have gored a daughter, according to this judgment (the judgment applying to goring of a *paterfamilias*) shall it be done unto him'. There is one other provision in the *Mishpatim* beginning with אוֹ, 'or', Exodus xxi. 36, which I have already shown to occur in a portion added to the original stock.[10]

Probably, then, Exodus xxi. 23 ff., the formula of retaliation, must be deemed an interpolation. But this does not solve the problem here raised at all. At most, we might say that it is not the original *Mishpatim* but only a later amendment in which we find the notion of retaliation as compensation. But even so, we still have to ask: What did the author of the amendment mean by representing the life, eye or wound of the criminal as taking the place of the life, eye or wound of the victim? It is only fair to add that, though an interpolation is extremely likely in view of what I have said, there does remain some slight doubt about it. For it is just conceivable that the sudden direct address, 'thou shalt give', was chosen even by the original author of the *Mishpatim* in order to emphasize his opposition to those practices which we come across in other Oriental codes, and which surely prevailed also among those for whom he wrote.

According to a familiar Rabbinic exegesis, the formula of retaliation does not enjoin literal retaliation at all but only compensation in money: the wrongdoer has to make good the damage that he has caused by payment, he has to pay the value of a life in the case of loss of life, the value of an eye in the case of the loss of an eye, and so forth. If this interpretation gave us the true, original meaning of the rule under notice, it would be easily intelligible why the idea of restitution is prominent. The law, on this basis, would aim at nothing but fair compensation, the preposition תחת, 'in the place of', would palpably be the one suitable word.

Yet it is difficult to believe that the formula of retaliation always had this gentle meaning. First of all, it should be noted that the exegesis outlined is not the only one. As regards the first member in the formula, 'life for life', there is a view within the orthodox tradition itself—perhaps it is the dominant view—that it is meant to apply to intentional killing, to murder, and must therefore be taken literally. In other words, while orthodox tradition is agreed on compensation in money in the cases of the loss of an eye, the loss of a tooth and other mutilations, in the case of murder Jewish law requires capital punishment, and a large body of opinion sees this requirement expressed in the clause 'life for life'. The Sadducees, however, interpreted as demanding literal retaliation even the further members of the formula, 'eye for eye, tooth for tooth', and so on; and though this was possibly due to their general attitude in favour of a literal interpretation of Scripture and against elaborate deductions such as were cultivated in the Pharisaic schools, yet we cannot be certain that in this case at least the Sadducean teaching does not reflect an earlier stage of the law.[11] Secondly, when we examine Exodus xxi. 22 ff. as it stands, uninfluenced by Rabbinic doctrines, we find that the offence dealt with in these verses looks very much like a malicious, deliberate offence, for which, given certain conditions, actual retaliation quite probably seemed the only adequate punishment at a remote period. Two men fight, and one of them hurts a woman with child. The verb used to denote 'hurting' is נגף. Wherever this is used with the accusative, it refers to a hostile, deliberate act: it occurs in this sense precisely in the *Mishpatim*—in xxi. 35, of one ox kicking another.[12] The nouns derived from

נֶגֶף in this sense, נֶגֶף and מַגֵּפָה, signify 'plague', 'blow' or 'defeat'.[13] The situation contemplated seems to be that one of the two men fighting hurts his enemy's wife in a most vicious manner. An analogous situation is dealt with in Deuteronomy xxv. 11 f. There also two men fight, and the wife of one of them interferes, seizing her husband's enemy by his private parts. Punishment in this case is severe: 'Then thou shalt cut off her hand.' It is true that the Rabbis in this case also interpret the law-giver as meaning compensation in money. But the text here is even less favourable to this exegesis than in Exodus xxi. 23 ff. At all events, there is no doubt that the crime of Deuteronomy xxv. 11 f. is committed intentionally, and I think that of Exodus xxi. 22 ff., too, must be regarded as a deliberate, malicious attack. Thirdly, if we hold that the formula of retaliation refers not to actual retaliation but to compensation in money, we arrive at the curious result that the criminal if he has caused 'mischief' is as well off as, or better than, if he has caused 'no mischief'. Verse 22 says that if there is 'no mischief', 'he shall surely be fined, according as the woman's husband will lay upon him; and he shall pay as the judges determine'. This rule speaks not of compensation but of a fine: and before the words 'and he shall pay as the judges determine' were added to the original portion of the rule—for I believe that they were added at some time, their purpose being to limit the powers of the offended husband and establish state supervision over the settlement of the affair[14]—evidently, the wrongdoer must have been in a very precarious position, since it is hardly likely that the husband never misused his right to fix the amount of the penalty. Before they were added, that is, the wrong-doer no doubt had often to pay enormous sums. In verses 23 ff. it is provided that if there is 'mischief', life shall be given for life and so on. This cannot conceivably be less than what is imposed on the criminal in verse 22. In fact, it must be more: it must be actual retaliation.

In attempting to find out about the earliest notions attaching to the law of retaliation, it is necessary, therefore, to proceed from an interpretation admitting the literal meaning of that law. I am not thereby dissociating myself from the orthodox

Rabbinic view. For while I claim that the formula of retaliation originally referred to actual retaliation, not a penalty in
money, I should like to make two reservations. In the first
place, it is the very object of this study to show that, even
in the earliest epoch open to inquiry, the idea of compensation
was important where we are inclined to notice nothing but
punishment. Consequently, when the Rabbis assigned to this
idea a prominent or exclusive role in the formula of retaliation,
they only worked out something of which at least the beginnings were there; they did not impose upon the text a line
entirely alien from it. Here it may be permissible to mention
that time and again, when a Rabbinic exegesis that at first
sight appears to be an arbitrary exploitation of Scripture is
subjected to a closer analysis, it turns out a genuine and
understanding, if progressive, use of the old material. The
Rabbis had to combine tradition and advance; they had to
base any advance on the fixed, traditional canon. This they
did with, on the whole, admirable insight and tact. If we
cannot allow the claim that the rules proposed by them are
always exactly the rules that the law-giver had in mind, yet
we can admit that their rules nearly always sum up and draw
the proper conclusions from the main tendencies of the law-
giver. In this sense at least orthodox Judaism may be upheld
even by a rationalist living in our age: the Rabbinic system
is the system of the Bible in that it represents and brings to
full life the essential teachings of the Bible. In the second
place, even extreme orthodoxy might concede that the formula
of retaliation referred to literal retaliation before it was made
part of the Torah. For there is nothing objectionable in the
assumption that it may have existed before. Accordingly,
even if the interpretation of the law as referring to actual
retaliation should be unacceptable for the time after the final,
complete revelation of the Torah, my argument may still be
upheld for any previous period. Similar considerations apply
also to what I am going to say about the law of retaliation as
occurring in Leviticus and Deuteronomy. I shall be content,
if necessary, to confine my thesis to that period before the
final revelation.

The interpretation here adopted of the formula of retaliation in Exodus is confirmed by the other two passages quoting the formula, Leviticus xxiv. 18 ff. and Deuteronomy xix. 21. For the Rabbis, these passages also refer to compensation in money, except, perhaps, in the cases of murder and attempted murder—if I may so call the crime of one who tries to cause somebody's death by bearing false witness against him. But it is obvious that the original meaning was very different. Of Deuteronomy xix. 21 it is sufficient at this stage to say that it comes at the end of the section dealing with the false witness: 'And thine eye shall not pity; but life shall go for life, eye for eye, tooth for tooth, hand for hand, foot for foot.' This sounds very firm: and when we remember how terrible a crime false accusation was considered in ancient times, and when we read in verses 19 f. 'Then shall ye do unto him as he had thought to have done unto his brother; so shalt thou put the evil away from among you; and those which remain shall hear, and fear', the conclusion that we have before us a law ordaining literal retaliation is unavoidable. However, the preposition used in Deuteronomy xix. 21 is not תחת, 'in the place of', but ב. The notion of compensation, if present at all, is not so manifestly present as in Exodus. I shall therefore defer the discussion of this text for the moment.[15]

As for Leviticus xxiv. 18 ff., the position is as complicated as interesting. I very much doubt whether in this section retaliation is restricted to intentional wrongdoing. Homicide is here paired off with the killing of another man's beast. He who kills a man, we are told, is to die, he who kills another man's beast is to pay for it; and, the law goes on, he who deprives a man of his eye or the like is to suffer the same. Now restitution for a beast has presumably to be made whether he who killed it did so intentionally or by accident:[16] and as there is no sign that the other cases regulated in this section should be treated differently, it seems that in them also the distinction between intentional and accidental wrongdoing is irrelevant. Other points support this view. The whole section under discussion forms part of a larger work concerned with priestly matters, sacrificial rites, festivals, offences against religion and so forth. In such a work, it is by no means surprising to find a law on homicide and allied cases that makes no distinction between him who kills with malice aforethought and him who kills, say, through negligence: it is certain that there were long periods when, in the eyes of the priests, killing as such, killing as shedding of blood, required atonement no matter what was the attitude of the person guilty of another's death. Genesis ix. 6 is a clear example of this principle: 'Whoso sheddeth the blood of man, by man his blood shall be shed.'[17]

The priestly character of the section from Leviticus under discussion is very pronounced. (1) The expression הכה נפש, 'to slay the life, the soul',[18] is used in xxiv. 17 f., both of the killing of a man and the killing of a beast. Literally translated, these verses run: 'And he that killeth the life of a man shall surely be put to death. And he that killeth the life of a beast shall make it good.' It is noteworthy that most or all texts of legal relevance where this expression occurs come from, or are influenced by, the priestly treatment of homicide. The expression occurs in Deuteronomy xix. 6 and 11, the law dealing with the right to protection in a city of refuge of the unintentional homicide: no doubt these rules came into existence at some sanctuary or other. In Genesis xxxvii. 21 also הכה נפש is to be found in what is at least a semi-legal context. Reuben, we are told, when his brothers wanted to slay Joseph, objected: 'Let us not kill him as to his soul.' His counter-proposal was to let him perish in a pit. Clearly, this contrast between slaying, shedding the blood of, a man—as a crime—and killing him by casting him into a pit and letting him starve to death—as less blameworthy—is based on sacral, priestly concepts. That Reuben's real intention may have been to save Joseph makes no difference. He reminded his brothers that they might get rid of Joseph in a manner not involving the crime of 'slaying the soul'; and they saw the point.[19] (2) The systematization of the law in bringing together the killing of a man and that of a beast is the kind of achievement typical of the priests. They were capable of these comprehensive schemata. No less typical, however, than the systematization as such is the peculiar way in which the two cases are here combined. They are combined under the maxim of נפש תחת נפש, 'life in the place of life'.

The A.V.'s rendering of the last few words of Leviticus xxiv. 18 as 'beast for beast' is incorrect: it must be 'life for life'. What the law-giver has done is clear. He has split up the formula of retaliation; he has taken the first member of the formula, 'life for life', separated it from the rest and put it by itself at the end of verse 18 so as to cover both homicide and the destruction of a beast. Verses 17 and 18 should be interpreted thus: capital punishment in the case of homicide, restitution in the case of the destruction of a beast—both according to the principle 'life in the place of life'.[20] The remaining members of his formula of retaliation the law-giver has relegated to verse 20, after the provision concerning cases like the loss of an eye or tooth. The offences of killing a man and killing a beast, then, are subsumed under a common principle, 'life for life'. Surely, only in a priestly system would the role of the נפש be emphasized in this fashion; only a priestly system would make the slaying of the נפש and the penalty for it the one governing idea of the two cases. (3) The treatment in verses 19 f. of the case where a man deprives another of an eye or the like is equally dominated by priestly notions. The offence contemplated consists in 'causing a blemish in one's neighbour'. This translation by the A.V. is excellent.[21] The Hebrew for 'blemish' is מום. It signifies the blemish making a priest unfit for service in Leviticus xxi. 17 f., 21, 23, and the blemish making an animal unfit to be sacrificed in Leviticus xxii. 20 f., 25, Numbers xix. 2, Deuteronomy xv. 21, xvii. 1. As blemishes of this kind were regarded almost any permanent deformities, blindness, lameness, a broken hand, etc. It is the causing of such a deformity in a person that constitutes the offence of the verses here analysed: the author thought in priestly categories, even though this particular law was to apply indiscriminately to priests and laymen. Once we recognize this factor, we can also explain the wording of the formula of retaliation in verse 20. It is highly significant. In Exodus, it may be recalled, the formula contains eight members, referring to life, eye, tooth, hand, foot, burning, wound and stripe. Of these, the last three may well be later than the others, at least, qua parts of this formula.[22] For they have regard not to definite limbs or organs lost but to various modes of hurting, hurting by burning, by wounding, by scourging.[23] In any case, the formula in Deuteronomy contains five clauses only, referring to life, eye, tooth, hand and foot, and in Leviticus also, as we shall presently see, the three modes of wounding are not mentioned. In Leviticus xxiv, we find the first member, 'life for life', separated from the others, in verse 18, as I have already pointed out. The rest of the formula is given in verse 20, but instead of four clauses referring to eye, tooth, hand and foot, there are three, referring to breach, eye and tooth. The only other passage in Leviticus using the noun שֶׁבֶר, 'breach', is xxi. 19. Here, a 'breach of the hand' and a 'breach of the foot' are specified as cases of מוּם, of 'blemish', resulting in unfitness for service as a priest.[24] Evidently, the author of the formula of retaliation in xxiv. 20 has replaced the two clauses preserved in Exodus and Deuteronomy, 'hand for hand, foot for foot', by the one, 'breach (*scil.* of hand or foot) for breach (of hand or foot)'.[25] He has replaced them, that is, by a priestly term, and, furthermore, he has given this priestly term the place of honour in his formula: whereas in Exodus and Deuteronomy hand and foot come after eye and tooth, in Leviticus שֶׁבֶר, 'breach', comes first and then only eye and tooth. The various modes of hurting specified in Exodus—burning, wounding, scourging— are not represented in Leviticus. The formula in Leviticus is concerned solely with the causing of a deformity in the priestly sense. But it is interested neither in smaller, curable wounds nor in the question precisely how the deformity has been caused, by a blow or by fire or in any other way.

The punishments laid down in Leviticus xxiv. 17 ff. are not, if the foregoing considerations are conclusive, limited to intentional wrongdoing. None the less there can be little doubt that, taken in its original meaning, this section also speaks of actual retaliation. The homicide, verse 17 says, 'shall surely be put to death'; and he who causes a blemish in another person, according to verses 19 f., 'as he hath done, so shall it be done to him...as he hath caused a blemish in a man, so shall it be done to him again'. It is hard to believe that these provisions are referring to mere restitution by payment; and I may add that if contrary to what I have suggested it is assumed that the law applies to deliberate crimes only, we get one more argument in favour of interpreting it as requiring literal retaliation. Destruction of a beast alone is to be settled by payment, and the difference between this case and that of homicide is made quite clear in verses 17 f. and again in verse 21: 'And he that killeth the soul of a man shall surely be put to death, and he that killeth the soul of a beast shall make it good....And he that killeth a beast, he shall make it good, and he that killeth a man, he shall be put to death.' With regard to the formula of retaliation, the result is that, as in Exodus and Deuteronomy, it expresses the demand that the wrongdoer actually suffer the same as his victim. Only the first member of the formula, 'life for life', has a wider meaning in Leviticus, owing to a systematization undertaken by the priests. As I pointed out above, this clause in xxiv. 18 is made into a general principle covering both homicide and the destruction of a beast. It therefore expresses a demand of actual retaliation when applied to the former case, and a demand of compensation when applied to the latter.

If I may repeat, as in Exodus and Deuteronomy, so in Leviticus, the formula of retaliation prescribes literal retribution for homicide and depriving a person of his eye, tooth or the like. On the other hand, as in Exodus (of this aspect of Deuteronomy I shall treat later), so in Leviticus, the formula of retaliation is worded as if retaliation were compensation. The preposition used is תחת, and a precise rendering must not neglect this: 'Life in the place of life, breach in the place of breach, eye in the place of eye, tooth in the place of tooth.' Actually, the fact that retaliation means or includes compensation is perhaps even clearer in Leviticus than in Exodus. We have seen that the priests made the maxim 'life in the place of life' govern both actual retaliation in the case of homicide and amends in the case of the destruction of a beast. Evidently, this extension of 'life in the place of life' to restitution in the latter case was possible only because the idea of restitution was prominent even in the native domain of the principle, in the domain of retaliation inflicted on the homicide. Professor Jolowicz, it is true, arrives at the opposite conclusion. His thesis is that the principle of compensation was not known to primitive lawyers; he notices the coupling of the provision about payment in the case of the destruction of a beast with the provision about retaliation in the case of homicide; and infers that even the former provision is dominated not by the principle of compensation but by the principle of retaliation.[26] This, however, is entirely overlooking the philological side of the question, the meaning of תחת discussed above, and that of שלם, 'to make good', to be discussed below.[27] It also leaves out of account the fact that, as I have shown, the maxim 'life for life' is only secondarily extended to payment for a beast; so that, even if it were correct that payment was thought of as retaliation at the time of the extension, we should still be without proof that this was the earliest way of looking at the matter. Professor Jolowicz proceeds from the English translation 'beast for beast', which obscures the origin of the clause as the first member of the formula of retaliation, and thus prevents one from seeing that it is only in consequence of a priestly systematization that it covers payment for a beast as well as punishment in the case of homicide. The truth is that, whatever part the notion of punishment may have played, in Exodus and Leviticus the law of retaliation is formulated and set in a mode leaving no doubt that, in the minds of the authors, retaliation involved compensation. Can this be explained?

In trying to account for this fact, I shall begin by examining the first member of the formula, 'life in the place of life', by itself. There are indications that it may at some date have stood alone. I have already remarked that the last three clauses of the formula in Exodus, 'burning for burning, wound for wound, stripe for stripe', may be an addition to the rest. If the first member, 'life for life', originally stood alone, the growth of the full formula would have taken place in three stages; the earliest stage having been 'life for life', the second 'life for life, eye for eye, tooth for tooth, hand for hand, foot for foot' (the last two clauses are replaced in Leviticus by 'breach for breach'), and the third the complete formula with 'burning for burning' and so on. However, I shall take into account also the possibility that the first clause 'life in the place of life' was from the outset combined with the following ones.

The first member of the formula of retaliation is 'life in the place of life'. We know of ancient Oriental laws according to which all that a man who had killed another man had to do was to supply the latter's family with one or more persons.[28] Under this system, in the case of homicide, one life was simply replaced by another. If there was a similar stage in Hebrew law, and if the clause 'life in the place of life' came into existence in that era, the wording would be easily intelligible. It should be remembered that, strange as those laws may seem to us, they are based on a notion, the notion of man as a 'fungible' being, which is perfectly natural and in many connections prevalent even in our day. The fact that we speak of it as an extraordinary thing if a person is irreplaceable only proves that most people are not so considered. A good example from the Bible of the idea of the replaceability of man in its wider application is furnished by Genesis iv. 25: 'And Adam knew his wife again: and she bare a son and called his name Seth (שת). For God, said she, hath appointed me (שת) another seed instead of Abel, whom Cain slew.' Seth, Eve felt, was granted her by God as a substitute for Abel (and it may be worth mentioning that he comes תחת, 'in the place of', Abel)— a line of thought that would be as acceptable now as it was then. The laws that imposed upon the murderer the duty to replace the victim merely show to what extremes the idea under discussion might be carried.

In Kings, two episodes are recorded where the phrase 'life in the place of life' is employed in a sense rather, though not quite, like the one just suggested; that is to say, where it refers to a real substitution of one man for another. Both times we are told about a guard who has to answer with his head for a prisoner doomed to death: if the prisoner escapes, the guard's soul is to be in the place of the prisoner's. In I Kings xx. 35 ff. the situation is as follows. Ahab has defeated Ben-hadad, King of Syria, with the help of God; yet, though God intended Ben-hadad's death, Ahab concludes a treaty with the former enemy and allows him to depart unharmed. Thereupon a prophet is sent to Ahab. The prophet pretends to be an ordinary man who comes to ask for the king's decision in a dispute. He tells the king how a fellow-soldier put him in charge of a prisoner: 'Keep this man; if by any means he be missing, then shall thy life be for his life, or else thou shalt pay a talent of silver.' The prisoner, however, escaped. The king replies that there can be only one verdict. At this point the prophet throws off his disguise and points out the moral of his parable. Ahab is the guard whom God put in charge of Ben-hadad; he let him escape, and now he himself will have to take his place. 'Thus saith the Lord, Because thou hast let go out of thy hand a man whom I appointed to utter destruction, therefore thy life shall go for his life, and thy people for his people.' Twice in this story do we find the clause 'life in the place of life' (the preposition used being תחת), once in the agreement, or rather, fictitious agreement, between the prophet and his fellow-soldier and once in the application of this to the position of Ahab. It may be observed—though it is not immediately relevant to my argument—that the words 'or else thou shalt pay a talent of silver', occurring in the agreement between the prophet and his fellow-soldier, most probably are an interpolation. They were added in a time when arrangements of the kind described by the prophet were deemed ruthless and immoral, and when composition had become customary in such cases. This alternative, this right of the guard to save his life by paying a fine, is not considered at all in the application of the parable. Surely, if the words belonged to the original story, we should expect something like 'therefore shall thy life go for his life and thy people for his people—unless thou sacrificest thy treasures': the whole procedure would be very much tamer and less impressive. In point of fact, the prophet foretells Ahab's inescapable destruction, which presupposes capital punishment without the possibility of composition also in the agreement between the prophet and his fellow-soldier.[29] It may be added that no such alternative possibility is mentioned in the other episode containing the phrase 'life in the place of life' and also concerned with the punishment of a careless guard, namely, II Kings x. 24.

To turn to this story, Jehu decides to slay the priests of Baal.

He waits until they are in their temple, assembles guards outside the building and warns them: 'If any of the men whom I have brought into your hands escape, he that letteth him go, his life shall be for the life of him.' Again, there is the clause 'life in the place of life' (with תחת, 'in the place of').

In these two pericopes, then, the clause 'life in the place of life' is used, not as in the Pentateuch as demanding retaliation in the case of homicide, but as demanding that a guard who lets a prisoner escape should take his place. It refers to substitution in our sense. This application of 'life in the place of life' would be quite understandable on the basis of the view that the principle came into existence at a stage of the law when a homicide had only to furnish one or more persons to the family of his victim. On the basis of this view, the principle even in the domain of murder did mean real substitution. One might even hold that the way in which the phrase is employed in Kings gives us a clue as to how that early rule concerning homicide developed into the law of the Pentateuch. One might hold, that is, that the original stage, when a homicide had to replace the victim by one or more persons, was followed by a second stage, when the penal element began to overshadow mere compensation and a homicide had himself to enter his victim's family; and that it is this second stage which is reflected in the application of the clause in Kings—for the negligent guard cannot replace the prisoner by supplying any person but has to take his place himself. The second stage, this argument might continue, would in course of time lead to the third, represented by the Pentateuch, when a homicide was claimed by the victim's family with a view, not to receiving him as substitute for the victim, but to putting him to death for his deed.

However, this is largely speculation. I have said that the application of 'life in the place of life' in Kings would be quite understandable against the background of a law under which a homicide had to supply one or more persons to the family of his victim. But I am far from maintaining that it would not be understandable without such a law. In fact, the difference between the case contemplated by such a law

and that contemplated in Kings is great enough to make a
connection appear highly doubtful. The former case is that
of a sound and valuable member of a family being killed. Here
the rule that the affair is to be settled by the delivery of one
or more substitutes certainly implies a somewhat extreme view
of the 'fungibility' of man. The case of Kings is that of a
hated prisoner being let loose, a prisoner destined to destruction. Here the rule that the prisoner is to be replaced by the
guard is far less surprising. The only use that was to be made
of the prisoner was putting him to death, and for that the
guard will do just as well. In other words, a man doomed to
death is considerably more 'fungible' than an ordinary person.
(True, even a man doomed to death is not entirely 'fungible',
since one usually dooms to death a particular individual, an
enemy; and from this point of view, any other person will not
quite serve the purpose. But in a way the guard who allows
a prisoner to escape has become an enemy.) Moreover, it is
well known how great a part is played in antiquity by the
idea of a surety that undertakes in certain circumstances to
suffer what, properly, another man ought to.[30] Considering
all this, it is perfectly possible that the clause 'life in the
place of life' is used in Kings spontaneously, without any
precedent in the law of homicide, to express the guard's
liability should his prisoner escape. Even the possibility that
the application in Kings is somehow based on the formula of
retaliation in the sense in which it occurs in the Pentateuch
cannot be absolutely ruled out, though I am not inclined to
rate it very high. It is just conceivable that there was a
principle 'life in the place of life' as demanding that a murderer be put to death; and that, since it involved the idea of
compensation (in a way to be explained), it could be transferred to the case of a guard taking the place of his escaped
prisoner.

To summarize the foregoing considerations, we have two
passages in Kings where the phrase 'life in the place of life'
refers to proper substitution in our sense, namely, the putting
of a negligent guard in the place of his escaped prisoner. This
may be taken as slightly supporting the suggestion, made
above, that the clause possibly came into existence under a

system that made a homicide literally replace his victim by supplying the latter's family with one or more substitutes. If this was the origin of the clause, it may have been retained even at a stage when retaliation had superseded compensation, when a homicide no longer replaced his victim but was liable to capital punishment. The clause 'life in the place of life' was applied to capital punishment even though compensation played here a far less obvious part than at the earlier stage. Such a survival of a technical ancient phrase even when, in strictness, it ought to be altered is nothing unheard of.

Yet we cannot leave the matter there. Quite apart from the fact that the evidence for the origin of the clause under a system of the kind described is extremely slender, two points are to be taken into account even if we accept it as sufficient. For one thing, the preposition 'in the place of' occurs not only in the first part of the formula of retaliation, 'life in the place of life', but also in all the following parts, 'eye in the place of eye', etc. In none of these following cases can there ever have been a system of real substitution of a sound organ for the lost one. 'Eye in the place of eye' must always have meant retaliation, and in spite of this we find the preposition 'in the place of', indicating compensation. One might perhaps say that the clauses 'eye in the place of an eye' and so on were simply worded on the model of 'life in the place of life', the impossibility of compensation being disregarded. But while this assumption is not utterly unreasonable, it is carrying the explanation on the ground of the inertia of language rather far. For remember what it implies: the phrase 'life in the place of life' came into existence as demanding the substitution by the homicide of a fresh person for the one that he had killed; the phrase was kept unchanged even when under the regime of retaliation it became very inexact; and now other phrases like 'eye in the place of eye' were modelled after it, though here there had never been anything else than retaliation. I do not think this is a satisfactory solution. For another thing, we have seen that, in Leviticus, the principle 'life in the place of life' is extended from the domain of homicide to that of the destruction of a beast. The principle here covers not only retaliation in the former case, but also amends by real compensation in the latter. This, as I have already observed, clearly shows that even when 'life in the place of life' was used as demanding retaliation, the notion of compensation must have been connected with it; otherwise it could not have been transferred to a simple case of reparation like amends for a beast. In other words, the idea expressed by the term 'in the place of', even in the domain of retaliation, was taken seriously, was not a dead letter having come down from an earlier period.

It follows that, however the first clause of the formula of retaliation, 'life in the place of life', may have arisen—whether it arose under a regime of real literal reparation in the case of homicide or whether it meant retaliation from the outset, whether it stood alone or whether it was always combined with the other clauses, 'eye for eye' and so on—the formula of retaliation as proposed in Exodus and Leviticus speaks of retaliation as compensation. The acceptance, by the family of a murdered man, of a living man to fill the gap (in accordance with some ancient Oriental laws concerning homicide) and the putting to death of a careless guard instead of the prisoner whom he let escape (the situation in Kings) are cases of substitution in our sense. The putting to death of a homicide and the plucking out of a man's eye because he has plucked out another's, in accordance with the law of retaliation in the Pentateuch, are not. Yet in Exodus and Leviticus the law of retaliation is worded and set in a fashion rendering it plain that, for those Hebrew law-givers, they were. It is this law of retaliation, in the form in which we have it before us in Exodus and Leviticus, that calls for explanation, and no theory as to the stages through which it may have passed before its appearance in Exodus and Leviticus will provide a complete solution.

The solution can probably be got by paying attention to an idea that seems to have been of much importance in early times—and not only in the Bible: the idea that if you deprive a man of a certain power or faculty, this power or faculty becomes yours. Traces of this idea are numerous in all literature, one might say, up to this day. A few passages from the Bible may serve to illustrate what I have in mind. I have to remark, however, that I am by no means claiming that in each case that I shall adduce the idea was present in the mind of the author or the person to whom the passage refers. Quite often, though a phrase may be used apparently expressing the idea in question, it is merely a phrase, emptied of most of its original content. On the other hand, even a phrase emptied of its original content usually has something to teach us about the notions of the period when it was first coined. Language frequently preserves valuable ancient material in this way. For my purpose it is sufficient to demonstrate that the idea existed at some time; and it matters little whether that was when the passage quoted was written, or when the events referred to in the passage occurred, or only when the phrase was created and employed in all earnest.

Here are a few examples. David accuses Saul who seeks his life without cause, 'Yet thou huntest my soul to take it.'[31] Similar expressions are to be met with fairly frequently, and it is very likely that לקח, 'to take', is used in them as denoting not only 'to take away from another man' but also 'to take to oneself, to capture'. He who murders a person captures, obtains control of, his soul, is the original meaning underlying the phrase in question: I do not say that this meaning must still be alive in the passage quoted, though there is nothing to show that it is not. Again, the enemies, the Psalmist complains, 'mark my steps, when they wait for my soul'.[32] Of the unfaithful prophets it is said that they are 'like a roaring lion ravening the prey; they have devoured souls; they have taken the treasure and precious things'.[33] It is a picture of men thriving on the corruption that they have caused; and the phrase 'to eat souls' strongly suggests the process of gaining wealth and strength by making others poor and weak. According to Balaam's prophecy, Israel 'shall rise up as a great lion, and lift up himself as a young lion: he shall not lie down until he eat of the prey, and drink the blood of the slain'.[34] This comparison is far from unique. It clearly has its basis in the belief that the strength of the conquered and slain goes to the victor. In fact we know that this belief was often given symbolic expression in ancient times by the victor's actually drinking of the blood of the vanquished.

Doubtless it was in view of symbolic acts of this sort that phrases like 'to drink the blood of the slain' became usual in the sense of 'to conquer an enemy'.

It is on these lines that I think an explanation of the formula of retaliation must be sought. (It may not be superfluous to emphasize that it is the formula alone which I am trying to explain. The actual phenomenon of retaliation as a whole is, of course, highly complex, and emotions like revengefulness or relief once retribution has been exacted play an enormous part.) The murderer gets hold of the murdered man's strength. But by taking vengeance and killing the murderer, the victim's family in turn seizes the strength of the offender. Where this belief prevails, retaliation does imply compensation. Two Biblical terms are of particular relevance in this connection since, unlike the passages cited so far, they have immediate reference to homicide and its punishment. The one is the expression דרש דם or דרש דמים, 'to require the blood'. It is used of God's requiring the murdered man's blood from his murderer.[35] This phrase, however loosely we may employ it nowadays, and however loosely it may be employed even in some passages of the Bible, could come into existence only on the basis of the belief that the murderer is in control of the murdered man's blood; only on the basis of this belief would people see in vengeance a demanding back, a 'requiring', of the blood that was shed. We have also to consider that the way in which God 'requires' the murdered man's blood is invariably by killing or having killed the murderer.[36] Here, then, language has preserved a term distinctly implying (at least at the time when it was coined) the notion that the soul of the slain comes under the sway of his conqueror; and the way in which Old Testament writers apply the term reflects the same idea that we find in the formula of retaliation—the killing of the murderer is a getting back of what has been lost. To him who causes a sinner's death by failing to warn him of the dangers of sin God says, 'But his blood will I require at thine hand.'[37] Possibly the notion that the person causing another's death obtains possession of his blood is no longer really present in the mind of the author of this passage. But the notion that God not only imposes a punishment on the

negligent watchman but also exacts compensation from him
for the sinner's soul undoubtedly plays some part.

The second term to be adduced is גאל הדם, which the A.V.
translates by 'the revenger of blood'.[38] Literally, however, it
signifies 'the redeemer of the blood' or, even more precisely,
'the taker back of the blood'.[39] The role of the גאל, the
'redeemer', in ancient law is of the greatest importance. Your
גאל is your nearest relative, who has the right and duty to
'redeem', to regain, for the family any property—property
taken in the widest sense—that you have lost. He has to
marry your widow if you die leaving no children; he receives
back any money that was unlawfully withheld from you and
not repaid to you during your lifetime; he has to buy back
any land that you are forced by poverty to sell; he has to buy
back even yourself if you have to sell yourself as a slave. As
גאל הדם, as 'taker back of the blood', the 'redeemer', I submit,
wins back the blood of his murdered kinsman from the murderer. For surely, this ancient technical term must at some
date have meant what it says; and, if so, it becomes intelligible
only by connecting it with that primitive belief I have outlined. The murderer has obtained control over the murdered
man's soul. So the גאל הדם has to redeem the dead man from
the power of the murderer. By killing the murderer, he takes
back the victim's soul. Vengeance is compensation.

In view of the expressions discussed, two of them directly
referring to homicide and its punishment, it can no longer be
surprising to find that the law of retaliation, as worded in
Exodus and Leviticus, speaks of retaliation as restitution. The
wrongdoer has deprived another person of some faculty—life,
eye, hand or the like—which means that he has added that
faculty to his own. By inflicting retaliation, the person harmed
or his family not only punishes the wrongdoer but regains the
faculty lost. It really is, from this standpoint, a matter of
exacting 'life in the place of life, eye in the place of eye, tooth
in the place of tooth, hand in the place of hand, foot in the
place of foot'. Three objections might perhaps be raised
against the thesis here advanced. In the first place, it might
be argued, there are two different ideas of compensation
involved in the cases which I have presented. Sometimes the

idea is that retaliation includes getting back what was lost, as, for example, when he who kills a relative's murderer is called 'the taker back of the blood'. If, however, we base ourselves on phrases like 'to drink the blood of the enemy', retaliation means getting back not what was lost, the blood of the murdered relative, but something else instead, the blood of the murderer. This objection does not seem to me very serious. We cannot expect absolute precision in matters of this kind. When the law of retaliation makes punishment imply compensation, to ask whether the compensation consists in receiving back the soul of the murdered man or the soul of the murderer would be too pedantic. Probably both ideas have something to do with the formulation of the law in Exodus and Leviticus: they were not strictly distinguished by primitive lawyers. Another objection might be that the expressions that I have adduced all refer to life and blood; but none of them shows that the same idea of seizing a man's faculty by depriving him of it attaches to other cases as well, to the case, for instance, where I deprive you not of your life but of your eye or hand. To this it is to be replied that there is a good reason why the notion that a person may appropriate another's soul by killing him should have left clearer marks in Hebrew language than the notion that a person may appropriate part of another's powers by, say, cutting off his hand. The reason is that anything connected with life and death is so much more important and impressive than minor affairs. However, there are perhaps a few dim traces even of the notion of a man subjugating, not the soul of another, but particular faculties. The wicked, we hear from the Psalmist,[40] come upon the pious 'to eat up his flesh'; Job asks his friends[41] why they must 'persecute him as God, and are not satisfied with his flesh'; and it is quite possible that when the thumbs of conquered chieftains were cut off, this was done not from mere cruelty but also on purpose to gain their strength.[42] Even in living languages we meet with phrases like 'to lose one's liberty, happiness, honour, to the enemy', 'to sell these goods to the highest bidder', 'to claim back these goods from the enemy' who has 'to give them back'. In Hebrew, there is, for example, the phrase לֵב גָּנַב, 'to steal a man's heart',

in the sense of 'to deceive a man'.[43] Such expressions render
it likely that the possibility of obtaining for oneself another
person's powers was in some remote age believed in quite
generally: you might gain not only another man's soul by
killing him, but also his strength by cutting off his hands and
so on. It must be this idea that underlies the clauses 'eye in
the place of eye, tooth in the place of tooth', etc., in the formula
of retaliation.

There is a further difficulty, concerning only the last three
members of the formula of retaliation as given in Exodus,
'burning in the place of burning, wound in the place of wound,
stripe in the place of stripe'. It is obvious that 'in the place
of' is here far more awkward than in the preceding clauses of
the formula. The preceding clauses deal with the loss of life
or limb, life, eye, tooth, hand and foot; they prescribe retaliation, or rather they lay down that the life or organ lost be
replaced by way of retaliation. But what about the last three
clauses, 'burning in the place of burning' and so on? You can
replace a life or organ lost, but you cannot properly speak
of replacing a wound. A wound is not anything lost, but a
damage inflicted, and you do not put anything 'in the place
of' a damage. Yet in Exodus we find enjoined 'burning in
the place of burning' and so on. I have suggested above that
the last three clauses of the formula in Exodus may well be
an addition later than the rest. They are mentioned neither
in Leviticus nor in Deuteronomy. Possibly, therefore, their
form is simply an imitation of that of the preceding clauses,
the author who added them not noticing the awkwardness or
not daring to give them a strikingly different form. But we
are by no means compelled to make this assumption. It is
true that 'burning in the place of burning' is less exact than
'life in the place of life' or 'eye in the place of eye', since a
wound, unlike a life or an organ, is never replaced. But
language, and in particular, archaic language, is not always
of scientific accuracy. The question may be reduced to simple
terms. An ancient lawyer wished to express the idea that,
say, a cut inflicted upon *A* by *B* should be made good by the
same cut being inflicted upon the latter. Are we to expect
him to say, as would be the correct way of putting it, 'the

loss resulting for *B* from a cut to be in the place of the loss that resulted for *A* from his cut', or are we to expect him to prefer the simpler though somewhat loose '*B*'s cut to be in the place of *A*'s cut'? The second alternative would convey the idea of compensation by retaliation clearly enough, and the slight illogicality surely would not disturb an ancient writer half as much as it would (or should) a modern.

It is perhaps worth while to mention a Rabbinic statement expressly describing the death penalty as having the function of monetary compensation. There is a principle in Talmudic law that capital punishment and compensation by payment are mutually exclusive.[44] He who is liable to capital punishment on account of a murder, for example, will not have to pay damages for any loss that his victim may have suffered before his death by, say, having had to stay away from work, doctor's fees and so on. The Rabbis go very far in the application of this principle. They apply it even if for particular reasons a criminal who has committed a capital offence cannot be executed. Accordingly, they apply it to the case of a burglar who intrudes into a house at night-time, prepared to kill the owner if necessary. For in this case the owner of the house is entitled, if he catches the intruder on the spot, to slay him. The Rabbis construe this right to self-help as a right to execute the death penalty. Of course, once the thief makes good his escape, the right no longer exists, nor can any court now inflict capital punishment. None the less the Rabbis declare the burglar free of any obligation to restore the stolen object or pay a fine. It is a case, in their eyes, where capital punishment has not been carried out for a special reason unconnected with the essential nature of the crime. Now some Rabbis seem to have regarded as basis for this decision the fact that the burglar 'has acquired the stolen object with his life'.[45] This statement reflects conscious recognition of the idea that the life of the wrongdoer itself constitutes a sort of compensation. Certainly, such an analysis becomes possible only in an age when criminal law, with punishment as the dominant factor, and civil law, with compensation as the dominant factor, are clearly distinguished. Only where this distinction is made can the absence of monetary compensation be justified by pointing out that the loss of life, or even the risk of its loss, must be accepted in lieu of payment. Yet it is conceivable that we have here very ancient notions coming to the surface, in however refined a form; and that the Rabbis only elaborate and put into words what had been a feature of the law all along—the idea that punishment includes restitution, that punishment itself compensates the party wronged for his loss.

Before going on to the formula of retaliation in Deuteronomy, it may be well to note that the belief which I suspect to underlie the formula in Exodus and Leviticus, namely, the belief that retaliation constitutes restitution, is not entirely irrational. Admittedly, there is a good deal of the magical behind concepts like 'the taker back of the blood'; but there is also a firm substratum of practical experience and shrewd calculation. The fact that an idea forms part of a system not scientific in our sense must not make us overlook its basis in everyday reasonable dealings. Let us remember, for example, that retaliation, roughly, does restore the original proportion of power between the two persons or families concerned. The difference between it and restitution proper is that it restores the original relation in a negative way, by depriving the wrongdoer of the same thing of which he has deprived the person wronged; while restitution is positive and gives back to the person wronged that which the wrongdoer has appropriated. But the original ratio of strength is restored through retaliation as well as restitution, and this, even from the rational point of view, constitutes an important similarity. Further, retaliation in a sense does put at the disposal of the man deprived of a limb, or the family deprived of a member, the same limb of the wrongdoer or the person of the wrongdoer. True, all that the man or family wronged can do is to cut off the wrongdoer's limb or kill the wrongdoer. Yet it is intelligible how an ancient lawyer might see in the proceedings an element of compensation even on rational reflection. Lastly, at times retaliation may produce even something like positive compensation. For a person or family, by exacting vengeance from an offender, gains in honour, security and influence. The loss is actually to some extent replaced: *que la fuerza de los valientes cuando caen se pasa á la flaqueza de los que se levantan,* says

Cervantes in *La Española Inglesa*. I am not urging that it is purely rational considerations which led to the idea of retaliation as compensation. I do urge that this idea is more rational than one might at first sight suppose.

In Deuteronomy xix. 21 the formula of retaliation occurs a third time, as the conclusion of the law concerning a false witness, who, it is laid down, is to suffer that fate which he had intended for the accused. The preposition used, however, is not תחת, 'in the place of', but ב. Why this form has been chosen is difficult to say. The range of ב is very wide indeed. In the passage under discussion it may simply mean 'because of, for the sake of': 'life because of life, eye because of eye' and so on. Or it may mean a little more than this, something like 'to atone for'; it is only natural that the signification of the particle should be coloured by the context. Or it may denote 'in accordance with, corresponding to': 'life corresponding to life, eye corresponding to eye', etc. This brings us rather near the idea of compensation and, in fact, ב can be used to express this idea. So it is very conceivable that this idea is present here just as much as in Exodus and Leviticus, where תחת is employed, and that we have to translate: 'life in compensation of life, eye in compensation of eye'.[46] If this meaning is intended, the difference between the formula in Deuteronomy and the formula in Exodus and Leviticus is small: the latter refers directly to the substitution of the wrongdoer's life, eye and so on for the life, eye and so on of the victim, the former more generally to the wrongdoer's life and eye making up for those of the victim.

Whichever of the various meanings of ב we prefer, I would not decide whether the formula in Deuteronomy is older or later than that in Exodus and Leviticus. Quite likely the law of retaliation existed in several slightly different forms from a very early time. One interesting possibility, however, may be specially considered. If in the Deuteronomic formula the preposition ב is used not as indicating compensation but, say, atonement ('life to atone for life, eye to atone for eye'), it is arguable that the author was deliberately discarding תחת, 'in the place of', in favour of ב, 'because of, to atone for'. In the first place, the formula in Deuteronomy refers to a false witness whose scheme has not succeeded. To him, the law ordains, it shall be done 'as he had thought to have done unto his brother'. It may well have appeared to the author of the Deuteronomic formula that to speak of compensation in this case was somewhat illogical, since as the accused has suffered no loss through the false witness—the latter's plot having failed—there is no room for compensation. In the second place, the idea of punishment as restitution may not have appealed to a Deuteronomist writer on more fundamental grounds. In Deuteronomy, the main objects of punishment, of which we are told again and again, are to extirpate sin and to deter any who might otherwise follow the example of the criminal. Even in the section concerning a false witness itself these two objects are clearly stated: 'So shalt thou put the evil away from among you, and those which remain shall hear, and fear, and shall henceforth commit no more any such evil among you.' With such a conception of retaliation the idea of retaliation as compensation of the person offended may well have seemed incompatible to a careful writer.[47]

In support of my main thesis, some observations of a more general nature may be useful. We have seen that at some date retaliation was thought of as constituting compensation: the party who had suffered the loss of a life, eye or the like was deemed to be compensated by the other party's suffering the same fate. I have attempted to suggest an explanation of this phenomenon. But whether the explanation is accepted or not, the fact is indisputable. This means that we find the principle of compensation dominating a series of cases which, to us, seem cases of punishment pure and simple. Now as I said at the beginning of this study, the prevalent view of modern historians is that civil law, governed by the principle of compensation, is a later achievement than criminal law, governed by the principle of punishment. Recently Professor Jolowicz, in an article already mentioned,[48] has declared that 'ancient systems deal with tort and the damages for it not so much quantitatively as qualitatively. The penalty is made to fit, not the amount of damage inflicted by the tort, but the nature of the tort itself'. This method of dealing with tort, Professor Jolowicz holds, was applied by the ancient lawyers not only to crime in the narrow sense but also to delicts causing economic damage only.[49] I have remarked before on the fundamental weakness of any theories of this kind.[50] Criminal law, with punishment, appears to us less civilized than civil law, with compensation. Hence we are inclined to think that the former must be older than the latter—a conclusion ultimately rooted in the liberal teaching of an ever-progressing mankind, but highly questionable when we go by the rigorous evidence of the sources. I have also gone into one of the detailed arguments advanced by Professor Jolowicz, the connection established in Leviticus xxiv. 17 ff. between 'life for life' in the sense of retaliation and 'life for life' in the sense of compensation for a beast killed. That connection, I have tried to show,[51] far from proving the absence of the idea of compensation from the provision concerning damages for a beast killed, is evidence that even when this section of Leviticus was composed retaliation was still seriously construed as compensation.

Of the further arguments relied on by Professor Jolowicz, the following seem to be the three principal ones. First, ancient laws, he points out, frequently demand restitution in kind, not in money. For a beast killed, for example, another beast is to be given, not the value in money. This, he thinks, is due to the primitive desire to have the penalty as analogous as possible to the tort.[52] It seems to me, however, that even if this desire plays any part—which is not impossible though one can hardly prove it—it would be rash to deny that the essential object of the laws in question is compensation. For one thing, unless there are definite signs to the contrary, surely we have to assume that any restitution, whether in money or in kind, is meant to effect compensation. There may be any number of other purposes in addition, but that of compensation obviously must be prominent. The mere fact that the wrongdoer has to give something to the person who has suffered a loss through him admits of no different interpretation. We have also to consider that from very early times delicts were often settled by the parties concerned in a peaceful manner. In those cases, the treaty between the two parties might be rather similar to sale, the wrongdoer 'buying' the thing destroyed or unlawfully taken away by him. The idea of compensation here might nearly oust any penal elements. As for restitution in kind in particular, I fail to see how compensation can be better achieved than precisely in this way. Clearly, payment of the value of a thing destroyed or stolen is a more, not a less, indirect method of compensation. Moreover, as Professor Jolowicz himself emphasizes,[53] money in our sense came into use at a fairly late stage. Before it came into use, it is evident that, wherever restitution in kind was possible (that is to say, wherever the object lost was a 'fungible' object), it simply was the sole natural way of compensating the party wronged. Why, if the main or only idea underlying restitution in kind was analogy with the offence committed, should the law not require the wrongdoer to sacrifice a beast? Why should it require him to return a beast to the man whom he has deprived of one? As a matter of fact, restitution in kind is the clearest example conceivable of the application of the principle of compensation.

In the second place, Professor Jolowicz refers to those laws which impose multiple restitution on the offender. Even here, however, while admitting the presence, or even predominance, of the idea of punishment, I do not think we are entitled to infer that the purpose of compensation is entirely absent. Professor Jolowicz adduces Exodus xxi. 37 (xxii. 1) and xxii. 3 (4),[54] saying that 'if a man shall steal an ox, or a sheep, and kill it or sell it; he shall restore five oxen for an ox, and four sheep for a sheep;...if the theft be certainly found in his hand alive, whether it be ox, or ass, or sheep, he shall restore double'. It is true that this gradation—(1) five-fold restitution of an ox stolen and killed or sold, (2) four-fold of a sheep stolen and killed or sold, (3) two-fold of any beast stolen but not killed or sold—cannot be explained as a result of the principle of compensation. Yet it can be shown, on the one hand, that the ideas of punishment and analogy between tort and damages for it also do not fully account for the provisions under discussion, and, on the other hand, that the principle of compensation plays a far from negligible part in them.

Three points may be mentioned. First, the distinction between him who has killed or sold the stolen animal and him who has not is not connected with any idea of analogy or the

like. I have submitted above[55] that theft originally was
regarded as proved only when the thief had used, that is
to say, killed or sold, the animal in question. The provision
making liable even the thief with whom the animal is found
alive dates from a later period. The lighter penalty in this
later provision is due chiefly to a change in the view taken
of theft: theft, from being a serious crime, gradually came to
be considered a very minor offence. Secondly, the contrast set
up between theft of an ox and theft of a sheep (a contrast
made only in the older provision but not in the later) may
indeed have something to do with irrational beliefs, such as
that the punishment for stealing a great thing should be
greater than that for stealing a small thing. It is not inconceivable, however, that there are some rational motives even
behind this strange distinction. The loss of an ox means the
loss of a working animal, that of a sheep does not. We know
from many examples how difficult primitive lawyers found
it to arrive at a sound method of assessing the value of labour
of any kind. The five-fold restitution of an ox may well
represent an attempt to take into account the higher working
capacity of that animal.[56] Considering that the same code, the
Mishpatim, in Exodus xxi. 19, lays down that he who wounds
another 'shall pay for the loss of his time', this assumption
can hardly be rejected on the ground that it presupposes too
advanced a state of legal ideas. If it is correct, then the
distinction between ox and sheep is based not only on the
principle of compensation but on the principle of compensation in a fairly subtle application. Thirdly, it must not be
overlooked that the provisions under notice contain the preposition תחת, 'in the place of', which I have analysed above.
The thief has to restore five oxen 'in the place of' the one
that he has stolen, four sheep 'in the place of' the one that
he has stolen. This manifestly suggests compensation. Furthermore, the word rendered by 'to restore' is a causative form
(Piel) of שלם (Kal). The latter means 'to be full, whole,
unimpaired'; and the causative form used in the provisions
here discussed means 'to make full again, to restore'. This
also distinctly refers to restitution. True enough, a thief has
to do more than merely to make good the loss that he has

caused. He is liable to multiple, not simple, restitution, and in this there lies a penal element. Nobody can say that the penal element is out of place: after all, theft, though causing economic damage only,[57] is an unpleasant offence which does deserve punishment. In any case, however, the penalty includes compensation, and the use of תחת, 'in the place of', and שלם, 'to make full, to restore', is philological evidence—if any were needed where a thief is forced to make amends to the person whom he has robbed—that the law-giver was conscious of the importance of restitution. Translations tend to obscure these features. The A.V. does not, and, for the sake of good English, probably cannot, do full justice to the force of תחת, 'in the place of'; and though in the particular provisions here concerned שלם is rendered, correctly, by 'to restore', in other provisions that also employ שלם, for example, in Exodus xxi. 36, the A.V. has 'to pay'. But when we examine Hebrew legal history, it is the original text that ought to be considered with all its implications, else erroneous conclusions are unavoidable.

At this point, an excursus on שלם, 'to restore', may be of some interest. I have already adverted to its character as a causative form of שלם, 'to be whole', and to the inference to be drawn from this fact: שלם means 'to make whole, to restore'. Now שלם is frequent in the oldest collection of civil laws preserved in the Bible, the *Mishpatim*, the Judgments, in Exodus xxi ff. There can be no doubt that the term itself is even older than the *Mishpatim* in which it is made use of, and thus we may venture a certain pronouncement upon what is surely the very earliest period of Hebrew law accessible to us, the period prior to the *Mishpatim*. We are safe in maintaining, that is, that even in that very earliest epoch the idea of compensation was formed, and could be expressed unambiguously by the causative mode of the root שלם. There is nothing startling in this, in my opinion, since the idea that he who has deprived another of something should make reparation, as I have already stated, seems to me a perfectly natural idea, to be expected at the most primitive stage just as much as at the most advanced. It may be worth drawing attention to the Latin verb *sarcire*, used in the XII Tables of the making good of a damage (*noxiam sarcire*). The verb comes from the root *sar*, suggesting 'to protect, to heal', the same root that appears in *salvus*.[58] From the use of this term in the XII Tables it is clear that the principle of compensation was thought of even in the remotest period of Roman law, the time before the first great legislation.

It might indeed be asked whether שלם, the literal meaning of which is 'to make full, to restore', has still got this meaning in the *Mishpatim*; or whether the idea of compensation is here perhaps ousted or obscured by other notions. If this were the case, it would follow, not that the principle of compensation was alien from primitive law, but on the contrary, that it existed at a very early stage and later only gave place, here and there, to different concepts. However, it is not the case. It is possible to demonstrate that שלם throughout the *Mishpatim* is used in statutes concerning restitution. More than this, it is possible to demonstrate that the verb refers to compensation wherever it occurs in a text of legal significance in the Bible; and further, that this meaning of the verb remains recognizable even where it is applied to non-legal situations, such as the repaying by God of an evil deed. In fact, it looks— but this is somewhat less certain than the preceding points— as if שלם were not far removed from its etymological sense 'to make whole', 'to restore', anywhere in the Bible, always suggesting literal restoration, that is to say, restitution in kind, restoration of the actual thing by which the whole in question has been diminished, not, say, payment for a beast of an equivalent amount of money.

Let us examine the texts. To begin with the *Mishpatim*, the term שלם occurs fourteen times, always referring to a person who has to make good a loss for which he is responsible; more precisely, to the owner of a pit that has caused the death of another man's beast,[59] to the owner of an ox that has killed another man's ox,[60] to the thief,[61] to the owner of animals that have grazed in another man's field,[62] to the owner of a field from which fire has spread to another man's land,[63] to him who withholds a deposit,[64] to the shepherd liable, or not liable, to make reparation for a beast that was stolen by a third party or perished,[65] and to the borrower of a beast liable, or not, to make reparation if it perishes.[66] In two of these rules, the preposition תחת, 'in the place of', is used to introduce the object to be replaced: in Exodus xxi. 36, saying that the negligent owner of an ox that killed another man's ox 'shall surely restore an ox in the place of the ox (destroyed)', and in xxi. 37 (xxii. 1), saying that a thief who has killed or sold the stolen animal 'shall restore five oxen in the place of the ox (stolen) and four sheep in the place of the sheep (stolen)'. There is simple restitution, with no penal or other element whatever coming in, in six cases (the pit,[67] the ox that has killed another ox,[68] animals grazing where they ought not to,[69] fire,[70] the shepherd from whom an animal is stolen,[71] the borrower of an animal[72]), multiple restitution in two cases (theft[73] and withholding a deposit[74]), and freedom from restitution—'he shall not restore'—obviously also with no penal object present, in two cases (the shepherd losing an animal through *force majeure*[75] and the borrower of an animal together with its owner[76]). Nowhere is there the faintest sign that שלם denotes anything but 'to restore', expressing the idea of compensation.

Actually, in all provisions but one the restitution contemplated is restitution in kind, literal replacement of the object lost by one belonging to the same species, or, in other words, compensation in the simplest and most palpable form, actual making full, restoring: and I may anticipate here a point to which I shall come back, namely, that the provision forming an exception is the sole exception not only in the *Mishpatim* but in the whole of the Bible. It is merely in view of this one case that I said above that I did not feel absolutely safe in confining שלם to the sense of 'to restore in kind'. Yet as we shall see, even this one exception may be due to an interpolation. In any case, in three provisions it is stated in so many words that restitution is to be in kind; in xxi. 36, according to which the owner of an ox that killed another man's ox has to 'restore an ox for the ox', in xxi. 37 (xxii. 1), according to which a thief who has killed or sold the stolen beast has to restore 'five oxen for the ox and four sheep for the sheep', and in xxii. 4 (5), according to which the owner of animals that grazed on another man's land has to restore 'the best of his field and the best of his vineyard' for the land devastated. Evidently, it would be carrying modern ideas into these ancient laws to ascribe to them any reference to payment in money. The wrongdoer, under them, has to make good the loss of an animal by delivering to the person wronged another animal of the same species (or several animals where punishment is intended besides compensation), the loss of a piece of land by delivering another piece of land. The remaining provisions containing the verb שׁלם, with the exception already mentioned, simply speak of the duty 'to restore', without specifying, in the manner of the three laws just quoted, that one thing is to be restored for another. We are told that a thief 'shall surely restore',[77] that he 'shall restore double',[78] that the person responsible for a fire 'shall surely restore the burned part of land',[79] that he who withholds a deposit 'shall restore double',[80] that a shepherd 'shall not restore' if an animal gets lost through certain types of *force majeure*,[81] that he 'shall restore' if an animal is stolen from the herd by a third person,[82] that he 'shall not restore an animal destroyed by wild beasts',[83] that the borrower of an animal 'shall surely restore' even in the case of *force majeure*,[84] and that he 'shall not restore' if the owner of the animal himself was looking after it.[85] It is fair to conclude that restitution in these rules means the same as in the three in which it is described at greater length, that is to say, restitution in kind, not by means of money.

Strong indirect support for this deduction is furnished, I think, by the fact that the term שׁלם is not used in five provisions in which, if it could refer to compensation in money or payment in general, we should expect to find it. It is not used in Exodus xxi. 19, laying down that he who wounds a man, thus causing him to be laid up for some while, 'shall give him his ceasing' or 'his sitting down', which means, in the words of the A.V., 'shall pay for the loss of his time'. Here restitution cannot be in kind: there cannot be a literal 'making full' or 'restoring'—compensation has to be rendered by means of money or in some other indirect fashion. Accordingly, the term used is נתן, 'to give', not שׁלם. Again, שׁלם is not employed in xxi. 22, laying down that he who hurts another man's pregnant wife, thus causing a miscarriage, 'shall surely be fined...and he shall give as the judges determine'. As in the case just discussed, the duty of the offender is expressed by נתן (he must 'give'), not by שלם (he cannot 'restore').[86] Nor is שלם to be met with in Exodus xxi. 30. Here it is provided that the owner of an ox that killed a man, even if guilty of negligence and therefore liable to capital punishment, may be allowed to 'give a ransom of his life'. Clearly, this is not a case of literal restitution, and the word used for 'to pay' is נתן, 'to give', not שלם. xxi. 32 deals with the case of an ox killing a slave and provides that the owner of the ox 'shall give unto the slave's master thirty shekels of silver'. This example is particularly illuminating. The money is obviously to be paid with a view to compensation. Yet the provision employs נתן, 'to give', not שלם. The latter verb, I suggest, could have been applied only if the law-giver had enjoined literal making up, say, 'the owner of the ox shall restore a male slave for the male slave killed and a female for the female'. Lastly, שלם is not to be found in xxii. 16 (17), which says that he who seduces a virgin shall marry her or at least, if her father does not accept him as son-in-law, 'shall weigh silver, according to the dowry of virgins'. Here, also, if שלם signified 'to pay' in general, it might have been used, though admittedly the expression 'to weigh silver' for 'to pay' is quite natural. That שלם occurs in none of the five provisions reviewed can hardly be accidental. In fact, when taken in conjunction with the other arguments pointing the same way, the absence of שלם from any rules which, though contemplating payment or even restitution, do not contemplate restitution in the very narrowest sense, restitution in kind, becomes highly significant: שלם throughout the *Mishpatim* has retained its original value.

Only in xxi. 34 do we find שלם as referring to compensation in money. The owner of a pit into which another man's animal has fallen 'shall restore, silver shall he return to the animal's owner, and the dead beast shall be his'. This is a definite injunction to pay for the animal destroyed in money, not to replace it by another animal. It is very possible, however, that the clause 'silver shall he return to the animal's owner', which, be it noted, uses השיב, 'to return, to give in return', not שלם, is an interpolation, inserted in an age when restitution in kind had become obsolete and superseded by monetary restitution. For one thing, the very fact that this is the only text in the Bible where שלם denotes a restitution other than in kind raises grave suspicion. For another thing, it is strange to find a code normally so economical as the *Mishpatim* stating the obligation of the owner of the pit twice, though once would do. Why should it be prescribed that 'he shall restore, silver shall he return', though either 'he shall restore' or 'silver shall he return' would do? Further, we have to consider that in the case, regulated in the same *Mishpatim* and similar to the one under notice in form and substance, where a man does not sufficiently guard an ox and the ox kills another man's ox (Exodus xxi. 36), the law is quite unambiguous in enjoining restitution in kind: 'he shall surely restore an ox in the place of the ox, and the dead beast shall be his'. There is no mention of silver here. The most decisive point, however, is that the words introducing payment in money may be eliminated when the statute will still make sense: indeed, it will make far better sense. These words are out of place in xxi. 34 as it stands, for the following reason. As it stands, the provision ordains that the owner of the pit should pay the value of a sound animal to the person who has lost an animal through him, but should receive the carcass of the animal destroyed. This is an unnecessarily clumsy procedure. Once you have payment in money, it would be very much simpler to make the owner of the pit pay the difference between a sound beast and a carcass, and to leave the latter to its original owner. The handing over of the carcass to the owner of the pit becomes intelligible, however, and even necessary, as soon as we omit the words 'silver shall he return to the animal's owner'. For now the provision demands restitution in kind. The owner of the pit has to deliver a sound animal, not money, to the person whose animal has perished. In this case, justice requires that the dead beast should go to the owner of the pit— otherwise its original owner would make a profit, obtaining a fresh animal and keeping the carcass.[87]

Evidently, the Rabbis noticed the difficulty, the unnecessary clumsiness of the procedure prescribed by xxi. 34 in its present form.[88] They solved the problem in a most ingenious way, by interpreting the clause 'and the dead beast shall be his' as meaning, not that the carcass shall go to the owner of the pit, but that it shall remain the property of its original owner; and by interpreting the words 'silver shall he return to the animal's owner' as meaning, not that the value of an animal shall be paid, but that the value of a living animal minus that of a carcass shall be paid. In short, they took the provision as laying down that the owner of the pit 'shall make amends, silver, i.e. the difference between the value of a living and the value of a dead beast, shall he return to the animal's owner, and the dead beast shall be his, i.e. shall continue to belong to its original owner'.

This is excellent law, but it is hardly the meaning that one would ascribe to Exodus xxi. 34 without the help of an elaborate system of hermeneutics. (1) It is clear from the analogy of xxi. 36 (where the owner of an ox that killed another ox has to supply a fresh ox for the dead one, 'and the carcass shall be his', namely, the person's making reparation) that, when the law says 'the dead beast shall be his', it means that it shall go to him who has to make reparation for a sound animal destroyed through his negligence. He has to make amends for the sound animal, but may keep the carcass. (2) If any confirmation of this were requisite, there is this additional consideration. Supposing the law meant to say that the difference between a living and a dead beast should be paid, why should it expressly lay down that the dead beast must continue to belong to its owner? The words 'and the dead beast shall be his' obviously refer to a change of ownership. They must mean that the dead beast should go to the person who makes amends for the loss of a sound animal. (3) It is a very heavy gloss on 'silver shall he return to the animal's owner' to maintain that these words signify 'the value of a sound animal minus that of the carcass shall he return to the animal's owner'. As a matter of fact, the Rabbinic interpretation only serves to bring into relief the difficulty created by the clause 'silver shall he return to the animal's owner': this clause seems to me to reflect an early desire, which was to be fully shared by the Rabbis, to adapt an antiquated rule of the *Mishpatim* to a more progressive state of the law, with restitution in kind ousted by damages in money. At all events, Exodus xxi. 34 is the only text where שלם has regard to a restitution other than in kind; and it is not too rash to claim that even here there is a strong possibility that the term once meant 'to restore literally', and that the present ambiguity is the result of an interpolation intended to emphasize the new method of compensation in money, but not going far enough to eliminate שלם and other features incompatible with the modern method.

Going on to legal passages outside the *Mishpatim*, we find שלם eleven times, again invariably used of a man who has to fill a gap for which he is responsible; more precisely, of a thief or one who appropriates or withholds somebody's goods in a mode similar to theft,[89] of a person who kills another's animal,[90] of a person who borrows money or stands surety for a borrower.[91] In all these cases, evidently, the idea of compensation is in the foreground; a fact not in the least altered by the presence of penal elements in some of them, such as theft, where more than mere simple restitution is required in settlement of the affair. Does שלם mean restitution in kind in all these cases? The answer, I believe, is in the affirmative. Restitution in kind is demanded in so many words in Leviticus xxiv. 18, where it is said that he who kills another man's beast 'shall restore it, life in the place of life'.[92] To introduce money into this rule is forcing our modern practice on an ancient statute. xxiv. 21 belongs to the same section. It speaks of the duty 'to restore it (the animal killed)', and there is no reason to refer this to payment in money. Nor is there any in interpreting II Samuel xii. 6, where a thief is said to be under the obligation 'to restore the lamb fourfold',[93] Ezekiel xxxiii. 15, where the wicked is admonished 'to return the pledge and restore what he hath robbed', or Proverbs vi. 31, where a thief is declared to be bound 'to restore sevenfold'.

Leviticus v. 16 and 24 (vi. 5) are less easy cases. Yet it is restitution in kind or something very like it that שלם signifies even here. To take the latter text first, verses v. 23 (vi. 4) f. expressly lay down that he who withholds another man's goods under a

false oath 'shall return (הֵשִׁיב) what he hath plundered or what
he hath deceitfully gotten or what was deposited with him or
what lost thing he found or all that about which he hath
sworn falsely'. This, unless we approach it under the spell
of monetary economy, means restitution in kind or, more
probably, restitution in an even narrower sense, in the sense
of restitution not of the same species but of the actual object
withheld: 'to return' here admits of no other, more progressive
explanation. The words following those just quoted, however,
are rendered by the A.V. as 'and he shall even restore it in
the principal, and shall add the fifth part more thereto'. In
the first part of this clause שִׁלַּם is used. The Hebrew for 'in
the principal' is בְּרֹאשׁוֹ, literally, 'by, for, its head'. If, as
seems likely, the A.V. by 'the principal' understands a sum,
namely, the value of the object in dispute, this rendering is
inexact. In view of the preceding clause it is clear that we
have to translate either 'and he shall restore it by itself,
bodily, and add...', which would signify return of the very
object withheld; or, though this is less likely, 'and he shall
restore it by its essence, heading, and add...', which would
signify restitution in kind, handing over an object of the same
species as the one withheld; or, conceivably, 'and he shall
restore it for its heading, in compensation of its heading, its
essence, and add...', which might signify either return of the
very object withheld or restitution in kind. On no account are
we entitled to turn the duty to restore into one to pay money.[94]
The fifth part, added as a penalty, may of course be payable
in money. But there is a fresh verb, הוֹסִיף, 'and he shall add
its fifth'; 'its fifth' is not governed by 'and he shall restore'.
It may be observed that the statute under notice is from a
larger code concerned with priestly matters. Now in other
priestly sections of the Pentateuch we find a good many rules
as to how things consecrated might be assessed by the priests
and their value in money be offered to the temple instead of
themselves. It is certainly significant that payment of the
value of a thing thus assessed is never once expressed by the
verb שִׁלַּם, but always in other ways, as by the verb נתן, 'to
give':[95] שִׁלַּם was unsuitable where it was not a matter of
actual making full, of actual restitution. In Leviticus v. 16, the

law-giver expresses himself more briefly than in v. 24 (vi. 5): the person withholding something due to the temple 'shall restore that concerning which he has sinned of holy property, and he shall add the fifth part thereto'. I suppose that here also return of the actual object withheld is what the law-giver has in mind; if not, the alternative is restitution in kind. There is nothing to indicate payment in money.

It remains to consider four texts which, at first sight, might appear exceptions to the rule but, in reality, are not, II Kings iv. 7, Psalm xxxvii. 21, Proverbs xxii. 27 and Sirach viii. 13 (16). In these four texts, שלם does indeed refer to payment of money. But the point is that payment of money and restitution in kind happen to coincide: *A* has lent money to *B*, and *B* or his surety now must repay it. So again, שלם does not signify payment or restitution in general but restitution in kind, literal restoration, filling a gap by an object of the same kind as the one missing. In II Kings iv. 7, Elisha tells the poor woman whom he has provided with oil: 'Go, sell the oil, and restore thy debt, and live thou and thy children of the rest.' It is clear that the debt is 'restored' with the money coming from the sale of the oil. From verse 1, however, it emerges that the debt worrying the woman is a loan or loans, presumably at a high rate of interest: 'Thy servant my husband is dead... and the lender[96] is come to take unto him my two sons to be bondmen.' Psalm xxxvii. 21 says, 'The wicked borroweth and restoreth not': a money debt. In Proverbs xxii. 27 there is a warning not to become a surety for another's debts, in case one may be unable 'to restore' and find one's very bed seized by the creditors: money debts. Sirach viii. 13 (16) says that if you stand surety for another, you should regard yourself 'as one who will have to restore'. In all these passages, payment in money constitutes restitution in kind. שלם has regard, not to payment in money for, say, a beast, but to payment in money for money.

This completes the list of legal texts with שלם. As for the non-legal use of the word, I can be very brief. There is I Kings ix. 25, recording how Solomon 'finished the house', where שלם manifestly has its literal meaning 'to make whole'. Not very different is Job viii. 6, where Bildad expresses the view that if Job were really pure, God would 'make whole the habitation of thy righteousness'. In a large number of texts שלם is used of the 'fulfilling' of a vow.[97] It would be outside the scope of this survey to go into the history of this notion. It is sufficient to observe that the term שלם is here very near its literal meaning, the idea being, roughly, that a vow is 'fulfilled, made whole, perfect, rounded off' by the act, by the delivery of the thing promised. Another series of texts[98] uses שלם of the 'requiting' of a deed, good or bad, very often by God. This also I cannot discuss at length. I would say only that here again the idea is compensation, restoring a balance, giving a man his due, returning a service or paying back an enemy in his own coin. (The ease with which one can express the idea in English or any other language is an indication of its universal character.) Moreover, the restitution is, so to speak, in kind: your deed or attitude is requited with a corresponding deed or attitude on my part.[99] This analysis of the meaning of שלם in the texts under notice is not vitiated by the possibility of all kinds of variation. You may, for example, 'return good in the place of evil'.[100] The writer who first coined this expression must have been a brilliant mind. But the mere fact that the preposition תחת is used proves that the fundamental sense of the verb is never lost sight of.[101]

After this excursus,[102] I proceed to the third argument adduced by Professor Jolowicz. He points out that there are provisions in the Babylonian and Hittite codes 'where the penalty is assessed neither in kind nor in the medium usual for penalties'.[103] This is no doubt correct, and it may be admitted that in some cases of this type the idea of compensation may be combined with others, even with irrational notions of a mysterious fitness of a certain medium for a certain tort. None the less, that the principle of compensation is present there can be no doubt: in all cases the offender has to pay the penalty to the person for whose loss he is answerable. If mere analogy between penalty and tort were intended, why should a law not provide, say, that the offender must bury or burn the appropriate amount of silver or corn, instead of providing that he must pay it over to the party wronged?

Actually, in some statutes it looks as if the unusual

medium were chosen for the very sake of accurate restitution. When, for example, a man responsible for the flooding of another man's field has to pay the penalty in corn, not in the more usual medium, silver, the reason may have to be sought precisely in the idea of compensation: it is corn that the owner of the damaged field has lost, it is corn that is to be supplied to him by the wrongdoer. In many cases, our scanty knowledge of the legal history of the old Orient in general should make us hesitate to draw conclusions of any sort. Take, for instance, a statute saying that he who steals a pregnant sow has to pay six shekels of silver for the sow and a measure of corn for every two pigs that she would have had. It is quite possible—only we are completely in the dark—that that portion of the rule which takes into account the exact number of pigs came into existence later than the main portion; originally, that is, there may have been just a fixed penalty for theft of a pregnant sow. If so, the difference in the medium may be due, not to an unusual medium being chosen for the pigs on some irrational grounds, but to silver having been the usual medium for penalties when the main rule was first composed, and corn having become the usual medium by the time that the exact number of pigs was declared relevant. Even if the statute as it stands dates from the same age and author, however, and even if for some reason or other silver was regarded as parallel to a sow and corn to a pig, the law would still be dominated by the principle of compensation: the person wronged is to receive the appropriate, analogous material for the sow stolen from him and the appropriate, analogous material for the pigs stolen from him—obviously he is to be compensated in as thorough a manner as possible according to the magical beliefs of the lawgiver. Professor Jolowicz himself recalls[104] that in the case of sale also 'one medium may be proper for one article, another for a different article'. Whatever may be the ultimate basis of these differences, nobody will deny that, in the case of sale at least, the idea of compensation, restoring or upholding the balance, giving and receiving one thing for another, equivalent to it, is absolutely essential.

It seems that primitive thought comes nearer than modern

thought to conceiving of the order under which a community
lives as a compact whole. The various aspects of a system are
closely interconnected, the several principles governing actions
or events are not scientifically worked out, delimited and shut
up each in a watertight compartment by itself. As a result it
often happens that where we, coming from the modern world,
at first sight notice only one idea, it is in reality a number of
ideas that are effective, only that one of them overshadows
the rest. I have already pointed out that it is far easier to
be struck by features characteristic of criminal law than by
features characteristic of civil law; and it may perhaps be
conceded that the former really are given more prominence
in primitive sources than they are nowadays. But civil law
notions are none the less in full play. I have presented an
extreme case, the formula of retaliation, and attempted to
show that even in this province, to which modern lawyers
apply nothing but criminal law principles, the idea of compensation was of real importance. This instance alone, it
is hoped, will be enough to indicate the true role of that
idea in early Hebrew law. It may be remarked, however,
that a glance through the sources will confirm how general
and deep-rooted the idea was that a criminal must pay for
his deed, and how general and deep-rooted that other idea,
which I have mentioned only incidentally in dealing with the
verb שלם, that the criminal is to be paid. Punishment constitutes compensation in both directions: the criminal, by
suffering punishment, is making restitution to the offended
party, and again, in suffering punishment, receives his due.
The two notions are so frequent, they appear in sources so
different in all other respects, they underlie terms so ancient
(such as שלם and השיב which, we have seen,[105] are both used
of the paying back a criminal in his own coin), and, it may
be added, they are of so universal a nature, occurring in the
ancient and modern literatures of all nations,[106] that we must
assume their existence right from the beginnings of any social
life. If that is so in the domain of crime, *a fortiori* the principle
of compensation must be considered prevalent in the domain
of peaceful dealings and settlement of torts causing economic
damage only; and, indeed, the evidence is all in favour of

this view. The idea that he who misappropriates or destroys another man's property has to compensate him for it, it is safe to say, belongs to the very oldest foundations of law.

Lafontaine tells us how Folly, by a wicked blow, deprived Cupid of his eyesight:

> *Nulle peine n'était pour ce crime assez grande :*
> *Le dommage devait être aussi réparé.*
> *Quand on eut bien considéré*
> *L'intérêt du public, celui de la partie,*
> *Le résultat enfin de la suprême cour*
> *Fut de condamner la Folie*
> *À servir de guide à l'Amour.*

In this fable—most perfect flower of modern rationalism—the various purposes of the penalty inflicted on Folly are clearly distinguished; and it is expressly stated that they were punishment proper, in accordance with the principles of public, criminal law, and compensation of the party wronged, in accordance with the principles of civil law. Yet if the author had not given this full analysis, could it therefore be doubted that both punishment of the criminal and reparation of the loss suffered by his victim were the objects of the sentence? To put the question in a less abstract form: can it be doubted that both the ideas of punishment and of reparation underlie the sentence of Zeus in Louise Labé's work from which Lafontaine seems to have borrowed, though neither of them is explicitly referred to?[107]

Meanwhile we command you to live together in harmony, without injuring one another. And Folly will guide blind Cupid and will conduct him everywhere it seems good to him to go. And as for the restoration of his eyes, after we have spoken of the matter with the Fates, a decision will be given.

NOTES

CHAPTER III

1 See p. 76.

2 The *Concise Oxford Dictionary*, s.v. sub-, takes the words 'subsequent' and 'succeed' under the heading of 'closeness' (with, for example, 'suburb'), and 'subsidy', 'subvention', 'succour', 'suffice' and 'sustain' under the heading of 'support' (with 'suffer'). This may indeed be defended, but it seems to me that the prefix here expresses also the idea of filling a gap, substitution.

3 For references, see Gesenius's *Handwörterbuch* and the *Lexicon*.

4 See pp. 132 ff.

5 See, e.g., A. Alt, *Berichte über die Verhandlungen der Sächsischen Akademie der Wissenschaften, Phil.-hist. Klasse*, LXXXVI, 1934, no. 1, pp. 34 ff.

6 According to the LXX, the case with 'no mischief' is the case where the child is not yet fit to live, that with 'mischief' the case where it would live, *i.e.* where the time of birth is very near. Seeing that the Hittite Code (I. 17 f.) distinguishes between hurting and making abort a woman pregnant in the sixth month and doing the same to a woman pregnant in the tenth month, I think it possible that in the LXX is preserved the original meaning of the distinction between 'no mischief' and 'mischief' in Exodus xxi. 22 ff. In the text I adopt the usual interpretation since the question does not affect my main argument. On the interpretation of the LXX, see Geiger, *Urschrift und Übersetzungen der Bibel*, 2nd ed., 1928, pp. 436 f. As for the Hittite Code's contemplating a pregnancy of ten months, it is interesting to note that the XII Tables do the same (IV. 4). Gellius says (*Noctes Atticae* 3. 16. 1) that *multa opinio est, eaque iam pro vero recepta...gigni hominem septimo rarenter, numquam octavo, saepe nono, saepius numero decimo mense.* Ancient medicine was not very clear about the problem, as is evident from the chapter in Gellius from which I have just quoted (3. 16, *Temporis varietas in puerperis mulierum quaenam sit a medicis et a philosophis tradita...*). Where a child is promised by God or a prophet in the Old Testament, the birth seems always to take place a year after the promise (Genesis xvii. 21, xviii. 10, 14, I Samuel i. 20, II Kings iv. 16 f.). One is reminded of the passage in Homer (*Odyssey* 11. 248 f.) where Neptune says to the nymph whom he has ravished:

Χαῖρε γυνὴ φιλότητι· περιπλομένου δ' ἐνιαυτοῦ

Τέξεις ἀγλαὰ τέκνα...

In the Talmud the view that gestation may last as long as a year is represented in Babylonian Yebamoth 80*b*. Further references are given by Rabelais in the course of his discussion of the birth of Gargantua, who, it may be recalled, was born in the eleventh month and even then only as a result of a series of strange accidents. Add the conversation between Compass and the two Boys in Webster's (?) *A Cure for a Cuckold*, Act 2, Scene 3.

7 See below, pp. 167 ff.

8 Paragraphs 209 and 210. Cp. the Assyrian Statutes 49.

9 D. H. Müller, *Die Gesetze Hammurabis und ihr Verhältnis zur mosaischen Gesetzgebung*, 1903, pp. 166 ff.

10 See pp. 85 f.

11 On the position in the time of the New Testament, see Daube, *Journal of Theological Studies*, XLV, 1944, pp. 177 ff.

12 Outside the *Mishpatim*, the verb is frequent of God's smiting the wicked. It is true that the verb may refer to the foot's hitting against something, unintentionally. But the object against which the foot hits is not expressed by the mere accusative (not 'to hit a stone', for example) but with the help of the preposition ב or עַל, 'at', 'against', 'upon' ('to hit against a stone'). Gesenius's *Handwörterbuch* says that in Proverbs iii. 23, נגף means 'to stumble' without ב. This is correct as far as it goes, but the reason why there is no ב is simply that the object against which the stumbling takes place is not specified: 'Then shalt thou walk in thy way safely, and thy foot shall not stumble.' If any object were named, it would have to be introduced with ב or עַל: 'Thy foot shall not stumble against, upon, a stone.' The *Lexicon* is more precise than the *Handwörterbuch* in saying that, in Proverbs iii. 23, the verb is used 'absolutely'.

13 נגף in Isaiah viii. 14 and Sirach xxxv. 20 (xxxii. 25) means 'stumbling', 'stone of stumbling'. This meaning of the noun is based on the use of the verb in the sense of 'to stumble'. I have already pointed out, however, that where the verb signifies 'to stumble', it does not govern the mere accusative.

14 The reason why I consider them added is that they conflict with the preceding part of the sentence, which lets the fine be fixed by the husband of the woman that was hurt. This inconsistency has been noticed before, and attempts have been made to get rid of it by emending the concluding words 'and he shall pay as the judges determine'. Any such emendation, however, only obscures what is a historical evolution of a well-known type. It is not a matter for lower criticism; the text as such is in order, but the disturbing last few words constitute an interpolation. Originally, the husband was free to exact any sum he liked (a regime by no means unheard of in antiquity). The interpolator brings the proceedings under the control of the state.

15 See, however, pp. 129 f.

16 This is also the Rabbinic doctrine. See, *e.g.*, Mishnah Baba Kamma viii. 1, at the end.

17 Maybe we ought to translate: 'for man his blood shall be shed'. The particle ב may be used in the same sense as in Deuteronomy xix. 21. On the latter text, see pp. 129 f.

18 I am aware of the inadequacy of this translation of נפש, but it will do for my purposes.

19 It looks as if, in ordinary language, הכה נפש had been used in the sense of 'straight, sheer, unadorned killing'. In Jeremiah xl. 14 f. we are told how Gedaliah was warned that Ishmael was being sent להכתך נפש—'to slay thee downright' we might translate. למה יככה נפש, Gedaliah's friend added: 'Wherefore should he be allowed simply to slay thee?' If this is correct, it is easily seen how, in language influenced by priestly thought, the phrase might be used of homicide involving the shedding of blood as opposed to, say, homicide by throwing a man into a pit; or, more generally, how in language so influenced the phrase might be used as emphasizing the fearfulness of the crime of slaying a soul. (I am not, however, deciding which is older, the ordinary use or that influenced by priestly thought.) This argument receives support from the use of the similar phrase רצח נפש, which signifies something like 'straight, sheer, unadorned murder' even in a legal text, Deuteronomy xxii. 26. Here the reason is stated why a woman betrothed to a man is not considered guilty if she is violated by another man far from a city: 'For as when a man riseth against his neighbour ורצחו נפש, and just murders him, even so is this matter.'

20 Luther's translation *Leib um Leib* is far preferable to the A.V.'s since it can be referred to both cases.

21 Luther, who speaks of *den Nächsten verletzen*, is here considerably less exact. As will presently be shown, all kinds of *Verletzung*, of wounding, do not fall under this law.

22 In other connections, they may be just as old as or older than the original portion of the law of retaliation. Two of the three modes of hurting appear next to one another in a very early pericope, Lamech's poem, Genesis iv. 23: 'For I have slain a man to my wounding, and a young man to my hurt' (or 'for, to avenge, my wound, for my stripe').

23 We do not really know the exact distinction between the three, but it is irrelevant to my argument.

24 Of the passages where the verb שבר, 'to break', is used, two deserve here to be mentioned, Exodus xii. 46 and Numbers ix. 12, laying down that no bone of the Passover sacrifice may be broken.

25 It is quite possible that 'breach of the hand, foot' means something worse than a broken hand or foot: it may well mean the loss of hand or foot. The Latin *membrum ruptum*, as opposed to the less fearful *os fractum*, seems to denote the loss of a limb. However, it must be considered that even a serious fracture must have been bad enough in ancient times and often have amounted to the loss, if not of the limb, at any rate of the use of the limb. It follows that when the author of Leviticus xxiv. 20 substituted 'breach for breach' for 'hand for hand, foot for foot', he was introducing priestly ideas and terminology but hardly changing the actual import of the older text.

26 *Cambridge Legal Essays*, 1926, p. 207. On some more general arguments advanced by Professor Jolowicz, see pp. 130 ff.

27 See pp. 133 ff.

28 See the first few paragraphs of the Hittite Code.

29 If the assumption of an interpolation should appear too rash, at least it will be admitted that the words here suspected are strikingly unemphasized, have no bearing on the lesson that Ahab is to be taught.

30 I have already remarked (see above, p. 59) on the importance of the ancient legal institutions of *vindex, sponsor*, hostages and the like for the history of the Christian idea of redemption through the sufferings of God. A relevant passage from the narratives of the Old Testament is Genesis xliv. 33, where Judah asks Joseph to enslave him in the place of, תחת, Benjamin. Job xvi. 4, 'If your soul were in my soul's stead (לו יש נפשכם תחת נפשי), I could heap up words against you', while not immediately referring to any legal institution, does presuppose a long history of the idea of one man suffering in place of another.

31 I Samuel xxiv. 11.

32 Psalm lvi. 7 (6).

33 Ezekiel xxii. 25.

34 Numbers xxiii. 24.

35 For references, see Gesenius's *Handwörterbuch* and the *Lexicon*. (In the latter, however, the limitation of דרש in the sense of 'to require' to God's actions is not mentioned.) Cp. above, p. 72, n. 132.

36 The case of Joseph's brothers, in Genesis xlii. 22, is no serious exception. Joseph decides to keep one of them imprisoned. They, thinking that they have killed Joseph, regard this as a punishment sent by God, and Reuben remarks: 'Behold, his (Joseph's) blood is required (from us by God).' It is probable that they despair of ever seeing again the one who has to stay behind—he is as good as dead. Moreover, slavery and death were in many respects equated in ancient thought. On this and some other aspects of the situation under notice, see below, pp. 241 and 252 f.

37 Ezekiel iii. 18, 20.

38 For references, see Gesenius's *Handwörterbuch* and the *Lexicon*.

39 On this point and some of the following observations, see above, pp. 40 ff.

40 Psalm xxvii. 2.

41 Job xix. 22.

42 Judges i. 6 f.

43 See Gesenius's *Handwörterbuch* and the *Lexicon*.

44 See, *e.g.*, Mishnah Ketuboth iii. 2.

45 See Babylonian Baba Kamma 114*b*, Babylonian Sanhedrin 72*a*.

46 Gesenius's *Handwörterbuch* classes the ב of Deuteronomy xix. 21 under the heading of ב *des Preises als des Mittels des Kaufes*, 'ב with reference to a price as the medium of purchase'. Similarly, the *Lexicon* says that we have here before us the ב 'of cost or price (the *Beth pretii*)'. If we proceed from this view, however, we are driven to one of two equally unlikely conclusions. (1) We may interpret the formula as providing that the wrongdoer must give away 'his life at the price of the wronged person's life, his eye at the price of the wronged person's eye' and so on. The idea of this would be that the wrong-doer chose the price at which he was prepared to lose his life, eye or the like; and that now he must take the consequences and lose his life at the price of the life that he took, his eye at the price of the eye that he took, and so forth.

Notes to Chapter III

The ‭ב‬, on the basis of this interpretation, would have regard to, not a compensation rendered by the wrongdoer to the wronged, but a compensation received, or better, exacted, by the wrongdoer from the wronged. He chose, as payment for his life, eye and so on that he was prepared to sell, the other man's life, eye and so on; now he must deliver the article sold, 'his life at the price of the victim's life, his eye at the price of the victim's eye', etc. I do not maintain that this interpretation is impossible, but it certainly is far from probable. (2) If we want to avoid having to refer the ‭ב‬ to a price received by the wrongdoer from the wronged, but still insist on rendering it as 'at the price of', the only course left is to make the wrongdoer and his victim change places in the formula; that is to say, to regard the first life, eye and so on mentioned in the formula as the victim's and the second as the wrongdoer's. This would give us 'the wronged person's life to be lost only at the price of the wrongdoer's life, the wronged person's eye to be lost only at the price of the wrongdoer's eye' and so on. The idea here would be the same as that at which I am arriving in the text by translating ‭ב‬ as 'in compensation of'; namely, the idea that the wrongdoer has to pay for the victim's life, eye and so on with his life, eye and so on. But the difference is that whilst the translation 'in compensation of' leaves the wrongdoer and the person wronged the places that they occupy also in the formula of Exodus and Leviticus ('the wrongdoer's life to be given in compensation of the wronged person's life', etc.), the translation 'at the price of', as I have already said, does not ('the wronged person's life to be sold at the price of the wrongdoer's life', etc.). Admittedly, it is not impossible that the author of the Deuteronomic formula did mean to put the wronged person's life, eye and so forth first and the wrongdoer's second. But again, it is anything but likely. As a matter of fact, I do not think the *Handwörterbuch* and the *Lexicon* intend seriously to advocate either of the two conclusions here presented; they are merely somewhat careless in classing the ‭ב‬ of Deuteronomy xix. 21, probably because the results to which a rendering of ‭ב‬ as 'at the price of' would lead were not fully considered. In any case, the translation of the formula given by the *Handwörterbuch*, *Leben um Leben*, is based on Luther and is unimpeachable, since the preposition *um* need not be interpreted as 'at the price of' but may signify, say, 'because of': 'the wrongdoer's life to be lost because of the victim's life' and so on. So the translation of the *Lexicon*, 'life for life, eye for eye', rests on the A.V. and is perfectly satisfactory.

47 The phrase 'skin for skin' to be found in Job ii. 4 (the preposition employed being ‭בעד‬) in all probability has no connection whatever with the law or even the idea of retaliation, though one might perhaps think so by the sound of it. The most likely interpretation of Satan's proposal to God seems to me to be: A man gives up only small things to protect himself from superficial pricks ('skin for skin') but he gives up all he has to ward off serious, thoroughgoing attacks ('but all that a man hath will he give for his life'); in spite of Job's behaviour so far, if God will only torture Job himself, he will cease being pious and patient ('but put forth thine hand now, and touch his bone and flesh, and he will curse thee to thy face'). Even if there should be a connection between the passage under notice and the formula of retaliation, its nature is obscure to me.

48 See above, pp. 114 f.
49 *Loc. cit.*, pp. 204 f.
50 See above, pp. 102 f.
51 See above, pp. 114 f. and 120 f.
52 *Loc. cit.*, pp. 205 ff.
53 *Loc. cit.*, pp. 210 ff.
54 *Loc. cit.*, pp. 206, 208.
55 See pp. 90 ff.
56 Cp. Rabbi Meir's view in the Mekhiltha on this statute.

57 In point of fact, there was a time when theft was not looked upon as a mere violation of economic rights. It would lead too far afield to go into this aspect of the delict as directed against the person.

58 See A. Vaniček, *Griechisch-Lateinisches Etymologisches Wörterbuch*, vol. II, 1877, pp. 1026 ff.

59 Exodus xxi. 34.

60 xxi. 36.

61 xxi. 37 (xxii. 1), xxii. 2, 3, 6 (3, 4, 7).

62 xxii. 4 (5).

63 xxii. 5 (6).

64 xxii. 8 (9).

65 xxii. 10, 11, 12 (11, 12, 13).

66 xxii. 13, 14 (14, 15).

67 xxi. 34.

68 xxi. 36.

69 xxii. 4 (5). In this case, there is perhaps a slight penal component, the law requiring the owner of the animals to make good the damage 'with the best of his field and the best of his vineyard'. We have to consider, however, that since it would as a rule be difficult to ascertain the quality of the field devastated by the grazing animals, the law-giver had to decide once for all how the question should be settled. The first chapter of the *lex Aquilia* comes to mind, which, as outlined above (see p. 76), dealt with a similar problem in a similar way. It provided that a man who killed another man's slave or beast should pay the highest value that the victim had had in the previous year.

70 xxii. 5 (6).

71 xxii. 11 (12).

72 xxii. 13 (14).

73 xxi. 37 (xxii. 1), xxii. 2, 3, 6 (3, 4, 7).

74 xxii. 8 (9).

75 xxii. 10, 12 (11, 13).

76 xxii. 14 (15).

77 xxii. 2 (3).

78 xxii. 3 (4) and 6 (7).

79 xxii. 5 (6).

80 xxii. 8 (9).

81 xxii. 10 (11).

82 xxii. 11 (12).

83 xxii. 12 (13).

84 xxii. 13 (14).

85 xxii. 14 (15).

86 I have shown elsewhere (*Tulane Law Review*, XVIII, 1944, p. 373) that, in the Mishnic treatment of delictal obligations, these more complicated cases of bodily injury, where restitution in kind is not possible, are relegated to the second place; and that it is in connection with the simpler cases of loss of property, where such restitution is possible and where the *Mishpatim* use the term שׁלם, that the Rabbis state their general principles of compensation.

87 Admittedly, the clumsy procedure of the statute in its present form does not by itself prove that there is an interpolation. This procedure arose when payment in money became usual but when what might be called the after-effects of the system of restitution in kind were still strong enough to prevent the immediate, full maturing of the monetary system: instead of simply paying for the damage caused, the owner of the pit paid the full value of a sound animal (as formerly he had handed over a sound animal), himself receiving the beast destroyed (as he had always received it). If there were no further indications making an interpolation probable, I should be satisfied with saying that the procedure under notice constitutes an interesting intermediate stage between restitution in kind and completely developed restitution by means of money. However, there are so many further indications (the meaning of שׁלם in all other Biblical texts, the use of השׁיב instead of שׁלם by the clause introducing money payment, the duplication 'he shall restore—silver shall he return', and the analogy of Exodus xxi. 36 with restitution in kind only) that I feel justified in suggesting that the statute originally referred to restitution in kind, and that it became an expression of the clumsy, intermediate stage only by the interpolation of the clause 'silver shall he return to the animal's owner'.

88 See the Mekhiltha.

89 Leviticus v. 16, 24 (vi. 5), II Samuel xii. 6, Ezekiel xxxiii. 15, Proverbs vi. 31.

90 Leviticus xxiv. 18, 21.

91 II Kings iv. 7, Psalm xxxvii. 21, Proverbs xxii. 27, Sirach viii. 13 (16).

Notes to Chapter III 153

92 For a detailed discussion of this passage, see above, pp. 110 ff.

93 The particular crime contemplated is the theft by a rich man of a poor man's only lamb, in Nathan's parable. There are indications that II Samuel xii. 6 is interpolated, coming as it does after the verdict of death in xii. 5 (a verdict possibly reflected in xii. 13, where the repentant David is told that he need not die). I have suggested above (p. 94) that there was a time when capital punishment of a thief was not unusual. Another problem is that the LXX has sevenfold restitution, not fourfold. The fourfold restitution is in accordance with the rule of the *Mishpatim*, Exodus xxi. 37 (xxii. 1): the rich man is represented as having slaughtered the stolen lamb. The sevenfold restitution recurs in Proverbs vi. 31, quoted in the text, p. 141, towards the bottom.

94 Luther's rendering is therefore preferable to the A.V.'s. He says '*das soll er alles ganz wiedergeben, dazu den fünften Teil darüber geben*', 'this all he shall return completely, and in addition give the fifth part'.

95 See, *e.g.*, Leviticus xxvii. 23, 'and he (who has sanctified a field which, for certain reasons, cannot be made over to the priests itself) shall give, ונתן, thine estimation in that day'.

96 The A.V. has 'creditor', Luther the much more pregnant *Schuldherr*.

97 For references, see Gesenius's *Handwörterbuch* and the *Lexicon*. The passive שׁלם (Pual) also occurs.

98 See Gesenius's *Handwörterbuch* and the *Lexicon*. Here, too, the Pual occurs.

99 The idea was carried to greater lengths in ancient thought than in modern. To His revengeful enemies God 'returns vengeance' (this, I think, is meant by Deuteronomy xxxii. 41, 43, where השׁיב is employed). Similarly, Zeus is praised as just, since he is νέμων εἰκότως ἄδικα μὲν κακοῖς, ὅσια δ'ἐννόμοις (Aeschylus, *Supplices* l. 3. 403 f.). As if God's punishment were on exactly the same level as the crime to which it is the reply. Cp. also II Samuel xxii. 26 f. = Psalm xviii. 26 (25) f.: 'With the merciful thou wilt shew thyself merciful, and with the upright man thou wilt shew thyself upright. With the pure thou wilt shew thyself pure; and with the froward thou wilt shew thyself unsavoury.' See, for a discussion of the problem in connection with the Greek sources, B. Daube, *Zu den Rechtsproblemen in Aischylos' Agamemnon*, 1938, p. 199.

100 See, *e.g.*, Genesis xliv. 4.

101 It is sometimes said, rightly in my opinion, that modern Hebrew has not the same force as Biblical. To give exact, detailed reasons for such a view is not easy, but the case of שׁלם is in point. In modern Hebrew, the verb means 'to pay' in general. It is not confined, as in Biblical usage, to the giving back of the very thing that is missing or at least to the giving back of the same kind of thing; and it thus has ceased to suggest the idea of 'making full, whole' to which originally it gave expression, and through which it was connected with certain other words coming from the same root such as שׁלום, 'peace'.

102 A full treatment of שׁלם would necessitate investigating also the other forms of the verb שׁלם, Kal, Hiphil and so on, its derivatives, and the role of the root in cognate tongues as well as possible influences exercised by it on the Hebrew. The foregoing remarks, however, will do for the purposes of this study.

103 *Loc. cit.*, pp. 208 f.   **104** *Loc. cit.*, p. 209.

105 See p. 144 and this page, notes 98 ff.

106 The infliction of vengeance is thought of as exaction of a debt, *e.g.* in Aeschylus: see B. Daube, *op. cit.*, pp. 106 f.

107 I am quoting the translation of E. M. Cox, *The Debate between Folly and Cupid* (by Louise Labé), 1925, p. 84.

Chapter IV

COMMUNAL RESPONSIBILITY

THE following observations are based on material from the Old Testament. But most of the conclusions reached, especially those of the second part of this study, bear on other early literatures. In the first part, attention is drawn to a case where communal responsibility is rejected, yet the corporate idea is still so strong that communal responsibility is replaced not by individual responsibility but by communal merit. The second part is intended to show that of the large number of cases usually taken under the heading of 'communal responsibility' by no means all deserve this description. There are cases which, though at first sight looking like communal responsibility, yet reflect an entirely different notion, which is here termed 'ruler punishment'. Briefly, in the case of communal responsibility proper, the community as a whole is deemed to be tainted by and answerable for the crime of any member (for example, a city may be answerable for a murder committed in its midst); while in the case of ruler punishment, the community suffers, not as answerable for the crime of a member, but as the property of a guilty ruler (for example, a sinful king may be punished by the plague decimating his people). It is hardly necessary to point out that these two notions belong to very different religious and political settings; that their history is not the same; and that it is essential to be clear about the distinction in dealing, say, with the family curse in Greek sagas or the evolution of the concept of original sin in Christianity.

Problems of Bible criticism are touched as little as possible. The main purpose of this study is to demonstrate the existence and meaning of certain ancient notions hitherto not, or insufficiently, recognized. How exactly they appear at various dates and in various sources is a further question, no doubt well worth investigating but not here raised.

I

The first great text on communal responsibility that a reader of the Bible comes across is the story of Abraham's intercession for Sodom and Gomorrah.[1] God, we are told, threatened to destroy these vicious cities. But Abraham urged Him that even if there were ten pious souls only living there, the two places ought not to be touched.

There is a remarkable feature in this episode. Abraham saw the injustice of communal responsibility; he saw that to exterminate the good with the bad would be wrong. Yet he did not infer that the proper thing to do would be to judge each person by his own deeds. What he asked was not that God should kill the wicked inhabitants of those towns and leave the righteous unhurt: it was that, if any righteous inhabitants—ten, to be precise—could be found, the towns should be spared altogether. In short, he replaced communal responsibility, not by individual responsibility, but by what may be called communal merit. To the idea that the righteous as well as the wicked members of a community might be punished for the sins of the wicked, he opposed the idea that the wicked as well as the righteous members of a community might be saved by the excellence of the righteous.[2]

That this concept was clearly shaped in his mind, not only vaguely adumbrated, is evident, in particular, from the first half of the dialogue; from Abraham's prayer, 'Peradventure there be fifty righteous within the city: wilt thou...not spare the place for the fifty righteous that are therein?', and from the assurance by God, 'If I find in Sodom fifty righteous... then I will spare all the place for their sakes.' As is to be expected, commentators have attempted to interpret away, or at any rate modify, the apparent extravagance of Abraham's demand. Rashi, for example, paraphrases some words used by Abraham thus: 'And though thou mayst say the good must not save the bad, why wilt thou kill the good?'[3] But these efforts, however justifiable on theological grounds, serve only to render more conspicuous the absence, from the actual Biblical account, of the principle of individual responsibility and the presence of that of communal merit. It is true that, in the end,[4] it so happened that God did specially consider a few individuals. But no reference to this course is to be found in the fundamental, conscious discussion on the problem between God and Abraham. Moreover, it should be noted that if Lot and his family had not left Sodom, they, too, would have perished, as, in fact, his prospective sons-in-law did.[5]

The point will become clearer by comparing another narrative in which God is entreated not to consume innocent and guilty alike, namely, the story of Korah's revolt against Moses and Aaron.[6] When God announced His intention to wipe out the whole people except Moses and Aaron, these two 'fell upon their faces and said...Shall one man sin and wilt thou be wroth with all the congregation?' This, indeed, was a request that the rebellion be dealt with on the basis of individual responsibility. Moses and Aaron besought God to strike at no one but the really blameworthy. But they did not introduce the notion of communal merit: they did not suggest that, as there were many more or less innocent, even the guilty should go unharmed. This is not saying that Moses and Aaron must necessarily have held views unlike Abraham's. That their request was not the same may well be accounted for by there having been, between the facts of the case of Sodom and those of the case of Korah, several important points of difference. I shall not, however, here specify them since this would involve too lengthy an analysis of the details of the two narratives. Similarly, individual responsibility, not communal merit, is the gist of commandments like 'The fathers shall not be put to death for the children, neither shall the children be put to death for the fathers: every man shall be put to death for his own sin.'[7] 'Every man', the injunction runs, 'shall be put to death for his own sin'; it does not run, 'The sinners shall live for the good works of the pious.'

How are we to explain Abraham's attitude? The answer, or part of it, seems to be that he wished to make God give up His plan, and chose the most natural and easy way of formulating his wish. God told him: I will raze these cities to the ground—they are vicious. Whereupon he replied: Preserve them—there may be a few good men. This was proposing the simplest alternative.

Was it? Was the pardoning of all really the most plausible
course when the punishing of all appeared unwarranted? Yes,
it was, if one assumption continued to be made—and here
we come to the crucial factor—the assumption that, for better
for worse, a community must be treated as a whole, no dis-
crimination between its various members being possible.
Abraham continued to make this assumption. He argued with
God, not because He was trying entire cities instead of individual persons (that fundamental objection did not yet occur
to him), but for the sole reason that His terrible sentence
might affect some men who deserved better. Should there
be a god-fearing remnant in the doomed towns, their annihila-
tion would be an injustice: therefore, in order to avoid wronging
it, the decision must be reversed—for the whole of the towns.
Instead of condemnation of Sodom and Gomorrah, there must
be acquittal of Sodom and Gomorrah.

Probably, communal thinking was so deep-rooted that
Abraham could think in no other way;[8] the method of
judging a city as one unit so unreservedly accepted that he
never questioned it as such. He noticed what deplorable
results this system might produce: but he did not discover
its real flaw, the ultimate source of those deplorable results.
So he criticized the results while, essentially, approving of the
system; or, to put it differently, he retained the current,
traditional method, only he applied it in a new way leading
to new conclusions. While he expressed horror at the idea
that 'the righteous should be as the wicked', his own proposal
implied neither more nor less than that the wicked should be
as the righteous. Fettered by the communal principle, he was
unable to take the direct step from communal responsibility
to individual responsibility: but keenly sensitive to the claims
of the righteous, he substituted communal merit for communal
responsibility. In a sense, it was a manner of progress to be
described as *imitation par opposition*.

I am not maintaining that it was merely in this manner,
and no other, that communal responsibility was overcome or
the idea of communal merit acquired prominence; nor even
that this must have been the starting-point. The very fact,
for example, of Abraham's being allowed to speak for his

brothers of lesser standing is strong indication that communal
merit, in one form or another, played some part long before
he asked God to rest on it the particular verdict on Sodom
and Gomorrah. What does seem plausible, though even this
no more than plausible, is that, in some ancient theologies
at least, Abraham's argument was the first to be used in a
conscious attempt to get rid of the unjust consequences of
communal responsibility, and in setting up communal merit
as a general, desirable basis for decisions.

It may be well to refer to a somewhat analogous case from
a very different province. Shakespeare's Shylock relied on the
strict letter of the law. It was pointed out to him how cruel
and unreasonable would be the execution of his design: yet
he would have his bond. Portia did feel that to let him proceed
would be abetting a crime; she failed to infer, however, that
there are contracts which a court simply ought not to enforce,
and that the contract in question was one of them. She solved
the difficulty by recognizing the bond but interpreting it just
a little too scrupulously: a pound of flesh, indeed, but not a
single drop of blood. Again, we have before us an instance of
imitation par opposition. It did not occur to Portia to question
the established, rigid rule that any bond is sacred, whatever
its contents, whatever the circumstances. She realized that this
rule might be the cause of unjust results. But she did not
reject it as such; she only saw to it that no wrong was done,
she only applied the old principles of strict law in such a way
—it was, true enough, a most artificial way[9]—as to make them
yield fresh and better results. Thus, her judgment does not
mark a direct step from a system of strict law to one of liberal,
flexible law. Essentially, she still adhered to the former; and,
in fact, she herself declared that she was beating Shylock on
his own ground:

> For as thou urgest justice, be assur'd
> Thou shalt have justice more than thou desirest.

It is, incidentally, this discrepancy between the method she
employed and the result she arrived at which must be considered the true cause of the prolonged controversy about the
value of her verdict. As is well known, Portia's judgment has

received as much praise from some as blame from others. For example, Ihering, disapproving, comments thus:[10] 'But a lawyer who criticizes the plot cannot but say: the bond was void since it stipulated for something immoral; the judge should from the outset have rejected it on this ground. Once he did not reject it, however,...it was a miserable trick...to pronounce the same man entitled to a pound of flesh from the living body but not entitled to the blood that must be shed to get the flesh....Who can help feeling that, with him (the Jew), the law of Venice has been outraged?' Kohler, on the other hand, approving, says:[11] 'It is a process of universal significance that the dramatist unfolds before our eyes: it is the triumph of the purified sense of justice over the dark night reigning during the previous period. It is a triumph hiding itself behind specious arguments and assuming the mask of false reasons because these are still necessary; but it is a triumph none the less, affecting not only the particular issue under notice but the whole history of law.' Both parties have submitted brilliant arguments, and it looks as if the feud might go on for ever. As a matter of fact, both parties are right. Portia wished to save Antonio, in spite of the bond; but she still thought in terms of a formalistic, strict law, and must therefore use, as best she could, the means provided by that regime to attain her end. Hence it comes that when we concentrate on the result, as most of those did who have praised her, we are satisfied; while when we concentrate on the method, as those did who have blamed her, we may find it ingenious but shall never find it sound.

It may be recalled that the first, famous part of the sentence was followed by a second part. This was based on a decree of Venice providing that an alien who sought the life of a citizen, unless the duke pardoned him, was to be put to death and his property to be confiscated. Had Portia founded on this decree also the first part of her decision; that is to say, had she, instead of 'upholding' the bond, simply decided that, in view of this decree, the contract was illegal and Shylock, not the merchant, had forfeited his life for making it; her judgment would indeed have to be regarded as directly setting aside the Jew's formalistic view of the law. But, then, had she done so, her judgment would not be nearly so intriguing as it is, and the play would be poorer by one of its most dramatic points. Actually, the second part of her sentence, the part based on the decree, is quite unexciting *qua* sentence, and derives all its interest from the consequences brought about by it: Shylock's plea that to lose his property would be as good as to lose his life, his enforced conversion, and so on.

I need hardly add, in conclusion, that if the story of Abraham's intercession reflects only the beginning of an advance as far as the evolution of legal methods is concerned, it embodies one of the greatest religious ideas ever conceived. The substitution for communal responsibility of communal merit, instead of individual responsibility, is a sign of a certain backwardness in regard to legal methods. But, from the point of view of religion, how magnificent is the idea that, far from the sinners drawing the pious to inevitable destruction, a handful of saints can render holy and save all the community! Certainly, few ideas have produced mightier effects in the course of Jewish and, indeed, non-Jewish history. The narrative discussed, with its combination of the primitive and the sublime, the one dependent on the other, illustrates well the mysteriously irregular path of human thought.

II

In modern literature, the term 'communal responsibility' is indiscriminately applied to two very different things, of which only one deserves that description. It may be well to begin by giving a few examples of the procedure that does deserve it. The Bible tells us [12] how Abraham asked God not to destroy Sodom if ten righteous people could be found there. 'That be far from thee', he exclaimed, ' . . . that the righteous should be as the wicked.' Evidently, this argument was directed against communal responsibility. Had there been a number of god-fearing men in the city, and had God destroyed it all the same, it would have meant treating the whole community as answerable for, or tainted by, the sins of a section. Again, there is a law in Deuteronomy [13] to the effect that if a murdered man is discovered lying in a field, and the murderer cannot be found, the elders of the nearest town have to bring

a sacrifice. This provision also is a landmark in the struggle
against communal responsibility. Were the ceremony prescribed in it not possible, God might treat the whole community as answerable for, or tainted by, the crime committed
by the one, unknown murderer. 'Lay not innocent blood unto
thy people of Israel's charge', is the prayer to be recited by
the elders.

But now let us consider a group of instances that ought not,
it is submitted, to come under the same heading as those
discussed. When David was presumptuous enough to count
his people, the prophet offered him the choice between three
kinds of punishment: seven years of famine, having to fly
before his enemies for three months, or three days of pestilence. The king chose the latter, and thousands of his men
died.[14] Whatever one's impression might be at first sight,
the governing notion here was not communal responsibility
(though, as we shall see later,[15] it was not entirely absent).
It would be wrong to say that all Israelites, because they
belonged to the offender's, David's, community, were regarded
as involved in the offence. At least, that cannot have been
the idea that the prophet had in mind. One of the penalties
proposed for choice, be it remembered, was that David should
have to fly before his enemies for three months. This, presumably, would not have troubled his ordinary subjects at all,
certainly far less than that terrible pestilence: it would have
troubled him alone. As a matter of fact, that pestilence, too,
however much it hurt the people, was intended as punishment,
not of the people, but of the king. It was he, not they, who was
to be chastised for his arrogance by their decimation. Supposing, in consequence of an earthquake, David had lost
70,000 silver coins instead of 70,000 men, or the plague had
seized his cattle instead of his men, or even it had seized his
slaves instead of free Israelites, it would never occur to us to
speak of communal responsibility. For we should see quite
clearly that there was David, the owner, and his coins or cattle
or slaves, his property; and that his sin was not laid to his
property's charge but it was damaged simply in order that he
should be impoverished. But, then, obviously, the mere fact
that he was made poorer by a host of men instead of coins,

sheep or slaves did not alter the direction of the vengeance: it was still he whom God meant to hit. In the case of Sodom, if God had killed even the righteous Lot and his family, He would have killed them, not in order to grieve the wicked—they were not likely to care—but on the basis of the communal principle: the whole city is responsible for crimes perpetrated in its midst. Similarly, in the case of a murdered man being found in a field, if God were not prepared to accept a sacrifice and turned against the nearest town, He would turn against it, not in order to punish the murderer—he might not mind at all—but to punish the town, which, on the communal principle, is responsible for a deed done within its boundaries. The situation in the case of David's census was totally different. Here God intended to strike at the real offender, David; only that the particular punishment inflicted happened to consist in slaying his men and not, as it might well have done, in depriving him of his money, cattle or the like. Of course, there was a reason why God took away his men and not his money or cattle. He had transgressed by counting, and boasting of the number of, the former: therefore it was fit that it should be the former by whose loss he was brought low. But this is only one more detail to confirm the interpretation here attempted. David, the 'owner', showed himself unduly proud of his men, his 'possessions': it was David, the 'owner', whom God confounded by falling upon them.

Actually, there is direct authority in the text for this point, on which I am insisting, that the 70,000 men were destroyed, not as responsible members of a sinful community, but *qua* David's property, like cattle—this is the reason why I have adduced this story before any other. David himself drew the comparison when he asked God to put an end to the sufferings of the innocent: 'I have done wickedly; but these sheep, what have they done?' True, what David mainly thought of, when he called his subjects 'sheep', was that they were incapable of grave sins (sheep are regarded as innocent[16]) and that they were in need of protection (good rulers are compared to shepherds[17]). But the implication of this clearly was that God was here killing people peaceful and helpless like sheep merely in order to punish their 'owner'.[18]

In short, David's census is an illustration, not of communal responsibility, but of individual responsibility: the sinner, David, alone was called to account. The special feature of the case is not any peculiar kind of responsibility, but a peculiar kind of punishment: he was punished, on this occasion, in a way that affected his people, human beings. We are not surprised when we find slaves being put on a level with any kind of dead property. But we ought to recognize that even relationships of less absolute power and subordination may give rise to situations and dealings very similar to those occurring in connection with slavery. The pestilence deprived David of 70,000 free Israelites just as a rich owner of slaves might be deprived of a vast number of slaves. If a label is needed for this type of retribution, we must call it, not communal responsibility, but punishment of a ruler by taking away or damaging his free subjects; or, for short, ruler punishment. I am afraid the expression 'ruler punishment', torn from the context, might be ambiguous: but I am introducing it for the sake of brevity. As may be seen from the argument, I do not mean by it—what I suppose the term as such might signify—liability of a ruler, guilty or innocent, for acts of his people. It ought to be quite clear that I use it as denoting the case where the wrong committed by a ruler is repaid to him by a move against those under his rule, by taking away or damaging his free subjects.

Two more events from the life of David may be mentioned, both connected with the affair of Uriah. The first is the death of the child whom Bath-sheba bore to her lover.[19] This was not communal responsibility, though it may look similar. The child was not killed because he belonged to a community with a sinner in its midst. Admittedly, there would be nothing startling in this: the idea that all members of a family are punishable for the unexpiated transgression of one occurs in many ancient narratives. But it does not in the narrative under notice. David, the actual offender, alone was made responsible. As God's messenger informed him, he himself would have perished had he not shown perfect humility; but his contrition moved God to mitigate His judgment and only to take away his child. All the time the child was ill,

David fasted and prayed for him. Clearly, it was David and no one but him—except, perhaps, Bath-sheba, his partner in the crime and 'co-owner' of the child—at whom the blow was aimed. He was deprived of the child he valued just as he might have been deprived of his most precious jewel. This, like the case of the census, was a case of individual responsibility: retribution was exacted from him who had committed the wrong. Only, as in the case of the census, the punishment was of a peculiar kind: the piece of 'property' by the loss of which the wrongdoer was punished happened to be a human being, and a free one at that. In the case of the census, it was a king who was chastised by the destruction of thousands of his people; in this case, it was a father (or a father with the mother) who was chastised by the destruction of his son. The correct heading for both cases is not communal responsibility, but punishment of a ruler by taking away or damaging his free subjects.

The other incident to be quoted is particularly instructive: it is the warning by the prophet that as David had committed adultery with Bath-sheba, so others would with his wives—an announcement foreshadowing the seizure of the king's harem by Absalom.[20] Was the prophet speaking in terms of communal responsibility? The question sounds absurd, and, as far as I know, nobody has suggested that, according to the prophet, David's women were being punished on that basis or, for that matter, were being punished at all: it is too manifest that David alone was intended, and made, to suffer. Yet, had the prophet foretold him the death of his wives instead of their capture by a rival, 'communal responsibility' would no doubt be the unanimous verdict in modern literature. But would the position be really different? Certainly not. Either the prophet had in mind retribution on the principle of communal responsibility, the women being made to answer for David's sin as members of his family; in that case, we must admit that it was they whom God meant to chastise, not only if they were killed, but even if they were carried off by the young prince. Or the prophet had in mind retribution on the principle of individual responsibility, David himself being made to answer for his sin;

in that case, we must admit that it was he whom God meant to chastise, not only if his women were taken by the prince, but even if they were killed. In actual fact, the latter interpretation alone can be correct. In the eyes of the prophet, David and no one but he deserved to be called to account; only he was to be hit in that peculiar manner I have tried to describe, by the loss of a piece of living, human 'property'. Punishment was inflicted on the basis of individual responsibility; only it took the form that I have labelled as ruler punishment. It has been shown how a king might be punished by the destruction of his men, and a father by that of his son: here we may see how the owner of a harem might be punished by the seizure of his women.[21]

There are two points rendering this case especially valuable. In the first place, as the women were not actually hurt, unlike the victims of the pestilence or Bath-sheba's son, the explanation of the punishment as an application of communal responsibility is *a priori* ruled out. But I have pointed out that it would make no relevant difference if they had been hurt. The case thus furnishes clear evidence that there was a type of punishment which, though free persons other than the real offender were affected, had nothing to do with communal responsibility; but must be accounted for by the fact that a sinner might be punished by being deprived of human 'property' (his men if he was a king, his son if he was a father, his wife if he was a husband) just as well as by being deprived of any other goods. Where this kind of punishment involved hurting the subjects (as it did in the first two instances discussed, but not in this third one), we ought not to be misled as to the essential meaning and direction of the blow, just as we are not misled where a man was humiliated by a decimation of his slaves. In the second place, the prophet's speech itself leaves no doubt that, for him, the women in the harem were that piece of 'property' by the loss of which David, the owner, was to be chastised. As the king had taken Uriah's wife, the prophet declared, so his wives were to be snatched from him. He was to be punished, that is, in a way fitting the crime. His crime had consisted in robbing the other man of his treasure—his 'one little ewe lamb', in the words of the parable (again, there is this comparison between a ruler's subjects and sheep[22]); so, in return, he was to be robbed of his treasure, his wives. Obviously, this signified, not communal responsibility, but precise retaliation by taking from the offender what he has taken from the wronged man. It was the same idea that underlies ancient rules such as that if a man tears out another's eye, he is to lose his own: there is no communal responsibility attaching to the eye, the responsibility is entirely its owner's, he alone is to be hit by the sentence though, in physical reality, his eye is affected.

The examples adduced so far are all from the domain of theology: in all of them it is a matter of God exacting retribution from a sinner. The following are from law proper, with society exacting retribution from a criminal. It will be seen that there, too, may be found that punishment of a ruler by taking away or damaging his subjects. As regards the parties concerned, naturally, in the province of law, we shall expect no cases of a king being deprived of his men (as David was after his census): it is difficult to imagine an ordinary provision laying down that if a king does this or that, a few thousand of his people are to be killed. What we may expect is cases of a father being deprived of his son (as David was of the child borne by Bath-sheba) and a husband being deprived of his wife (as David was of his harem). Again, as regards the occasions on which this type of punishment is chosen and the way it is applied, we shall not, in law proper, expect it to be inflicted for arrogance (as it was in the case of David's census), nor shall we expect a man to have to lose his son for committing adultery (as David lost the child borne by Bath-sheba). What we may expect is to find this type of punishment serving the purpose of exact retaliation, the purpose of taking from the offender what he has taken from his victim; what we may expect, for example, is to find a husband being deprived of his wife because he has deprived another man of his wife (as David's harem was appropriated by Absalom because he had appropriated the wife of Uriah).

In the *Mishpatim*, the Judgments, one of the earliest codes of the Bible, it is ordained that, given certain conditions, the owner of an ox which kills a free person shall be put to death;

and the law adds, somewhat mysteriously, that this rule is to apply also if the ox kills a free person's son or daughter.[23] The mysterious addition is by no means an empty phrase. According to the Code of Hammurabi, if a builder works badly and the house collapses and kills its owner, the builder is to be put to death: but if the owner's son is killed, it is the builder's son who is to be put to death.[24] As was pointed out some forty years ago,[25] the provision about the son and daughter in the *Mishpatim* is directed against this kind of practice. It is always the owner of the wild ox himself—thus we have to understand the text—never his son or daughter, who is to lose his life. This interpretation, it seems to me, is confirmed by the fact that the rule about son and daughter does not show the usual form of rules in the *Mishpatim*. Whilst most other rules begin with כי or אם, 'if' (the former being put at the opening of a section, the latter introducing special cases within each section), the rule about son and daughter begins with או, 'or'. The most probable reason is that it did not belong to the original stock from which the greater part of the material of the *Mishpatim* was taken, but constitutes an amendment, replacing a different regulation that was much closer to that of the Code of Hammurabi. The only other provision in the *Mishpatim* beginning with או, 'or', is Exodus xxi. 36, which I have already shown to belong to a section added to the original stock.[26] Now when we ask what is the striking element in that older regulation, or in that still preserved in the Code of Hammurabi, the answer will have to be, not communal responsibility, but ruler punishment. It is not as if the law treated as answerable and tainted all members of the guilty person's family. If that were the case, clearly, there would be no reason why it should not be the owner of the ox, or the builder, himself, or his wife, who was to be killed for the offence; whereas, in point of fact, we are expressly told that it must be his son if he has caused the death of another man's son and his daughter if he has caused the death of another man's daughter. Moreover, if there were communal responsibility, it would be difficult to see why it should not be applied where the person killed by the wild ox, or by the house that collapses, is a *paterfamilias*; whereas we are told that, in this case, it is the owner of the ox, or the builder, himself who is to be put to death. The conclusion is obvious. The only person regarded as answerable is the owner of the ox or the builder, that is to say, the actual offender. But, in order to achieve precise retaliation, if the victim is another man's son or daughter, the law punishes him by depriving him of the same piece of 'property' of which he has deprived the other man—and this means the putting to death of a third human being, a third free person who, being under the *potestas* or *manus* of the culprit, is treated almost as if he were his slave. The son of the wrongdoer is destroyed, not as guilty, but as the guilty man's 'property'.[27] The essential idea behind this regulation is no other than that which governs the old rules of retaliation in cases like a torn-out eye or a cut-off limb.

There is perhaps a further provision in the *Mishpatim* directed against ruler punishment; I mean the provision saying that if a man hurts a woman with child and she not only miscarries but dies or suffers serious harm herself, 'thou shalt give life for life, eye for eye, tooth for tooth...'.[28] This direct address, 'thou shalt give', is very unusual in the *Mishpatim*; the usual form would be, 'he shall give'. As in the case just discussed, the uncommon form may be explained by assuming that the rule which belonged to the original stock, and which spoke of the wrongdoer in the third person, has been ejected and replaced by a better; by the one, in fact, which we have now before us. The Assyrian code seems to lay down that if a man hurts a woman with child, under certain circumstances his own wife is to be hurt in the same way.[29] It is true that the precise text of this law is not established. But the main idea recurs in another law of the code of which we do know the text in full, and which says that if a married man violates an unmarried woman, that woman's father may take his wife from him and offer her to anyone[30]: one is reminded of David's wives being given to Absalom for his adultery with Bathsheba. Similarly, the Code of Hammurabi provides that if a man strikes a woman with child and she dies, his daughter shall be put to death.[31] The injunction in the *Mishpatim*, 'thou shalt give life for life...', quite possibly abolished some practice like the Assyrian and Babylonian. From now, this may have been the point of the innovation, punishment was on no account to affect the wrongdoer's wife or daughter; whatever harm might have come to the woman whom he hurt, his women should not suffer for it.[32] Yet it would not be correct to conclude that the earlier system, which resembled the Assyrian and Babylonian, and according to which the wrongdoer's wife or daughter might have to suffer, was based on communal responsibility. Under that earlier system no less than under the new one it was the offending individual alone who was called to account. The point of the abolished system, as of the Assyrian and Hammurabi's, was that it aimed at strict retaliation and, therefore, required that the offender should incur the same loss (the loss of a wife or daughter, namely, or of his wife's health—the women of a man's household being here deemed very much the same as slaves) that he had inflicted on the other man.

The foregoing remarks may suffice to show that when we find the family or compatriots of an offender being hurt by the punishment following the offence, this may be due to either of two different things. It may be the result of a certain type of responsibility, communal responsibility, as when the whole town in the fields of which a murder has taken place is considered in some sense guilty; or it may be the result of a certain mode of punishment, punishment of a ruler by taking away or damaging his free subjects, as when a man who causes the death of another man's child is deprived of his own. The two things must not be mixed up with one another: ruler punishment is far from confined to cases where the principle of communal responsibility is applied. Actually, for the sake of clarity, all the instances I have given above have been so chosen as to illustrate this. That ancient rule, for example, according to which a man who causes the death of another man's child is to lose his own is definitely based on individual responsibility: he who has perpetrated the crime, the father, and no one but he, is to be punished. It is only in consequence of the particular mode of punishment inflicted that, in physical fact, a third party is hurt. It should be added, however, that, very naturally, ruler punishment is possible also where communal responsibility prevails. The destruction of the Egyptian firstborn is a good enough example.[33] It is based, to some extent at least, on the idea of communal responsibility: all Egyptians alike are made answerable by God, not only Pharaoh and his active accomplices, but even 'the captive that was in the dungeon'. And the mode of punishment is that which is here termed ruler punishment: the Egyptians are punished by losing each his most valuable 'property', his firstborn son. In a sense, indeed, the case of David's census also is a combination of ruler punishment with communal responsibility. For it was not David alone who was being punished by losing his subjects, but David and his house. This is evident from the prayer by which he implored God to stop the pestilence: 'These sheep, what have they done? let thine hand...be against me and against my father's house.' The entire house of David was guilty because of David's sin—on the basis of communal responsibility. It was punished by a decimation of the people—on the basis of ruler punishment.

Should any further support be required of the thesis here maintained (namely, that one has to distinguish ruler punishment from communal responsibility), it is to be found in a notion well known from ancient literature: the notion, that is, that when a ruler's subjects are unlawfully attacked, even though they be free men it is the ruler, not themselves, whose rights are being infringed. It was 'out of the hand of Jehoahaz', the king of Israel, that the Syrians snatched some cities, not from the inhabitants of the cities themselves;[34] it was Uriah, not Bath-sheba herself, whom David wronged by stealing her; and according to the Assyrian law which I have quoted and which deals with the rape of an unmarried woman by a married man, it is the woman's father, not herself, who may offer the criminal's wife to the public, just as under the *Mishpatim*, if a woman is hurt and miscarries, it is her husband who fixes and receives the fine for the offspring lost.[35] All that evidently has no connection with communal responsibility; it is a natural thing in a system under which the people of a king, or a man's wife, or his children, are, up to a point, his 'property', not unlike slaves. To attack that 'property' is to attack the king, the husband, the father, much as to attack a herd of cattle or a slave would be to attack the owner. But this notion, with which all historians are acquainted, and of which notable traces remain in present-day law, is the exact counter-part of that of ruler punishment. Just as it may be the ruler, not his free subjects, whose rights are violated by an unlawful attack on the latter, on his living, human pieces of 'property', so it may be he who is punished by disasters affecting them.

One question arises. Why, it may be asked, if the suggestion propounded is correct, should ruler punishment, punishment of a ruler by taking away or damaging his free subjects, differ, in one interesting respect, from punishment affecting ordinary property, money, cattle or slaves? For it looks as if there were a difference. Where a man is punished by being deprived of some of his ordinary property, as a rule, it is handed over to the person whom he has wronged; from now that person is to own and enjoy it. A thief, for instance, who has stolen a sheep and slaughtered it, will have to return four other sheep to the victim of his theft, according to the *Mishpatim*.[36] In the cases reviewed above, on the other hand, where the 'property' in question is the free subjects of a ruler, the people of a king, a man's wife or child, the 'property' is not given to the person wronged to remain, safe and sound, in his hands, but it is damaged or destroyed: the unsuccessful builder of Hammurabi's code, for example, has not to transfer his son to the man the death of whose son he has caused—his son is simply killed. Why is that so?

The answer is easy to find. Of ordinary property, broadly speaking, one piece is as good as another. It is reasonable, therefore, that a man who has interfered with another man's property should make amends by replacing what he has taken or damaged, by giving another, or several other, sheep for that which he has stolen, and so on. Difficulties, however, are bound to crop up as soon as we come to irreplaceable goods. An eye, for instance, is not replaceable like a sheep: the damage done by tearing out a man's eye just cannot be made good in the real sense of the phrase. In such cases, ancient systems sought to meet the requirements of justice by providing that the wrong-doer, as he could not replace the victim's eye, should at least lose his own.[37] Here lies the solution to our question. The free subjects of a ruler, his men if he is a king, his wife if he is a husband, his son if he is a father, are nearly always regarded as falling in that category of irreplaceable goods. Consequently, if a builder causes the death of somebody's son, or if a man violates somebody's daughter, he cannot make amends by giving the father his own child or wife to occupy, from now onwards, the place of the destroyed or damaged 'property'. As in the case of a torn-out eye, since actual replacing of the wronged man's 'property' by the offender's is impossible, justice, in ancient times, was achieved by inflicting the same measure of destruction on the offender's as he had inflicted on the wronged man's: the builder's son was to be put to death, the wife of the debauchee to be offered to anybody.

There are, however, noteworthy exceptions to the rule that free subjects are considered irreplaceable, and they furnish decisive confirmation of the view here advanced. The Hittites, for example, appear to have deemed free persons almost as 'fungible' as cattle or slaves: under the code of Boghaz-keui a man whose wife or child has been killed, or even a family a grown-up male member of which has been killed, can demand no more, it seems, than that the murderer hand over four members of his own household (besides the corpse).[38] Again, he who wounds a man has to supply a substitute for the time that the wounded man is unable to work.[39] This is ruler punishment, punishment of a ruler by taking away his free subjects: and, in this case, the 'property' is neither destroyed nor damaged. One is in fact tempted to speak here of property without the use of inverted commas. The free subjects are here treated exactly like money, cattle or slaves: the owner transfers them to the wronged family, by way of restitution in kind, as under a provision of the *Mishpatim* a thief has to give four sheep for that which he has stolen. Indeed, the only difference, according to Hittite law, between punishment in case a free man has been killed and punishment in case a slave has been killed seems to be that four persons have to be given for the former, and only two for the latter.[40] Yet the Hittite case is by no means unique. Where larger units than the family are concerned, in particular, free subjects may, in certain connections, be regarded as replaceable even in our age. It is quite conceivable even now that a monarch who has been deprived of a number of subjects through the unlawful incursions of a neighbouring prince should require the cession of the same or a larger number in compensation. In the Middle Ages at any rate, and right up to the French Revolution, that a feudal lord should be punished by having to give up, or that he should generally deal in, free subjects was far from unheard of.[41] From these extreme instances of ruler punishment, with the ruler having to transfer his subjects like cattle or slaves, it is a far cry indeed to communal responsibility, the making answerable the whole of a community, all equally and as equals, for a crime committed by any member.

Having, as I hope, established the distinction between communal responsibility and ruler punishment, I hasten to add that, in many cases, it is difficult to decide which of the two ideas has produced the result recorded; more than that, in many cases it is undeniably both ideas that have been at work at the same time. I have said that God's wreaking vengeance on all Egyptians, even 'on the captive that was in the dungeon', is an example of communal responsibility: the whole nation was treated as answerable for, and tainted by, the crimes committed against Israel and its Lord. But very probably, a secondary purpose at least of the decimation of the Egyptians was to strike at Pharaoh as their ruler, their 'owner'. Here, then, the two notions, that of communal responsibility and that of ruler punishment, are closely interwoven. Further, I have said that when David's men perished through a pestilence, the main object was to impoverish him, their king, for his arrogance. Yet there are signs that the notion of the whole people being under a curse as a result of the census, of their being made answerable themselves for the offence, is not altogether absent from this narrative. Curiously enough, these signs are stronger in Chronicles than in Samuel. It is only in the version of Chronicles that Joab, warning the king against the census, says, 'Why will he be a cause of trespass to Israel?', or that we are told how 'God was displeased with this thing; therefore he smote Israel.'[42] Thus, again, the ideas of communal responsibility and ruler punishment seem here to merge into one another. There are numerous instances like this. Whereas in the narrative of Isaac at Gerar the idea of communal responsibility is relatively undiluted, Abimelech assuming that if any member of the nation had taken Rebekah, the whole nation would have been guilty,[43] in the similar stories of Abraham in Egypt and at Gerar the idea of ruler punishment also seems to come in, however faintly. The kings of Egypt and Gerar took Sarah, Abraham's wife, into their harems, believing her to be his sister only; whereupon God inflicted diseases on them and their households. It appears that these plagues were not sent merely in application of the principle of communal responsibility; it was not merely that the two nations were tainted by a sin in their midst. There was also the object of punishing the actual wrongdoers, the kings of Egypt and Gerar, by making their wives sterile, their 'property' useless.[44]

I cannot here go into the many very complicated cases of this kind. At the risk, however. of confusing where I should wish to enlighten, I have to state a little more fully what is their nature and how they can be explained. It may be noticed that there are two ways in which communal responsibility and ruler punishment may be combined. The one, very simple, I mentioned above[45] and am not now concerned with. It is the case where men, made responsible as members of a community, are for some reason or other punished in that peculiar mode that I am calling ruler punishment, i.e. by having their free subjects damaged or destroyed. For example, when God slew the firstborn in Egypt, the Egyptians, one may say, were called to account by Him as members of a sinful nation (communal responsibility), and their punishment consisted in the loss by each of them of his most valuable 'property', his eldest son (ruler punishment). Or the whole house of David was deemed guilty on account of his census (communal responsibility) and punished by a pestilence killing off a large number of the people (ruler punishment).

There is, however, another way in which communal responsibility and ruler punishment may meet, or better, clash, and this alone I am here considering; namely, the case where men are made responsible as members of a community, but, at the same time, we can discern within that community a ruler on the one hand and all the rest as his subjects on the other, the former to be the main loser by the misfortunes befalling the community. When God slew the firstborn in Egypt, the Egyptians were called to account by Him as members of a sinful nation (communal responsibility). At the same time, however, Pharaoh occupied the place of ruler and the rest of the people were his subjects; and the death of the firstborn was intended not only as a punishment of the Egyptians *qua* members of a sinful nation (communal responsibility) but also as a blow against Pharaoh, the wicked ruler of the land (ruler punishment). Or again, we have seen that while the main object of the pestilence inflicted on Israel was to punish the guilty ruler, David (ruler punishment), yet the idea that the entire people was tainted by the census did play some part (communal responsibility). It is in cases like these, where the same group is considered communally responsible and yet divided into ruler and subjects, the latter's disasters being regarded as so much damage done to the former's 'property', that there is a real tension between communal responsibility and ruler punishment. Logically, these cases are most unsatisfactory; logically, we might argue that if the Egyptians or Israelites were punished on the basis of communal responsibility, as members of a guilty nation, they cannot have been decimated, like cattle, as Pharaoh's or David's, the wrongdoer's, 'property'; and if they were decimated, like cattle, as Pharaoh's, or David's, the wrongdoer's, 'property', they cannot have been punished as themselves guilty. But life and literature are not always governed by strict logic. The tension under notice, the clash of communal responsibility and ruler punishment, in general reflects a tension in the structure of the community concerned. To take the example of the Egyptians and Pharaoh: on the one hand, the Egyptians, as depicted in the Bible, were a community of free men, capable of making decisions, of performing good deeds and committing crimes, and so on. Judged from that point of view, they might well be made answerable, all of them, for what they did to the Israelites. On the other hand, they had a king, Pharaoh, who directed the policy of the country and to whom, in a sense, they belonged. Judged from this point of view, it was Pharaoh who deserved to be punished and, as a great king, might be most terribly hit by the loss of his 'possessions', by a decimation of his free subjects. An age like ours, in which what is *au fond* largely a struggle between communal responsibility— 'We fight a guilty nation'—and ruler punishment—'We fight the nation in order to destroy the rulers'—has assumed enormous dimensions and importance, and in which all variations and combinations of the two ideas are to be found (including the interesting situation—no less frequent in antiquity than now—where the representatives of one idea consciously or unconsciously masquerade as representatives of the other), surely should have some understanding for this.

As already remarked, I cannot here examine all cases, or even groups of cases, of this type. One important class, however, I wish to draw attention to: the family curse, perhaps one of the most frequent cases where we may have difficulty in deciding whether the basis of the result is communal responsibility or ruler punishment, and where quite often it is both. In modern treatises on the subject, the family curse is invariably taken to be an illustration of the principle of communal responsibility pure and simple. But the instances when this is the sole idea behind it are rare indeed. Unfortunately, the problems involved are too knotty to be here elaborated. Suffice it to say that the head of a house at any given time, and especially the founder or would-be founder of a famous house, was regarded in ancient times as something of the ruler, of the principally interested 'owner', of the house, even of the as yet unborn generations. Hence it comes that nearly always when a family curse is being announced to an offender, the idea of communal responsibility, of all members of the family being answerable for, and tainted by, his offence, appears side by side with the idea of ruler punishment, of his being punished, as the actually guilty individual, by the disasters to befall his sons and grandsons. When Eli was told that 'there shall be not an old man in thine house for ever',[46] no doubt both notions were at work: the idea that his whole family was tainted by the crimes committed by himself and his sons, and the idea that he, as the first great chief of the house, was to be punished by the misfortunes to visit his descendants. Again, when David, after his adultery with Bath-sheba, was warned by the prophet that 'therefore the sword shall never depart from thine house',[47] one of the under-lying ideas may indeed have been that the whole family was answerable for what he had done; but, in this case, the idea of ruler punishment was unquestionably predominant—David, the first founder of what he hoped would be a famous line, was to be punished by the calamities befalling his successors.[48] According to Holinshed, Kenneth—whose life Shakespeare used for *Macbeth*—having attained his end, heard a voice at night-time: 'It shall therefore come to pass, that both thou thyself, and thy issue, shall suffer worthy punishment, to the infamy of thy house and family for evermore. For even at this present are there in hand secret practices to dispatch both thee and thy issue out of the way, that other may enjoy this kingdom which thou doest endeavour to assure unto thine issue.' The entire house shall be infamous, the voice declares: this is communal responsibility. But, evidently, it is chiefly the murderer Kenneth, or Macbeth, himself whom the fall of his house is meant to hit and the prescience of it is meant to torture: this is ruler punishment. And the latter idea is in the foreground, for the descendants, communally respon-sible, are quite nameless, almost a shadow.

I need hardly add that what is true of the family curse is true also of hereditary blessing: and the very fact that it can be shown to apply to hereditary blessing in turn supports the observations made with regard to the family curse. Abraham, for showing himself willing to sacrifice Isaac, his beloved son, to God, was promised, 'I will multiply thy seed as the stars of the heaven...and thy seed shall possess the gate of his enemies.'[49] This meant communal merit (corresponding to communal responsibility) inasmuch as the whole family was treated as sanctified by what one member had done. But it also meant 'ruler reward' (corresponding to ruler punishment), reward of the present head of the house and its first founder, inasmuch as his 'property', his house, was to be increased in

order to please and repay him, as an individual, for his splendid
act of faith. According to Holinshed, the three weird sisters
address Banquo thus: 'Yes, we promise greater benefits unto
thee, than unto him, for he shall reign in deed, but with an
unlucky end: neither shall he leave any issue behind him to
succeed in his place, where contrarily thou in deed shalt not
reign at all, but of thee those shall be born which shall govern
the Scottish kingdom by long order of continual descent.'
This means that providence favours Banquo's house in its
own right: a communal blessing. But it also means that
providence, in favouring Banquo's house, is kind to him, the
ancestor. Indeed, nothing could be clearer than this, for the
three sisters say that they have good news for Banquo, yet he
himself, they say, is not to reign: the good news consists in the
promise of the kingdom to his offspring—it is a ruler blessing,
he is blessed by the good fortune to come to his descendants.

There is a rough test (it is far from infallible) that sometimes enables us to see whether the infliction of a family curse
rests on the idea of communal responsibility or on that of
ruler punishment: we can, when we come across the announcement of a family curse, ask ourselves whether the curse would
have been imposed even if the offence in question had been
done by a minor member of the family. For example, would
the prophet have cursed David's house even if an insignificant
son of his had committed adultery? If the reply is 'Yes', then,
clearly, the idea of communal responsibility is predominant:
for then, clearly, the idea is that the offence of any member of
a family affects all equally. If the reply is 'No', however,
there is a presumption that the curse is meant mainly as a
punishment of the offending individual, and that if third
persons are affected it is only because he is treated as their
'owner' and they, his subjects, as his 'property', by whose
destruction he can be most effectively struck. The same test,
of course, may be applied to cases of family blessing, such
as that of Abraham. Would his house have been blessed even
if any of his near relatives had performed a good deed, or
was it not rather a blessing chiefly intended to reward himself,
as an individual? I believe the answer in the majority of
cases would have to be something between 'Yes' and 'No',

but nearer 'No'; which implies that in the majority of cases we have at least to consider whether the notion of ruler punishment is not the main element, rather than that of communal responsibility. A frequent complication, however, is that the same writer, when he concentrates on the life of the ancestor of an unfortunate house, may think of the curse chiefly as ruler punishment, as it would be from the point of view of the ancestor, from the point of view of the man somehow sovereign of the whole house; while, when he goes on to describe the lives of the various descendants and how the curse worked out in each case, he may think of their sorrows as springing chiefly from communal responsibility, as they do from their point of view, from the point of view of men each a fully recognized, independently acting and suffering being. The same complication arises in connection with hereditary blessing. Where God promises Abraham that his descendants will be fortunate, the emphasis mostly lies on the reward given to the individual Abraham in form of a fortunate seed—ruler reward. Where the fulfilment of this promise in the lives of his descendants is depicted, the emphasis mostly lies on their belonging to a fortunate line. Abraham's interest is no longer predominant, theirs is just as great—all members of the house share in the communal merit.

The reservation that the ideas of communal responsibility and ruler punishment may form the joint basis of one result, or that it may be impossible to pronounce which of them forms the basis, does not mean that quite frequently it is not clearly this idea or that which is solely responsible. When a whole town is made answerable for a murder committed in its midst, it is definitely communal responsibility; when a builder who has caused the death of a child has to lose his own, it is definitely ruler punishment. In any case, the question whether, and how far, we have before us one idea or the other ought always to be put. For the two have very different histories and reflect very different religious, social and economic factors. As the only object of these pages is to establish the distinction between them, I do not propose to pursue this subject any further. I shall only, in conclusion, call attention to a few items, selected more or less at random, to

show that the distinction is important not only as such but
also as leading to further deductions.

For one thing, the two ideas have not the same origin.
True, in some connections, one of them may conceivably
have evolved out of the other. It is possible, for example,
though anything but likely, that the idea of all members of
a family being answerable for what one of them does somehow
grew from the idea that the *paterfamilias* may be punished
by having his subjects destroyed or damaged; and it is
probable that, when a democratic community came under the
control of a dictator (or a narrow class), the idea of communal
responsibility in certain domains changed into the idea that
the ruler might be punished by having to lose his subjects.
Be this as it may, in most cases the development of one idea
from the other is out of the question. The communal responsibility of a city for a murder committed within its boundaries
certainly does not go back to any kind of ruler punishment.
Its main basis is the very practical and rational consideration
that, at a certain stage, the best means of ensuring order is
to force all citizens to take an active, personal interest in the
prevention and discovery of crime, that is to say, to threaten
them all with evil consequences should anything untoward
happen. In modern times, the same rational element underlies
the making responsible by a power occupying an enemy city
of the entire city in the case of sabotage. Undoubtedly the
threat of a collective fine or of the shooting of hostages taken
from all groups of the population, however reprehensible on
moral grounds, very often produces the desired effect. Again,
the punishment of a man who has violated another man's
wife by taking away his own does not go back to any kind
of communal responsibility. There is a certain stage where a
husband is regarded as his wife's master, a wife as something
like her husband's property; and where justice seems to require
that if a man meddles with another's 'property', he should
be punished by a similar interference with his own. The
origins of the ideas of communal responsibility and ruler
punishment are different. As it would lead too far afield,
within the scope of this study, to trace them, I shall say no
more about them.

Similarly, the factors making for the abandonment, partial or complete, of the two ideas are not identical. No doubt, the main element in all attacks directed against them is the same: the feeling, namely, that no man should suffer except for his very own sin. When David asked God to stop the pestilence, he was asking Him to stop ruler punishment; and his main argument was that his subjects were blameless and should not, therefore, be hurt: 'Lo, I have sinned...but these sheep, what have they done? let thine hand, I pray thee, be against me.' The ceremony to be performed when a murdered man is discovered near a town is destined to avert communal responsibility; and here, too, the main argument is the innocence of those who, if communal responsibility were applied, would suffer: 'Our hands have not shed this blood, neither have our eyes seen it', such is the prayer to be recited by the elders of the city. But, except for this idea that no man should be harmed unless it were for his own offence, it is very different factors which make for the weakening of the two notions of communal responsibility and ruler punishment; or, more precisely, it is different factors which bring to active life that consciousness of the injustice of suffering innocently in the two cases. Communal responsibility goes where the bonds holding together a unit are loosened (or, what is the same, where the individuals composing a unit acquire more and more independence), where the view of the contagiousness of sin recedes into the background, and also where a unit comes to be regarded as so impotent as no longer to be capable of responsibility. That the ceremony prescribed in Deuteronomy in case a murdered man is found near a city is possible shows that the city is no longer considered, in this connection, as an indivisible unit (the bonds holding together the individual citizens are loosened) and that the crime of murder is no longer considered as absolutely corrupting all that come into contact with it (the view of the contagiousness of sin—or better, certain sins—is disappearing): the guilty and innocent can now be separated from one another. A rational factor in this development is the growth of a city into a settled organization, with peace and security prevailing, and perhaps a police force detailed to keep down crime. In such circumstances, it is no longer necessary to hold all citizens under a threat in case of any murder being committed; just as, once complete order can be restored, a military power in occupation of enemy territory need no longer resort to collective fines and the shooting of hostages. Or another case: if a democracy becomes a monarchy, or aristocracy, and the king, or ruling class, alone is now made answerable where all citizens would have been answerable before, it is because the citizens are now insignificant, the king, or leading group, deciding for them and bearing the consequences of any actions (the community is no longer capable of responsibility). Ruler punishment, on the other hand, goes where the power of the ruler over his subjects becomes less absolute (or, what is the same, where the subjects become his equals). When David entreated God not to continue killing his subjects for their ruler's offence, he was thereby recognizing his subjects as, in certain respects, real men like himself. He still called them 'sheep', since they were incapable of acting for themselves, used to looking up to him as their master and protector, and, above all, not prone to the sin of arrogance for which the pestilence had been sent. He perceived, however, that they were not like inanimate property at all, but would bleed if pricked and die if poisoned.[50]

It is not my task here to set out the circumstances in which the bonds holding together a unit are loosened,[51] the view of the contagiousness of sin disappears, a unit becomes incapable of responsibility, or the power of rulers over their free subjects grows less absolute. From what I have said, it is easy to see that communal responsibility will persist longest in the religious and political sphere, where composite bodies, not individuals, form the centre of interest and the idea of the contagiousness of crime, of *miasma*, is prominent even in our time. In the political sphere, nowadays, this idea of course assumes a less mystic form, but it would be rash to say that it is not a very real force. According to Deuteronomy xiii. 13 (12) ff., if the inhabitants of a city turn idolators, the entire city, including cattle and even houses, is to be utterly destroyed: 'and there shall cleave nought of the cursed thing to thine hand'. That, in politics, it is nations, races, parties

as such which are called to account by their enemies, that
it is difficult for an individual belonging to an outlawed group
to escape the communal fate by appealing to his personal
blameless behaviour, is too commonplace to require substantiation. No doubt there are good reasons for the survival
in all these cases of communal responsibility. For one thing,
as a matter of practical expediency, very often the only way
to stop subversive religious and political activities is by
striking at the group in which they originate as a whole. To
try to confine measures to those individuals who can be proved
guilty would make the defence of the system in power impossible. For another thing, it is a fact that the attitude of
one member of a group is apt to influence that of another.
Even modern parents who are in favour of individual responsibility in law frequently take part in social ostracism of a
family a member of which has committed theft, afraid lest
the other members may have caught some of the spirit of
the actual offender and give it to their children. In matters
of religion and politics the danger of heretical ideas being
contagious is particularly strong. In contradistinction to
communal responsibility, ruler punishment may well occur
in a completely non-religious, or secularized, and non-political
sphere, while no less usual than communal responsibility in
religion and politics.[52] For the punishment of a ruler by
damaging or destroying his free subjects may be an effective
mode of punishment whether the offence committed is religious
(such as David's census, for which he was punished by a
pestilence) or political (such as a war made by a dictator or
a rebellion made by a pretender, for which the punishment
might consist in a decimation of his subjects) or private (such
as a builder's miscalculation that causes the death of a child,
for which in Babylonian law he was punished by his own
child's death); and again, this may be an effective mode of
punishment whether the ruler in question is a communally
responsible body (such as the Egyptians when they lost each
his firstborn son, or the house of David—if we regard his
entire house as the object of God's anger—that was to be impoverished by the pestilence) or an individual (such as David
when he lost the child borne to him by Bath-sheba). In other

words, ruler punishment may be of importance even where it is individuals, not a group of people, on whom interest is focused.

Thus, the decay of communal responsibility and the decay of ruler punishment take place at different times and in different ways—though, indeed, they may happen to coincide in a particular case. Ruler punishment may well persist where there is no trace of communal responsibility. In the Code of Hammurabi and the Assyrian and Hittite codes we have found several examples, the builder, the man who hurts a woman with child, the married man who rapes an unmarried woman, the murderer who gives a few substitutes to the wronged family; and in the *Mishpatim* ruler punishment seems to be just abolished. Yet there are few signs in these legislations of the idea that the whole community is answerable for, and corrupted by, the crime of one. Again, communal responsibility may well persist where no trace is left of ruler punishment. In Deuteronomy, communal responsibility in case of a murdered man being found near a town is just abolished; and it is still present in the law, quoted above, under which an idolatrous town is to be razed to the ground, and other laws, such as the rule that he who builds a house must make a battlement round the roof, 'that thou bring not blood upon thine house if any man fall from thence'.[53] Yet there are few signs in the laws of Deuteronomy of ruler punishment.

With the history and background of the two ideas so different, it becomes essential to ask questions such as: Against which idea is the famous injunction 'The fathers shall not be put to death for the children...' directed,[54] communal responsibility or ruler punishment? Or against both? Which idea had the prophets in mind when they prophesied Israel's downfall to its wicked kings?[55] Did they mean that the kings would be punished for their sins by their people's ruin (ruler punishment)? Or that the whole people would have to answer for the sins committed by its rulers (communal responsibility)? Or both? Which is the idea chiefly underlying the curse pronounced upon Adam? In the treatment of original sin by ancient and medieval writers, when is the idea of communal responsibility predominant and when that of ruler punishment? I suppose that the distinction suggested above[56] would be found to play a great part here: where a writer has chiefly in mind Adam himself, the curse is apt to assume the form of ruler punishment, Adam being punished by his descendants having to labour and die; where a writer has chiefly in mind the descendants, the curse is apt to assume the form of communal responsibility, the whole of mankind being tainted by, and answerable for, the sin committed by one of them. Even in the treatment of salvation through Jesus, similar trends are observable. A writer considering the doctrine from the point of view of Jesus will say that God pardoned mankind for the sake of Jesus—ruler reward; a writer considering the doctrine from the point of view of mankind will say that mankind itself was affected, purified, by Jesus' action—communal merit. These questions could be multiplied only too easily. We shall never understand the distribution of responsibility in any regime or the meaning of certain penalties so long as we mix up communal responsibility and ruler punishment. In fact, we shall never understand the structure of a society and the interpretation put upon it by its philosophers and historians without appreciating the difference between the two things. One word of warning, however, may not be amiss since I myself, in order to avoid problems too hard for me, have not here heeded it. Both communal responsibility and ruler punishment are phenomena so near the vital interests of a society that it would be too much to expect the society concerned to be quite clear, or even outspoken, about them. In examining the sources, therefore, we have to attempt to find out how far the interpretation given fits the facts. One tribe may have exterminated another because the aims of its chieftain seemed dangerous or simply because it possessed desirable pastures. But the historians of the victorious tribe might invent, or dwell on, a crime perpetrated by one member of the vanquished tribe, and justify the war by the principle of communal responsibility. Or the facts may be that a father is pursued by bad luck, which, in a patriarchic society, must reflect on the children. There is a temptation here for lookers-on to describe these indirect consequences as a deserved punishment of the father, as ruler punishment. Enough of this—the complications possible, and even normal, are many and not easy to tackle.

The thesis here advanced applies to non-Jewish sources as well as to Jewish. There is a vast amount of modern literature dealing with the family curse in Greek sagas, for example, and it all suffers from the defect that ruler punishment is not distinguished from communal responsibility: wherever a third person is hurt in consequence of the punishment of a crime, communal responsibility is the label most readily attached to the case. In a recent book on Aeschylus, the author says,[57] with reference to the curse lying on the house of Atreus, that originally 'for those who think in terms of communal responsibility, a father is, so to speak, directly affected by the suffering of his son'. The truth is that in the sagas of the house of Atreus, as in many others, there are two ideas playing each an important part: the idea that any member of the house is responsible for the sins committed by any other, and the idea that a father and, particularly, the first founder of a house may be punished by the destruction of his 'property', his descendants. These ideas sometimes are almost blended into one; sometimes this may be in the foreground; sometimes that. (I have repeatedly mentioned that, where a family curse is announced to the first founder of a house, it is often his punishment as 'owner' of the house that receives the emphasis, whereas in the descriptions of the working out of the curse, in the descriptions of the later generations, it is the membership of a corrupted family, communal fate, that stands in the foreground.) But the distinction ought to be recognized—be it only in order that we may draw the right conclusions as to the structure of the group in question and the view that ancient writers took of it. To leave the topic of family curse, the same author adduces the first book of the *Iliad* as an illustration of communal responsibility,[58] following, in this, the universally accepted interpretation. He is right, but he misses just a subtle element. For the army is visited by a pestilence not only because they must all suffer for the grave sin committed by some of them (though this is the main reason); but also (though this is here only a very secondary motif) because this decimation of the army is a terrible blow for the actual sinners, the sons of Atreus, the leaders of the war. The latter element comes from the domain of ruler punishment.

Notes

CHAPTER IV

1 Genesis xviii. 20 ff.

2 Neither here nor anywhere else in this study do I mean to suggest that the communal principle was at any time applied to every kind of community or offence. It would, however, lead too far afield to go into the question of its scope. I may remark that expediency seems to play a large part in the delimitation of the principle.

3 To quote a very different author, Romanelli also, in his *Massa' ba-'Arab* 14, first half, alludes to Abraham's argument as in favour of individual responsibility, preservation of the good and punishment of the bad. He describes how Muley Yazid entered Tetuan as ruler in 1789 and planned to have all Jews killed; but one of his counsellors warned him: 'That be far from thee to slay the righteous with the wicked. Shall not the judge according to the law of Mohammed do right? Let thy hand be upon them that rebel against thee.'

4 So we learn from Genesis xix. 12 ff.

5 After Korah's revolt also, those who wished to avoid destruction had to go away from his and his men's tents (Numbers xvi. 23 ff.). As we shall presently see, however, in that case it was individual responsibility on which Moses and Aaron insisted from the outset.

6 Numbers xvi. **7** Deuteronomy xxiv. 16.

8 But I should like once again to call attention to what I have said in the second note of this study, as to the limitations of the communal principle.

9 For, obviously, to decide that the contract gave the Jew no drop of blood was an interpretation, not genuinely literal, but sophistic and chosen with the object of helping one party and crossing the other.

10 *Kampf ums Recht*, first published 1872, 22nd ed. 1925, pp. 59 f.

11 *Shakespeare vor dem Forum der Jurisprudenz*, 1883, p. 90.

12 Genesis xviii. 23 ff. **13** xxi. 1 ff.

14 II Samuel xxiv, I Chronicles xxi. **15** See pp. 173 f.

16 Isaiah xi. 6. **17** Ezekiel xxxvii. 24.

18 In medieval and modern Jewish literature, however, the verse appears where communal responsibility proper is to be combated. Romanelli, in *Massa' ba-'Arab* 14, first half, says that when in 1789 the new emperor of Morocco expressed the wish to have all Jews killed, one of his counsellors told him: 'Let thy hand be against them that wrong thee; but these sheep, what have they done?'

19 II Samuel xii. 13 ff. To anyone doubting David's piety on account of his crimes let Dr Johnson make answer: 'Sir, are you so grossly ignorant of human nature as not to know that a man may be very sincere in good principles, without having good practice?'

20 II Samuel xii. 11 f., xvi. 22.

21 I need hardly point out that the position of women in a harem was something between freedom and slavery in most respects.

22 Again, as in II Samuel xxiv. 17 and I Chronicles xxi. 17, the idea of innocent helplessness is predominant.

23 Exodus xxi. 29 ff. Cp. above, pp. 105 f.

24 Paragraphs 229 f.

25 D. H. Müller, *Die Gesetze Hammurabis und ihr Verhältnis zur mosaischen Gesetzgebung*, 1903, pp. 166 ff.

26 See above, p. 86. I have also pointed out before (see pp. 98 f.) that the assumption of various strata in a code of the Pentateuch is not necessarily in conflict with orthodox Jewish teaching. For it is nowhere denied that there are elements in the Pentateuch which can be found also in other systems and may go back to a period long before the final giving of the Torah.

27 According to D. H. Müller, *op. cit.*, p. 168, what the rule under notice does is 'to shift the guilt from the parents to the children' (*die Schuld von den Eltern ab und den Kindern zuzuwälzen*). This explanation is quite wrong, but only to be expected so long as ruler punishment is not distinguished from communal responsibility.

28 Exodus xxi. 23 ff. See above, pp. 105 f.

29 Par. 49.   **30** Par. 54.   **31** Par. 210.

32 Cp. D. H. Müller, *op. cit.*, pp. 152 f.

33 Exodus xi f.   **34** II Kings xiii. 25.

35 Exodus xxi. 22. See above, p. 108.

36 Exodus xxi. 37 (xxii. 1).

37 Cp. above, for a detailed discussion of the *lex talionis*, pp. 102 ff.

38 I. 1. See above, p. 116.

39 I. 10.   **40** I. 2.

41 See, *e.g.*, H. Mitteis, *Lehnrecht und Staatsgewalt*, 1933, pp. 586 ff.; and especially p. 586, n. 188, where the author warns us against assuming that a certain gift of vassals in the eleventh century could not have taken place unless the vassals were unfree.

42 I Chronicles xxi. 3, 7. But in Samuel as well as Chronicles the opening verse of the narrative speaks of Israel as the object of God's anger: II Samuel xxiv. 1, I Chronicles xxi. 1.

43 Genesis xxvi. 10.   **44** Genesis xii. 17, xx. 9, 17 f.

45 See above, pp. 169 f.

46 I Samuel ii. 32.   **47** II Samuel xii. 10.

48 A number of Jewish authorities, ancient and living, hold that the penalty of *Kareth*, which, according to the Torah, is inflicted by God for certain most grave transgressions, consists in the offender's house being doomed to eventual extirpation. I am convinced that an analysis of their remarks would show that the notion of ruler punishment plays a very great part. (On the probable origin of the penalty, see Daube, *Symbolae Friburgenses in honorem Ottonis Lenel*, 1931, pp. 249 ff.)

49 Genesis xxii. 17.

50 There is another passage in the Bible where God is asked to attack a man directly and not by striking at his subjects, Job ii. 4 f. But the request there springs from a very different attitude. David asked God to punish him personally and not by slaying his subjects, because he no longer regarded his subjects as like dead property. In Job, Satan asks God to torture the hero personally and not by slaying his family, because he knows that having one's body hurt is worse for most men than losing one's property, even the dearest: the idea that it is not right to treat free subjects as 'property' and to hit the 'owner' by damaging them is not here present at all.

51 'I talked of the little attachment', Boswell records, 'which subsisted between near relations in London. "Sir, (said Johnson,) in a country so commercial as ours, where every man can do for himself, there is not so much occasion for that attachment. No man is thought the worse of here, whose brother was hanged."'

52 I must apologize for using the terms 'religious' and 'political' in their traditional, popular sense. I am fully aware, of course, that, say, a husband's *potestas* over his wife and children has religious and political foundations; and that, from this point of view, any ruler punishment (even, for example, the provision that a builder who causes the death of another man's child is to lose his own) is religious and political.

53 xxii. 8.

54 Deuteronomy xxiv. 16. Cp. II Kings xiv. 6, Ezekiel xviii (in particular xviii. 19 f.).

55 *E.g.* II Kings xxi. 10 ff.   **56** See p. 179.

57 B. Daube, *Zu den Rechtsproblemen in Aischylos' Agamemnon*, 1938, p. 156. The words are: *In solcher Denkform* (referring to the most ancient view of *Kollektivhaftung*, communal responsibility) *wird der Vater gleichsam direkt betroffen, wenn der Sohn leidet.*

58 *Loc. cit.*

CHAPTER V

SUMMUM IUS—SUMMA INIURIA

I

WHEREVER there exists any kind of administration of justice, people will soon realize that a man who makes, or receives, a declaration has to be very careful if he wants to be quite sure of its ultimate legal effect; and the same, of course, is true of all manner of legal business. A man may believe that the promise he is giving has one meaning, but later be told by the judge that it has another; or he may enter into an agreement on the assumption of the existence of certain facts, which afterwards turn out not to be as assumed. There are many ways in which such a discrepancy between *verba* and *voluntas*, or letter and spirit, or act and intent, can come about; and a not infrequent one seems to be that the two parties to a contract wish to cheat one another. Very naturally, the temptation to take advantage of a person's lack of forethought must be particularly great in an age when it is permissible to interpret the words of an agreement in a strict and narrow fashion, and when a formal undertaking is considered valid no matter by what trickery you have been led to give it. The Spartan king, Cleomenes, concluded a truce with Argos for thirty days; but he broke it by night, the truce having been made for thirty *days*. Q. Fabius Labeo, for the Roman senate, arbitrated a boundary dispute between Nola and Naples. He interviewed the parties separately, appealed to their generosity and induced them to make substantial concessions. In the end, there was a large strip of territory left between Nola and Naples, which Labeo awarded to Rome. By the time of Cicero, both these cases were regarded as cases of fraud and as illustrating the maxim *summum ius summa iniuria*.[1] The jurists had come to see that an over-subtle, over-scrupulous construction of the law produced results no different from those that would spring from lawlessness. *Existunt etiam saepe iniuriae calumnia quadam et nimis callida sed malitiosa iuris interpre-*

tatione; ex quo illud 'summum ius summa iniuria' factum est iam tritum sermone proverbium. The history in Roman law of the problem of *verba* and *voluntas* has been the subject of much discussion during the past few years. I may, perhaps, be forgiven for drawing attention to a Biblical narrative which is dominated by this problem, though the commentators do not appear to have noticed it. It is the story of the sale of his birthright by Esau.[2]

It should be observed that four at least of the other tales of Jacob culminate in the appeal by the subtler disputant to those rigid, formalistic principles which may so often be found governing the legal or religious transactions of ancient peoples. There is, to begin with, the story of the blessing.[3] Of his two sons, Isaac preferred Esau; it was Esau on whom he intended to confer his best blessing. But Isaac was blind; and Jacob, whose skin was smooth, made himself hairy like his brother, by covering his hands with the skins of goats. Then he asked his father for his blessing. Isaac, indeed, touched him to make certain that it was Esau. He was misled, however, by the hairy skins of goats, and gave his best blessing to Jacob. When he discovered the truth, it was too late: the blessing once uttered was beyond recall. This is an obvious case of error as to identity, an error, moreover, induced by sheer fraud. Yet it pays the deceiver to deceive, since what he obtains in the proper form cannot subsequently be taken from him. Rabbinic attempts to blunt the edge of this story—for example, by saying that the blessing was valid only since ratified by Isaac after he was informed of the fraud[4]—indicate the legal and moral progress made between the period when the story was composed and the Talmudic era; and unquestionably when we make use of the story as part of the whole Biblical system of religion, we have to adopt the Rabbinic explanations. But they cannot alter the original significance of the narrative.

None the less, Jacob went not unpunished. Nemesis ordained that he himself should be tricked into an error as to identity and have to abide the result.[5] For seven years he served Laban, being promised the hand of the latter's younger daughter, the lovely Rachel, as his reward. At last the wedding-feast was celebrated. But at night, when he was to receive his bride—no

doubt with her veil lowered, according to Oriental custom—
Laban substituted his elder and less beautiful daughter. In
the morning Jacob found himself irrevocably bound to Leah.[6]
The structure of this case is strangely similar to that of the
case of the blessing. It is safe to assume that the original
audience did connect the two stories and enjoy so striking an
instance of exact retaliation. They may well have chuckled
even over such details as that whilst Jacob's stratagem was
to act his elder brother, he in his turn was deceived by Leah's
acting her younger sister.

In the next two narratives here to be adduced the point is
the deriving advantage from an overstrict, artificially literal
interpretation of a contract or statement. Some time after
Jacob's wedding, a new arrangement was made between him
and his father-in-law.[7] Jacob agreed—most generously, it
seemed to Laban—to continue to look after Laban's flocks
without getting any share of them. One thing only he demanded. All spotted goats should be removed from the main
stock: it would be very few, the Syrian goats being nearly all
brown. They should be kept at a distance of a three days'
journey and be taken care of by Laban himself, in order to
make impossible any interbreeding between them and the
main stock. If after that any spotted goats were born amongst
those entrusted to Jacob, an extremely unlikely contingency
in the ordinary course of nature, they should be his. Jacob
carefully observed the letter of the agreement. He never laid
hands on a brown goat; he never coupled the brown goats
with spotted ones. Yet, by some clever devices,[8] such as
placing coloured rods in the drinking troughs during the
breeding season, he caused the strongest of Laban's animals
to bring forth spotted kids. As the contract, or rather, the
express words of it, did not provide against this, Laban could
only look on helplessly. The fourth narrative of this kind will
be discussed at length below;[9] but the point here of interest
may be summarized. The Bible tells us how, eventually, Jacob
fled from his employer, taking his family with him; and in
the course of the negotiations that followed, he once more
benefited by the fact that it was the letter of a declaration,
not its apparent, natural meaning, which counted. As she

was running away with her husband, Rachel carried off her father's idols. Laban after a hot pursuit overtook the fugitives and accused them of theft. Jacob, however, vehemently repudiated the charge, swearing: 'With whomsoever thou findest thy gods, he shall not live.' A terrible curse this was. Yes; but, as the Bible repeats no less than three times, Laban was not able to *find* the idols. The curse consigning to death him with whom they were *found* could not, therefore, produce any ill effects.

There is yet a further story worth mentioning in this connection. For, though the case recorded is neither one of error nor one of strict interpretation of a statement, yet it does clearly presuppose the absolute validity of solemn pronouncements. I am referring to Jacob's wrestling, in a lonely night, with a mysterious stranger.[10] Towards morning, the stranger asked Jacob to let him go: spirits of the night must vanish at dawn. Jacob, however, held him fast till he had extracted a blessing from him. The blessing was none the less valid for being given under duress.

It is submitted that the story of the acquisition by Jacob of Esau's birthright belongs to the same class as the four cases of fraud discussed, Jacob receiving Esau's blessing, Laban disposing of Leah instead of Rachel, Jacob securing Laban's goats and his oath in the matter of Laban's idols. For what we have before us is a case, not merely of squeezing a famished man (as is generally supposed), but also of dishonesty, of consciously profiting by an error of the other party. According to the commentaries, Esau returned from the hunt hungry and weak, and Jacob availed himself of this opportunity to extort from him his birthright for some paltry lentil soup. But this cannot be all. Even if it were, the narrative would still furnish an example, somewhat parallel to the episode of the wrestling with the stranger until he bestowed a blessing on Jacob, of a declaration being valid though made under great stress. But it is not all. The current interpretation, while correct as far as it goes, leaves four points unexplained: (1) Why did Esau not ask for the lentil soup by name? He asked for 'that red dish'. The explanation sometimes offered that he was so greedy as to be unable to utter the words 'lentil soup' does not seem good enough. (2) Why are we not told in the first part of the story that the dish in question was lentil soup? It is not till right at the end that the nature of the dish is revealed. No real explanation of this odd feature has been attempted. (3) Why did Esau repeat the word 'red'? If we translate literally—as we ought to in a serious analysis of a narrative—he asked for 'that red, red dish'. Minor and major emendations of the text have been proposed, but they are all—emendations. Actually, in this case to emend seems particularly rash, since, according to the Bible, it was because of his use at that juncture of the word 'red' that Esau received the name 'Edom'; to this I shall come back presently. (4) Above all, why did Esau remark on a later occasion, namely, on discovering how Jacob had obtained their father's blessing, that Jacob 'had overreached him twice', once when he took from him his birthright and another time when he secured the blessing?[11] According to the usual interpretation, Jacob did not resort to fraud when he made Esau part with his birth-right. Yet, the Hebrew verb here rendered by 'to overreach', עקב, distinctly refers to sly and crooked behaviour.[12] Indeed, a derivative of the verb, עקבה, 'subtlety, fraud', seems to be used to denote the attitude of one who makes an ambiguous, misleading declaration, a declaration, that is, not dissimilar to that of the Roman general who concluded an armistice for thirty *days*.[13] Moreover, Esau himself paired off the case of the birthright with that of the blessing as though the essential features were the same. No solution of this difficulty has been advanced.

Let us briefly examine the story. An introductory note informs us that Esau was a huntsman, fond of venison, whereas Jacob was an ordinary shepherd. After this, the main part of the tale begins. One day Jacob boiled a certain dish. He had hardly finished when Esau arrived in a state of exhaustion and begged to be allowed 'to gulp some of that red, red food'. As observed above, he did not call the dish by its name, nor, at this stage, is there any remark in the narrative to enlighten us, the readers, on the subject. It is reasonable to conclude that Esau was ignorant of the nature of the dish; and that, at this stage, we also, the readers, are not meant to know, though, indeed, we are meant to suspect, that something is wrong. What, then, did Esau think Jacob was preparing? Red, in Hebrew literature, as in most others, is the colour of blood.[14] The Hebrew word for 'red', in particular, is not only etymologically connected with that for 'blood',[15] but also of a very similar sound: אדם signifies 'red', דם 'blood'. Esau, in his request, repeated the word. In fact, the word being אדם, '*adom*, he was called אדום, '*Edom*, the Bible says, for ever after. It must have been the colour of blood that struck him and roused his desire. It should be noted that he asked, not to be given 'to eat' or 'to drink' (אכל or שתה), but to be given 'to gulp'. The Hebrew word, לעט, suggests bestial wildness.[16] Besides, we have been told at the beginning of the story that Esau was greedy of venison. Evidently, he thought that Jacob was preparing a blood-broth, a dish to which antiquity ascribed special powers of reviving a tired body and the fare, it may be recalled, of the Spartan warriors.

It is probably superfluous to point out that we must not ask why Esau, if he thought it was blood-broth, did not explicitly state that he wanted blood-broth. For had he done so, there would have been no story to tell. The word 'blood-broth' would have appeared in the agreement, and Jacob in that case could not, of course, have performed his part by serving lentil soup. As it was, Esau bought 'that red, red dish', when, on the letter of the contract, Jacob's position was safe. We need only remember how important it is even under our present-day law not to point at an object displayed in the shop window, but to buy by description and make quite clear the purpose for which we are buying the article in question (since only if we observe these precautions have we any prospect of redress should the object acquired disappoint our expectations) to see what an enormous difference it would have made if Esau had expressed himself more accurately, and how shockingly careless he was.

To go on with the story, whether Jacob merely made the best of an unexpected chance, or whether, as is more likely, he had already planned the fraud when he started cooking the dish, is of small moment. Next in the narrative comes the preliminary agreement between the brothers. Jacob said Esau

might have the dish, provided he would give his birthright
in exchange; and Esau replied that he had no objection to this
bargain. (The word used for Esau's part in the bargain is
מכר, 'to sell'. He 'sells' his birthright for Jacob's dish. This
confirms, what we know from other texts[17] and what would
be likely even without positive textual evidence, that ancient
Hebrew law, or at least ancient Hebrew language, did not
make the Roman technical distinction between *emptio ven-
ditio*, the sale of an object for a price in money, and *permutatio*,
the exchange of one object for another. The verb מכר, 'to
sell', is applied even where the price is not in money.) With
this informal agreement, however, Jacob was by no means yet
content. Esau, he insisted, must renounce his birthright by
a solemn oath; indeed, he must take this oath before he could
have his meal. This little incident is not without significance.
Had Jacob been satisfied with a purely informal agreement,
Esau, it is to be supposed, would have made no scruple, so
soon as he noticed the swindle, to declare the whole transaction
null and void. But an oath, Jacob knew, would remove any
danger of this sort; it would lift the contract into the realm
of the absolute; and Esau's promise would stand regardless of
the means used in eliciting it. One is reminded of the famous
instance of *dolus* recorded by Cicero.[18] The owner of a villa on
the shore of a lake invited a prospective buyer to dinner. On
the day of the visit, he got a large number of people to row
about on the lake pretending to be catching fish, and the guest
declared himself ready to pay a high price for the house.
A simple, informal sale, however, was not what the owner
wanted. For sale gave a so-called *bonae fidei iudicium*. This
meant that, in any law-suit arising out of a sale, the judge
would have to take into account not only the agreement itself,
but also the accompanying circumstances, and to deliver the
fairest decision possible. The fraudulent vendor of the villa,
therefore, could never, on the basis of a mere, informal sale,
have hoped to succeed in enforcing payment. For this reason
he suggested to the buyer that they should at once confirm
the sale by a formal 'literal contract'. A 'literal contract'
gave a *stricti iuris iudicium*. It was a transaction, that is,
which—at any rate, at the time when the case under notice

occurred—had to be treated by the judge as fully valid even if it had clearly been brought about by fraud. The visitor agreed thus to confirm the sale. Accordingly, though it did not take him long to detect that there was no fish in the lake, he had no choice but to pay the sum promised. It would lead too far afield here to raise the question why legal systems find it useful to have forms of contract or declaration which, once gone through, cannot be challenged on the normal grounds. Suffice it to say that, in ancient Hebrew law, an oath was at least as radical a confirmation of an agreement as a 'literal contract' was in Rome.

Esau swore the oath as required. Only now do we learn, only now did he learn, what Jacob had in his pot: lentil soup. So it was for that that he had bartered away his birthright! The complete silence of Esau upon finding himself outwitted, and his doing nothing but very ordinary actions, are most impressive and almost introduce into the story a touch of the tragic. There is an interesting stylistic parallel to this 'and he ate and drank and rose and went, and thus Esau despised his birthright',[19] at the close of the chapter of Saul's visit to the witch of Endor. This narrative, full of the most dramatic events and describing how Saul heard of his and his sons' death to take place the next day, ends with the simple words, 'and they ate and rose and went that night'.[20] But there was no redress for Esau. Well might they call him 'Edom' after the colour, red, that had led him into the trap. Well might he remember this piece of deception when Jacob later overreached him once again and snatched the blessing that ought to have gone to the huntsman.

On that coupling by Esau of the two cases, a word may here be added. We have seen that in both stories, that of the birthright as well as that of the blessing, the misleading a man in order to profit by his error is a prominent feature. Regarding the question what exactly was the type of error committed, it is true, modern text-books would distinguish. Isaac's error when blessing Jacob, as has already been noted, may be described as an error as to the identity of the person before him. Esau's, on the face of it at least, was an error as to the qualities of the subject-matter of the contract. It is highly doubtful, however, whether this distinction played any part in the minds of the old hearers of these tales. To them, if they speculated on the point at all, it may well have appeared that, fundamentally, it was a matter of simulation, assuming another person's identity, both times. That they must have classed as impersonation Jacob's conduct in the affair of the blessing, when he presented himself as Esau to his blind father, is obvious. (Needless to repeat, the case of Leah replacing Rachel in the night of the wedding is precisely analogous.) But it should be remarked that Jacob, in a sense, adopted the guise of Esau even when, in the affair of the birthright, he had to deal with Esau himself. He made what resembled a blood-broth, the kind of dish that would normally be prepared by Esau, who had an immoderate craving for it. It may be said that Jacob seemed to be hairy, like his wild brother, when he asked Isaac for his blessing; he seemed to be boiling a blood-broth, in the manner of his wild brother, when he bought the birthright from that very brother. This close analogy may, indeed, be due to mere coincidence. But I am much more inclined to think that we can trace through it a very ancient notion; and that in both stories is reflected the same belief in the virtue of imitation, impersonation, the belief, namely, that, by acting another person, you can succeed to his place.

Be this as it may, it emerges that, on the basis of the interpretation here proposed, the two stories of the blessing and the birthright have their essential features in common: the use made by Jacob of the formalistic principles of ancient law and religion (Isaac's blessing, though brought about by fraud, is irrevocable, and so is Esau's oath), and the exploitation by Jacob of the uncommon lust of his antagonists for venison and blood (Isaac loves, and ascribes special powers to,[21] his hairy son's venison, and Esau asks to be given 'to gulp that red, red food'). Actually, we should perhaps speak of one essential feature only. For, ultimately, the use made by Jacob of the formalistic principles and the exploitation by him of his antagonists' lust for venison are the consequence of, and meant to illustrate, one and the same thing: the superiority of Jacob, the 'plain man dwelling in tents', over his hunting brother.

Jacob, experienced in the subtleties of 'jurisprudence' and 'theology', beats Esau, with his primitive, stupid appetites.

This result, the fact that the two stories of the blessing and the birthright are, on my interpretation, centred upon the same ideas or idea, seems to me to be greatly in my favour; not only because, as already mentioned, the Bible itself classes both incidents under one heading, as cases of fraud, but, possibly, also for the following consideration. In the Bible as it stands, the two stories are separate stories, one following the other: first Jacob managed to make Esau sell him his birthright, then he managed to make Isaac confer on him the blessing which had been intended for the firstborn. There is here a problem. One of the two stories looks superfluous. If the purchase of the birthright from Esau gave Jacob the rank of the firstborn, why did he exert himself to get that special blessing? Conversely, if a way could be found of getting that special blessing, why did he exert himself to buy the birthright from Esau? In Rabbinic literature, a number of suggestions are made designed to show why both transactions were requisite (few difficulties escaped the notice of the Rabbis), and I do not say that they are absolutely untenable. Yet surely there is a strong possibility that the two incidents at some date were not told as following one another, but that each was told as a complete, sufficient explanation and justification of the prominent position of Jacob; that they were, in fact, two versions of what had been one account of the origin of Jacob's good fortune. If this is so, it furnishes an additional argument for the interpretation of the story of the birthright here advanced. For if this is so, we have to ask what was the gist of the original account, and on the basis of my interpretation an answer can be given: the original account of the beginning of Jacob's pre-eminence in some way or other represented Jacob as availing himself of the weakness of his opponents, of Esau's and Isaac's blind fondness of game and helplessness in regard to the intricacies of a formalistic regime. The present two versions, of the birthright and of the blessing, grew out of this single account. In the process, they became more and more different from one another. The story of the birthright, for example, became an explanation of the name Edom as well as of Jacob's hegemony. But the principal traits of the original account were retained; and the upshot of the one is still so much like that of the other—Jacob's acquisition of the rights of the firstborn—that their appearance in the Bible as successive events remains a stumbling-block. This is not attacking the orthodox doctrine of Judaism. I am not maintaining that the events did not happen exactly as recorded. The question of the growth of the tales of Jacob and the question of the events lying behind them are two different matters. I have dealt only with the former.

In conclusion, a word of warning may be useful. No greater mistake can be made than to argue that, since the narratives here reviewed—the stories of Jacob and Laban and Jacob and Esau—invariably lead up to the triumph of the party abusing certain formalistic principles of law, the characters described, and even the authors of the descriptions, must have been primitive men who did not see the flaws in their system. The exact opposite is true. The impostors celebrated in these anecdotes knew very well what they were doing—so did Till Eulenspiegel when he became apprenticed to a baker, asked the unnecessary question what he should bake, received the angry answer 'Owls and monkeys', and did bake owls and monkeys instead of bread—their victims knew very well how they had been trapped, and the story-tellers what elements formed the mainspring of the plot. The mere fact that such incidents were taken note of and handed down, as tragedies or comedies, from one generation to the other, is sufficient proof of this; and it is doubly proved by the very subtle manner in which the tales are told. Those people were wide awake to the problem of *verba* and *voluntas* and similar difficulties. The proper question for us to pose is not, 'Why did they not see that there might be an alternative to that strict, pedantic kind of law?' (though this seems the usual question to ask nowadays, explicitly or implicitly), but, 'Why did they apply, in some branches of the law at least, those strict, formalistic principles although they were fully aware—for I repeat, they were—of the possibility of unjust results?' It is not intended here to attempt an answer.

II

It is generally assumed that *vestigii minatio*, the hot pursuit of a thief and the search of his house under certain formalities, was a practice peculiar to ancient Indo-European systems. (The expression *vestigii minatio*, to be found, for instance, in the *Lex Salica*,[22] may be admitted in this study on account of its brevity.) *La chasse au voleur correspond à des pratiques répandues chez tous les Indo-Européens, et probablement anté-rieures à l'époque des grandes migrations*—thus a scholar sums up what has since become a widely accepted view.[23] It is on the basis of this theory that historians continue carefully to collect all traces of *vestigii minatio* that can be detected in Indo-European sources.[24] Without detracting from the value of these works, it may be questioned whether the premisses from which they proceed are tenable. Quite apart from the fact that the connection between the Indo-European peoples is one of language rather than of common descent or common civilization—at least we are very much in the dark concerning the latter two points—it ought to be borne in mind that there are certain customs likely to grow up whenever and wherever a certain stage of political and economic development is reached; customs, that is, determined less by the specific characteristics of a race than by material environment.

Vestigii minatio may well be one of them. If a man has been with me and after he has gone I miss a valuable object, the natural thing for me to do is to follow him whether I am Indo-European or Semitic. It is not only that my first impulse will dictate this procedure. There are special reasons for taking immediate steps in the case of theft—as contrasted, say, with the case of my visitor smashing a vase or killing an ox of mine. In the case of theft, unless I catch the thief in the act, the difficulties of proof will increase considerably. The thief will take care to dispose of the stolen thing. Moreover, even if he does not and is discovered in possession of it at some later date, he will probably have prepared some excuse or other: for witnesses of the offence there are usually none. It may be recalled that, as I have shown above,[25] the earliest version of the *Mishpatim* regarded theft of an animal as proved only if the thief had sold or slaughtered it, not if it was still alive in his possession. All these problems can be avoided, at all events mitigated, if I catch the thief on the spot, or failing this—and here *vestigii minatio* comes in—if I go after him while the scent is hot. He will have no time to get rid of his booty nor, when caught within a very short space of time, will he have many convincing excuses at his disposal. *Vestigii minatio*, so to speak, extends the period during which I can catch a thief red-handed, without being faced by all the complications that accumulate once there is a definite interval between act and accusation; or as the Romans might have put it (and did very nearly put it, as will be seen later on[26]), *vestigii minatio* serves to keep the theft *manifestum*, fresh, easy to prove. Clearly, we should not be surprised to find this recognized in any system, Indo-European or other, prior to the time when the existence of a modern numerous police force rendered the question of proving theft very much easier. On the other hand, intruding into a man's house always was and still is regarded as a serious offence all over the world. We may therefore expect that, if a thief once reaches his home without being caught, any system, Indo-European or other, will prescribe a ceremonial to be observed by the pursuer in pushing his claim. No law would allow you to enter my premises at any time of the day or night and in any manner that you choose, under the pretext that you suspect me of having robbed you. The ceremonial prescribed may vary in many respects according to the character of a people, the material and moral state of civilization and historical accidents. But it will normally include measures to parry chicanery or even fraud on the part of the accuser and, on the other hand, to ensure the conviction of the accused if guilty.

The Bible contains three instances of *vestigii minatio*: Laban's pursuit of Jacob whose wife had stolen his idols,[27] Joseph's pursuit of Benjamin with the object of convicting him of the theft of his cup,[28] and Micah's pursuit of the Danites who had stolen an image and other sacred objects from his sanctuary.[29] The former two cases both culminate in the triumph of the fraudulent party who knows how to make use of the inflexible, formalistic principles of law and religion. I shall devote to

them most of the remaining part of this study, though ven-
turing to turn aside here and there and deal at some length
with the way in which problems and ideas similar to those
governing the Biblical narratives reappear far away, in Roman
law. Before starting on this inquiry, however, let us cast a
glance at the third case, Micah's pursuit of the Danites. There
is little to say about it since it came to a premature end; but
even the little may be worth setting down.

First, the objects stolen by the Danites were sacred things,
Micah's 'graven image, and the ephod, and the idols, and
the molten image'. (Might we add the priest looking after
them? He was invited to come with them, and, realizing
that the thieves were many and Micah's friends few, accepted.)
Rachel also stole sacred things, Laban's idols, and Benjamin
was accused of stealing the cup with the help of which Joseph
practised divination. This is more than sheer coincidence. It
is indeed doubtful whether we are entitled to infer that *vestigii
minatio* was limited to theft of holy things, and that if a minor
type of theft had been committed, the victim had to institute
the ordinary, slower, less war-like proceedings. But it is safe
to infer that theft of anything sacred was deemed a particularly
grave offence and, on the other hand, that sacred things were
favourite objects of theft, were in great demand. In support,
I would refer to Achan's theft of some of the booty of Jericho,[30]
which had been withdrawn from secular commerce—accursed
or consecrated. His punishment is well known, though it is true
that there were exceptional elements in the situation. I may
also mention that, while the *Mishpatim* have no special rules
on theft of holy things, other Oriental codes have.[31] Secondly,
Micah started on his pursuit immediately on noticing the theft,
which was, it seems, the same day. In a system that has
vestigii minatio, it is reasonable to set a time limit after which
ordinary proceedings only can be instituted. The whole point
and justification of *vestigii minatio* is that the offence is not yet
really completed: the thief is still in the act, in a sense, and
self-help therefore still admissible. But, obviously, there is less
to be said for *vestigii minatio*, for example, when a year or two
have elapsed since the crime was committed. In this case, the
normal routine of justice—whatever it may be, a meeting of the

clans or a court of elders or the like—is to be preferred. At any rate, Micah began his pursuit the same day that the theft was committed. It does not follow that the time limit was one day or less. It may have been a week or so—I shall have to return to this question in discussing the affair of Laban's idols.[32] But that there was some time limit is probable. Thirdly, Micah took his neighbours with him. The importance of witnesses throughout a *vestigii minatio* is easily explained. The aim of *vestigii minatio* is to keep the theft *manifestum*, to get the thief red-handed, so to speak, although he has already left the place, to get him, that is, in such a way that the evidence is crushing, and to deal with him ás one caught in the act. For this witnesses are indispensable. It would not do to allow you to come to me unaccompanied, slay or otherwise ill-treat me, and later, when my relatives or I go to law, defend yourself by saying that I had robbed you. That would make it too easy for anyone to murder his enemy without risk of punishment. No, if you want to catch me red-handed even though I have already left your place, you have to collect witnesses and, more or less literally, to show them the footprints leading from your stable, which is empty, to mine where I am just shutting up your ox. They are necessary to supervise the proceedings, or there would be nothing to prevent foul play.

There is, however, a further no less important object in calling witnesses, an object that has nothing whatever to do with legal niceties. *Vestigii minatio* is a kind of self-help. The party offended opposes the offender. That is a dangerous undertaking, particularly in an era when a thief caught in the act has to expect severe treatment. A thief pursued by *vestigii minatio* is in a desperate situation and as a rule has little to lose by offering resistance. Obviously, it would not be advisable for a man to pursue a thief without a sufficient number of witnesses, or rather, friends, who could, if need be, defeat the criminal and his men by force of arms. It is interesting to note that the verb used in the narrative under discussion of the 'being summoned' of the neighbours, נִזְעַק, in all the other three texts in which it occurs refers to the 'being summoned' to battle of those liable to military service.[33] So near one another lay the provinces of legal contest and war.

Can we always say with confidence where the one began and the other ended? (Can we always say it in our day?) There is much the same indefiniteness about the ancient Germanic hue and cry or *Gerüft*, and the Greek γόος. Should any further confirmation of this warlike role that the pursuer's friends had to play, and of their necessity for a successful *vestigii minatio*, be required, the story of Micah's pursuit itself provides it. For his pursuit, we are told, ended in a most miserable fashion. The Danites, when he overtook them with his neighbours, simply defied him; they simply told him, 'Let not thy voice be heard among us, lest angry fellows run upon thee, and thou lose thy life, with the lives of thy household.' They did not deny the theft, they did not even excuse it. They just sent him packing—there is no milder word for it. 'And the children of Dan went their way.' They turned their backs on him and went on, without bothering any further. 'And when Micah saw that they were too strong for him, he turned and went back unto his house.' Thus right broke down before might. Our only consolation is—and the point is of some significance— that it was right asserted, not in the ordinary forms of law, but by way of *vestigii minatio*, by way of what might be called legalized self-help.

To proceed now to an examination of Laban's pursuit of Jacob, the Bible records that Jacob and his wives, aware of the resentment evoked by their newly amassed riches, decided to run away from Laban and his clan. As they left, Rachel stole her father's, Laban's, penates. On the third day, Laban was informed of the flight. He immediately collected his kinsmen (the Hebrew word used is אח, 'brother', but it often has the wider meaning of 'kinsman'[34]), followed the fugitives and came up with them after a journey of seven days. Most legal detail occurring up to this point of the narrative has already been referred to. First, Rachel stole her father's idols; she stole sacred objects, that is—a particularly heinous offence. Secondly, Laban started on his pursuit on the third day after the crime and overtook the culprits after another seven days. Possibly this means that he was just in time. I have said that it would be a sensible rule to lay down that *vestigii minatio*, if it was to entitle the pursuer to examine the suspected person's house, had to be entered upon within a short period of the theft. Three days would be a reasonable limit, and so would be a further seven days for the chase itself. Later, the matter would become too uncertain, the crime could no longer be regarded as *manifestum*, and it would be only fair to make the victim of the theft proceed in the ordinary way, with no self-help permitted. Thirdly, Laban took his kinsmen with him. Their dual role as warriors and witnesses is no less noticeable here than in the case from Judges. Laban himself told Jacob that if he did not use force it was only because God had warned him not to do so in the previous night.[35] As for the legal side, it is clear from the text that both Laban's and Jacob's kinsmen were present at the search of the latter's tents. When Laban was about to enter them, Jacob said, 'Before our brethren discern thou what is thine with me':[36] the examination of another man's house was a delicate affair, for which witnesses were indispensable. (I have shown above, in a different connection,[37] that the term הכיר, 'to discern', is technical of the formal finding out of, and making a statement about, a piece of evidence, and, in particular, of the formal recognition of one's stolen property in another person's hands. The verb is used of the owner of stolen things 'recognizing' them in a third party's—not the thief's—house in Mishnah Baba Kamma x. 3, though by the time that this provision was laid down *vestigii minatio* was most probably obsolete.) Further, it is Laban's relatives who, together with Jacob's, would have had to pronounce judgment if the images had been discovered. As soon as the search had ended in Laban's failure, Jacob ironically asked him to show any of his property that he had found: 'Set it here before my brethren and thy brethren, that they may judge betwixt us both.'[38]

The most interesting part of the episode, from the point of view of legal history, is the *quaestio* itself, Laban's entry into Jacob's tents and the search. We are told that Laban charged Jacob with theft, and that Jacob replied 'With whomsoever thou findest thy gods, let him not live', or more precisely, 'he shall not live' (the Hebrew being לֹא יחיה). He then invited Laban to go through the tents.[39] Evidently, theft of sacred things, if *manifestum*, or kept *manifestum* by immediate pur-

suit, was a capital crime. This is not surprising. I have shown[40]
that in Hebrew law, originally, any theft seems to have been
considered a capital offence. As regards theft of sacred objects
in particular, it is punishable by death under the Code of
Hammurabi, for instance, even if not *manifestum*; and I have
already referred to Achan who was put to death together with
his whole family for appropriating some of the consecrated
booty of Jericho. As regards *furtum manifestum*, we have seen
that the *Mishpatim*, otherwise not unduly severe in this matter,
allow you to kill a thief caught in the act, even if no sacred
objects are concerned. No wonder, therefore, that in the narrative of Laban's pursuit—as also in that of Joseph's pursuit
of his brothers to be examined below[41]—where both elements,
manifest theft and theft of a sacred object, are combined, the
punishment envisaged should be death.

Maybe Jacob, by saying that the person convicted 'should
not live', meant no more than to promise Laban to kill, or
rather to surrender to be killed, the person convicted. We shall
see below[42] that such a promise was made by Joseph's brothers
when they were accused of having stolen his cup. I incline to
think, however, that Jacob went further; and that the words
'he shall not live' constituted an oath, a curse. He surrendered
the person convicted, not to Laban, but to divine vengeance.
Had he intended only to allow Laban to kill the person convicted, a phrase like מות ימות, 'he shall surely die', or יומת, 'he
shall be killed', would be more natural—as Joseph's brothers
said ומת. (It is true that the injunction 'Thou shalt not let
live' seems equivalent to 'Thou shalt kill' in, say, Exodus
xxii. 17 (18).[43]) Moreover, theft is one of those offences in connection with which oaths had to be taken very frequently
in ancient systems. Theft is always committed in secret, and
the traces of theft can be obliterated more easily than those
of many other delicts. In ancient times, with the police less
efficient than nowadays, to compel a man charged with theft
to take an oath must have been a useful method of overcoming
these difficulties. So long as an oath was deemed to be of
unfailing effectiveness, few thieves would be prepared to risk
it: they would prefer to give up what they had stolen. If an
exceptionally reckless thief did swear falsely, he might indeed

be able to keep his booty; but at least he would know, and his opponents would know, that some day or other divine punishment would surely overtake him. In the *Mishpatim*, we find two provisions enjoining a man to take an oath, or submit to an oracle, to clear himself of the suspicion of being a thief.[44]

Admittedly, in the case of *vestigii minatio* an oath was perhaps less necessary than in most other situations arising out of a theft. For as there took place immediate pursuit of the suspect culminating in an examination of his house, it might well be held that the truth would come to light without an oath: if the man pursued was the thief, it might be held, the missing object would be found, and if it was not found, he was not the thief. In fact, Roman law, as I shall try to show,[45] prescribed no oath in the case of *vestigii minatio*. Nevertheless, in other systems, such as Greek law, an oath was usual even here;[46] and I can think of several reasons why even here it was considered right that the person whose house was to be searched should swear to his innocence. In the first place, I have repeatedly mentioned how close *vestigii minatio* was to a real feud or punitive expedition. A stage can be imagined at which, roughly speaking, the footprints leading from the pursuer's dwelling to that of the pursued were regarded as adequate proof of the latter's guilt; and when the pursuer with his friends simply treated their opponents as *fures manifesti*, without bothering to search their tents or listen to any defence. The introduction of an oath to be sworn by the accused would mean a considerable progress in those circumstances: it was a safeguard against methods too summary, it prevented the pursuer from dealing with the pursued as a *fur manifestus* before he had had any chance of defending himself, it opened the 'legal' part of the proceedings, the search of the house to be followed by a proper judgment. (When I speak of 'the introduction' of this oath, I am not implying that at a definite date people decided that it was better to have it. Much more probably, the development was gradual. The party pursued, if weaker than the pursuers, would try to dissuade them from attack by any means conceivable. The taking of an oath might sometimes help and, in course of time, it became the normal thing to do.) In the second place, an

oath to be taken by the accused before the examination
of his house must be useful once a distinction begins to be
made between theft committed by a *paterfamilias*, a head
of a family, himself, and theft committed by one of his subjects. I shall presently have to say more about this. Here
it is sufficient to point out that a curse pronounced by the
paterfamilias against the guilty person renders it easier, even
if the object in dispute is discovered in his house, to accept
the plea that it was not he who stole it but an irresponsible
member of his household. Certainly, the same effect might be
achieved by the *paterfamilias* declaring himself willing to surrender any guilty subject to the other party, not to divine
vengeance: and we shall find this very rational declaration in
the case of Joseph's brothers.[47] But there may have been a
time when an oath, delivering the guilty person to divine
retribution, was a better, surer method of inducing the pursuers to make a distinction between the *paterfamilias* and some
wicked member of his family.

There is still a third reason why Hebrew law and other Eastern
systems may have prescribed an oath even in *vestigii minatio*,
a reason of a more fundamental nature, extending far beyond
the province of law. It looks as if at some period it had
been considered important that a man who was to die for a sin
or crime should submit to, accept, the sentence. I cannot here
go into the history and ramifications of this idea; it is very
widespread, plays a part in many connections, and much too
little, if any, attention has so far been paid to it. To some
extent, it was probably due to the belief that only if the guilty
man had accepted the verdict would his blood not be upon
those who put him to death.[48] In the case of a person openly
charged with a capital offence, such as one accused of being
a *fur manifestus* of a sacred object, it would be best to have
his consent before the verdict was delivered, before it was
certain, that is, whether it would be a sentence of death or an
acquittal. Now again, it might be said that this consent could
be given without an oath—as indeed it was by Joseph's
brothers, whose pursuit by Joseph's steward will be discussed
below.[49] But at an earlier date an oath may well have been
deemed the only full submission to the sentence. For an

oath was more than an expression of willingness to suffer punishment if the verdict was one of guilty; an oath was self-damnation, it was certainly the most effective exoneration of those who might have to execute the sentence. It may be remarked that when Nathan visited David after his adultery with Bath-sheba, and induced him to say of the cruel thief of the parable, 'As the Lord liveth, the man that hath done this thing shall surely die',[50] this, as interpreted by Nathan, meant a curse uttered by David against himself: without knowing it, he delivered his own death-sentence. Or to take another narrative discussed before,[51] when Ahab had allowed the defeated Syrian king to depart in peace, a prophet came to him, pretending to be a soldier that had let a prisoner escape for whom he had pledged his life. Ahab's reply was, 'So shall thy judgment be; thyself hast decided it', intimating that the 'soldier' had accepted sentence of death. Thereupon the prophet turned the tables on Ahab and made use of the same idea: he put off his disguise and foretold Ahab's own doom. Here also we are meant to understand that Ahab himself called divine vengeance upon his head.[52] It is this idea of the submission of the accused to the verdict, or rather, of the self-surrender of the accused to divine vengeance should his guilt be proved, which, I suppose, was another factor making for the introduction of an oath to be taken by the suspect in the course of *vestigii minatio*.

It seems likely to me, then, that Jacob, in saying that the person convicted of the theft of Laban's idols 'should not live', uttered a curse; and I would call attention to the fact that the Rabbis, who knew Hebrew, thought so too, even though this interpretation was not convenient for them—I shall have to come back to this.[53] No objection against this view can be raised on the ground that there is no explicit invocation of a supernatural power contained in the words 'he shall not live'. Certainly, had Jacob exclaimed, 'he shall be cursed before the Lord', the meaning would be clearer—at least, for modern readers. We have to consider, however, that for instance the formula יחי המלך, 'the king shall live', in I Samuel x. 24, is unquestionably more than the expression of a benevolent wish, is more even than a wish addressed to God (the A.V. very reasonably introduces God, though the Hebrew text has no express reference to Him, and translates 'God save the king'): it is also a kind of charm, designed actually to ensure the life of the king. On the other hand, I want to emphasize that the practical difference in the case of Jacob's declaration between a surrender of the person convicted to divine retribution and a promise to surrender him to Laban to be killed could not be very great. If the words 'he shall not live' primarily meant the former—as I think likely—they did not exclude surrender to Laban. On the contrary, it was no doubt understood that Laban would be justified in putting the thief to death—for the thief would be outlawed or outreligioned. If the words quoted meant the latter, a promise to surrender the person convicted to Laban to be killed, the notion that the culprit was cursed before God would not necessarily be absent. The practical consequences, the actual conduct to be adopted by the parties on the basis of the declaration in question, must have been very much the same whether it was an oath or no.

Whether it was an oath or no, the declaration made by Jacob formed a defence in more than one way. It should be noted that Jacob did not say, 'Thy gods are not in my house; if they are found, treat me as a thief.' He said, 'With whomsoever thou findest thy gods, let him not live.' In other words, he surrendered (no matter whether to Laban or God) that person alone who had committed the crime, he would not be held liable—beyond the obligation to surrender the culprit—even if the things were found, so long as they were found with somebody else. This is a point of the greatest significance. We may assume that in an earlier era, if the missing things were discovered in the domain of the accused, of a head of a family, he could not defend himself by alleging that some subordinate member of the household had stolen them. He was answerable for the theft or, what is virtually the same, the whole household was communally answerable for it. In that earlier era, if the missing sacred objects were found in the course of a *vestigii minatio*, we may assume that the *paterfamilias* responsible and his entire family were at the mercy of the other party: no further questions were asked as to who might actually have committed the offence. Jacob's declaration reflects a more advanced stage, a stage at which individual responsibility was about to oust communal responsibility in this section of the law. I say that the former was about to oust the latter: it had not yet completely superseded it. The traces of the earlier regime here postulated are still distinctly noticeable in the story under discussion. I need only refer to the fact that it was Jacob, the chief of the family, who was formally charged with the theft by Laban: 'Wherefore hast thou stolen my gods?'[54] It was Jacob, the chief of the family, who, the proceedings having resulted in his favour, triumphed: 'What is my trespass? what is my sin, that thou hast so hotly pursued after me? Whereas thou hast searched all my stuff, what hast thou found of all thy household stuff?'[55] More than this, if the stolen goods had been discovered, it would have been Jacob, the chief of the family, against whom sentence would have been passed. This is quite clear from his ironical invitation, after Laban's unsuccessful search, to deliver the verdict: 'What hast thou found of all thy household stuff? set it here before my brethren and thy brethren, that they may judge betwixt us both.'[56] 'Betwixt us both'—Jacob, and no one else, was in the dock. But the point is that the sentence would have had to permit Jacob to hand over to justice the individual person convicted of the offence, Rachel, and thus to ward off further punishment from himself and the rest of the family. He would have been entitled, to use a term from Roman law, to *noxae deditio*, to surrender for punishment of the actual wrongdoer. With the words here analysed, 'With whomsoever thou findest thy gods, let him not live', Jacob not only invited retribution should the idols be found, but also indicated the exact limitation of retribution.

The narrative under notice illustrates a period of transition as far as *vestigii minatio* is concerned, the period of the momentous change from communal responsibility of the household to individual responsibility of the offender alone. That we have before us not an isolated, exceptional case but a case typical of the prevalent notions of a certain time, a case representing a definite stage in the development of ancient Hebrew law, is probable enough from general considerations. It is confirmed by the fact that we may notice a very similar tension between communal responsibility and individual responsibility in the story of Joseph's *vestigii minatio*, undertaken in order to convict Benjamin of the theft of his cup—a chapter to be analysed below.[57] I am, however, deliberately bypassing the problem of dating that time. Highly important though it may be, it is not essential in this connection where I am concerned merely with interpreting a narrative and showing its relative place in the history of Hebrew legal thought, but not with giving an absolute chronology of legal institutions. In solving the problem, one would have to attempt to establish whether the period reflected in the legal presentation of the case is that of the author of the pericope or that of the events underlying his account. Possibly one would find traces of both, but that might involve too fine-spun theories.

Here a brief observation may be inserted about a question from Roman law. In Roman law there was a system of 'noxal' actions: if a child or slave had committed a delict, the father or master, the *paterfamilias*, had either to pay damages or surrender the wrongdoer to the party offended. It is generally agreed now that when these 'noxal' actions were introduced, their meaning was that the party offended had the right to take vengeance on the guilty child or slave, but the *paterfamilias* could buy off the vengeance; and this regulation, it is argued, points back to a time when the latter possibility did not yet exist, when the delict of a child or slave was inevitably followed by the infliction of vengeance on him, the wrongdoer.[58] In other words, originally, if a subordinate member of a household committed a delict, he and only he had to take the consequences, had to suffer retribution; later the 'noxal' actions grew up, under which the *paterfamilias* was entitled to save the child or slave by offering amends for the delict committed.

I believe this view is correct as far as it goes. Only a case like Laban's *vestigii minatio* makes me think that there may have been a stage even earlier than that at which the offended party simply inflicted retribution on the guilty child or slave. Laban, we have seen, addressed his complaint to the *paterfamilias*. Indeed, no matter in the hands of which particular member of his family the stolen goods would have been detected, it would always have been Jacob, the *paterfamilias*, who would have played the part of the accused; it would always have been he and his family who would have been exposed to vengeance—had it not been for that saving clause made use of by Jacob, according to which a *paterfamilias* could clear himself and his family by surrendering the individual person convicted of the delict. From these facts I concluded that, at the earliest stage traceable on the basis of this narrative, if a subordinate member of a household had committed a delict, the *paterfamilias*, or better, the entire family was called to account. It was a time of clan against clan. It did not matter whether a head of a family himself or one of his subjects had committed theft: the party offended took vengeance on the whole community from which the wrong had emanated. It was not until much later that vengeance was restricted to the individual culprit, be he *paterfamilias* or child or slave. This restriction meant a triumph of individual responsibility of the actual wrongdoer over communal responsibility of the *paterfamilias* together with his entire household. The case of Laban versus Jacob, I have tried to show, reflects the law at a point between the two poles outlined: in some ways the idea of communal responsibility was still alive, it was still Jacob who was accused, it was still he and his whole family who were threatened, but already they could escape the worst by handing over the person actually guilty.

Now I would suggest that the same development took place in Roman law. General opinion is right in saying that when the 'noxal' actions were introduced, the object was to make it possible for a *paterfamilias* to save his guilty child or slave by buying off the vengeance; it is also right in saying that, before they were introduced, this possibility did not exist and vengeance was inflicted on the guilty child or slave. But I would add to this that, under a regime even prior to this, vengeance was inflicted on the entire household or clan a member of which had committed a delict. We have, that is, not two but three stages in Roman law, and a dialectical materialist might find here as neat an illustration of his doctrine as any of those current. First stage: No matter whether a delict was committed by the *paterfamilias* himself or a subordinate member of the family, the party outraged inflicted vengeance on the *paterfamilias* or, what comes to the same in this era, the entire family from which the offence had proceeded. Second stage: Vengeance was inflicted only on the actual wrongdoer, so that if a subordinate member of a household had offended, it was he alone on whom the other party took vengeance.[59] (The story of Laban versus Jacob is to be placed somewhere between these two stages.) Third stage: The 'noxal' actions entitled the *paterfamilias* to save a subject guilty of a delict by paying damages. The third stage, in a sense, was a return to the first on a higher level: a return to a kind of responsibility of the *paterfamilias* for delicts of his subjects, though a vastly different kind from that prevalent at the first stage, namely, a responsibility incurred by the *paterfamilias* in his own interest, on purpose to save his child or slave, and leading not to destruction by the other party but merely to an obligation to pay the other party. I cannot here go into the question whether there is any evidence of the first stage in Roman sources themselves, evidence independent of comparative law. Suffice it to remark that we ought perhaps to look for it in the international field since, plainly, it is in international relations that the situation of clan against clan remained long after it had ceased to dominate the law operating within the state. It may be added, for the sake of exactitude, that in classical Roman law a step was taken even beyond the third stage described above. The relationship under the 'noxal' system between the two alternatives open to a *paterfamilias*, surrender of his subject or payment of damages, gradually changed. Whereas the 'noxal' actions, at the time that they were introduced, meant that the *paterfamilias* might save his subject by offering damages, in classical law the idea was that a *paterfamilias* was liable for delicts committed by his subordinates, that is to say, was bound to pay damages, but that he could get rid of this liability by surrendering the culprit.[60]

Jacob cursed (or, if his words are not regarded as an oath, promised to kill or deliver to be killed by Laban) the actual wrongdoer only: 'he shall not live'. However, I ought to say that he seemed to do so. For—and here we come to the climax of the narrative and to that feature on account of which it is to be grouped with all the other stories of Jacob showing the truth of *summum ius summa iniuria*—there was just a little flaw in his declaration, which Laban was not sharp enough to notice and have put right. His curse was formulated in such a manner that not even the actual wrongdoer, Rachel, suffered any harm (or, if we take it as a promise of surrender, it was formulated so that it did not bind him ever to hand her over). I have shown above[61] that the exploitation by the subtler of two parties of the formalistic principles of ancient law plays an enormous part in the cycle of stories concerning Jacob. The subtler party defeats the simpler by making use of the fact that certain words and acts are of strictly binding force quite irrespective of any accompanying circumstances. It was in this way that Jacob obtained the blessing that Esau ought to have obtained: by means of a clever fraud he induced his father to bestow his best blessing on him, and once the blessing was uttered, it was beyond recall. It was in this way that Leah obtained the husband that Rachel ought to have obtained: by means of a clever fraud Jacob was induced to consummate marriage with the former, and once joined to her, he was her husband. It was in this way that Jacob collected his magnificent herds. His contract with Laban allowed him to take from Laban's herds a certain type of kids, very rare as a rule, but he found a method of making the strongest animals produce just that type: as this was not against the letter of the agreement, there was nothing that Laban could do. It was in this way, as I have attempted to demonstrate,[62] that Jacob acquired the birthright from his brother. He bought it for 'a red, red dish', looking like a dish of blood but, in reality, lentil soup: as the letter of the contract was in his favour, there was nothing that Esau could do. Here I wish to suggest (what I have already briefly referred to[63]) that it was in this way that he protected Rachel when she had stolen her father's idols. 'With whomsoever thou findest thy gods, he shall not live', thus Jacob swore (or promised). Very well, but Laban, as we are told not less than three times, did not *find* his gods. Jacob consigned to destruction him with whom Laban would *find* his things, not him who had them. Laban, who by this time should have been more cautious, was satisfied with this declaration: therefore, when he failed to *find* his things, the thief had nothing to fear.

'And Laban went into Jacob's tent, and into Leah's tent, and into the two maidservants' tents; but he found them not.' Laban started his investigation in the wrong tents, in Jacob's, Leah's, Bilhah's and Zilpah's. We shall find exactly the same wrong start in the case of the search of Joseph's brothers. The authors of those tales knew how to heighten the excitement of readers or audience. 'He found them not', is the upshot of this first phase. 'Then went he out of Leah's tent, and entered into Rachel's tent. Now Rachel had taken the images...and sat upon them. And Laban searched all the tent, but found them not.' The second phase also concludes by 'and he found them not'. But Rachel had to do something to prevent her father from searching the camel's saddle on which she sat, covering the stolen idols. 'And she said to her father, Let it not displease my lord that I cannot rise up before thee; for the custom of women is upon me. And he searched, but found not the images.'[64] Rachel was not only lovely but also shrewd:[65] it may be noted that she did not say to her father, 'You cannot search this saddle', which would have aroused his suspicions, but she said, 'I cannot rise up before thee', which served the same purpose as the other formulation would have served and involved a little flattery besides. So the story finishes with a third 'he found not the images'. Jacob's fearful oath (or promise) 'he shall not live' was made ineffective since he had added 'with whomsoever thou *findest* thy gods'.

Two objections might perhaps be raised against this interpretation. First, the wording of the declaration made by Jacob was, it appears, perfectly usual. As we shall see,[66] Joseph's brothers also, when accused of theft, agreed that 'with whomsoever...it (the cup) be found' was to be punished, and it is clear that they did not think of escape by relying on a literal construction of the clause. Is it conceivable, it might be asked, that a guilty person got off by means of the normal form of an oath or promise? This objection does not seem to be too serious. I do not see why a certain declaration should not have been made a thousand times without any ulterior motive until, one day, some particularly cunning fellow came along and used, or misused, it in an unexpected fashion. Many generals must have concluded an armistice for so and so many days both before and after that one who concluded an armistice for thirty *days*, attacking the unsuspecting enemy in the night.[67] Many persons charged with theft in the course of *vestigii minatio*, both before and after the case of Jacob, may have consented to the destruction of him with whom the goods were found, and only the one Jacob spoke of him with whom they were *found*. In fact, the more ingenious a man, the fewer alterations of the forms ordinarily observed he would need for attaining his end. A stratagem is none the worse, on the contrary, it is all the better, for being based upon the normal course of proceedings.

My thesis might be attacked on a different ground. The Rabbis interpret Jacob's words 'he shall not live' as an oath, a curse, rightly I think.[68] But they go on to suggest[69] that this curse was fulfilled, that Rachel died a premature death. No doubt if the Bible did say that Rachel died prematurely in consequence of Jacob's oath, my view that she escaped because the oath referred only to him with whom the gods were *found* would be disproved. The Bible, however, does not say so. In the Bible, the *vestigii minatio* undertaken by Laban ends in utter failure for him and a complete triumph of Jacob and Rachel. Nowhere is there any indication that Rachel's death— recorded four chapters after the *vestigii minatio*[70]—took place as a result of Jacob's curse, or even that it took place before the proper time. The truth is that, for the Rabbis, the idea of dodging justice, and particularly divine justice, by an over-literal, artificial, dishonest construction of a clause was un-bearable. They, therefore, had to give effect to the curse, and I am not denying that this was the right way, in their age and from their theological and moral point of view, of dealing with the narrative. I feel, however, that it confirms rather than weakens my case. It shows that they saw that there was here a problem; and while they solved it by cutting the Gordian knot and maintaining that Jacob's oath did kill Rachel, as historians we have to ascribe the escape of the couple to the validity at a certain stage of civilization of rigid, formalistic methods of interpretation. I have already pointed out[71] that this validity of formalistic methods by no means indicates any primitive frame of mind; and that the very existence of those narratives celebrating men who knew how to avail themselves of the methods under notice to discomfit their antagonists is conclusive evidence that the consequences possible under such a system were fully realized. It would, however, be outside the scope of this study to inquire how these methods came to prevail even though people were aware of their nature and the results to which they might lead.

One detail is noteworthy. Had the Rabbis taken 'he shall not live', not as a curse, but as a promise of Jacob to kill or surrender to Laban to be killed the person convicted, it would have been rather easier for them to moralize the narrative. They might have urged that the final treaty between Jacob and Laban, concluded after the examination of the tents was finished,[72] cancelled any previous obligation of either partner; and that, accordingly, whether Jacob then knew or at some later time found Rachel in possession of the idols, he was no longer bound to kill her or hand her over to Laban. For a modern historian, even this explanation would sound somewhat forced, but the Rabbis would probably have found it more satisfying and easier to argue than the view that Rachel died prematurely. However, this way was barred as soon as they interpreted 'he shall not live' as an oath. An oath would not, of course, be affected by a later treaty between Jacob and Laban: an oath, bringing in God, if it once hit a person, remained in force whatever you might subsequently do about it. That the Rabbis saw in Jacob's words an oath, a curse, though it was less convenient for them, seems to me to be a point in favour of this interpretation, as I have said before.[73]

According to the Biblical account as we have it, Jacob did not know that Rachel had stolen the idols; indeed, we are told so *expressis verbis*.[74] It follows that, in swearing an ambiguous oath or giving an ambiguous promise, Jacob was the innocent instrument of his wife. It was she alone who took advantage of the wording of the declaration that had to be made by the *paterfamilias* before a search began, 'With whomsoever thou *findest* thy gods, he shall not live'; she alone who hit upon the idea that, provided she concealed the penates so that they could not be *found*, the oath or promise would be neutralized. I cannot help thinking, however, that there may have been a pre-Biblical version of the story differing from the Biblical in this respect. More precisely, considering the style of Jacob's performances in general and the whole clever conduct of his defence against Laban in particular, it seems likely that, in an earlier version of the narrative discussed, he was consciously averting the risks of a curse or promise from the responsible person, Rachel.[75] If that is so, the Bible, by inserting the remark 'for Jacob knew not that Rachel had stolen them (the gods)',[76] has somewhat improved the moral standard of the tale: at least there was no trickery on the part of Jacob, at least there was no misuse of legal forms by the *paterfamilias* representing the accused household. But, clearly, as a folk-tale, as a popular story, the narrative would gain, Laban's defeat by a subtle construction of 'with whomsoever thy gods are *found*' be more impressive and amusing, if Jacob knew of the theft. At all events, Tremellius Scropha knew.

III

Tremellius vero Scropha, thus we are told by Macrobius in his *Saturnalia*,[77] *cognominatus est eventu tali. Is Tremellius cum familia atque liberis in villa erat. Servi eius, cum de vicino scropha erraret, subreptam conficiunt. Vicinus advocatis custodibus omnia circumvenit, nequa efferri possit: isque ad dominum appellat restitui sibi pecudem. Tremellius qui ex vilico rem comperisset, scrophae cadaver sub centonibus collocat, super quos uxor cubabat. Quaestionem vicino permittit. Cum ventum est ad cubiculum, verba iurationis concipit: nullam esse in villa sua scropham nisi istam, inquit, quae in centonibus iacet, lectulum monstrans. Ea facetissima iuratio Tremellio Scrophae cognomentum dedit.*

The point of this anecdote is remarkably similar to that of the story just analysed: here as there the stolen object, search for which is about to be made, is hidden in a woman's bed, with the woman covering it, here as there the man searching for it is misled by an oath apparently adequate, but in reality capable of an interpretation under which it can do the thief no harm. The actual contents of the oath in the Roman story, true enough, differ from those of Jacob's. But this is unavoidable. The Roman story is designed to account for the name of Scropha. Consequently, it is a pun on the word *scropha* that is wanted, it is by making an improper use of this word that the thief is to baffle his pursuer. The main structure of the two narratives is the same.

This is not asserting that the anecdote told by Macrobius cannot be genuinely Roman. In Rome as well as in Israel *vestigii minatio* is sure to have produced numerous funny situations, and even more numerous jokes about funny situations that might have, even though they did not, come about. The contrast between a pursuer blind with rage and sorrow (as the pursuer would normally be) and an ingenious thief (and thieves would often be crafty) is excellent material for comedy. We have, therefore, to expect stories employing this material in all countries. Moreover, there are characteristic differences between the two tales in question, besides the one already mentioned between Jacob's oath and Scropha's oath. Whilst in the Bible Rachel herself commits the crime, the Roman matron does not participate in it. Rachel steals a sacred thing, her father's idols, Scropha's servants steal a sow. In the Biblical story the proceedings are witnessed by the kinsmen of the parties, in the Roman story the *custodes*— probably the *custodes villae*[78]—assist the search, that is to say, officials or semi-officials. In fact, the warlike features of the Biblical story are altogether absent from the Roman: there is no threatening of the entire community of the thief, there is no indication of theft being considered a very grave offence at all, but an orderly, peaceful examination of the house under official supervision. Finally, the taboo on women during the menses, which prevents Laban from approaching Rachel, is not to be found in the story of Tremellius Scropha. Here the correct attitude of Romans towards women suffices to keep the neighbour away from the spot where the stolen object is hidden; as Webster's Jesuit, in England, is safest in a lady's room—'the modesty of the *Poursuivant* has only forborne the bed, and so missed him'.

Yet, though it may well be that the anecdote of Macrobius

is of native Roman growth, its similarity to the story of Jacob and Laban is great enough to make one wonder whether a genetic connection is not at least a possibility; whether it must not be regarded at least as possible that the jest in which the story of Scropha culminates comes from the Orient. It is well known that myths, sagas and anecdotes, if adopted by one nation from another, are at the same time modified so as to fit the environment and way of thinking of the borrowing party. Most of the differences outlined above could be easily understood in this way, as due to a Romanization of an Eastern tale. The substitution in Macrobius of a secular object of theft for the idols, of the *custodes* for the kinsmen witnesses, of the normal Roman procedure for the fiercer, more primitive expedition of a clan, and of the Roman respect for married women in general for the Biblical taboo setting apart women during the menses—all this might naturally happen in the course of borrowing and revising a narrative from the Orient.

The same process of adaptation might account for that divergence which probably strikes one most, namely, the leading role of Tremellius Scropha and the innocence of his wife in the Roman story, as compared with the initiative of Rachel and the minor part played by her husband in the Bible: the wife of a distinguished Roman citizen was not supposed to steal, was not supposed to behave like Rachel. Two further considerations make this particular divergence appear less weighty. First, the Roman story seeks to explain the origin of the family name of Scropha. No wonder that the eponymous hero should be placed in the foreground. Secondly, I suggested above[79] that Jacob's part as a mere blameless instrument of his wife, far from being an essential trait of the Biblical narrative, looks like an innovation. There may have been an older version where he was a real accomplice in the offence much like Tremellius Scropha; and, if so, it may be from that pre-Biblical version that the Roman anecdote is descended. As for the difference of Scropha's oath from Jacob's, I have already pointed out that it is unavoidable. It must be the dishonest construction of the word *scropha* that forms the climax of the Roman story, intended as it is to account for the name of the family Scropha. (One is reminded of Esau, who is called Edom for being trapped by his brother's literal interpretation of the words 'the red, red food'.[80] Of course, Tremellius Scropha is not trapped by, but traps, his opponent.) The important point is that in both stories, the Biblical and Roman, there is the same exploitation of a formalistic principle, according to which you are justified in ascribing a certain meaning to your declaration even though it is not the meaning that the ordinary addressee would ascribe to it, provided it agrees with the letter. This also has to be observed that the pun on *scropha*, necessary in the Roman story, cannot have been difficult to hit upon. It is of a most simple character: it requires little skill to use the word 'sow' in the ambiguous fashion in which Scropha uses it. Actually, the author of the anecdote had not even to invent this use. It seems to be an old element in comic literature. In the *Acharnians*, a man of Megara puts his daughters in a sack and tries to sell them as χοῖροι, as little pigs.[81]

In fact, some little details of Macrobius's anecdote rather point to a source more like the Biblical version. Whilst Tremellius Scropha plays the chief part in the Roman story, it is still not himself but members of his family, his slaves, who commit the actual theft. This feature, not at all essential to the story, may be a remnant of the Biblical tale with Rachel as the actual thief. It has, indeed, the appearance of a remnant; or more cautiously, if we regard it as such, a certain weakness in the Roman story becomes intelligible. In the Biblical tale, Rachel, guilty of theft and afraid of punishment, is anxious to find a way out. She does find one by hiding the stolen things in her camel's saddle and lying down on them—a means not proper, it is true, but understandable in the circumstances. In the Roman story, the delict is committed by the slaves, not by Scropha's wife: a Roman matron would not steal a sow. As a result, however, her role has become an entirely silent one and no longer naturally follows from the course of events. As she has done no wrong and perhaps does not even know what has happened, it is only an idea of her husband's that involves her in the business. Certainly the story is not only weakened by this change but also very much vulgarized: the obscene mode of concealing the stolen object is resorted to not by a desperate woman, for the sake of her own salvation, but by a man—one is almost tempted to say, for the sake of acquiring a surname.

There is another point that requires attention. As far as we can see, there was no oath in Roman law in the case of a search of a house for stolen goods; yet Tremellius Scropha takes an oath, like Jacob. Admittedly, I have no more than an argument from silence for the position in Roman law. But, then, if there was no oath, we can hardly expect more than— not to find it. At any rate, Gaius, who speaks of the search at some length,[82] makes no mention of an oath. It is true that P. Huvelin takes a different view from the one here advocated,[83] basing himself on a passage from *Poenulus*[84] and one from the *Aeneid*.[85] Neither of them, however, seems to me conclusive, and I may here state my reasons.

First, for the passage from *Poenulus*. For one thing, it is possible that Plautus is here following the pattern of a Greek comedy.[86] Great care, therefore, is required in deducing from this passage the existence of a provision in Roman law of which there is no sign in the legal sources. For another thing, there is no question in *Poenulus* of a legally prescribed or customary oath, nor even, as it seems, of a search at all. The situation is this. Agorastocles wishes to remove a pretty young lady from the power of a greedy pander. For this purpose he has sent a slave of his, Collybiscus, to the pander, well supplied with money. Collybiscus has had to pose as a free man and the pander, of course, has invited him into his hotel. In the presence of some fellows, who had been made familiar by Agorastocles with the whole scheme and been bribed to act as witnesses, Collybiscus has paid the pander 300 silver coins. He has taken care not to haggle over the admission fee, since the more the pander receives from him, the higher the penalty will be that he incurs when his action is construed as theft. Thereupon the pander has shown his guest in. At this juncture Agorastocles appears on the scene. The plan is going well, and he makes a speech to his witnesses expatiating on what is to follow, though they know it as well as he. He tells them how he is going to ask the pander whether his slave is not staying with him, having brought him 200 silver coins. The pander

cannot know that his visitor Collybiscus is a slave of Agorastocles, and will be absolutely thrown off the track by hearing
of a different, and smaller, sum of money, 200 silver coins
instead of 300. He is sure to deny that Agorastocles's slave is
with him, sure to deny that he received any of Agorastocles's
money, and by these denials will make himself guilty of theft.
Indeed, as he will be caught before the offence can be said to
be fully completed, with the witnesses who have seen him
take the slave and money still on the spot, he may be considered as caught in the act, as *fur manifestus*, which means
that he will become the *addictus* of Agorastocles.[87] After this,
it will be easy for the latter to get his lady. I need not discuss
the question, which may occur to the reader, whether and how
far, in the age of Plautus, a man who took away another
man's goods and, surprised in the act by the other, denied that
he was appropriating his things, could later, when he realized
the position, defend himself by pleading that he had acted in
good faith, that is to say, that at the time of the denial he had
not known the goods to be the other's property. The pimp
most definitely could not thus defend himself, since no praetor
or judge would have believed him. Here is the part of the
speech that contains the line which Huvelin adduces in support of his theory:[88]

Agorastocles. *Vidistis leno quom aurum accepit?*
Advocati. *Vidimus.*
Agorastocles. *Eum vos meum esse servom scitis?*
Advocati. *Scivimus.*

. . . .

Agorastocles. *Si exierit leno, quid tum? hominem interrogem*
meus servos ad eum veneritne?
Advocati. *Quippini?*
Agorastocles. *Cum auri ducentis nummis Philippis?*
Advocati. *Quippini?*
Agorastocles. *Ibi extemplo leno errabit.*
Advocati. *Qua de re?*
Agorastocles. *Rogas?*
quia centum nummis minus dicetur.
Advocati. *Bene putas.*
Agorastocles. *Alium censebit quaeritari.*
Advocati. *Scilicet.*
Agorastocles. *Extemplo denegabit.*

Advocati.	*Iuratus quidem.*
Agorastocles.	*Homo furti sese adstringet.*
Advocati.	*Hau dubium id quidemst.*
Agorastocles.	*Quantum quantum ad eum erit delatum.*
Advocati.	*Quippini?*
Agorastocles.	*Diespiter vos perduit.*
Advocati.	*Te quippini?*

The point of this dialogue is that Agorastocles, highly excited, talks very much, but says very little that is not perfectly obvious to his witnesses. They, on the other hand, with their complete indifference—after all, they are just rabble expecting to be paid for their role—their monotonous echo, their uniform confirmation of his proposals, serve as a contrast, as a foil.[89] This being so, one ought not to overrate the significance of an isolated exclamation on their part. If Agorastocles says that the pander will flatly deny having seen his slave and the witnesses reply, *Iuratus quidem*, 'Even on oath', this does not mean that the pander is forced by law to swear an oath, but that for once, in this case, he will really feel blameless. In other words, the witnesses merely approve Agorastocles's forecast: a free translation of *Iuratus quidem* might be 'Indeed, he will'. In fact, when it comes to the encounter and Agorastocles asks the pander for his slave and money, the pander simply answers that he knows of neither. He takes no oath, nor is any required to make him a thief: his mere denial is enough. If an oath were necessary, it could not possibly be omitted in this scene; but there is no trace of it.[90] For that matter, it should be noted that in the scene towards the beginning of the play,[91] where the whole stratagem is first suggested to Agorastocles by his cleverest slave, Milphio, no reference to an oath is to be found. Milphio foresees that the pander will deny having Collybiscus and any of Agorastocles's money with him, thus laying himself open to the charge of theft, but he does not hint at the necessity of an oath: further confirmation that the words *Iuratus quidem* do not reflect any legal institution. How precarious it is to argue from such a casual exaggerated remark in a comedy is shown by a passage occurring in the last scene of *Poenulus*.[92] Here Agorastocles and the pander meet again, and the latter, now utterly crushed by the misfortune described above and others that have since befallen him, entreats the former not to go to law. He offers to pay back the money that he has obtained and to swear that he meant Agorastocles no harm. *Tum autem aurum tuom reddam quod apud me est, et iusiurandum dabo me malitiose nil fecisse, Agorastocles.* This oath obviously has nothing to do with law, and Huvelin, needless to say, does not hold that it has; it is neither prescribed nor customary, but just an oath offered by the pimp on the spur of the moment, in the hope that it may help to pacify his antagonist. Yet it is at least actually mentioned by the pander (though even here he does not get as far as to swear it), which is more than one can say of that other oath, of real importance in Huvelin's view.

Quite apart from all these arguments, however, I very much doubt whether a search in the technical sense takes place, or is alluded to, in this comedy at all. Agorastocles so posts his witnesses that they can watch the pander accept the money from Collybiscus and show the latter into his hotel. Immediately this has happened, Agorastocles comes himself and asks the pander whether he has taken his property. The pander goes into the trap and replies in the negative: whereupon the witnesses point out that the money is in the very purse that the pander is carrying, Agorastocles seizes it and pronounces him a manifest thief. As soon as the pander realizes the truth, he submits to his defeat, and Agorastocles fetches his slave out of the house.[93] This looks to me like a scheme designed to convict the pander of theft, and, if possible, of *furtum manifestum*. But I cannot see here any reference to a technical search. Accordingly, even if the pander did swear to his innocence—which he does not—it would still be highly questionable whether there was any connection with ceremonies observed in the course of a search of a house, Roman or Greek.

Similar considerations apply to the text from the *Aeneid* cited by Huvelin. The saga of Hercules and Cacus here narrated is due to Greek inspiration. Consequently, it is *a priori* dangerous to use it for the reconstruction of Roman law, unless, indeed, there are special reasons for doing so. As far as I can see, there are none. But even if we knew that the particular passage concerned was based on Roman life, it would not show that the accused had to take an oath before the search of his house. Cacus, a formidable monster, has stolen the bulls of Hercules. Hercules manages to penetrate into his cave and after a fearful struggle to strangle him. Here the text goes on:[94]

> *Panditur extemplo foribus domus atra revolsis,*
> *abstractaeque boves abiurataeque rapinae*
> *coelo ostenduntur, pedibusque informe cadaver*
> *protrahitur....*

It is the word *abiuratae* that Huvelin thinks bears out his theory, though indeed he admits that it is only *un lointain souvenir du serment purgatoire.*[95]

What does this word mean? Obviously, Virgil does not want us to understand that the monster's cave was ever searched before Hercules conquered him; nobody would have risked it. The word in question, therefore, cannot refer to an oath taken in the course of a *vestigii minatio* prior to Hercules's intervention. No less absurd would be the idea that Cacus ever took an oath in an ordinary process before a court of law. There remain only two possibilities. The one is that Cacus has taken an oath, sworn to his innocence, while being chased by Hercules. This is what Huvelin assumes.[96] It may be correct, but can hardly be admitted as proof that the law required a formal oath at the start of a search. When we read those lines in which Virgil describes the panic terror by which Cacus was seized on finding Hercules after him,[97] it becomes clear that, if indeed he took an oath, he was induced to do so by his fear, and by the hope that Hercules might abstain from pursuing him any longer, much rather than by a provision of the law.

It is anything but certain, however, that *abiuratae* implies an oath at all. In fact, there are two difficulties rendering this interpretation unlikely. In the first place, Virgil, though depicting the chase in all detail, makes no mention of a disclaimer on the part of Cacus. Why he should have omitted it had he thought of it is difficult to see. It would have added to the liveliness of the scene, and without it *abiuratae* is in the air, referring back to a disclaimer not mentioned and not, I think, very easily supplied by the reader. In the second place, Hercules finds in the cave *boves* and *rapinae*, that is to say, his bulls and other treasures hoarded by Cacus. Of the former Virgil says that they are *abstractae*, unlawfully alienated from their owner, misappropriated, withheld. Surely, the symmetry of the line would be upset if he said of the latter that they were disclaimed during the chase, that Cacus, caught by Hercules, had sworn that he did not know of them; the symmetry of the line requires that *abiuratae* should signify more or less the same as *abstractae*, should mean that the treasures are ill-gotten, unlawfully withheld from their owners. Hercules finds 'the bulls that Cacus has taken away and the treasures that he has misappropriated', this would seem an interpretation doing justice to the poet. It is, indeed, the most probable interpretation, and the one that has the authority of Servius. He, in his commentary on Virgil, remarks, rightly I believe: *abiurare est rem creditam negare periurio. Sed hoc isto loco non congruit: unde modo abiuratas rapinas contra ius retentas intellegamus. Alii abiuratas abductas atque alieni iuris factas, alii fraude et furto abductas tradunt.* This unprejudiced rendering, the essential part of which was apparently undisputed in the time of Servius—for the two paraphrases he quotes agree in rejecting any reference to an oath—seems to me the most acceptable one. The words *abiuratae rapinae* denote all the possessions of Cacus, acquired by violence and fraud, and now won by Hercules.

There is a point not noticed by Lewis and Short[98], but worth considering in forming an opinion about this passage from the *Aeneid*: *abiurare* has the sense of 'to hold back fraudulently, to misappropriate', with no oath implied, even in legal language, though I cannot find this usage before the early half of the fourth century. A decree of Constantine, dating from 319,[99] deals with property without an heir, of which the emperor makes a gift to somebody. In this case it is important to prevent the fiscal officers from taking a few odd bits for themselves, before handing the property over to the donee. The decree ordains: *Iubemus quotiens iure suadente aliquorum bona ex officio tuo fuerint occupata, breves eorum plenissimos ad... comitem...mitti, ne fraudibus Caesarianorum imminuantur vel petentibus aliquid abiuretur.* Again, a decree of Maiorianus, of 458,[100] is directed against those who find ways and means of appropriating possessions without an heir though they should go to the exchequer. *Cum enim caduca bona...privato aerario competere videantur, occultata quibusdam fraudibus aerarii nostri commodis abiurantur.* Actually, there is one constitution, issued by Theodosius in 424,[101] where *abiurare* simply signifies 'to withhold', not even 'to withhold wrongfully'. This decree reminds people of the law that garments made entirely of purple may be worn only by the imperial household. Anyone else who owns such garments must hand them over to the exchequer. *Nec est*, the decree goes on to say, *ut quisquam de abiurato pretio conqueratur, quia sufficit calcatae legis impunitas.* Which means: Nor should it be regarded as a reason for complaint that we are going to pay no compensation, that we are 'withholding' the price of the garments surrendered,[102] since we are lenient enough in letting off the persons concerned the punishment that they have deserved for violating the law.[103]

In all probability, then, Roman law had no oath in the case of a search of a house for stolen goods. If Tremellius Scropha takes an oath none the less, this may betray the foreign origin of the story. Admittedly, the argument is far from conclusive: there is no reason why he should not swear to his innocence on his own initiative, with no law coming in. But the suspicions about the oath seem to receive support from one or two internal points, from evidence, that is, concerning the position of the oath within the Roman anecdote itself. This position is somewhat unnatural. In the Biblical narrative, Laban charges Jacob with theft, whereupon Jacob swears an oath and allows Laban to examine the tents. It is not till the search is almost over that Tremellius Scropha takes his oath. The course of events in the Biblical narrative is perfectly intelligible. The taking of an oath here is an integral element of the search; it takes place, very reasonably, at the beginning, an expression of the consent of the *paterfamilias* to the destruction of the person convicted, and a safeguard against attack on the entire community. In the story of Scropha, however, the oath has lost its weight and even its sense. It is no longer a legal procedure that cannot be dispensed with, it is not even a spontaneous reply of the accused to the charge. Scropha waits till they are arrived in the bedroom before he swears *nullam esse in villa sua scropham*.... This is a weakness in the story. The oath here merely serves to exhibit a trick played by Scropha on his opponent: as this trick is based upon the double meaning of *scropha*, henceforward to be the name of the family, the oath has to be taken in the bedroom, at a point where it does not fit. I have said above that whilst in the Biblical tale it is essential that the theft should be committed not by Jacob but by Rachel, in the Roman tale the fact that the slaves, not Tremellius Scropha himself, steal the sow is of no significance; and that Rachel's role is more natural than that of Scropha's wife. Similarly, it may be added, Jacob's oath comes where it is required by the situation, Scropha's is unmotivated.

From the foregoing discussion it appears possible, though no more than possible, that the anecdote related by Macrobius is borrowed from the Orient, more precisely, that it goes back to some version of the case of Laban versus Jacob. Here, however, we come up against a serious problem. Huvelin is of opinion[104] that Macrobius is telling a true story: that search of Tremellius Scropha's house and his ambiguous oath, Huvelin asserts, did actually occur about the middle of the second century B.C. If this were correct, or even if it could be made probable, my suggestion that the tale may come from the East would have to be given up. As a matter of fact, however, Huvelin's theory seems quite untenable. His argument is that Varro introduces his friend, the agronomist Cn. Tremellius Scropha, as a speaker in his *De Re Rustica*,[105] and makes him observe that his grandfather, who was quaestor about the middle of the second century B.C., was the first to be called by the strange surname of Scropha. But, clearly, this proves at most that the family did not receive the name before the middle of the second century B.C., not that Macrobius's account of the origin of the name is historical. Huvelin puts too much confidence in the veracity of this kind of anecdote. Again and again it happens that an imaginary aetiology is provided for an existing, queer name. Certainly, incidents similar to that described by Macrobius may well have occurred in Rome and created a predisposition to the invention, or borrowing from abroad, of the story. But this does not make the story true. In fact, we have what amounts almost to positive evidence that the events depicted by Macrobius did not take place. The agronomist Scropha, in Varro, also gives an explanation of the surname of Scropha, and it is entirely different from the one given by Macrobius:

> *Avus meus primum appellatus est Scropha, qui quaestor cum esset Licinio Nervae praetori...hostes, arbitrati occasionem se habere victoriae, impressionem facere coeperunt in castra. Avus, cum cohortaretur milites ut caperent arma atque exirent contra, dixit celeriter se illos, ut scropha porcos, disiecturum, id quod fecit. Nam in eo proelio hostes ita fudit ac fugavit ut eo Nerva praetor imperator sit appellatus, avus cognomen invenerit ut diceretur Scropha.*

I doubt whether we need accept as historical either of the two explanations, Macrobius's or Varro's. The name in question may have been taken from swine-breeding, may have been given to a farmer who went in for it and made it profitable.[106] But, if we have to choose, Varro's account has much more the semblance of truth than that of Macrobius. Huvelin rejects it on the ground that it is more honourable, more in favour of the family concerned: it must have been invented, he says, by the agronomist Scropha, in order to replace the discreditable explanation. But though this argument is very plausible considered by itself, it does not hold good when we examine the special data of the case under notice. To begin with, Varro has, or at least says he has, his explanation from a grandson of the eponymous hero himself. There is not the faintest indication that he knows about the explanation given by Macrobius, not the faintest indication that his own explanation is meant to replace the other. Indeed, the current, popular explanation of the name in his time seems to have been to derive the name from swine-breeding—I have already remarked that it may well be the right explanation—for it is to this derivation that the agronomist, in Varro, opposes his story.[107] In Macrobius, on the other hand, the anecdote forms part of a section *ex professo* dealing with queer names. This significant contrast alone should be enough to make us hesitate to prefer

to Varro's account one to be found 450 years later. But there
is more than this. In Varro's story, the ancestor of the Scrophas
does in fact compare himself with a *scropha*: he exclaims *se illos,
ut scropha porcos, disiecturum*. From comparison to nickname is
not far. In Macrobius's version, it should be noted, it is only the
thief's wife to whom the comparison refers: there is no other sow
in his house, Tremellius Scropha swears, than the one in bed.
The point is not very important, since even an incident like
that described by Macrobius might quite easily lead to people
calling the family by the name of Scropha. We may remember
that Edom came by his name, according to a Biblical aetiology
discussed above,[108] not by reason of a comparison at all, but
because he had carelessly sold his birthright for 'a red dish'
instead of blood. Yet it is a small additional detail in favour
of Varro's version, which makes it so very natural that the
ancestor of the family should have received, or rather adopted,
this surname. The decisive consideration, however, seems to
me to be this. Varro's story is founded on the specific career
of a specific individual, on the career as an army leader of the
quaestor Tremellius Scropha (though it may be worth observing
that the picture which the quaestor uses for his comparison
is traditional, occurring in Plautus[109]). Macrobius's story is
abstract, schematic, transferable. It might be told of whoever
was the first to be called Scropha, a feature that clearly shows
that the name caused the story and not the story the name.

To sum up, it has to be admitted that for once, by way of
exception, the explanation of a name more creditable to its
bearer is older than the obscene alternative. (What a reflection
on human nature that the opposite should be the rule!) If one
of the two stories told to account for the name Scropha must
be historical, it is Varro's more honourable one. And is this
result not to be preferred also for a more general reason?
Varro's Scropha is a quaestor of soldierly manners and ways
of expression such as may well have lived in the second
century B.C. But would it not be most surprising if Macrobius's
version were true and a high Roman official of that period
had taken a *facetissima iuratio*?

The episode related by Macrobius is not historical, and we
are free to hold that, possibly, it is descended from the tale

of Laban's idols—be it in its exact Biblical form or some other. Varro, far from showing that the episode occurred in the second century B.C., helps us to fix a *terminus post quem*: the story of Scropha the swindler must have been invented, or taken over from foreign literature, after the time of Varro, who, it is evident, did not know about it. The exact date it is impossible to establish: it may lie anywhere between Varro and Macrobius. Nor is it possible to say precisely how the story came over to Rome, if indeed it did come from abroad. Supposing it did, the most likely assumption would be that the stratagem constituting the substance of the Biblical tale was a current motif in the Orient—just as was the motif of Hercules and Cacus, for instance—and was conveyed to the Romans by way of Greece. There is, however, still another, though remote, chance. Macrobius was a friend of the family Symmachus. He moved in a circle, that is, which was certainly well acquainted with the Bible. There is, perhaps, a remote chance that the story of Scropha was composed by a member of this circle under the direct influence of the Biblical narrative. It is hardly needful to repeat that this view is not precluded by the existence of non-Hebrew elements in the anecdote of Scropha. I have said above that when a tale is adopted by one nation from another, it is usually also adapted. In the case here in question, the author of the story of Scropha would have taken from the Bible only the main idea and outline of the trick. Maybe it is worth mentioning that the anecdote of Scropha, in Macrobius's *Saturnalia*, is told at a symposium of the circle of that Symmachus who was the great pagan opponent of bishop Ambrosius of Milan. It is true that, as a rule, the scene that Macrobius lays for the presentation of his stories has nothing to do with the sources from which they are derived. Nevertheless, a few of them he may actually have heard at the Symmachus's or read in collections of stories and jests put together by a member of this group. As for the general question whether such a thing was possible, it is sufficient to recall that frescoes depicting Biblical scenes in caricature have been discovered at Pompeii: they must be as early as the first century A.D., for Pompeii was destroyed in A.D. 79.[110]

IV

If the story of Laban's penates is an example of a *vestigii minatio* brought to nought by a trick on the part of the thief, the saga of Joseph contains a case of an innocent person being convicted through a trick on the part of the accuser.[111] The sons of Jacob, we are told, were about to return from Egypt to Canaan after their second visit. They were not yet aware that the great Egyptian minister, who treated them so kindly, was their brother Joseph, and the latter decided to exploit their ignorance on one more occasion before he would make himself known to them. He had his divining cup, the cup that he used for predicting the future, put into Benjamin's sack, seeing to it that they did not notice. They left the residence but had not gone far when Joseph's steward overtook them and charged them with the theft of the cup.

Up to this point,the narrative, as far as legal procedure is concerned, more or less follows the pattern found in the two other accounts of a *vestigii minatio*: the offence alleged consisted in the theft of a sacred object from a palace, and the pursuit was taken up with the least delay possible, namely, 'when they were gone out of the city, and not yet far off'.[112] When we ask, however, who it was that pursued them, the answer is not, as in the two stories considered above, the victim of the offence with his clan, but Joseph's steward; and, unless the author of the narrative omitted to mention further witnesses because he thought their presence so natural that it was superfluous to mention them, Joseph's steward pursued his brothers by himself. It is only a small point, but we shall do well to remind ourselves in time that the narrative under notice is even more difficult to analyse from the technical, legal point of view than those concerning Rachel and the Danites. An even greater proportion of the incidents recorded, that is, may have to be explained as due to the particular situation, not to any general rules of law or custom. The detail in question seems to be an example of this kind. It would be rash to infer from it that a *vestigii minatio* could ever be undertaken without witnesses, so long as the parties concerned were ordinary citizens. Joseph's steward set out alone—if we do not regard the presence of witnesses as implied. But very probably this was possible only because of the exceptional position of his master, who was a powerful man, ruling the state in the name of Pharaoh. No resistance, no prevarications were to be expected in this case. The Bible tells us how his brothers prostrated themselves before Joseph each time they were admitted to his presence;[113] the last occasion, indeed, was when they had to appear before him after the 'stolen' cup had been discovered in Benjamin's sack.'[114] This is sufficient illustration of his exalted position.

As in the case of Laban and Jacob, the pursuer, on overtaking the pursued, charged them with theft, to which the latter replied by pleading not guilty and declaring themselves punishable in case the charge should be proved: 'With whomsoever of thy servants it (the cup) be found', the brothers said to Joseph's deputy, 'both let him die, and we also will be thy lord's bondmen.'[115] It may be recalled that Jacob, when accused of theft by Laban, uttered what I have argued was in all probability a curse against the person convicted.[116] Here we find a more rational wording of the defence. וָמֵת, 'let him die', is not a curse. The verb is often used in this or some equivalent form in statutes imposing capital punishment on an offence and in threats addressed by one person to another.[117] וָמֵת means 'he shall be killed', 'he shall be executed'—almost as if it were יוּמַת. This is not denying that, at some remote date, even this expression may have constituted a kind of execration. I doubt whether it ever really did, since it seems to me that even in the earliest times people relied on God's intervention only in the case of crimes with which they could not possibly deal in any other way, and there is no sign of a special connection of the verb with such crimes. At any rate, in the narrative here discussed, if there should be any magical element left in וָמֵת, it is decidedly very much weaker than the rational element. The interpretation of וָמֵת as 'he shall be executed' is confirmed by the rest of the sentence, which distinctly refers to a penalty to be inflicted by human agency: 'and we also will be my lord's bondmen'. It follows that the brothers, unlike Jacob, handed themselves over not to divine vengeance, but to a secular power. Instead of invoking the wrath of God should they be convicted, they merely gave their consent to punishment by Joseph in case of conviction.

I have already suggested that this appears to reflect a later stage, when, roughly speaking, self-damnation had become acknowledgment of liability. One advantage that the latter must have had is illustrated by the narrative itself. In contradistinction to self-damnation, a rational acknowledgment of liability admitted of a precise, well-considered statement of the punishment to be inflicted. Where an accused man took an oath, he could hardly say more than what Jacob said, namely, that the person convicted 'should not live'; he could hardly make such a detailed proposal to the supernatural powers as that the actual thief should be destroyed and his relatives become slaves. Where, however, a mere secular acknowledgment of liability had superseded the curse, there was no reason why details of any sort should not be introduced. Joseph's brothers could explain with great preciseness what they deemed the proper consequences if they were found guilty. Yet, essentially, we have the same thing in this case as in that of Laban and Jacob (and a good many other narratives of the Old Testament—I pointed this out before[118]): the accused men themselves pronounced the fate that they merited if the charge preferred against them should be established.

Joseph's brothers, as we have seen, declared that if the cup were found with any of them, the thief should lose his life, all the others become Joseph's slaves. Joseph's steward, however, modified this proposal in two respects; though, in accordance with Oriental politeness, he opened his protest by expressing complete assent, 'Now also let it be according unto your words.'[119] (One is reminded of the way in which the negotiations between Abraham and Ephron about the purchase of the cave of Machpelah were conducted.[120]) The thief, he held, should be enslaved, not killed, while all the others should remain entirely unmolested. Later, when the cup had been found with Benjamin and the brothers were taken before Joseph, they abandoned the idea of the death penalty for the thief, but still considered that they were all answerable to Joseph: they now said that they all regarded themselves as

Joseph's slaves. But Joseph insisted that only the actual thief, Benjamin, had forfeited his freedom; the others, he said, should return to Canaan.[121]

These differences between the punishment proposed by the brothers and that proposed by the steward and Joseph, and between the punishment proposed by the brothers when talking to the steward and that proposed by them when talking to Joseph, make a nice puzzle for a legal historian. Let it be emphasized again: it would be a wrong approach to the problem to try and say that it was this attitude or that which corresponded to the legal practice of the time. The situation was absolutely exceptional, the various moves of the parties were largely dictated by their respective personal interests, and we must not jump to conclusions. We need only reflect on the general trend of the divergences, just pointed out, between the punishment suggested by Joseph's brothers and that suggested by Joseph or his steward to realize how unusual the position was: for the general trend is that Joseph's brothers, the party accused, chose a severer punishment, and Joseph, the accuser, a more lenient one, surely not a typical controversy in a criminal court. Nor is it surprising that the parties should have acted in an extraordinary manner. To mention only a few of the complications: Joseph was accusing, and convicting, his brothers of a theft that he knew they had not committed. At the same time he wished to frighten them only, not to hurt them. He was particularly fond of the one branded as the actual thief, Benjamin, since Benjamin, like himself, was Rachel's son. The others also were connected with Benjamin by a special tie, having pledged themselves to bring him back safely to Jacob. And there was this further anomalous feature about the brothers that they constituted a body, a family, but one without a *paterfamilias*—except that the role of a *paterfamilias* was to some extent undertaken by Judah, who spoke for them all. This is enough to account for a good deal of deviation from the accepted rules of law.

If we apply these considerations to the details of the story, we might argue somewhat as follows. Joseph's brothers, when charged with theft by the steward, admitted a communal responsibility should the cup be found. Not only should the actual thief lose his life, they said, but even the others should become Joseph's slaves. Jacob, it may be remembered, replying to Laban, admitted liability of the actual thief only. The reasons for the attitude of the brothers may have been, first, that they formed a group of equals, not a family with a *paterfamilias*, and secondly, that they felt quite innocent and wanted to show it. A third point must be added. The author of the narrative probably intended to focus attention on the steward's and Joseph's opposite view, namely, that only the actual thief was to be called to account. This view, however, also was connected with the peculiar situation in which the parties found themselves. It suited Joseph to single out Benjamin, his beloved brother of the same mother, and the one person without whom the others could not possibly go back to their father. Similarly, when first accused of theft by the steward, the brothers, certain that the cup would not be found with them, declared that the thief deserved nothing less than death. The steward and Joseph were satisfied with keeping him as slave. Even this substitution of enslavement for the death penalty, it seems, answered Joseph's purpose. Years before his brothers had thrown him into a pit, and gone home to Jacob with a piece of his coat dipped in blood as evidence that he must have fallen victim to a wild beast; but it had not been a convincing story.[122] This time, before they left for Egypt, Jacob exacted a solemn promise from his sons not to lose Benjamin as they had lost Joseph.[123] Joseph knew that it was impossible for them to face their father without Benjamin: it had been most difficult for him to force them to bring Benjamin into Egypt.[124] He also knew that nothing could be worse than his threat to keep him back as slave. For this meant that they would have to tell Jacob once again that they had left a son of his—and of Rachel's—somehow, somewhere. The true object of Joseph in insisting on punishing Benjamin alone, and punishing him by enslavement, was not to make it easier for his brothers, but to embarrass them. Moreover, that Joseph should have pronounced sentence of death against Benjamin, however little in earnest, very likely appeared repugnant to the author of the pericope.

There remains the problem that the brothers, while speaking of the death penalty for the thief when first charged by the steward, later, when before Joseph, changed their minds and held that they all, the thief too, ought to become Joseph's slaves. This is easily explained. They spoke of the death penalty so long as they were convinced that the cup would be found with none of them. By the time that they appeared before Joseph, they were treated as guilty, the cup had been found, the charge was proved. Now, of course, they would not say that the thief, who was Benjamin, should be killed: Benjamin was most precious to them. Now they desired that they should all remain together, even though it had to be in slavery.

However, though it would be unwise to attempt to deduce the exact rules of law of the period from the steps taken by the parties in this narrative, we are certainly justified in seeing reflected in those steps the legal ideas current at the time. More precisely, to whatever extent the parties were influenced by their personal aims, it is obvious, for example, that neither of them would have referred to the death penalty or enslavement if the offence in question had been considered, as it was in later times, a minor delict, to be made good by a fine in money. Again, there would have been no talk of communal responsibility if such a thing had been unheard of in this connection, and the same is true of individual responsibility. What we may infer, then, from the narrative is the poles between which the practice of the period must have moved, the kind of punishment that was thought possible, and (most important of all) the direction in which the law was developing. The results thus gained will be deemed all the more reliable since they are consistent with those at which I arrived in discussing the conflict of Jacob and Laban.

To begin with, clearly, the thief of a sacred object, if caught in the act or through a *vestigii minatio*—the purpose of which, as shown above, was to keep the offence fresh, manifest—was liable to severe punishment, the death penalty or enslavement. In the story of Laban's *vestigii minatio*, we found only the former.[125] Here enslavement is introduced as an alternative. This is an indication of the way in which the law was shaping. Originally, we may assume, the proper punishment for a manifest thief was death. In course of time, it was replaced by enslavement. Three factors at least must have contributed to this evolution. First, it should be observed that, throughout antiquity, death and enslavement were looked upon as modes of punishment closely resembling one another in their essential features. The Roman jurists, indeed, used the phrase *poena capitalis* and similar expressions to denote either punishment by death, punishment by loss of liberty or punishment by loss of citizenship.[126] I need not here investigate the ultimate basis of this view—an undertaking that would involve inquiring into the most fundamental notions of life, death, the status of man and so on prevalent in the ancient Mediterranean countries. Suffice it to register the bare fact that a close affinity was felt to exist between the death penalty and enslavement. Secondly, as for the punishment of theft in particular, in all probability, enslavement played a certain part even in the earliest epoch, when the entire family was held responsible if any member had committed theft. It is hardly credible that the proceedings (if such a civil term may be used of the measures taken in the case of manifest theft) should inevitably have ended in a wholesale massacre of the guilty family. The *paterfamilias*, true enough, may have had to be eliminated. But of the others, no doubt some were usually spared and retained as slaves. Thirdly, it is only natural that, in the case of theft, death punishment should in the end have given way altogether to enslavement. In primitive times, theft, like most crimes perpetrated in secret, was regarded as a terrible offence. You simply could not tolerate a man breaking into another's house or enclosure in an age when there was no police, when your private domain had to be jealously guarded against all kinds of attack, and when undisturbed confidence between neighbours was vital for the peaceful life of a community. As communities became bigger and some sort of police was organized, that touchiness about the inviolability of one's private domain and that necessity of mutual confidence grew less and less. Theft came to be considered an offence directed chiefly against property, not against the person and the community. Once this stage was reached, it was far more rational for a victim of theft to make the thief—even the manifest thief—a slave, and thus obtain compensation in addition to punishing him, than just to put him to death.

The narrative discussed shows us theft on the road from a capital offence to a petty delict of the civil law. For Joseph, enslavement was an adequate way of dealing with manifest theft of a sacred cup. I have already said[127] that the same general tendency is discernible in the *Mishpatim*. There we find an earlier statute concerning theft—ordinary theft, not manifest or of a holy object—imposing upon the thief a fourfold or fivefold penalty according to the kind of animal stolen; and a later statute imposing only a twofold penalty. By the age of the Rabbis, theft had become entirely a matter of civil law. Exodus xxii. 1 (2) f. was interpreted by them as giving you the right to slay a thief caught in the act only if you had reason to believe that he was out to murder you: that is to say, it was no longer for the offence of theft as such, in whatever form, that a thief forfeited his life. Enslavement persisted solely in the case of an insolvent thief—but in this he was not much worse off than any insolvent debtor.[128] It may be worth mentioning that the evolution in Roman law seems to have been very much the same. The XII Tables lay down that a *fur manifestus* should become the bondman, the *addictus*, of the man whom he tried to rob. This regulation no doubt superseded one under which a manifest thief might be killed. There exist quite a few traces of that earlier regime: even under the XII Tables, if it was a slave who was caught in the act, he was thrown from the Tarpeian rock.[129] In classical law, however, only a fourfold penalty in money was imposed on a manifest thief—though later, when the state publicized more and more branches of private law, and there was a large proletariate, criminal proceedings appear to have become prominent again.[130]

As regards the question of communal or individual responsibility, the narrative of Rachel's theft led me to conclude[131] that at some remote date, if a *vestigii minatio* ended in the discovery of the missing article, no further questions were asked as to which member of the family pursued had stolen it: the *paterfamilias*, or, what was the same in that era, the entire household was answerable for the offence. By the time of Laban versus Jacob, however, though a good many features of the older system survived, a *paterfamilias* could free himself and his family from responsibility by giving up the actual wrongdoer. The story of Joseph's *vestigii minatio* provides support for this thesis. Whatever the precise law of the time may have been, we can observe a tension in legal thought between the claims of communal responsibility and those of individual responsibility, and a movement towards rejecting the former and recognizing only the latter. Joseph's brothers would not have admitted communal liability, even though their peculiar situation favoured this attitude, had such a thing never been known in practice; nor would Joseph have insisted on individual liability, however much his private aims influenced him, had such a thing been quite unimaginable.

Actually, I think we may, without being incautious, go a little beyond this very general conclusion: at least two further points, it seems, can be made. In the first place, the narrative here examined suggests—what is plausible also from *a priori* considerations—that there was in some systems a stage between communal responsibility of a family and individual responsibility of a member of a family; namely, a stage where, though the whole family was held responsible, yet a difference was made—those not guilty being punished less severely than the actual culprit. The first verdict pronounced by Joseph's brothers, when they did not foresee that the cup would be found with them, was, as we saw, that the thief should be put to death, all the others enslaved. I have said that, in proposing this sentence, they were guided by private motives rather than the law. Still, the sentence does show that people could conceive of some legal regulation midway between communal responsibility and individual responsibility. I do not maintain that all law, or even Hebrew law, must have gone through a period with this regulation on the journey from communal responsibility to individual. All I mean to claim is that, from the case under notice, it is probable that the transition from the former to the latter was not always sudden and completed without much wavering, hesitation and compromise. In a previous study I have dealt at length with a different instance of a regime somewhere between communal responsibility and individual responsibility, the chapter of Sodom and Gomorrah, where it is communal merit that is opposed to communal responsibility.[132]

In the second place, Joseph, when he insisted on individual responsibility, introduced his plan, not simply as a different practical method of settling the affair, and not even as a different legal principle, but as the only plan in harmony with the requirements of religion and ethics. To the suggestion advanced by his brothers that all should be his slaves, he replied: 'God forbid that I should do so; but the man in whose hand the cup is found, he shall be my servant; and as for you, get you up in peace unto your father.'[133] To avoid misunderstandings, I may repeat again that his immediate motive in espousing individual responsibility, far from being of a splendid, prophetic character, was to embarrass his brothers, who would put up with anything rather than having to leave behind Benjamin as a slave in Egypt. None the less it remains true that he referred to that idea as an inviolable demand of real justice; that, to his brothers, he pretended to be obeying a fundamental rule of divine law; and that he could do so only if he might reasonably expect them to appreciate this view (or, to use more critical language, if the author of the narrative might expect his public to appreciate this view). It follows that the story under notice constitutes a testimony, not merely of a semi-conscious legal development from communal responsibility to individual responsibility, but of serious reflection and argument on the merits of the latter. Without this, there would have been no basis for Joseph's ostensibly horrified rejection of the proposal to enslave all his brothers, no basis for his claim to be acting in accordance with a great principle if he kept Benjamin only. Indeed, the very fact, which I have just adverted to, that he could speak in such strong terms in favour of individual responsibility although he was not *ex professo* dealing with problems of religion and law, although the question of communal or individual liability formed only a small incidental element of the case before him, and although his attitude was determined largely by the personal object that he pursued, shows clearly with what *élan* the idea of individual responsibility must have been advocated on occasions lying behind this narrative. It even looks as if the principle had gained recognition only after a real struggle.

The result thus emerging, incidentally, should be carefully noted by those who contend that the idea of individual responsibility did not become a factor in the history of Hebrew thought before the 'Deuteronomic' period, that is to say, the seventh century, or possibly not even before Jeremiah and Ezekiel. I do not intend to discuss the problem in any detail. It does, however, strike me as surprising that the narrative of Joseph should never be considered in this connection. This narrative is universally regarded as belonging to the 'Yahwist'; no 'Deuteronomic' revision has been noticed. As I have tried to show, individual responsibility appears here as a great ideal to be upheld: 'God forbid that I should do so', namely, judge on the basis of communal responsibility, are the words put into Joseph's mouth. In view of this, the whole theory outlined which affirms the lateness of this principle in the sources of the Bible seems to me extremely doubtful.[134]

Before leaving the problem created by this tension between the death penalty and enslavement, and between communal responsibility and individual, I have to consider whether the solution might not be sought on lines different from those on which I proceeded. One might, for example, argue (though, as far as I know, it has never been done) that the tension discussed is the result of a conflation of two or three sources. According to one tradition, one might hold, the brothers were threatened with capital punishment, according to another with enslavement only; according to one tradition, they were all liable to punishment for the theft of the cup, according to another, he alone was liable who was deemed the actual thief, according to a third, perhaps, while they were all liable to punishment, the actual thief was to be punished more severely than the rest. The story before us, which makes these several ideas clash with one another, on the basis of this view, would be an ingenious if somewhat clumsy combination of various traditions.

If I were writing a full history of Hebrew law, I should have to examine the possibility of such a solution most carefully.

For a full history of Hebrew law would involve attempting an exact chronology of legal institutions and ideas, and, evidently, if we want to give an exact chronology, we must find out where and when a certain institution or idea made its first appearance. My object, however, is merely to bring out certain trends and notions as such, merely to show the relative position in Hebrew legal development of a narrative like the one under discussion, but not to try and give absolute dates. For my purpose, therefore, the question of whether there may be several traditions behind the story in its present form is of little relevance: I am by-passing the critical problem.[135] Assuming that the narrative as it stands is due to a conflation of different sources, my main conclusions would hardly be affected. The only serious difference would be that I should have to speak of a 'redactor' of the narrative instead of an 'author'. But it would still be true that, at some stage of Hebrew law, namely, in the time of the redactor, death punishment in the case of manifest theft was giving way to enslavement, communal responsibility to individual responsibility: otherwise the redactor would not have made the hero exclaim, 'God forbid that I should do so, but the man in whose hand the cup is found, he shall be my servant'. This exclamation reflects a definite tendency, of however many sources the chapter may be composed. Another difference would be that, instead of saying that the author of the narrative wavered between the older practice of death punishment and communal responsibility and the more progressive practice of enslavement and individual responsibility, we should have to say that the redactor combined the older sources referring to death punishment only and communal responsibility only with the later sources referring to enslavement only and individual responsibility only; and that he showed his preference by assigning the more progressive views to Joseph. But none of this means an essential divergence from the results that I reached without dividing the narrative into different sources. The point is that, whether we ask 'How was it that the author presented the case in the way he did?' or 'How was it that the redactor combined his sources in the way he did?', the reply will be very much the same.

There is a second possibility, which is less easy to dispose of, the possibility that the different points of view represented in the narrative analysed may indicate a conflict between Hebrew law and Egyptian law. The punishment, one might perhaps maintain, that Joseph's brothers declared themselves willing to suffer in case the cup were found with them was in accordance with Hebrew law; whereas Joseph's counter-proposals were made in accordance with Egyptian law. If this could be proved, it would indeed largely vitiate my conclusions: obviously, it would be wrong to use a conflict between the systems of law of two different countries as a basis for establishing an evolution within one of them.

However, for one thing, it seems to me very unlikely that the narrative is intended to depict a clash of the systems of Egypt and Palestine. Were such a thing intended, we should expect a remark like 'For it is the custom of Egyptians to do this, not that'—just as we are told that Joseph and the Egyptians with him did not eat the same meal 'because the Egyptians might not eat bread with the Hebrews, for that is an abomination unto the Egyptians'.[136] (Even if we found a remark to this effect, the question would arise how far it was really Egyptian law that was being applied.) For another thing, even supposing that Joseph's attitude was determined by Egyptian law, the narrative is a Hebrew one. It was a Hebrew author who understood the meaning and implications of the substitution of enslavement for the death penalty and, above all, of individual liability for communal or something between communal and individual. Consequently, even so, though no direct conclusions as to the progress of Hebrew law would be permissible, the fact would remain that somewhere, at some time, it was a Hebrew writer who had to describe the various possible ways of treating the offence in question and to whom, it is clear, the one, the stricter way, appeared less just than the other, the more lenient way.

I now go on to the climax of the story, the discovery of the cup with Benjamin and its consequences—the portion, that is, on account of which I have included the narrative in this study, concerned with the working of formalistic principles when carried to an excess, to the point of *summum ius summa iniuria.* Joseph's steward examined the luggage of the brothers of his master: they were only too ready to show him all. Just as Laban had started by investigating the tents of Jacob, Leah, Bilhah and Zilpah and only then proceeded to Rachel's tent where the stolen objects were concealed, so the steward searched the eldest of the brothers first, then the second eldest and so on, until at last he came to Benjamin. Quite apart from the fact that this delay renders the story more exciting, there was a good reason why the steward should not seize upon Benjamin too soon. He had to pretend not to know what he knew, he must be careful not to show that he expected to find the cup in Benjamin's sack. In any case, he succeeded, it would seem, in appearing innocent of fraud. When the cup was discovered, the brothers returned with him to the city without a murmur. There is no indication that they suspected foul play.

They returned with him to the city. More than that, they admitted that their crime was established. They rent their clothes as people would do whom a great disaster had befallen (and, incidentally, the custom that a man accused or convicted of a capital offence should wear mourning persisted throughout antiquity in the Mediterranean countries [137]), and in their pleadings before Joseph made no attempt to deny that they were rightly to be treated as thieves: 'What shall we speak', Judah said, 'or how shall we clear ourselves? God hath found out the iniquity of thy servants; behold, we are my lord's servants.' [138] It follows that, once a *quaestio* properly conducted had led to the discovery of the missing article, the charge was proved. I would not assert that there may not have been one exception, namely, the case where the party accused could show that the accuser himself had put the object in question into the accused's house or tent. It is just conceivable that a plea of fraud on this ground would be admitted. In the narrative under notice, the problem does not arise—which is the reason why there must remain some uncertainty as to what the legal regulation would have been: Joseph's brothers did not know that he himself had his cup put in Benjamin's sack, and even had they guessed it, they would not have been able to show it. Therefore, they could not think of advancing

an *exceptio doli* to this effect. My impression, however, is that
the law of the time made no provision even for this extreme
case. At any rate, it is obvious that no excuse of any other
kind was possible. The brothers could not defend themselves
by contending that some third person must have played them
a trick. The *quaestio* was a recognized method of arriving
at the truth; and, on a formalistic view, it was irrefutable
evidence.

It is important to remember that on at least two more occasions
in the life of Joseph the old, rigid doctrine of evidence was
of decisive influence on the turn of events. I have discussed
in detail the use that his brothers had made of the rule
governing the relation between a shepherd and the owner of
the flock entrusted to him, namely, that the former should
not be liable for an animal which he could prove, by sub-
mitting its remnants, to have fallen victim to wild beasts.[139]
Joseph's brothers, we have seen, took his coat to their father,
after dipping it in the blood of a kid slaughtered for the purpose, thereby getting rid of any responsibility. Their father
might have his suspicions: but the evidence was unimpeachable, his sons were proved blameless. The other example
suggesting a regime of formalistic evidence that I have in
mind is the decision of the brothers to cast Joseph into a pit,
instead of 'slaying his soul' or 'shedding his blood'.[140] Though
Reuben's aim in proposing this course may have been to save
Joseph, the rest of the brothers clearly desired his death. Why,
then, did they prefer to let him perish in a pit rather than
slay him on the spot? I do not want to go into this question
to any length. An important factor certainly was the religious
fear of shedding blood, blood being deemed a holy force, the
seat of the soul.[141] But another point also comes in, not unconnected with that just mentioned, and it is sufficient here
briefly to draw attention to it. On the basis of a certain type
of formalistic evidence, unless you had shed a man's blood in
the literal sense, you were not made answerable for his death.
Blood must have flowed or else you were not considered guilty,
the charge was not established. Accordingly, if you were able
to contrive a man's death without shedding his blood, you had
not killed him. It is highly probable that some such system,

or at least the popular reminiscence of some such system, underlies the passage discussed. Be this as it may, the result of a *quaestio* counted as absolute proof of guilt or innocence. In the eyes of the law, Joseph's brothers, in possession of the missing cup, were guilty.

With all due reservation, I venture to submit that whoever collected the cycle of tales of the patriarchs may have seen and emphasized and enjoyed a close parallel, or rather contrast, between the narrative of Joseph's pursuit and that of Laban's. In the first part of this study, it may be recalled, I suggested[142] that the way in which Jacob was deceived on the night of his wedding must have been regarded by an ancient audience as a precise and amusing retaliation for the way in which he himself had deceived Isaac in order to obtain the blessing intended for Esau. Jacob had pretended to be Esau and thus received the blessing; once this was conferred on him, it could not be cancelled. But later, Leah pretended to be Rachel and thus became his wife; and once he had taken her to wife, the marriage was valid. Nemesis worked in a wonderfully subtle fashion. I cannot help feeling that there is a similar relation between the story of Laban's idols and that of Joseph's cup. The former narrative tells us how Jacob and Rachel escaped punishment as a result of a formalistic, dishonest interpretation of the words, 'With whomsoever thou findest thy gods, let him not live.' Laban did not *find* his gods, his *quaestio* was unsuccessful, the innocence of Jacob and Rachel was established and they had to fear neither secular vengeance nor divine. The latter narrative tells us how Jacob's and Rachel's beloved son Benjamin incurred mortal danger as a result of the formalistic, dishonest use, by Joseph, of the words, 'He with whom it (the cup) is found, shall be my servant.'[143] Joseph did *find* the cup, his *quaestio* was successful, the offence of Benjamin was established and lifelong slavery was the fate that he had to expect. According to the former story, Jacob and Rachel, the thieves, triumphed in consequence of the formalistic character of the *quaestio*, which made their stratagem possible; according to the latter, their youngest son very nearly perished in consequence of the formalistic character of the *quaestio*, which made the pursuer's

stratagem possible. Should the early listeners not have connected the two incidents? In the long run, then, for the
author of the final cycle at least, that theft of the idols was
not left without its due retribution.

And here, a further inspection of the attitude of the Bible
to the result of Joseph's *quaestio* becomes necessary. I have
explained that this result was conclusive evidence of Benjamin's offence. The brothers made no attempt to prove their
innocence once the cup was discovered. An article, and a
sacred one at that, had been declared missing soon after they
had left the residence; pursuit had been taken up without
delay; they had been overtaken within a short distance from
the city; they had been charged with theft; they had repudiated the charge, offered to show the pursuer all their be-
longings and pronounced themselves guilty in case the missing
object should be found with them; it had been found, and
there was no more to be said about it. Was there no more to
be said about it? From the strictly legal point of view, no:
the case was finally decided. But we should get a wrong idea
of the situation if we did not ask ourselves what the parties
concerned (or, to use critical language, the author of the narrative) thought about this strikingly unjust verdict. Indeed,
though the answer to this question may have no direct bearing
on the problem what was the law of the period—for it cannot
alter the fact that the result of a *quaestio* was accepted in a
rigid, formalistic manner—yet it will, I believe, throw some
light on the general trend of legal argument in that age, on
the forces behind the evolution of Hebrew law and on the
methods adopted by certain circles at least to deal with difficulties like those resulting from formalistic proofs.

To begin with, then, it is necessary to emphasize that the
injustice of the verdict was clearly realized. I have remarked
before[144] on a tendency among some scholars to conclude that
when ancient lawyers assigned to certain words, acts or events
an absolute legal effect, brushing aside as irrelevant special
circumstances which, in modern law, would deprive them of
such effect, they were not aware of the possibility or nature
of these special circumstances; and I have expressed the view
that this conclusion is completely fallacious. The very fact

that Jacob's, Laban's and Joseph's achievements in the way of misusing the formalistic principles of law and religion were considered worth telling and handing down from one generation to the other—or the very fact that the exploit of the Roman general who, having concluded a truce with the enemy for so and so many *days*, attacked in the *night* was recorded and preserved—in my opinion is sufficient evidence that the problem of formalism was seen. In the case of Joseph's *quaestio*, in particular, there is a good deal of additional evidence. Joseph deliberately brought about a miscarriage of justice: he knew that he had himself ordered the cup to be put into Benjamin's sack. Again, his brothers knew that they had not stolen it. In the end, Joseph did not go as far as to execute the punishment to which, being proved guilty, they were liable. There cannot be the shadow of a doubt that the parties themselves, and whoever told and whoever heard the story of this trick, were fully conscious that a *quaestio* had here led to the conviction of an innocent man. Under a formalistic regime, the conviction stood: but it was seen to be the conviction of an innocent man all the same.

The weakness of formalistic methods of evidence was recognized, just as was the weakness of the strictly binding force of certain legal acts and words. At this point, however, a most remarkable feature of the argument of the story-teller becomes apparent. The weakness was recognized: but, far from being attacked or even regretted, it was made the basis for a profound doctrine of divine retribution, it was turned into strength. Joseph's brothers regarded the outcome of the *quaestio*, though it was incorrect and unjust in the ordinary sense, as correct and just inasmuch as it was a punishment, in their view, that God inflicted upon them for their crime against Joseph, whom they believed a slave or dead in a far away country. It may be recalled that on a previous occasion, when they had gone down to Egypt for the first time, Joseph had accused them of espionage. Though they had felt perfectly innocent as far as this specific charge was concerned, yet they had admitted among themselves that they did deserve being ill-treated: ' And they said one to another, We are verily guilty concerning our brother (Joseph), in that we saw the anguish of his soul when he besought us and we would not hear (but threw him into a pit and sold him); therefore is this distress come upon us.'[145] In a higher sense, then, they had felt the accusation to be just, or more precisely, to be an act of unerring, divine justice. Had they not refused mercy—somewhat like this must have run their argument—to Joseph when, innocent enough, he pleaded with them; and was it not in order that they should be refused mercy now when, innocent enough, they pleaded with that Egyptian minister who chose to look upon them as spies? It is very much the same kind of idea that we find in the narrative of the *quaestio*. When they appeared before Joseph after the cup was discovered, Judah exclaimed: 'What shall we say unto my lord?...God hath found out the iniquity of thy servants.'[146] These words contained a double meaning. Judah meant not only that he and his brothers were proved guilty of having stolen the cup, but also that, despite the fact that they had not stolen it, the decision was, in a sense, right. 'God hath found out the iniquity of thy servants'—this was an admission not only of the technical conclusiveness of the evidence by which the charge of theft was established, but also of the justice of God, who in this way, 'delaying but not forgetting', visited their past misdeeds upon them.

Here we have arrived at the main idea on which the author of the narrative rested his solution of the problem of formalistic evidence. It is the idea that God is always just, that He always metes out to you the fate that you deserve—though, indeed, His ways may not always be as direct as ours, and He may wait a long time before He decides on vengeance; but when it comes, His vengeance will be all the more effective and fitting your offence. Accordingly, even the seemingly un-merited disaster is to be explained by reference to this prin-ciple. To apply this line of thought to the *quaestio*: in the eyes of the author of the narrative, or of Judah and his brothers, the *quaestio* had not ceased to be an ordeal producing an irrefutable and, what is more, a just result. Only it was an ordeal on a higher level than it presumably had been when it was first introduced. If you were found guilty of theft, this now did not necessarily mean that you had in fact committed theft. They knew that, in this respect, the evidence might be deceptive.

But it did mean that you deserved your punishment. Formalistic evidence received its justification, that is, not from the
assumption that it was infallible in the ordinary sense—it
obviously was not—but from the assumption that there existed
a supreme court which, in one way or another, repaid every
wrong that you did, but would never let you incur any suffering unless you had done a wrong. This theology, we might
say, interpreted the sentence pronounced against the innocent Benjamin and his brothers as a case of *summa iniuria
summum ius*. In being condemned unjustly, they were only
receiving their due.

It is dangerous to try and discern in an early narrative like
this qualities typical of Jewish law and theology right down
to our time. Nevertheless, if I were for a moment permitted
to throw caution to the winds, I should suggest that there
are at least three points in the method adopted to overcome
the difficulties of formalistic proof which we meet with again
and again in Biblical and Talmudic writings. In the first
place, there is a curious conservatism. The ancient rule that
the result of a *quaestio* is conclusive for or against the guilt
of the accused is maintained. Now, as before, if the missing
article is found in the course of a properly conducted *vestigii
minatio*, the charge is established; and presumably, if it is
not found, the charge fails. No attempt is made, not a single
word is said, to show up the unreasonableness of this rule.
What is done is something quite different: the rule is given a
fresh sense. Whereas formerly the *quaestio* was deemed a highly
reliable means of getting at the truth of the specific matter in
dispute, now it is only one of the innumerable ways in which
God may unmask a villain, be it for the particular offence in
question or be it for another crime, perpetrated, maybe, long
before. But the principle that on the outcome of the search
should depend conviction or acquittal of the accused remains.

The second point that one would like to call characteristic is
what admirers (and I do not hesitate to range myself with them)
might describe as confidence in God, though sceptics might
brand it as escapism into theology. The rigid system under
which a man convicted on the ground of a *quaestio* has no
more defence, instead of being realistically opposed, is tolerated

in the belief that God will see to it that no hardship ensues. It is often pointed out, both by admirers and sceptics, that there is a school of Jewish and Christian teaching that prefers to see a religious purpose in injustice and suffering rather than lead a frontal, secular attack. Something of this spirit would seem to be observable in the narrative examined. Formalistic evidence may lead to the conviction of a man innocent of the crime with which he is charged—thus much is admitted: this need not worry us, however, since God would not allow a person to be found guilty if it were not in accordance with justice on a higher plane.

Lastly, the *quaestio* is judged from a rationalistic point of view. If there ever was an element of magic in it, if it ever was held that a *quaestio*, perhaps in consequence of some ceremony or other, would inevitably distinguish between the thief and the innocent, this element is entirely gone. The *quaestio*, I have said above, remains an ordeal. But it now is an ordeal consistent with a rationalistic attitude, an ordeal only in the sense that God is just, that man is sinful, and that when God makes you undergo sufferings, this must be for some sin that you have committed. Any magic that may have attached to the *quaestio* has become religion—*ratio* probably being the distinctive feature of religion as contrasted with magic. If it be objected that I am seeing too pure a rationalism in this narrative, I would refer to a little significant detail. Joseph, it should be noted, when his brothers were led before him by the steward who had conducted the pursuit, told them that he had had no difficulty in deciding that they must be the thieves: he had found it out by supernatural means. 'What deed is this that ye have done? wot ye not that such a man as I can certainly divine?'[147] These words, uttered by him who had himself smuggled the cup into Benjamin's luggage, constituted a strong gibe at divining by magic and similar hocus-pocus, and must have been understood thus by all that heard the story. In fact, the motif almost reminds one of Voltaire.

The first two of the three points just outlined, it is true, namely, the conservatism and the settling of a difficulty by the interposition of theology, should perhaps be considered typical of the religious groups dominating the Bible rather than of ancient Hebrew law proper. I have already stated[148] that when the Bible regards law under the aspect of religion, it does not always follow that the same was the case in the legal circles of the Hebrew state. The institution under discussion, *vestigii minatio*, seems to furnish another illustration of a discrepancy of this kind. In the Biblical tale of Joseph, the injustice possible where formalistic evidence prevails is got rid of with the help of a religious doctrine, the doctrine that, in a higher sense, no injustice can occur, since God will protect the good and let misfortune befall the wicked only. Law proper, however, does not seem to have been satisfied with this solution. How exactly it progressed we do not know. But we know, first, that the Biblical instances of *vestigii minatio* are all to be found in early narratives, those of Jacob and Laban, of Joseph and his brothers and of the Danites (in the latter narrative, as I have shown above,[149] the procedure is cut short by the successful refusal of the thieves to submit); and secondly, that even in the oldest Rabbinic sources, *vestigii minatio* is no longer to be met with. So whatever the precise evolution may have been, and however many various factors may have contributed, the end was that formalistic evidence was abandoned. According to Talmudic law, a man in whose house you discover goods stolen from you is always entitled to prove that he is not the thief but that, for example, he has bought them from a third person. He is entitled to prove this whether you call on him months after you first became aware of the theft, or immediately on his leaving you and your noticing that the goods are missing: there is no procedure by which he can be deprived of the right to advance any special defence that he may think will exonerate him.[150]

To some extent, then, the way in which formalistic evidence is vindicated in the narrative of Joseph is peculiar to the theological authors of the Bible, not to the early Hebrew lawyers. It is none the less conceivable that the first serious attempts to rectify miscarriages of justice were made by these theological groups, though they confined themselves to spiritual means; and that it was largely due to their initiative that the lawyers were able to take up the struggle in the secular field and finally to abolish the *quaestio* from the law proper. One thing at any rate the theological authors of the narrative had in common with the lawyers, a perfectly rationalistic view of the matter. That given, there might still be a conflict between a religious solution—making God take charge of the system and see that no injustice was done—and a practical solution—replacing formalistic proof by a freer, more liberal assessment of evidence. But the main thing was to recognize the problem and the necessity of dealing with it by some rationalistic method: and this recognition is fully present in the narrative of Joseph.

The happy end of the pathetic little story of Joseph's pursuit of Benjamin is well known. When the tension was at its highest, when his brothers thought that the only mitigation of the punishment that they might hope for was that Joseph would keep back as slave Judah instead of Benjamin, Joseph stepped out of his disguise, forgave his brothers for what they had done to him, and asked them to come and stay with him in Egypt, themselves and their father Jacob. But all this is quite outside the topic of history of law however much the concept of law be stretched, and I must not linger on one of the finest dénouements in world literature.

V

We have seen that *vestigii minatio* occurs in Hebrew law as well as in Indo-European law; not indeed because it was introduced 'before the epoch of the great migrations'[151]—we know very little about them—but because it necessarily grew up wherever there existed a certain state of society, no matter what part of the world it was. No better confirmation of this can be desired than the way in which the story of Hercules's pursuit of Cacus and, quite probably, that of Laban's pursuit of Jacob travelled from one people to the other. Such transmission would hardly have been possible had the elements from which these tales were made up not been universal. That a man who noticed that a valuable object had just been stolen should hurry after the thief, without waiting for the slow machinery of the courts, was understood everywhere.

In fact, the main problems arising in this situation are so similar in all ancient systems that the Biblical examples of *quaestio* analysed above may help us to greater clarity about the Roman law on the matter. In both the case of Laban versus Jacob and that of Joseph versus his brothers, a major problem, as I have tried to show, was the problem of the position of the *paterfamilias* or, one might say, of communal or individual liability. On the one hand, there are strong traces of a time when a legal argument did not differ too much from a feud. That was the time when a *paterfamilias* could not defend himself any further once the missing article was found in his house. Once it was found, he was made responsible, or rather, he and his entire family were treated as enemies: there was no selection of that particular member of the family who had committed the theft. On the other hand, it is important to note that Jacob's oath confined punishment to the particular person convicted, 'With whomsoever thou findest thy gods, let him not live' (the ambiguity of the wording may be disregarded in this connection); and that Joseph most emphatically stuck to the principle of individual responsibility, 'But the man in whose hand the cup is found, he shall be my servant.' Surely, we may expect to find the same problem demanding a solution in early Rome. Again, in the case of Laban versus Jacob, the thief succeeded in thwarting the search: the missing article was concealed too well to be found. Tricks of this kind must have occurred in Rome also, and it is unlikely that any legal rules could stop a thief from resorting to them. Finally, in the case of Joseph versus his brothers, there was the problem of the conclusiveness of the result of a *quaestio*. The cup was discovered with Benjamin; but Benjamin had not stolen it, it was smuggled into his bag by a third person—in fact, the accuser himself. I have argued that, at the period of this story, the law did not yet admit any special excuse if the article in dispute turned up in the course of a *vestigii minatio*. The person in whose possession it was found could not say that he and his family had not stolen it, but that they had bought it unaware of its nature or that it had been put in their house without their knowledge. The *quaestio* was accepted as final proof. At the same time, however, I observed that the possibility of an injustice being done under this regime was fully realized. Joseph's brothers 'solved' the problem by a religious method. They held that the result of the search, which proved them criminals, was right in a higher sense: they were criminals, having dealt cruelly with Joseph, and this was their reward. But secular jurists could not be content with this, and I have stated that as the methods of evidence became freer, the positive result of a *quaestio* more and more assumed the character of a mere presumption of guilt, instead of that of an absolute, final verdict of guilty. This difficulty, this question how far discovery of the missing object showed the accused a thief, how far he might be allowed to defend himself by reference to a third party from whom he had received the object, must have played as big a part in Roman law as in Hebrew.

I propose, therefore, to survey the Roman ground, bearing in mind the problems and tensions that we come across in the Biblical narratives. The best way seems to be first to go through the relevant passages in Gaius and Justinian paragraph by paragraph. They are by far the most outspoken sources in this branch of the law, and only a careful interpretation of the texts can lead to anything like a convincing result. Moreover, it is Gaius's presentation of the law that has caused so much controversy among historians as to the course of evolution that the Roman *quaestio* took.

As is well known, Gaius, in *Institutes* 3. 186 and 191, says that the XII Tables imposed a threefold penalty upon a man with whom the missing goods were found through a search conducted in the presence of witnesses; while in 3. 192 he says that the XII Tables deemed a theft manifest if the missing goods were found through a search conducted under certain formalities— *nudus quaerat, licio cinctus, lancem habens.* The difference in punishment is great, for it may be recalled that a manifest thief was liable to being scourged and adjudged to the other party. The prevalent doctrine at present seems to be that Gaius here contradicts himself, erroneously ascribing to the XII Tables two procedures which never existed at the same time, but represent successive stages of the law. The investigation conducted *lance et licio* alone, it is held, goes back to the XII Tables; the less formal search, with witnesses, must be of later origin. Gaius simply was careless or ignorant enough to credit the XII Tables with both these procedures.[152]

Some authorities, however, disagree with this rather facile explanation.[153] It is hard to believe, they contend, that Gaius, author of a commentary on the XII Tables, should have made this mistake. I would add that the contradiction assumed by the prevalent theory is so obvious that even Gaius, who was not hypersensitive to slight inconsistencies, would not have been guilty of it. According to the conservative view, the XII Tables must have spoken of two alternative modes of search. One of them, more formal, led to the treatment of the accused person as a manifest thief, the other to a penalty in money. This view will be accepted if reasons can be given why there should have been two different procedures at the same time. Such reasons, I submit, are not lacking.[154]

The discussion of theft in Gaius's *Institutes* begins in 3. 183: *Furtorum autem genera Servius Sulpicius et Masurius Sabinus quattuor esse dixerunt, manifestum et nec manifestum, conceptum et oblatum; Labeo duo, manifestum et nec manifestum; nam conceptum et oblatum species potius actionis esse furto cohaerentes quam genera furtorum; quod sane verius videtur, sicut inferius apparebit.*

Even from these remarks on classification, one or two conclusions as to the nature of *furtum conceptum*, the case of stolen things found by a search, may be drawn. Above all, it is certain that *furtum conceptum* here cannot refer to the discovery of stolen goods in the hands of the thief as thief. For if it did mean this, Labeo would not have denied its character as a class of *furtum*, nor would Gaius have accepted his opinion. *Furtum conceptum* must denote the discovery of the goods with someone not, or not necessarily, the actual thief. A second conclusion to be drawn is that there must be a close 'relationship between *furtum conceptum* and *furtum oblatum*: the two are clearly connected with one another by the lawyers. Finally, the question may be raised—though it obviously cannot be answered on the basis of this text alone— whether the difference in classification mentioned by Gaius does not reflect a difference in law. In other words, the fact that the earlier jurists, Servius and Sabinus, have one classification and the later, Labeo and Gaius, another suggests that, for some reason or other, very possibly through a change in legal notions, the traditional doctrine became outmoded.

In 184 Gaius deals with the first class, *furtum manifestum*, in 185 with the second, *furtum nec manifestum*. These paragraphs are of no immediate relevance to my topic. In 186 and 187 he describes the two pseudo-*genera*, *furtum conceptum* and *furtum oblatum*. *Conceptum furtum dicitur, cum apud aliquem testibus praesentibus furtiva res quaesita et inventa est. nam in eum propria actio constituta est, quamvis fur non sit, quae appellatur concepti. Oblatum furtum dicitur, cum res furtiva tibi ab aliquo oblata sit eaque apud te concepta sit, utique si ea mente data tibi fuerit ut apud te potius quam apud eum qui dederit conciperetur. nam tibi apud quem concepta est propria adversus eum qui optulit, quamvis fur non sit, constituta est actio, quae appellatur oblati.*

This text confirms the conclusions that I have just reached in interpreting 3. 183. First, Gaius expressly states that both actions, *furti concepti* and *furti oblati*, may be brought against a man *quamvis fur non sit*. Secondly, the two actions are closely related with one another, the latter being available to a person compelled to pay under the former. A man in whose house the stolen article is discovered, and who, on an *actio furti concepti*, has to pay threefold damages to the owner, may claim indemnification by an *actio furti oblati* from him who has put him in possession of the article concerned. As for the evolution lying behind the difference in classification between the Republican jurists and those of the Principate, this will become clear when we examine Gaius's exposition somewhat more critically.

For it looks as if we might distinguish at least two strata in his account. As we shall soon see, when we come to 3. 191, according to Gaius, both the *actio furti concepti* and the *actio furti oblati* were given by the XII Tables. In view of all that we know of that code, however, it is hardly likely that it did more than briefly state when these actions should lie and what their results should be. In other words, while there is no reason to doubt that the brief definitions (*conceptum furtum dicitur cum apud aliquem testibus praesentibus furtiva res quaesita et inventa est—oblatum furtum dicitur cum res furtiva tibi ab aliquo oblata sit eaque apud te concepta sit*) and the threefold damages which 3. 191 says must be paid under these actions do substantially, though not in form, represent the law of the XII Tables, the further, detailed explanations (that is to say, with regard to *furtum conceptum, nam in eum propria actio constituta est, quamvis fur non sit, quae appellatur concepti*, and with regard to *furtum oblatum, nam tibi apud quem concepta est propria adversus eum qui optulit, quamvis fur non sit, constituta est actio, quae appellatur oblati*) in all probability represent Gaius's comment or the comment of his source—which may or may not be in exact accordance with the notions prevalent at the time of the XII Tables. Gaius himself formulates these explanations as glosses, meant to elucidate the law (*nam actio constituta est*), not as provisions directly taken from the statute. Similarly, the restriction on the *actio furti oblati*, namely, the rule that it should lie *utique si ea mente data* (*res furtiva*) *tibi fuerit ut apud te potius quam apud eum qui dederit conciperetur*, gives the impression of an addition later than the XII Tables—which may or may not be a faithful paraphrase of the law that they had laid down. Quite apart from the fact that no other provision of the XII Tables is preserved so carefully describing a mental state necessary for a verdict of guilty, it is significant that no equivalent restriction is mentioned in connection with the *actio furti concepti*. We should expect that, if the XII Tables had been so scrupulous in protecting an innocent person from the *actio furti oblati*, they would also have provided that he with whom a missing object was found might be sued *utique si sciens eam* (*rem furtivam*) *celaverit*.

Assuming, then, that the main features recorded by Gaius, and they alone, correspond to the law of the XII Tables, the following picture emerges. According to the XII Tables, if a search carried out in the presence of witnesses results in the discovery of the missing object, an *actio furti concepti* lies against the man in whose house it has been discovered, no matter whether or not he is the actual thief. This means a compromise of a kind typical of the XII Tables. On the one hand, the methods of evidence are still fairly formalistic. Once a *quaestio* has taken place and ended in the article being found, the owner of the house is considered responsible: he cannot escape liability by saying that a third party sold or gave him the thing, or smuggled it into his house, or the like. On the other hand, the man in whose house the object has been discovered is no longer treated as a manifest thief. We shall see below that at some earlier time he had been so treated, losing his freedom or life. Under the XII Tables, he is to be sued not by an *actio furti manifesti*, but by an *actio furti concepti*, leading to threefold restitution, a far more lenient punishment. The XII Tables, that is, while upholding the rigid principle that he who is shown in possession of the object by a *quaestio* has to answer for it, yet, by mitigating the penalty, do take into account the possibility that he may not be the actual thief, but may have received the object from a third party, perhaps even without suspecting anything wrong.

It might perhaps be argued that it is for a different reason that the XII Tables do not put *furtum conceptum* on a level with *furtum manifestum*. They are contemplating, it might be argued, not the possibility of a third party, an outsider, being the actual thief, but the possibility of the wife or a son or a slave of the *paterfamilias* accused being the actual thief. It is most improbable, however, that this should be the motive behind the milder view taken of *furtum conceptum*. Theft by a *filiusfamilias* or slave is regulated in the XII Tables in special provisions. No doubt some of them are lost. But even from those that we have it is clear that no more than 'noxal' liability is imposed by the XII Tables on a *paterfamilias* for a theft committed by a member of his family: unless he offers to pay damages (which, of course, he cannot do in cases where the law deems a monetary settlement inadequate), he has to tolerate the infliction of vengeance on the guilty member.[155] That is all. It follows that when the XII Tables lay down that *furtum conceptum* be dealt with more leniently than *furtum manifestum*, it is not because the article discovered may possibly have been stolen by a member of the family, not the *paterfamilias* himself—this possibility is provided for in the special rules just referred to—but because the article discovered may possibly have been stolen by a third party, not the man in whose house it is found. The latter may have got hold of it in a great many ways, ranging from receiving, as the thief's accomplice, to buying in perfectly good faith.

Strong support for the interpretation here attempted is furnished by the *actio furti oblati*. It is an action to be brought by him who has had to pay threefold damages on an *actio furti concepti* against the person—if there is one—who has put him in possession of the article concerned. This confirms the view that the reason why the XII Tables distinguish *furtum conceptum* from *furtum manifestum* is not the possibility of the theft having been committed by a member of the family, a son or a slave, but the possibility of its having been committed by a third party, an outsider. It is only in the latter case that an *actio furti oblati* can operate at all: no action for indemnification could be instituted by a *paterfamilias* against a member of his own family. Further, and more generally, by the *actio furti oblati* is confirmed the view that the *actio furti concepti* is not directed against the actual thief only. If it were, the *actio furti oblati* would be senseless. If the *actio furti concepti* were directed against a man *qua* thief, there would be no point whatever in giving him a remedy against a third party. Obviously, then, the authors of the code are aware that the *actio furti concepti*, though in many cases it will reach the actual thief, in many others will reach one who merely obtained the stolen goods from someone else. In fact, it is probable that the XII Tables contemplate the possibility of their having been obtained in all innocence. I think it most unlikely that if a dishonest receiver only were contemplated, a special action would be put at his disposal to recover damages from the actual thief. I do not mean to say that the XII Tables do not allow a man to bring an *actio furti oblati* unless he obtained the article in good faith. Difficulties of evidence at this stage of the law make it impossible to examine in each individual case whether the person condemned under an *actio furti concepti* is honest or not. What I do mean to say, however, is that the XII Tables, in allowing a man condemned under an *actio furti concepti* to claim redress from whoever gave him the goods, seem to take into account not only the case where he is not the actual thief, but the case where he is not even a fraudulent receiver: they seem to contemplate the chance that a man may be condemned under the *actio furti concepti* who, perfectly innocent, has become involved in the affair entirely through the trickery of a third party. It is in order to achieve some measure of justice in this deserving case, it would appear, that the *actio furti oblati* is recognized, even at the risk of its helping a dishonest receiver also.

Just as an *actio furti concepti* lies whether he with whom the article is discovered is the actual thief or not, and whether, if he is not the actual thief, he obtained the article in bad faith or unwittingly, so, under the regime of the XII Tables, an *actio furti oblati* is available to him condemned on an *actio furti concepti* whether the man who put him in possession of the article did so with *dolus* or without. No doubt, even at this period, the *actio furti oblati* is intended to hit him who acted in bad faith, preferably, indeed, the actual thief. But bad faith is not a necessary condition of the action in any given case. Justice as yet is rough and ready. Provided he who has had to pay the penalty of an *actio furti concepti* had the goods from a third party, he may bring the *actio furti oblati*, even if the third party should happen to be innocent.

A modern lawyer might ask whether there is a further similar action for him who has been condemned under an *actio furti oblati*, but had obtained the object from yet another outsider. For example, stolen goods are discovered in my house and I am condemned to pay damages under an *actio furti concepti*; I successfully bring the *actio furti oblati* against you, from whom I had the goods; may you, if you had them from somebody else, bring a further action against that man? Most probably not. Under the XII Tables, it seems, there are just two actions, and there the matter has an end. A person defeated by an *actio furti concepti* may claim indemnification from the person who has put him in possession of the article—but there is no further regress. Thus the loss must occasionally fall on the shoulders of an innocent man. In most cases, however, an *actio furti oblati* will lead to one who is at least an accomplice of the actual thief. That now and then an innocent man should have to suffer is the price paid at this stage of civilization for a smooth, reliable and peaceful working of the machinery of justice.

On the other hand, the guilty will often escape. An *actio furti oblati*, it should be noticed, may be brought only if there has been a condemnation on an *actio furti concepti*. This is quite clear from Gaius's account: *oblatum furtum dicitur cum res...oblata sit eaque apud te concepta sit.* In other words, if I have, say, bought a plough from you and find out that you have stolen it from a neighbour, unless he conducts a search and successfully sues me with an *actio furti concepti*, I cannot sue you with the *actio furti oblati*. Forfeiture of the penalty of *furtum conceptum* is an essential requirement for an *actio furti oblati*. Once I have forfeited the penalty, I have an *actio furti oblati* against you whether or not you are guilty of theft or similar dishonesty.

To sum up, according to the XII Tables, if stolen goods are found in a man's house as a result of a search conducted in the presence of witnesses, an *actio furti concepti* lies. It lies irrespective of any special circumstances: the positive outcome of the search is still decisive, still sufficient to make the owner of the house a *fur*. In fact, the penalty, threefold damages, is higher than the penalty for what one might call ordinary theft, *furtum nec manifestum*; the case is still rather serious. At the same time, account is taken of the possibility of the owner not being the actual thief and perhaps not even a fraudulent receiver. This is done in a somewhat clumsy manner: in the first place, the threefold penalty is far more lenient than the punishment of *furtum manifestum* that had once been imposed on a man convicted by a *quaestio*, in the second place, if he obtained the object from a third party, he can recover the penalty forfeited by an *actio furti oblati*. This action also lies irrespective of special circumstances: though its purpose is to throw the loss on the actual thief, yet it lies whenever I have had to pay damages under an *actio furti concepti* in respect of a thing that you brought into my house. It is intended, that is, to compel you to indemnify me if you have smuggled the thing into my house without my knowledge, or have sold it to me because you knew or suspected that there was something wrong; but it lies even if you have sold it to me in perfectly good faith. The fact that an object that I had from you has been searched for in the presence of witnesses, has been discovered and has led to my condemnation in an *actio furti concepti* is still decisive, is still sufficient to make your giving it to me an offence, to make you a *fur*.

The system outlined is reflected in the names of the two actions, and conceivably to a greater extent than has hitherto been seen. The action against a person in whose house the missing article is found is called *actio furti concepti*. This, if we follow the interpretation of the Roman jurists,[156] means 'an action on the ground that the stolen thing has been seized in the house of the defendant'. The discovery through a search constitutes the basis of the action; there is no reference to any state of mind; and the choice of a wording analogous to *actio furti manifesti* and *actio furti nec manifesti* suggests that a man made responsible on this basis is regarded as, in a sense, a *fur*. Yet the very existence of a special name shows that the distinctive problems of the situation are recognized, in however crude a fashion they may be solved. Again, the action against a person who has brought stolen goods into a house where they are found is called *actio furti oblati*, meaning 'an action on the ground that the stolen thing has been brought into the house of the plaintiff'. The putting a man in possession of a stolen article which is later discovered is the basis of the action. It constitutes a wrong, an *offerre*, one might translate, 'an infliction of the stolen article on a man', no matter whether done with *dolus* or without—though, as I have tried to make out and as the name itself indicates, the law-giver has in mind primarily him who acts in bad faith. As in the case of *furtum conceptum*, the choice of an expression analogous to *actio furti manifesti* and *actio furti nec manifesti* suggests that a person liable under the action is considered a *fur*.

Of the name *actio furti concepti*, however, I think an alternative explanation is possible. It may, I think, originally have signified 'an action on the ground that the stolen thing has been received by the defendant'. Two arguments seem to speak in favour of this interpretation. For one thing, it would make the name more closely parallel to *actio furti oblati*. The act expressed by *oblati* is the offence committed by the defendant: he has brought the thing into the house of the plaintiff, he has committed an *offerre*. Now if we take *actio furti concepti* in the traditional way, the act expressed by *concepti* is not the offence committed by the defendant, but the result of the search conducted by the plaintiff: he has seized the thing in the defendant's house. If, however, we render *actio furti concepti*, against tradition, by 'an action because of stolen goods received', *concepti* refers to the offence committed by the defendant in this action, his receiving the stolen object, precisely as *oblati* refers to the offence committed by the defendant in an *actio furti oblati*. The one would be 'an action because of stolen goods received', the other 'an action because of stolen goods brought'. For another thing, I have shown above that the *actio furti concepti* grew up when it was felt that to treat a man in whose house the missing article had been detected as a manifest thief was unsatisfactory. Might it not happen that he was not the actual thief at all but had only been given the article by a third party, perhaps without even suspecting any offence connected with it? It is tempting to suppose that the case in view of which the action arose, the case where he in whose house the object was discovered had only obtained it from a third party, determined the name of the action: 'an action on the ground that the stolen thing has been received'.

There are indeed serious considerations against this explanation. I can find no evidence in extant texts showing that *concipere* was ever used in the sense of 'to receive stolen goods'. Moreover, the Roman jurists unanimously explain the word as 'to seize stolen goods in the course of a search'. To the first objection I might reply that the Latin language changed a great deal in the period between the XII Tables and the second century B.C., when our main sources begin to flow; that there is nothing *a priori* improbable in the assumption that an intensive form of *capere*, at the time of the XII Tables, meant 'to receive stolen goods'; and that one might think of reasons why the term was gradually superseded in this meaning by verbs like *recipere* and *suscipere*. As for the second objection, too much weight need not be attached to the philological efforts of the Roman jurists. Their explanation of *concipere*, like many similar ones, seems to date from the first century B.C.[157] It is not, that is, a very ancient, decemviral piece of teaching, but a creation of the young, pre-classical jurisprudence arising in the late Republic. These late Republican interpretations and etymologies of early words and phrases need not be considered as infallible. Still, it must be admitted that the alternative explanation of the name *actio furti concepti* here suggested, while quite possible, is considerably less likely than the one given in the Roman sources and so far unchallenged by modern historians.

Looking now at Gaius's, or his source's, remarks on this machinery, we find that while on the whole he maintains the system of the XII Tables, some highly significant changes have crept in. The most striking of them is that, according to Gaius, condemnation under an *actio furti concepti* does not by itself entitle you to bring an *actio furti oblati* against the man who put you in possession of the incriminating article. You may sue him only *si ea mente (res) data tibi fuerit ut apud te potius quam apud eum qui dederit conciperetur*. Under the XII Tables, I concluded, though the purpose of the *actio furti oblati* was to throw the loss on the actual thief or at least a dishonest accomplice, yet the methods of evidence were too undeveloped to admit of an examination of the defendant's mental state in each individual case. Thus even a man who had given another a stolen article in all innocence, having himself, say, bought it in the market, would be liable to pay damages: it was not possible to do justice in such exceptional situations. This is different under the regime prevalent at the time of Gaius. The purpose of the *actio furti oblati* is now taken account of, made the criterion, in each given case. Unless the defendant has acted in bad faith, he will not be condemned on an *actio furti oblati*. Each case is judged on its own merits: a defendant may show that he is innocent even though *prima facie* appearances may be against him. It is a sound development not only from the ethical point of view but also from the point of view of commerce. Surely, it can never have been encouraging to a trader to know that, whenever he sold anyone an object with the history of which he was not thoroughly familiar, he was running the risk of being sued with an *actio furti oblati*. Under the system described by Gaius, so long as a trader is honest, he is running no risk of this kind.

It should be noticed, however, that if Gaius's account is complete, the *actio furti concepti*, in contradistinction to the *actio furti oblati*, does not require *dolus* even at this stage. An *actio furti concepti*, even under the regime outlined by Gaius, lies whether the man in whose house the missing thing is discovered is guilty or innocent. This is a most suggestive feature of the system. Evidently, the rigid rules of responsibility disappeared from the *actio furti oblati* before they disappeared from the *actio furti concepti*. Why? Because the former is one degree removed from the *quaestio*, the search of a house in the presence of witnesses. In the case of the *actio furti concepti*, it was more difficult to loosen the fetters of formalist evidence. The result of the *quaestio* had always been decisive irrespective of the mental state of the defendant: it was hard to break this rule. The *actio furti oblati* was not so closely connected with the search. It was brought by a man who, condemned under an *actio furti concepti*, sought to obtain redress from him who had given him the article in question. Here it was easier to bring in ‘subjective’ elements and gradually to make bad faith in the defendant an essential condition of a successful claim.

The fact that, in Gaius's system, bad faith is an essential requirement of the *actio furti oblati* but not of the *actio furti concepti* produces one curious result. Under this regime, a man condemned on an *actio furti concepti* may sometimes obtain no redress even though he is innocent, having obtained the article from a third party. For example, if *A* steals an object and sells it to *B*, who is in good faith, and *B* sells it to *C*, in whose house it is discovered, *C* may be sued with an *actio furti concepti*, since this action does not require *dolus*; but he cannot recover damages from *B* by an *actio furti oblati*, since this action does require *dolus*. I have shown above that under the earlier system of the XII Tables, when both actions were available irrespective of the mental state of the defendant, similar injustice might be done to a defendant in the *actio furti oblati*: in the case just put, *C* could recover damages from *B*—since the *actio furti oblati* also lay even if the defendant had acted in all innocence—but *B* had no further remedy to get back the threefold penalty from the thief or the accomplice who had sold him the article. The history of law is not exclusively governed by logic, and it takes a long time for a more or less coherent and just regulation to come about in matters so complicated as the one under notice.

There is, indeed, a possibility that Gaius's account is not quite complete, that it does not fully represent the law of his period. In other words, it may well be that, in his age, *dolus* on the part of the defendant had to be proved both in an *actio furti oblati* and in an *actio furti concepti*. That he omits to mention the point in describing the latter action is true. But it is quite conceivable that he does so because he did not find it in his source. He was doubtless capable of a piece of negligence of this kind. His source, we may hold, was written at a time when *dolus* was not yet a requirement of *actio furti concepti* (here the result of the search was still decisive) but only of *actio furti oblati*. By the time of Gaius, *dolus* was essential in both, only he failed to bring his source up to date.

In any case, it is easy to see, even on the basis of Gaius's exposition, in what direction the law was going. According to the XII Tables, an *actio furti concepti* lay no matter whether the defendant was guilty or not; yet by prescribing a more lenient penalty than in the case of *furtum manifestum*, and by allowing an *actio furti oblati* if a third party had put the defendant in possession of the object concerned, the XII Tables to some extent mitigated the injustice done to an honest defendant. The *actio furti oblati* also lay whether the defendant was guilty or not. In Gaius's system, however, the latter action is confined to the case where the defendant, when putting the plaintiff in possession of the article, acted in bad faith. It is easy to see that, in postclassical times at least, but possibly already under the actual law practised in the period of Gaius, the question of *dolus* in the *actio furti concepti* would be treated on the model of the *actio furti oblati*; that is to say, gradually the *actio furti concepti* must also have ceased to lie unless the man in whose house the thing was found had known that it was stolen. I shall adduce below a text from Justinian confirming this conclusion.

Before doing so, however, I have to draw attention to another divergence between the system of the XII Tables and that of Gaius. Gaius says that the actions of *furtum conceptum* and *furtum oblatum* lie even if the accused is not a *fur*: *quamvis fur non sit*. This is quite correct in a certain sense, for both the XII Tables and the law of the age of Gaius: in both periods, neither the defendant in an *actio furti concepti* nor the defendant in an *actio furti oblati* need be the actual thief and, under the XII Tables, neither of them need even be dishonest at all. (Under the system of the time of Gaius, at least the defendant in an *actio furti oblati* must have shown *dolus*. Therefore, if he had been really accurate, Gaius could not have said that he need not be a *fur*. Any *contrectare* constituted *furtum* in the age of Gaius, and a man who gives me a stolen article in order that it should not be found with him, even though he may not have stolen it himself, surely commits a *contrectare*. The remark that an *actio furti oblati* lies *quamvis fur non sit qui optulit* dates from a time when the action did not yet require *dolus*. Gaius was not accurate enough to strike it out or modify it in accordance with the new development. What he meant is clear, however: he meant that it lay even though the defendant had not actually stolen the object.) Yet, in another sense, for the time of the XII Tables, the clause *quamvis fur non sit* is hardly tenable. Roughly speaking— and I am well aware of the inadequacy of my formulation—as regards the practical application of the system, it is true that a man not a *fur* might be condemned under an *actio furti concepti* or *oblati*; but not so as regards the 'theory' of the system. As I have attempted to show, on the one hand, the XII Tables impose a threefold penalty only on *furtum conceptum* and allow a man to obtain redress by an *actio furti oblati*, thus recognizing the possibility of a condemnation of one who is not the actual thief, and perhaps not even a fraudulent receiver. But, on the other hand, the penalty is higher than for *furtum nec manifestum*, ordinary theft. Moreover, the outcome of the search is still absolutely decisive for an *actio furti concepti*; and similarly, in an *actio furti oblati*, he who brought the goods into the house where they were found may plead no special circumstances by way of excuse. This means that, while fairly far-reaching efforts are made to prevent injustice being done, yet the formalistic side of the procedure of *quaestio* has not yet been overcome. In short, I think that a man condemned under an *actio furti concepti* or *actio furti oblati* at the time of the XII Tables is still considered a *fur*—despite the growing realization that he need not in fact be one. It was probably the jurisprudence of the late Republic and early Principate which analysed the system more confidently and freely, arriving at the conclusion, and stating it, that you might have to pay threefold damages even though you were not a *fur*.

This theoretical development, I believe, this abandonment of ancient formalistic theory, lies at the bottom of the difference in classification mentioned by Gaius and referred to above. Servius and Sabinus, the latter of Capito's school, maintained the earlier view that *furtum conceptum* and *furtum oblatum* were proper modes of theft. They stuck to the doctrine that there were four *genera* of theft, all fundamentally on the same level, *furtum manifestum, nec manifestum, conceptum* and *oblatum*. But Labeo preferred, maybe introduced, a more modern classification, taking account of the fact that in an *actio furti concepti* or *oblati* you might be condemned though you were not guilty. He declared *furtum conceptum* and *furtum oblatum* to be *species potius actionis furto cohaerentes quam genera furtorum*: these two actions, he said, were connected with theft but not properly on the ground of theft. Gaius, though Sabinist, accepts Labeo's classification; no wonder, since this must have appeared the only sensible one to a lawyer of the second century—with a proviso to be added below.

There may, however, have been another factor contributing to the evolution. In the XII Tables, the noun *furtum* means not 'the offence of theft' but 'a stolen article'. So long as the word had this meaning, it was quite in order to enumerate as parallel *furtum manifestum, furtum nec manifestum, furtum conceptum*, 'a stolen article seized in the defendant's house' (or possibly, at some time, 'a stolen article received by the defendant'), and *furtum oblatum,* 'a stolen article brought into the defendant's house'. Used in this sense, the expressions *furtum conceptum* and *furtum oblatum* did not necessarily imply any dishonesty on the part of the defendant. When, however, the word *furtum* acquired the meaning 'the offence of theft', there arose a problem. For, as soon as it was seen that the actions *furti concepti* and *furti oblati* might be available even against a perfectly innocent person, it must have struck the jurists that these were not *furta,* cases of theft, properly so called, and that only *furtum manifestum* and *furtum nec manifestum* fully deserved that appellation. This may well have been a further consideration making for Labeo's teaching that there were two real classes of theft only, with *furtum conceptum* and *furtum oblatum* as allied cases.

As a matter of fact, by the time of Gaius, the situation had undergone a further change, at least as far as *furtum oblatum* is concerned. This action now required *dolus*; and the *actio furti concepti,* if it did not yet require it, was certainly moving in the same direction. Had Gaius been subtle, he would have realized that at least *furtum oblatum* was now a proper kind of theft, in line with *furtum manifestum* and *furtum nec manifestum*; and he would have rectified Labeo's doctrine accordingly. But he was not subtle. (As already remarked, he ought not to have described the *actio furti oblati* as lying against a man *quamvis fur non sit.*) We shall see that Justinian did regard both *furtum conceptum* and *furtum oblatum* as real theft, subsuming them under *furtum nec manifestum.*

It may be well at this point to look briefly at post-classical law and see where the development traced so far led to in the end. It is well known that in the post-classical period the old formalistic methods of evidence were generally superseded by freer proceedings. In the course of this evolution, the *quaestio* lost more and more of its weight. The eventual result was that a thief not caught in the act of stealing, or a person who knowingly possessed or transferred to another person stolen goods, was dealt with as a *fur nec manifestus,* no matter whether the offence was proved in the ordinary way or through a search in his house: a search, that is, was deemed no different now from any other manner of proof. Justinian, in *Institutes* 4. 1. 4, tells us: *Sed hae actiones, id est concepti et oblati. . . in desuetudinem abierunt.*[158] *cum enim requisitio rei furtivae hodie secundum veterem observationem non fit, merito ex consequentia etiam praefatae actiones ab usu communi recesserunt, cum manifestissimum est quod omnes qui scientes rem furtivam susceperint et celaverint furti nec manifesti obnoxii sunt.*

This paragraph, it should be observed, besides giving us a survey of the post-classical history, supports some of the conclusions at which I have arrived above, in discussing the classical and pre-classical systems. Three points may be mentioned. In the first place, Justinian expressly states that the fate of the actions *furti concepti* and *furti oblati* was determined by the fate of the *quaestio*. I have shown above how, as the search as such became less and less important, the part played by these actions became more and more problematic. From Justinian we learn that when the *quaestio* as a distinctive mode of evidence disappeared, the actions *furti concepti* and *furti oblati* disappeared with it. In the second place, Justinian assumes that both the *actio furti concepti* and the *actio furti oblati* had required *dolus* on the part of the accused. This is clear from his explanation that the actions are now superfluous because all who deal with the stolen article *scientes*, in bad faith, may be sued by an *actio furti nec manifesti*. The result which I reached above was that *dolus* was a condition at least of the *actio furti oblati* by the age of Gaius; and that, if it was not a condition of the *actio furti concepti* as well by then, it must have become one before long. In the third place, I have argued that the *actio furti concepti* from the outset lay not against the actual thief as such, but against anyone in whose house the stolen object was discovered, be he the actual thief or a fraudulent receiver or even an innocent dupe of the thief's; and that the *actio furti oblati*, though its aim was to get at the thief, yet for a long time did not admit of an examination of the mental state of the defendant, and even in classical law lay against a fraudulent receiver as well as against the actual thief. This is confirmed by Justinian's view that the actions had been available not only against the actual thief, but against whoever *rem furtivam susceperit et celaverit*.

In fact, it is important to note that, if we take the text literally, Justinian does not think of the actual thief at all: *suscipere et celare* describes the deed of one who obtains the article from a thief, not the deed of the thief himself. Certainly, it is not impossible that the omission of the actual thief is just due to carelessness in formulating the paragraph under notice. I am inclined to believe, however, that there is more behind it. Justinian, I think, was under the impression that the actions *furti concepti* and *furti oblati* had been given exclusively against receivers.[159] To him, the rule that if the goods were found with the actual thief the case gave rise to an *actio furti nec manifesti* was probably so obvious that he did not remember that things had at one time been different. Retrojecting this rule into a former age, he thought of *furtum conceptum* and *furtum oblatum* as confined to *suscipere et celare*, to the case, that is, where the defendant was not the actual thief but only the receiver of the missing article.

Going on with Gaius, we are told of a further kind of *furtum* in 3.188: *Est etiam prohibiti furti actio adversus eum qui furtum quaerere volentem prohibuerit.* Here we learn that an action lies against the owner of a house who will not allow his house to be searched for the missing article. It is clear, both from Gaius's account and the name of the action itself, that the very act of preventing a *quaestio* constitutes the basis for this action. It does not matter whether or not the goods in question actually are in the house: the owner, by refusing to admit the search, becomes liable to the penalty of *furtum prohibitum*. This is perfectly reasonable. What strikes one as strange is not the existence of a provision about this kind of *furtum*, but, on the contrary, its omission from the catalogue of 3.183 considered above. In that catalogue, Gaius, as we saw, enumerates the various *genera* of *furtum*, *manifestum*, *nec manifestum*, *conceptum* and *oblatum*, but *furtum prohibitum* is not mentioned. The reason for this will emerge later. I should like to say, however, that, in examining the history behind the classical system, great importance should be attached to this feature. For it is from classification and arrangement that we may often draw the surest conclusions about the evolution of a branch of the law, since they are apt to be left intact even where the actual rules governing the matter undergo alterations.

Besides the sudden appearance of another *genus* of *furtum* not referred to before, there is a second slightly curious point to be remarked, namely, the name of the delict, *furtum prohibitum*. Whether we proceed from *furtum* in the sense of 'a stolen object' or in that of 'the offence of theft', *furtum prohibitum* as denoting prevention of a search is odd: we can translate it neither as 'a prohibited article' nor as 'a prohibited theft'. No doubt language is capable of amazing abbreviations; and to talk of 'a prohibited article' or even of 'a prohibited theft' when, in fact, it is the person trying to recover his property who has been prohibited from searching for it (Livy 1. 7. 7 makes Cacus *prohibere Herculem* who is looking for his bulls, just as Gaius refers to *prohibere furtum quaerere volentem*) is probably not the worst that may happen. Nevertheless the expression *furtum prohibitum* does look like an artificial growth, later than and modelled after the four terms in the classification of 3. 183, *furtum manifestum* and so on.

Having thus defined five groups of theft, *furtum manifestum, nec manifestum, conceptum, oblatum* and *prohibitum*, the latter without announcing it in 3. 183, Gaius informs us how each of them is punished. On manifest theft, he tells us in 3. 189, the XII Tables had imposed capital punishment. But the praetor, to whom this seemed too severe a treatment, introduced fourfold restitution in his edict. In 3. 190, Gaius deals with *furtum nec manifestum*. In this case, the penalty laid down by the XII Tables, twofold damages, has not been changed by the praetor. Of the significance of the threefold damages to be paid in the cases of *furtum conceptum* and *oblatum* I have already spoken. Gaius in 3. 191 says that this penalty, like that of *furtum nec manifestum*, was taken over by the praetor from the XII Tables without change. I have argued that this threefold fine puts *furtum conceptum* and *furtum oblatum* between the most serious offence of *furtum manifestum* (capital in the XII Tables and involving fourfold restitution under the edict) and the other extreme, *furtum nec manifestum* (involving twofold restitution ever since the XII Tables). There follows, in 3. 192, the punishment of *furtum prohibitum: Prohibiti actio quadrupli est ex edicto praetoris introducta.*

Two points should be observed. In the first place, the

praetor, according to Gaius, took a very serious view of the matter. The penalty of *furtum prohibitum* is the same as that of manifest theft; it is fourfold restitution. Surely, what one would expect is that a man refusing to admit a *quaestio* would forfeit the threefold damages of *furtum conceptum*. In point of fact, he is put on a level with a manifest thief. No explanation of the system that does not account for this fact can be deemed satisfactory. As I shall attempt to demonstrate, it is to be accounted for as ultimately coming from the machinery laid down by the XII Tables.

In the second place, the praetor did not, as in the case of *furtum manifestum*, find a penalty in the XII Tables which he mitigated in his edict. Gaius says that he introduced a new action altogether: *prohibiti actio...ex edicto praetoris introducta*. In other words, the XII Tables contained no action on the ground of the prevention of a search. What are we to make of this? Was it possible, under the regime of the XII Tables, for the owner of a house to resist a *quaestio* without risking any unpleasant consequences? The answer to this question is to be found in Gaius 3. 192 and 193: *Prohibiti actio quadrupli est ex edicto praetoris introducta. lex autem eo nomine nullam poenam constituit; hoc solum praecipit, ut qui quaerere velit nudus quaerat, licio cinctus, lancem habens; qui si quid invenerit, iubet id lex furtum manifestum esse....Quae lex tota ridicula est; nam qui vestitum quaerere prohibet, is et nudum quaerere prohibiturus est, eo magis quod ita quaesita re et inventa maiori poenae subiciatur.* The XII Tables, it is true, provided no action in case the person accused did not allow his house to be searched. But they did not overlook or tolerate this situation. They laid down that, in this case, a more ceremonial procedure should be resorted to. Moreover, they declared that, should the stolen object be discovered in the course of this second, more ceremonial procedure, the matter should be treated as a manifest theft—which, at the time, meant capital punishment.

Here I have to turn aside for a moment to consider a theory worked out by F. De Visscher[160] and quoted with some approval in recent discussions on the subject.[161] Like many authorities,[162] De Visscher claims that the XII Tables can have had only one mode of search, a ceremonial procedure *lance et licio*, and that this was later replaced by an informal investigation *testibus praesentibus*. But De Visscher goes much further than that: he thinks that this view is reconcilable with Gaius, in fact, that it is the view of Gaius himself. From *Institutes* 3. 192 f., the text just cited, it appears, he says, that Gaius assigns to the XII Tables one kind of search only, the ceremonial kind, which gave way, at some date, to the classical, informal one. De Visscher's argument runs as follows. Gaius criticizes the XII Tables for providing no action should the ceremonial procedure be resisted by the accused (this is correct); Gaius tells us that the praetor corrected this fault of the XII Tables by introducing the *actio furti prohibiti* (this is also correct); the *actio furti prohibiti*, however, lies, not in the case of prevention of the ceremonial procedure, but in the case of prevention of the ordinary, informal, classical search (this is also correct); since Gaius—thus De Visscher concludes—assumes that a defect of the XII Tables concerning prevention of the ceremonial procedure could be cured by a remedy available in the case of prevention of the informal procedure, he must have regarded these two modes of search as one and the same institution—ceremonial in the age of the XII Tables, informal in the classical age (this is incorrect).

The argument is ingenious, but, for one thing, it culminates in a *non sequitur*, and for another thing, it means flying in the face of the text. The *non sequitur* is obvious. Certainly, Gaius records that the praetor, by giving a remedy against prevention of the informal search, closed a gap left by the XII Tables in the case of prevention of the ceremonial search. It does not follow by any means that Gaius looks upon the two modes of search as equivalent. If the XII Tables had two different kinds of search (as I maintain they had), the more ceremonial one to be conducted where the informal one had been resisted; if they gave no action (as I maintain they did not) in case the second search was also resisted; and if the praetor found (as I maintain he did) that this system did not work because the second search was in practice resisted just as frequently as the first: why should he not have dealt with the problem by doing without the second search and giving an action as soon as the first, informal search was prevented? This would be, in the eyes of Gaius, correcting a fault that the XII Tables made in the case of prevention of the ceremonial procedure by allowing an action in the case of prevention of the informal investigation. But it leaves us with two procedures in the system of the XII Tables, and that is how Gaius sees it.

The decisive proof that he does assume two lies in the plain text of 3. 192 f. Gaius starts by saying that the praetor introduced an action in case a search *testibus praesentibus*—the only kind of search mentioned so far, in 3. 186—was prevented by the owner of the house. He goes on to remark that the XII Tables had no such action, but 'laid down only this that he who wished to conduct a *quaestio* should conduct it naked, with *lanx* and *licium*'. The natural interpretation is that, under the XII Tables, a person whose first search, informal save for the presence of witnesses, had come to naught, instead of having an action, had to proceed to a second, more ceremonial search. Still, it may be admitted that, on a slightly artificial interpretation, the text up to this point could be harmonized with De Visscher's thesis: we might take it as meaning that the XII Tables dispensed with an action because 'they were satisfied with prescribing that the search—the only search, the search mentioned in 3. 186—should be conducted with *lanx* and *licium*'. Things become less favourable to De Visscher's theory when we examine Gaius's statement that the regulation of the XII Tables is absurd since *qui vestitum quaerere prohibet, is et nudum quaerere prohibiturus est*. Again, the natural interpretation is that, according to Gaius, the XII Tables prescribed a second, ceremonial search in case the first, less formal one failed: this scheme Gaius considers inadequate, arguing, somewhat amused, that an owner of a house who resists the first search, when his opponent is dressed, is certainly going to resist the second, when his opponent is naked. Again, however, the words might just bear the meaning required by De Visscher, though the interpretation would here be even more forced than that which he has to put on *hoc solum*. . . . It might just be possible, that is, to regard Gaius as speaking of one search only, to regard him as saying that the XII Tables ought not to have relied on the ceremony

attached to their search—their only search, the search mentioned in 3.186—seeing that one capable of resisting a dressed
man, a search without a ceremonial (alien to the XII Tables,
on this exegesis), would not mind resisting a naked man, a
ceremonial search (the only search of the XII Tables).

But I do not see any conceivable way of reconciling with
De Visscher's theory the final clause of Gaius's criticism, *eo
magis quod ita quaesita re et inventa maiori poenae subiciatur.*
Here Gaius explains that the ceremonial search of the XII
Tables will be resisted all the more determinedly as it is likely
to lead to 'a greater penalty'. A greater penalty than what?
There is absolutely no answer to this question on the basis
of De Visscher's construction—unless we suppose that Gaius
wrote something completely different from what he had in
mind. De Visscher, it may be recalled, urges that Gaius is
here speaking of the only search of the XII Tables, the search
with *lanx* and *licium*. If the stolen thing is found in the course
of this search, Gaius says, there is capital punishment. But
in comparison with the punishment of what offence is this
punishment greater, a *maior poena*? At this point, then, the
natural interpretation proves the only possible one. Gaius
ascribes to the XII Tables two procedures, an informal one,
mentioned in 3.186, and leading, if the article is discovered,
to a threefold penalty, as we are told in 3.191, and a ceremonial one, to be adopted if the first one is resisted by the
owner of the house, and leading, if the article is discovered,
to capital punishment. To this machinery Gaius has to object—
quite reasonably, from his point of view—that it seems senseless: a man who opposes the first search, where the risk consists
in a threefold fine only, will be all the more obstinate in face
of the second search, which involves the risk of a far greater
penalty—a greater penalty, namely, than the first. It may
perhaps be added that all details of the text support this
interpretation. For example, the words *ita quaesita re* clearly
allude to a kind of search by which the article is not looked
for *ita*, is not looked for with *lanx* and *licium*, but in a less
formal manner. Whatever the truth may be as to the exact
history and relation of the two modes of search, De Visscher's
thesis that Gaius himself thought of them as equivalent, as

one and the same institution, the one going back to the XII Tables, the other replacing it in the edict, is utterly untenable.

Let us resume the analysis of Gaius. Gaius informs us that, under the XII Tables, if the ordinary search *testibus praesentibus* was prevented, there was no action *furti prohibiti*, but a more ceremonial search with *lanx* and *licium*. Needless to say, it is highly probable that there had to be witnesses also for the second procedure. When Gaius says, with reference to the first, that an *actio furti concepti* lies if the article is found in the presence of witnesses, he does not thereby indicate that in the second witnesses were unnecessary. Far from it. What he means is, on the one hand, that even an *actio furti concepti* lies only if the article has been discovered in the presence of witnesses, that to this extent even the ordinary, first search is formal, that even an *actio furti concepti* cannot be brought if the article in question has been found entirely by chance, without any people having been asked to attend (in this case, the person from whom the object has been stolen must be content with the ordinary remedy, namely, the *actio furti nec manifesti* against the thief); and, on the other hand, that the ordinary, first search requires nothing but the presence of witnesses, requires no elaborate ceremonial. To read into Gaius's words a denial of the requirement of witnesses for the second, more formal *quaestio*, however, would be rash indeed. Be this as it may, the question does not affect the main point: the XII Tables, according to Gaius, prescribed two kinds of search, the second, more ceremonial one to be adopted if the first one had been resisted. This scheme Gaius declares to be absurd: would not the second search, he asks, be opposed just as much as, or even more than, the first?

In actual fact, when the law was first enacted, it no doubt was perfectly sound. At the time of the XII Tables, though an informal *quaestio* might be successfully prevented by the owner of the house to be searched, the same was certainly not true of the *quaestio* with *lanx* and *licium*. This ancient, traditional procedure, presumably of a semi-sacred character and with all the power and prestige of secular and religious authorities to support it, would hardly be resisted by the most desperate criminal, and, where it was, the state would be in a position to overcome the resistance. In the fifth century B.c., the difference between an informal search and the search with *lanx* and *licium* was not a difference between a man who has his clothes on and is respectable and a man who has no clothes on and is ludicrous (so it looked to Gaius), but a difference between a comparatively slight and private affair and one involving the interest and peace of the community. In short, at the time that the XII Tables were promulgated, the gap assumed by Gaius did not exist. If the owner of a house refused to allow it to be examined *testibus praesentibus*, there followed a second, more ceremonial procedure, which to resist was out of the question.

But how did the XII Tables come to recognize two modes of search? Here we have the *crux* of the problem. As is well known, early law is far less varied than modern law. That there should occur in the XII Tables two different kinds of *quaestio*, a less formal one and a ceremonial one, at first sight appears out of keeping with the general character of an ancient system. It is really this point that lies at the bottom of all attempts to refute the historical account given by Gaius. It is really this notion that the XII Tables could not possibly have had one *quaestio* on top of another which has led to the now prevalent view that Gaius is mistaken, that only one *quaestio* goes back to the code and that the other replaced it at a later stage. The XII Tables, it is argued, a simple, primitive law, can have put only one, ceremonial procedure at the disposal of a person claiming a stolen object. If the object was found in the course of this search, the sole kind of search at the time, the owner of the house was treated as a manifest thief.

The fallacy of this argument, quite apart from its inconsistency with Gaius, lies in the fact that the XII Tables are not such a simple, primitive law. It is quite true that if we had to conceive of them as standing at the very beginning of Roman law, of their authors as the very first people to think in legal terms at all, to find two kinds of *quaestio* would be rather surprising. But this is the wrong way of looking at that legislation. In point of fact, there is a long legal history behind the XII Tables: the recent discovery of a new fragment of Gaius, with its information about *sponsio*, should convince even the most sceptical. This being so, we must not wonder at an accumulation of *quaestiones*: the two modes of search have to be, and can be, explained as the result of an evolution preceding the code.

It is, indeed, safe to assume that, at some date before the XII Tables, a ceremonial search conducted with *lanx* and *licium* was the only kind of *quaestio*. In that period, we may suppose, the search formed the end of a *vestigii minatio*, of an immediate pursuit of the man suspected of having carried away an article—a pursuit very much like the one we know from the Bible. The pursuer, when he reached the dwelling of the pursued, had to observe elaborate rites in conducting his investigation. If the missing article was found, the case was deemed proved; indeed, since *vestigii minatio* kept the offence flagrant (I have discussed this above[163]), the matter was regarded as *furtum manifestum*, with all the terrible consequences for the thief. Gradually, however, an alternative mode of search arose, which was applied when a proper *vestigii minatio* could not take place. Supposing, for example, a man stole an object from another man, but this was not noticed till three months later, by which time immediate pursuit with hue and cry and ritual search was no longer admitted. In this case, the reasonable thing for the victim of the theft to do was to collect witnesses and carry out an examination of the house of the suspect in a quieter, less formal fashion.[164] But clearly, if the article was discovered in this manner, there was far less justification for treating the owner of the house as a manifest thief. For one thing, there was neither the warlike atmosphere nor all the ritual that attached to a search with *lanx* and *licium* coming at the end of a *vestigii minatio*. For another thing, where a considerable period had elapsed between theft and search, the possibility of the owner of the house not being the actual thief at all was evidently much greater; even if the missing article was found with him, there was a strong chance that he had only received it from the thief, perhaps in complete innocence. It might perhaps be argued that the possibility of his being innocent existed even if the object was found after a *vestigii minatio*. The story of

Joseph's cup smuggled into Benjamin's bag is a case in point: there was immediate pursuit then and yet Benjamin was innocent. Gaius himself, in 3.193, refers to a tradition according to which a person conducting a ceremonial search has to hold a *lanx* in his hands in order not to be able to smuggle the object that he claims into the house and put it somewhere where he may then 'discover' it: whether or not this is the right explanation of the *lanx*—it probably is not—it shows that tricks like that of Joseph were not unknown in Rome. However, broadly speaking, it remains true to say that, if an article was found in the course of a *vestigii minatio*, the likelihood of the person pursued being blameless was very much smaller than if an article was found in the course of a search *testibus praesentibus*, long after the theft had been committed. The very transmission of the story of the trick played by Joseph on his brothers testifies to its exceptional nature.

We may assume that the two kinds of search, the ceremonial connected with hot pursuit and the less formal in other cases, co-existed for a long time. We may also assume that they did not co-exist without trespassing the one on the province of the other. And it is obvious that, on the whole, it was the less formal kind that must have gained more and more ground and the ritual one that must have lost correspondingly. For, evidently, the less formal kind offered advantages to both parties—not to mention the community, which was not disturbed by it. The pursuer was not compelled to prove that all conditions of a proper *vestigii minatio* were fulfilled, nor had he to go through the elaborate ancient ceremony. The person whose house was to be searched did not risk being treated as a manifest thief, but, even if the object in question was discovered, might expect to be heard when he pleaded that it was brought to him by a third party.[165]

The XII Tables, by their regulation, probably did not much more than crystallize the practice of the time, with some bias in favour of its more progressive elements. The respective spheres of application of the informal procedure and the ceremonial procedure were definitely fixed, in the way outlined by Gaius. It was a compromise between the two kinds of search, and a very reasonable one. A man suspecting goods stolen from him to be in the house of another man, the code lays down, may search that house in the presence of witnesses; and, if the goods are found, an *actio furti concepti* lies for threefold damages. As I have already stated, the point of this relatively light penalty is that the person convicted by the search is not dealt with as a manifest thief. The possibility of his having obtained the incriminating object from a third party is taken into account. Indeed, the law does even more for an innocent person. It provides that if the owner of the house had the goods from a third party, he may sue him by an *actio furti oblati* and recover the fine that he has had to pay. Even some such right of regress the XII Tables quite possibly found established in current practice. Only in the case where an informal search is resisted does the law-giver retain the ancient procedure with all its harshness; only in this case is he unable and unwilling to introduce a quiet action leading to a money penalty. For, in this case, the owner of the house produces himself the warlike situation which necessitates public intervention, the semi-sacred procedure. Moreover, in this case, there is little to be said against treating the owner of the house as a manifest thief should the article turn up. By opposing the first search, he puts himself in much the same position as a man suspected of an offence just committed: the matter becomes flagrant, a fresh, hot affair. Most important of all, it is quite natural to regard a man as guilty if the thing is found with him by a second search, after he has prevented the first. The defence that he has only received the object from someone else does not sound plausible in this situation; and though exceptional circumstances could be imagined in which he might be innocent despite all this, the XII Tables make no allowance for them. In fairness it ought to be remarked that even nowadays, if a man prevented the lawful inspection of his house and the missing article were afterwards discovered in his possession, a judge would be strongly inclined to deem the evidence against him conclusive. In the period before the XII Tables, when there was only the search conducted with *lanx* and *licium* and, in case of discovery of the stolen thing, inevitably leading to treatment of the accused as a manifest thief, the institution must have worked unfairly. In the XII Tables, clearly, it is restricted to its proper domain.

In this way, then, the system of the XII Tables as Gaius depicts it becomes perfectly intelligible. It is possible to understand this system without attributing any mistake to Gaius or twisting his text—either of which courses really means shaping a history of one's own. Since, however, consistency with the sources is not always regarded as a good argument, I hasten to add that the explanation that I have attempted seems to me far more likely even on general grounds than the prevalent view. Admittedly, it is very tempting to argue from the simple character of early legislations; to say that the XII Tables would not have mentioned two different forms of procedure for the search after a stolen article; and that, of the two forms given by Gaius, one was used from this year to that and the other from the moment that the first was dropped. But reality is more complicated than this. However much such a development might be in accordance with some modern theories, it seems to me far more likely, even on general grounds, that the older form of procedure was not replaced by the new one on a certain definite day, at one stroke. The new one grew up gradually, as a rival, struggled for recognition by the law. Then they existed side by side, all the time the new form encroaching on the domain of the old. The XII Tables represent the last stage of this co-existence of the two. The new kind of search is now the ordinary search, the old, ceremonial procedure is confined to the case where the new one fails: it is the last corner left to what had at some remote time been the sole mode of *quaestio*, the last occasion on which the ancient, lively and serious ritual once again comes to life. To explain away this co-existence for the reason that it does not suit pre-conceived doctrines of the nature of ancient codes appears to me injudicious, not only in view of the conflict thus produced with Gaius, but also because the account given by Gaius sounds life-like, real, whereas the one substituted for it in modern literature sounds academic, unreal.

It is easily seen why the system of the XII Tables, though progressive and sound when introduced, was eventually succeeded by the classical one. The ceremonial procedure with *lanx* and *licium*, already playing a minor part in the code, soon became completely antiquated. Suffice it to mention three reasons for this. First, the community probably disliked being drawn into a quarrel between two citizens about a missing article. Secondly, a milder view was gradually being taken of theft in general, which made all that elaborate ceremony and the capital punishment attached to it seem out of place. Thirdly, as time went on and Rome became a modern, cool-headed community, that ceremony itself no doubt began to lose its glamour. People ceased to respect the semi-sacred apparatus, and, obviously, as soon as their implicit acceptance of and submission to the old form weakened, its very purpose was frustrated. Other forms might live on even when no longer believed in: the procedure with *lanx* and *licium* could not. As we have seen, this procedure was resorted to when the first, ordinary search had been resisted. At the time of the XII Tables, this was an adequate regulation, since no one would dare or be suffered to resist the ritual search with *lanx* and *licium*. But as soon as the respect for this ritual search went, the regulation became senseless: a man would now resist the ceremonial procedure just as much as the ordinary one. (For this incredulous age, then, Gaius's criticism would be justified. The point is that, at the time of the XII Tables, things had not reached this stage yet.) There may have been other reasons, but it is not necessary to go into them. The fact is that the procedure with *lanx* and *licium* fell into disuse. It is sometimes said that Gellius, *Noctes Atticae* 16. 10. 8, gives us the exact date when it disappeared, namely, on the enactment of the *lex Aebutia*.[166] As a matter of fact, however, Gellius is not quite so clear. His words are: *Sed enim cum 'proletarii' et 'adsidui' et 'sanates' et 'vades' et 'subvades' et 'viginti quinque asses' et 'taliones' furtorumque quaestio 'cum lance et licio' evanuerint, omnisque illa Duodecim Tabularum antiquitas, nisi in legis actionibus centumviralium causarum, lege Aebutia lata consopita sit....* It is not certain that by *illa antiquitas* Gellius means to refer to the institutions mentioned in the first part of the sentence: he may mean 'all the well-known ancient lore of the XII Tables' in general. Even if he does refer to the institutions of the first part of the sentence, including the search with *lanx* and *licium*, he would give us only a *terminus ante quem*: he does not imply that the old search may not have fallen into disuse long before the *lex Aebutia*, though it was that statute which formally and finally abolished the antiquated institutions. I think that all we can say with confidence is that the ceremonial procedure with *lanx* and *licium* died out centuries before the classical era. It may well have been abrogated by the *lex Aebutia*, but it is also possible that it became obsolete before and it is also possible that it became obsolete after.

In any case, when the old procedure with *lanx* and *licium* died out, something had to be done about the case where the first, ordinary search was prevented. The praetor solved the problem in the obvious way. The proceedings were no longer carried to a further stage, there was no longer a second *quaestio* to follow if the first one had failed. The act of prevention of the ordinary search itself was now considered adequate evidence of the accused person's guilt, the act itself was made the basis for a penalty no matter whether the missing article was actually in possession of the owner of the house or not: and the praetor created the *actio furti prohibiti adversus eum qui furtum quaerere volentem prohibuerit*. He could do this with a conscience all the easier since capital punishment had by this time completely disappeared from the domain of theft. The *actio furti prohibiti* was only for a monetary penalty and thus, even if it might in exceptional circumstances hit a man not the thief, the consequences were not as terrible as they would have been under the former regime. Here, then, is the classical system: a search informal except for the presence of witnesses and leading, in case of discovery of the stolen goods, to an *actio furti concepti* for threefold damages; and, should the search be resisted, not a second search leading, in case of discovery of the stolen goods, to capital punishment, but immediately an *actio furti prohibiti* based on the very act of resistance.

However, the law thus abolished has left some traces, and here at last I come to the answer to some questions raised above. To begin with, the *actio furti prohibiti* carries the same penalty as the *actio furti manifesti*, fourfold damages. Why?

I have said above that, if we disregard the historical background and look only at the classical system itself, we should expect a threefold fine: he who resists an examination of his house forfeits the penalty of *actio furti concepti*, without any further ado. On the basis of the development as I have tried to outline it, the fourfold penalty becomes easily explicable. The praetor substituted the *actio furti prohibiti* for the old ceremonial search which, if the article was found, involved treatment of the owner of the house as a manifest thief. Under the new regime of the edict, once the informal search was resisted, no further enquiry was necessary as to the guilt or otherwise of the accused. The act of resistance itself was deemed sufficient to warrant the treatment that, previously, had followed a discovery of the missing article in the course of a second *quaestio*: he who resisted incurred the penalty of *furtum manifestum*, a fourfold fine. Clearly, this fourfold fine of *furtum prohibitum* is strong confirmation of the thesis here advanced: the action took the place of the obsolete procedure with *lanx* and *licium*, at the end of which, if the owner of the house was found guilty, stood his punishment as a manifest thief. In the *actio furti prohibiti* he was dealt with as guilty of manifest theft even on the act of resistance itself.

Another trace of the pre-classical evolution is to be seen in the absence of *furtum prohibitum* from the classification of various kinds of theft recorded by Gaius. As already remarked, it is only *furtum manifestum*, *furtum nec manifestum*, *furtum conceptum* and *furtum oblatum* that appear in it. Why, I asked above, is *furtum prohibitum* not mentioned? The reason now is clear. Only the four kinds of theft appearing in the classification were traditional *genera* of theft: there was *furtum manifestum*, when the thief was caught in the act, *furtum nec manifestum*, 'ordinary' theft, *furtum conceptum*, when an object was found in the course of a search, and *furtum oblatum*, when the owner of a house in which a stolen object had been found sought redress from the person who had brought the object to him. The second, ceremonial search involved no special kind of theft: it was an appendix to *furtum conceptum* and *furtum oblatum*, and, if the result was positive, the case was regarded as *furtum manifestum*.

It was only when the praetor created the *actio furti prohibiti* that a fifth kind of *furtum* came into being. But this praetorian kind never received a place in the traditional classification based on the old civil law. Similarly, in the arrangement of the matter in Gaius, *furtum prohibitum* occupies the position of a case subordinate to *furtum conceptum* and *furtum oblatum*. In describing the nature of the various kinds of theft, Gaius deals with *furtum manifestum* in 3. 184, with *furtum nec manifestum* in 3. 185, with *furtum conceptum* in 3. 186 and with *furtum oblatum* in 3. 187: then, in 3. 188 only, comes the edictal, secondary case of *furtum prohibitum*. Again, in giving the penalties, he deals with *furtum manifestum* in 3. 189, *nec manifestum* in 3. 190, *furtum conceptum* and *furtum oblatum* in 3. 191, and then only, in 3. 192 ff., with *furtum prohibitum*.

I have stated above that classification and arrangement are important criteria, since they often remain even where the actual law changes. Applying this to the problem under notice, I would say that nothing perhaps is more damaging to the prevalent view denying the ancient origin of the actions *furti concepti* and *furti oblati* than the classification and arrangement to be found in Gaius. It is one thing to claim that Gaius made a mistake and erroneously ascribed to the XII Tables actions in truth of later origin (though even such a theory ought not, I feel, to be adopted unless there are overwhelming arguments in its favour). It is quite another thing to neglect the classification and arrangement of the different actions in Gaius. The classification—which goes back at least to the time of Servius—proves that the actions *furti concepti* and *furti oblati* belong to the old, civil law stratum, whereas the *actio furti prohibiti* does not. The arrangement—which also may well be pre-Gaian—points to the descent of *furtum prohibitum* from that appendix to *furtum conceptum* and *oblatum*, the second, ceremonial *quaestio*. Had Gaius been more profound and original than he was, he would have amalgamated the several strata of the law with one another, would have modified the traditional classification so as to cover *furtum prohibitum* as well as the other kinds of theft, would have put *furtum prohibitum* after *furtum conceptum* and before *furtum oblatum*. From the point of view of a modern historian, it is fortunate that he was incapable of thoroughly revising his predecessors. For it is precisely the irregularities in his account that enable us to reconstruct the development of the law.

It may perhaps be permissible to add here a remark on a certain form of law used by the XII Tables in their section about *furtum conceptum*; for it seems to me that although it is a question concerning primarily the manner of legislation, by understanding it we may gain a little more insight into the matter. Gaius, we have seen, in 3.192 tells us that, according to the XII Tables, if the missing article was found in the course of the second, ceremonial procedure with *lanx* and *licium*, 'this was *furtum manifestum*': *iubet id lex furtum manifestum esse*. It follows, if Gaius is reliable, that the XII Tables in this case did not expressly state the punishment to be inflicted on the criminal; they did not expressly say that the person convicted should be flogged and adjudged to the victim of the theft—which was the penalty of *furtum manifestum*. Instead of doing this, they simply gave the name of the offence that was committed, they simply subsumed the state of facts concerned under a certain category, they simply declared that the facts constituted *furtum manifestum*; leaving it to the reader and user of the code to draw the obvious conclusion, namely, that the offender had to be treated as a manifest thief, had to be flogged and adjudged to his opponent.

That Gaius is here reliable there can be no doubt. First, there is the general consideration that he was an expert on the XII Tables: he wrote a commentary on them and what he says of them in his *Institutes* is usually sound. Secondly, the XII Tables used the method that we find in the case under notice also in other cases. It is sufficient to adduce the well-known provision about the slaying of a thief who comes at night-time (VIII. 12): *Si nox furtum faxsit, si im occisit, iure caesus esto.* Here also we have subsumption of the facts under a legal category rather than direct statement of the consequences of the deed for the person accused. Had the latter method been chosen, the code would have had to say something like 'he who has killed the thief shall not be liable to vengeance'. An example from early Roman law outside the XII Tables is furnished by the statute concerning murder, ascribed to Numa: *Si qui hominem liberum dolo sciens morti duit, paricidas esto.* Whatever the precise meaning of *paricidas* may be, it must be an established category of offence or offender under which the statute classified the wrong in question. Instead of directly describing the penalty to be imposed, the legislator stated the crime constituted by the facts with which he had to deal. Thirdly, we come across the same method in other ancient systems. In fact, we come across it not only in law but also in religion, medicine and so on; and it would be a problem well worth investigating whether law did not take over the method from one of these. When the Bible declares a thing clean or unclean without specifying the consequences—because they are supposed to be known—it is exactly the same method as is applied in the XII Tables when they declare an object discovered with *lanx* and *licium* to be a *furtum manifestum.* Ancient medical treatises, Egyptian and Babylonian, frequently present a case and, before proceeding to state the cure or prognosis, give a general diagnosis, of which the cure or prognosis is an evident consequence.[167] Again, it is essentially the same method as the one in the XII Tables here analysed. Fourthly and lastly, what speaks decisively in favour of the veracity of Gaius's account is the fact that there was discussion among the jurists, long before his time, as to how that provision of the XII Tables declaring a certain case to be *furtum manifestum* was to be explained. In 3. 194, Gaius speaks about this discussion: *propter hoc tamen quod lex ex ea causa manifestum furtum esse iubet, sunt qui scribunt....* It should be observed that he almost literally repeats what he has said of this rule in 3. 192 (*iubet id lex furtum manifestum esse*). Moreover, he mentions two explanations of the provision, one that he rejects and one that satisfies him, as we shall see presently. Both of them have this in common that they seek to account for the code's pronouncing a case not really manifest to be manifest: that is to say, they both presuppose a provision in the XII Tables which, instead of directly laying down the punishment to be inflicted on the owner of a house caught out through the second search, merely classed the case as *furtum mani-festum*. In view of all this, I may repeat, there can be no doubt that we have to follow Gaius as regards the detail in question. The XII Tables, instead of saying that he with whom the missing article was found in the course of a *quaestio* with *lanx* and *licium* should be flogged and adjudged to the other party, stated the category to which the crime belonged. I shall not go much further into this form of law. From what I have remarked it will be seen that it is a form raising manifold problems; a form, moreover, the existence and nature of which should not be overlooked by anyone interested in the development of legal thinking and legislation in general and concerned to get at the hidden springs behind it.

One point only I would draw attention to since it is somewhat more closely connected with the main topic of this study. Gaius tells us that the XII Tables declared it to be a case of *furtum manifestum* if the missing article was found in the course of the ceremonial procedure with *lanx* and *licium*. This regulation is perfectly understandable when we look at the matter as it must have stood at the time of the legislation. The old procedure, which at some remote date before the XII Tables had been the only kind of *quaestio*, forming the climax of a *vestigii minatio*, a hot pursuit of the thief, by the time of the XII Tables persisted only in one case, namely, if the accused man offered resistance to an ordinary, informal examination of his house and a second search became necessary. In this case, however, all the primitive apparatus and all the primitive atmosphere celebrated their last triumph. The resistance offered to the first search turned the affair into a desperate matter of life and death. If the article was discovered now with *lanx* and *licium*, it really was *furtum manifestum* in the traditional sense, catching the thief while the scent was hot. The legislator, in laying down that if an informal search was prevented the procedure with *lanx* and *licium* should be resorted to, and that this should mean the risk of being treated as a manifest thief for the recalcitrant owner of the house, took the notion of *furtum manifestum* in its established, usual meaning.

It is only natural, however, that as time went on, as the

origin of the procedure with *lanx* and *licium* in *vestigii minatio*, immediate pursuit, was forgotten, and as that procedure it- self lost all its specific significance and became obsolete, the jurists came to wonder about the provision of the XII Tables under notice. There was nothing like a hue and cry now with a hunt of the suspect to prolong the 'freshness' of his act; no search now was of a warlike character; and the question arose among lawyers how the XII Tables could say of a set of facts which obviously—obviously to these later jurists— did not constitute *furtum manifestum* that it did. Gaius, in 3. 194, records the discussion: *Propter hoc tamen quod lex ex ea causa manifestum furtum esse iubet, sunt qui scribunt furtum manifestum aut lege intellegi aut natura: lege id ipsum de quo loquimur, natura illud de quo superius exposuimus. sed verius est natura tantum manifestum furtum intellegi; neque enim lex facere potest ut qui manifestus fur non sit manifestus sit, non magis quam qui omnino fur non sit fur sit, et qui adulter aut homicida non sit adulter vel homicida sit; at illud sane lex facere potest ut proinde aliquis poena teneatur atque si furtum vel adulterium vel homicidium admisisset, quamvis nihil eorum ad- miserit.*

As is to be expected, the explanations of the jurists are not historical in our sense. It did not occur to them to say that the XII Tables declared the case manifest because, in that age, it was, whereas now it had ceased to be so. On the other hand, it was difficult, at least for the earlier commentators, to argue that the XII Tables called a set of facts *furtum manifestum* which, in reality, was not. The view rejected by Gaius seems to represent a fairly early—let us say, second or first century B.C.—way out of this dilemma. There were really, the jurists reasoned, two kinds of *furtum manifestum*, one that was so by nature, the flagrant deed, and one that was so by virtue of a law, namely, the offence of him with whom stolen goods were found through an examination with *lanx* and *licium*. This solution of the dilemma admitted that the *furtum manifestum* of the provision under notice was not the *furtum manifestum* proper, which people would naturally have in mind when speaking or hearing of *furtum manifestum*; yet it still insisted that what the XII Tables called *furtum manifestum* was *furtum manifestum*—though of a different kind, *furtum manifestum lege*.[168] The weakness of the theory is easily seen: it begs the question, for what it ought to tell us is precisely the meaning of a *furtum manifestum lege*, the reason for the code's regarding a case as *furtum manifestum* though it is not *furtum manifestum* by nature. The solution preferred by Gaius, but most probably taken over by him from an earlier source,[169] was more rational and independent. It now was admitted not only that the *furtum manifestum* of the provision in question was not *furtum manifestum* proper, but also that it was no *furtum manifestum* at all. No statute, it was argued, could alter the nature of things, no statute, therefore, could make a *furtum manifestum* of something that simply was not. The conclusion drawn was that what the code meant was that the case should be dealt with as if it were *furtum manifestum* even though, in reality, it was not: this kind of rule, indeed, any law-giver might make use of. The whole discussion reminds one strongly of the modern nineteenth-century controversy about the essence of legal personality. Gaius seems to take up the position of the Fictionists: the XII Tables, he says, feigned the case concerned to be *furtum manifestum*. But quite apart from the interest the matter has for the history of Roman legal science, it does shed some light on the evolution of the law of *furtum conceptum* as traced above: the case of a man convicted as a result of a *quaestio* with *lanx* and *licium* appears as *furtum manifestum* in the XII Tables; it still ranks as *furtum manifestum* in the theory rejected by Gaius, but only as *furtum manifestum lege*, keeping its place only on the ground of an artificial and laborious argument; and it is definitely considered to be something quite different in the theory that Gaius holds himself.

This concludes my examination of Gaius, by which I hope I have shown that a not unlikely historical development may be arrived at without violent eliminations or corrections of large parts of his account. I have now to supplement my remarks by going into the evidence outside Gaius. The first text to consider is Justinian's *Institutes* 4. 1. 4. The first half of this text, containing definitions of *furtum conceptum*, *furtum oblatum* and *furtum prohibitum*, is literally taken from Gaius.[170]

It is interesting to note that Gaius's historical parenthesis recording the decemviral regulation of the case where a search is resisted, with the old procedure by *lanx* and *licium*, is not quoted by Justinian. After defining the three kinds of theft just mentioned, however, Justinian brings a further kind that appeared in the edict of the praetor, though Gaius does not refer to it. *Praeterea poena constituitur edicto praetoris per actionem furti non exhibiti adversus eum qui furtivam rem apud se quaesitam et inventam non exhibuit.*

This action obviously filled a gap left by the others, more precisely, by the *actio furti prohibiti*. The latter, it will be recalled, lay when examination of a house was prevented. But what was to happen if the search itself was allowed, but resistance was offered on the missing article being found? What was to happen if the owner of the house refused to surrender the object discovered by a search? Clearly, this was a situation very similar to that arising in the case of a prevention of the *quaestio*; and there can be little doubt that, if ever it came about under the regime of the XII Tables, the consequence was that the person claiming his property now resorted to the second, ceremonial procedure with *lanx* and *licium*, just as he would have done had he been refused admission into the house from the outset. Yet the facts did not completely fit into the scheme of the *actio furti prohibiti*. This action was directed *adversus eum qui furtum quaerere volentem prohibuerit*, and the *formula* was no doubt worded accordingly. As a result, a man who had not opposed an investigation but refused to hand over the object discovered, if he was sued by an *actio furti prohibiti*, might successfully plead that the *formula* did not cover him: *non prohibui*, he might object, *furtum quaerere volentem*. It was in order to bar this way of escape that the *actio furti non exhibiti* was introduced. Justinian does not tell us what was the penalty involved; but it is fairly certain that it must have been the same as in the case of *actio furti prohibiti*, fourfold damages.

Why does Gaius not refer to the *actio furti non exhibiti*? It is not impossible that it was not created till after he had written his work. The case contemplated by the action cannot have been frequent. Once a search resulted in the discovery of the missing article, surely, as a rule, the owner of the house would be prepared to give it up. It is true that, if very obstinate, he might now plead that it was not identical with the object looked for, but even this can only have occurred comparatively rarely. Perhaps, then, the action had never become necessary before. I think it far more likely, however, that the action is pre-Gaian. Gaius may have omitted it either because it was not very important, being used less often than any of the others discussed by him, or because he did not find it in the sources from which he compiled his *Institutes*. This seems to me the most probable answer. The work which he took as a model for his own mentioned only the *actio furti prohibiti* but not the *actio furti non exhibiti*: the latter, designed, as we have seen, to fill a gap left by the *actio furti prohibiti*, was not introduced till some time after Gaius's precursor wrote, and Gaius was not thorough enough to bring his account up to date by adding the further action. It is worth observing that there is a slight but suggestive divergence in Justinian between the wording of the definition of *furtum prohibitum* and the wording of the definition of *furtum non exhibitum*. The former, Justinian says, lies *adversus eum qui furtum quaerere testibus praesentibus volentem prohibuerit*, the latter *adversus eum qui furtivam rem apud se quaesitam et inventam non exhibuit*. The two phrases are so similar to one another in form that it appears highly probable that the second was modelled after the first. Yet there is this difference that in the second the stolen article is called *res furtiva*, whilst in the first it is called *furtum*. This may be taken as an indication—though admittedly several other explanations of the difference are conceivable—that Justinian took his definition of *furtum non exhibitum* from a source less ancient than that from which Gaius, and, through Gaius, Justinian, took the definition of *furtum prohibitum*. In other words, by the time that the action *furti non exhibiti* was created, the term *furtum* in the sense of 'stolen object' seems to have been more or less ousted by *res furtiva*, a stage that had not yet been reached when the *actio furti prohibiti* came into being. If this is so, it confirms the conclusion just reached, namely, that *furti non exhibiti* is later than *furti prohibiti*.[171]

Justinian does not quote that part of Gaius which tells us about the penalties to be imposed on the various kinds of theft connected with a *quaestio*. He was satisfied, we may suppose, with a brief description of the sphere of application of these actions, but, as they were no longer law, thought it superfluous to go into the precise fines to which they led. I have already stated that, in the second half of *Institutes* 4. 1. 4, he explains that *furtum conceptum* and *furtum oblatum* no longer exist in his time.[172] It may now be added that, as is only natural, we hear the same of *furtum prohibitum* and *furtum non exhibitum*. These actions also, Justinian records, are obsolete: *Sed hae actiones, id est concepti et oblati et furti prohibiti nec non furti non exhibiti, in desuetudinem abierunt*, thus we are told in 4. 1. 4. The reason for the disappearance of the actions *furti prohibiti* and *furti non exhibiti* is plain. There was no use for them when, on the one hand, the police was ready to conduct and, if necessary, enforce any search, and, on the other hand, the discovery of stolen things by a search had ceased to carry any particular consequences whatsoever. Even *furtum conceptum* and *furtum oblatum*—or rather, what had once been *furtum conceptum* and *furtum oblatum*—now led to a double penalty only, like any kind of theft not manifest; and so, like any kind of theft not manifest, the action available when a stolen object was found after the owner of the house had offered resistance to a search, and the action available when a stolen object was found and the owner of the house refused to surrender it, both led to a double penalty. But the mere act of resisting a search no longer constituted a special kind of *furtum*. This is not saying that it gave rise to no legal disadvantages, such as, given certain conditions, punitive measures taken by the authorities under public law: but these had no specific connection with the law of theft.

A very brief survey of the remaining texts will suffice. As regards classification of theft, the later view preferred by Gaius, namely, that *furtum conceptum* and *furtum oblatum* are not two classes of theft proper, is accepted by Justinian in 4. 1. 3: *Furtorum autem genera duo sunt, manifestum et nec manifestum. nam conceptum et oblatum species potius actionis sunt furto cohaerentes quam genera furtorum, sicut inferius apparebit.*[173] The later view alone is quoted in the *Digest*, in 47. 2. 2, from the commentary of Gaius on the provincial edict; whether Gaius in this commentary mentioned also the earlier view there is no means of knowing. The text of *Digest* 47. 2. 2 is simply, *Furtorum genera duo sunt, manifestum et nec manifestum.* Curiously, there seems to have been a branch of tradition preserving the old classification into four equivalent *genera* throughout the classical age; unless we consider the reappearance of this classification in Paul's *Sententiae* and the late *Gai Epitome* as due to the late classical and post-classical inclination to simplify and systematize things—it was easier just to enumerate four *genera* than to explain that there existed two categories of theft proper and two actions merely connected with theft, but not really on the ground of theft. Moreover, it must be remembered (what I have already referred to above[174]) that, in a sense, the classification into four equivalent *genera* became correct again in the late classical period, as it had once been correct in the pre-classical one. During the latest stage of their existence, even the actions *furti concepti* and *oblati* required *dolus* on the part of the defendant; the latter did so already by the time of Gaius. Once this requirement was established, there was no longer any reason to deny the character of *furtum conceptum* or *oblatum* as theft in the strictest sense. In any case, Paul, *Sententiae* 2. 31. 2 (= *Collatio* 7. 5. 3), says: *Furtorum genera sunt quattuor, manifesti, nec manifesti, concepti et oblati.* And *Gai Epitome* 2. 11. 2 says: *Furtorum autem genera sunt quattuor, manifesti, nec manifesti, concepti et oblati.*[175] It should be remarked, incidentally, that nowhere do we come across an attempt to get *furtum prohibitum* into the classification, not to mention *furtum non exhibitum.*

The old procedure with *lanx* and *licium* is mentioned several times, notably in Festus 117[176] and in Gellius 11. 18. 9, to be quoted below,[177] and 16. 10. 8, quoted above,[178] the text where we are told about the abolition of the ceremonial procedure. One passage only in the *Digest* seems to be concerned with what form remained in the classical *quaestio*, that is to say, with the witnesses, *Digest* 22. 5. 12, from Ulpian's commentary on the edict:[179] *Ubi numerus testium non adicitur, etiam duo sufficient: pluralis enim elocutio duorum numero contenta est.* If this refers to the search *testibus praesentibus*, it means that two are enough to entitle a man to the *actio furti concepti* (or *prohibiti* or *non exhibiti*) if the other conditions are fulfilled. Paul, *Sententiae* 2. 31. 22, however, ought perhaps also to be adduced in this connection: *Qui furtum quaesiturus est, antequam quaerat, debet dicere quid quaerat et rem suo nomine et sua specie designare.* This rule in all probability goes back to the earliest stage of *quaestio*, though its exact form and scope may have been different at different times. It is natural: even before the law made a duty of it a pursuer, on overtaking the pursued, would tell him what he believed him to have carried away. He does so in all Biblical cases of *vestigii minatio*, hardly in pursuance of a definite, legal injunction. And it is reasonable: without it, I could search your house at any time under the pretext that 'something' belonging to me might be there. It is odd that such a detail should be preserved just in Paul's *Sententiae*. One can think of reasons accounting for this, but I do not propose here to enquire into them.

As for penalties, we find confirmation of Gaius's account of the procedure with *lanx* and *licium* in Gellius 11. 18. 9. He says, in conclusion of his paragraph about the decemviral treatment of *furtum manifestum*, that *ea quoque furta quae per lancem liciumque concepta essent proinde ac si manifesta forent vindicaverunt.* This is in entire agreement with what Gaius tells us. It is in agreement with him even in the interpretation of the rule as declaring, not that the case in question is manifest theft, but that it must be dealt with as if it were manifest theft. This is strong support for the opinion which I expressed above,[180] to the effect that Gaius did not himself invent the 'Fictionist' explanation of this law of the XII Tables.[181] The classical penalties of *furtum conceptum* and *furtum oblatum*, threefold damages, are mentioned, first, by Gaius himself in the fourth book of his *Institutes*, 4. 173;[182] secondly, in Gellius 11. 18. 12;[183] thirdly, in *Sententiae* 2. 31. 14, though this passage is corrupt.[184] In none of these texts, however, do we find anything about *furtum prohibitum* or *non exhibitum*.

What little we learn about the history and nature of *actio furti concepti* and *actio furti oblati* is in perfect harmony with the results reached above on the basis of Gaius. It is true that Gellius does not refer to these two actions in 11. 18. 6–9, where he deals with the XII Tables. But why should he, seeing that he does not pretend to depict the entire system of that code? In fact, in the second half of 11. 18. 12 he does clearly imply that they are of ancient origin: *Sed quod sit 'oblatum', quod 'conceptum'*, he says, *et pleraque alia ad eam rem ex egregiis veterum moribus accepta...qui legere volet inveniet Sabini librum cui titulus est De Furtis.* Justinian's definitions in *Institutes* 4. 1. 4 are simply taken from Gaius 3. 186 and 187. Paul, *Sententiae* 2. 31. 3, 5 (= *Collatio* 7. 5. 4, 6[185]), defines both him who may be sued and him who may sue with an action *furti concepti* or *oblati*: *Concepti actione is tenetur apud quem furtum quaesitum et inventum est. oblati actione is tenetur qui rem furtivam alii obtulit, ne apud se inveniretur....Concepti is agere potest qui rem concepit, id est invenit. oblati is agere potest penes quem res concepta, id est inventa est.* This agrees with what Gaius tells us; and it is noteworthy that, as in Gaius, the requirement of *dolus* is stressed only in the case of *furtum oblatum* (*ne apud se inveniretur*), not in that of *furtum conceptum*. The only significant difference from Gaius is the omission of the requirement of witnesses for a search. Paul says nothing like *testibus praesentibus*. This may well represent a stage when the *quaestio* had become even less formal than it was in Gaius's period. It should be remarked that *Collatio* 7. 5. 4, otherwise a faithful version of *Sententiae* 2. 31. 3, has merely *est inventum* for Paul's *quaesitum et inventum est*. Here, then, the reference to a *quaestio* is dropped altogether. This must have happened in the post-classical era, when the search had lost all its specific relevance. *Furtum conceptum* now denoted any discovery, even an accidental one, of one's missing goods in another man's house. As by this time all kinds of theft that were not manifest were equally punishable by a double fine, the laxer application of the notion of *furtum conceptum* involved no practical consequences. I shall presently have to discuss the same point in *Gai Epitome* 2. 11. 2.

This is the only text that remains to be examined. Here are the definitions given in it: *Conceptum furtum dicitur cum apud*

*aliquem alterum res furata invenitur. Oblatum furtum dicitur
cum res furtiva alicui ita a fure datur ut apud ipsum furem
inveniri non possit.* It is evident that this is mainly a re-hash of
Gaius 3. 186 and 187, with omission of portions not absolutely
necessary and substitution of common terms for less common
ones (*datur* for *oblata sit*). These and a few other minor changes
are easily explained by the fact that, first, the *Epitome* forms
part of a code, not of a work destined for students, and secondly,
while in all other parts of the *Lex Romana Visigothorum* we
get both the original Roman source and an *Interpretatio*, the
Epitome of Gaius has to do for both: it is itself a modernized
edition of the original *Institutes*. But they are changes affecting
only the form. Strangely enough, even here *dolus* does not
appear as a condition of the *actio furti concepti*. This does not
prove that it was not a condition in the actual law of the time:
the modernizer of the original Gaius may simply have been
negligent.

There are, however, four deviations that may reflect material
changes in the law, or at least in legal theory. In the first
place, the *Epitome*, after defining *furtum manifestum* and
furtum nec manifestum, goes on to say, in the passage just
quoted, that *conceptum furtum* is the case where the stolen
object is found *apud aliquem alterum*. The original Gaius has
simply *apud aliquem*, without *alterum*. Now I have tried to
show[186] that the *actio furti concepti* was never confined to the
case where the stolen thing was found with the thief. It always
lay irrespective of whether the owner of the house was the
actual thief or had only received the thing from a third party.
In fact, it was the latter situation that was chiefly contemplated by this action. However, if we take the text of the
Epitome literally, it goes further: it means that the action is
directed exclusively against a man not the actual thief.[187]
Very probably, this *apud aliquem alterum*, this restriction of
the action to the case where the defendant is neither *fur
manifestus* nor *fur nec manifestus*, is not just due to careless
wording. Very probably, the rule that the actual thief, unless
caught in the act, should be sued by an *actio furti nec manifesti*, and should be sued by this action no matter how the
offence was proved—even if it was proved by an examination

of his house, that is—was so firmly established by the time
of the *Epitome* that *furtum conceptum* had to be interpreted
as referring to discovery of the article with somebody not the
actual thief. This could be done all the more easily since it
made no difference in practice. By this time, all kinds of
theft not manifest led to twofold damages; consequently, if
the person with whom the missing article was found was the
actual thief, he gained nothing by being sued with the *actio
furti nec manifesti* instead of *furti concepti*.

The second material deviation is that, while Gaius gives the
actio furti concepti if the object *testibus praesentibus quaesita et
inventa est*, the *Epitome* gives it if the object *inventa est*. This is
hardly a merely formal abbreviation. As in *Collatio* 7. 5. 4, since
what little form there had remained in the classical *quaestio* is
now gone and the search of a house has lost all relevance,
the reference is dropped. According to the *Epitome*, any discovery of the stolen object in another man's house makes the
case a *furtum conceptum*: no search in the presence of witnesses, indeed, no deliberate search at all, is required. I have
already said, in discussing *Collatio* 7. 5. 4, that at a time when
even *furtum conceptum* leads only to a twofold penalty, the
extension or restriction of its scope at the expense or in favour
of *furtum nec manifestum* is of no practical moment whatever.

In the third place, the *Epitome*, defining *furtum oblatum*, says
that the incriminating object is brought *a fure*; Gaius says that
it is brought *ab aliquo*. Certainly, both emphasize that for the
action to lie the man who brings the object must act with
evil intent. But the *Epitome* speaks of the thief, Gaius of
anyone. The most probable explanation of the divergence is
that the *Epitome* prefers to put the most frequent case,
namely, the case of stolen goods sold by the thief himself.
It does not follow that any restriction of the scope of *furtum
oblatum* is intended. There is, however, another possibility.
By the time of the *Epitome*, all thefts not properly manifest,
that is to say, *furtum nec manifestum* proper, *furtum conceptum*
and *furtum oblatum*, were dealt with in the same way, as
furta nec manifesta, punishable by a twofold fine. Accordingly,
accurate distinctions were no longer indispensable; indeed,
they became impossible. Anyone who, though aware of its

nature as a *res furtiva*, kept or transferred an article might now be called a *fur*. We have seen above [188] that, whilst Gaius, on the authority of Labeo, distinguishes *furtum conceptum* and *furtum oblatum* from theft proper, the *Epitome* no longer does, quite rightly for its period. It is possible, therefore, that *a fure* is meant to be quite as comprehensive as *ab aliquo* in the original Gaius: a person guilty of *furtum oblatum* was a thief in the strictest sense even though he had not himself stolen the object. In any case, I do not think that on either of the two explanations of the difference any change in practice need be assumed.

Finally, according to Gaius, an *actio furti oblati* lies only if the stolen thing *tibi oblata sit eaque apud te concepta sit*; according to the *Epitome*, it lies even before the object has been 'concepted', namely, as soon as *alicui datur*. Here, indeed, we may well have before us a considered and practically important extension of the *actio furti oblati*. If you knowingly put me in possession of a stolen article, I may sue you even before I have become involved in a charge. This would be quite reasonable in an age when, for one thing, the *quaestio* had lost all relevance, when it was no longer the *quaestio* that set the whole affair in motion, and when, for another thing, the public, penal aspect of theft and allied offences was predominant: a man transferring stolen things in bad faith deserves punishment on this very ground.

NOTES

CHAPTER V

1 Cicero, *De Officiis* 1. 10. 33.   2 Genesis xxv. 27 ff.

3 Genesis xxvii.

4 The Rabbis see an indication of this in the concluding clause of Genesis xxvii. 33. The whole verse runs thus: 'And Isaac (on Esau's arrival) trembled very exceedingly, and said, Who? where is he that hath taken venison, and brought it me, and I have eaten of all before thou camest, and have blessed him? yea, and he shall be blessed.' The last few words, in the eyes of the Rabbis, are a confirmation of the blessing.

5 Genesis xxix. 21 ff.

6 Jewish exegetes sometimes assert that Jacob must have wanted to keep Leah as wife: if he had not, they say, he could have made use of a husband's right, mentioned in Deuteronomy xxiv. 1, to dismiss his wife without suffering any inconvenience. This may be so, though for one thing we do not know

whether divorce was as easily effected in the period of Jacob as in that of Deuteronomy (Abraham's dismissal of Hagar cannot be adduced since Hagar's status was not the same as Leah's); and for another thing, whatever the law may have been, we have to consider that Jacob was probably wise in risking no open quarrel with Laban at the time, when the least result would have been his losing Rachel as well as Leah. Laban, for one, seems to have been fairly certain that Jacob could not send Leah back; otherwise his trick would have been too risky. I cannot help feeling that while there is every justification for using the story as illustrating Jacob's meekness in school and synagogue, from the historical-literary point of view it is fundamentally wrong to make much of the technical possibility of a divorce. It is like arguing that Demaenetus need not have let himself be dragged away by his wife from the lovely Philaenium (Plautus, *Asinaria* 5. 2. 909 ff.), seeing that he had not been transgressing the law and, in any case, divorce was easy enough in Athens or Rome; or that Portia's verdict might have been successfully appealed against on the ground that she delivered it posing as Doctor Balthasar, whereas in fact she was not only a female but a female without any University degree whatsoever.

7 Genesis xxx. 25 ff.

8 The question what zoology has to say about them is obviously irrelevant to my argument. I am concerned solely with the view that the author of the narrative in question took of events.

9 Genesis xxxi. 17 ff. See pp. 205 ff.

10 Genesis xxxii. 25 (24) ff.   **11** Genesis xxvii. 36.

12 Leaving aside the controversial passage Hosea xii. 4 (3), which may mean 'In the womb (from the outset) he (Jacob) overreached his brother' (with allusion to the very text under discussion, Genesis xxvii. 36) or 'In the womb he took hold on his brother's heel' (with reference to Genesis xxv. 26), there is Jeremiah ix. 3 (4): 'Take ye heed every one of his neighbour, and trust ye not in any brother; for every brother will utterly overreach, and every neighbour will walk with slanders.' The etymological meaning of עָקַב seems to be 'to slink after somebody': it is connected with עָקֵב, 'heel' (see Gesenius's *Handwörterbuch* and the *Lexicon*).

13 The word occurs in II Kings x. 19, where we are told how Jehu, resolved to exterminate the priests of Baal, proclaimed a great feast for their god: 'And Jehu gathered all the people together, and said unto them, Ahab served Baal a little, but Jehu shall serve him much. Now therefore call unto me all the prophets of Baal, all his servants, and all his priests; let none be wanting; for I have a great sacrifice to do to Baal; whosoever shall be wanting, he shall not live. But Jehu did it in subtilty, to the intent that he might destroy the worshippers of Baal.' It should be noticed that Jehu deliberately chose formulations like 'Jehu shall serve Baal better than Ahab' or 'I have a great sacrifice to do to Baal'. The priests took, and were intended to take, these promises as being in their favour. Jehu, however, meant them in the opposite sense. But, on the basis of over-literal interpretation, he did not lie. For he did plan to serve Baal, he did plan to bring him a huge sacrifice—by slaying his priests in his temple.

14 Isaiah lxiii. 2, II Kings iii. 22.

15 See Gesenius's *Handwörterbuch, s.v.* אָדַם. It matters little, however, whether this is the correct etymology or not (it is not mentioned in the *Lexicon*). For, in the first place, a pun or allusion based on the similarity in sound between אָדַם, 'red', and דָּם, 'blood', would be equally possible whether the two words were genetically connected or not. In the second place, for an ancient writer this similarity in sound, coupled with the fact that the colour of blood is red, would probably be sufficient evidence of an intimate relationship between the two words.

16 See Gesenius's *Handwörterbuch, s.vv.* לְעֵט and לְהֵט, and the *Lexicon, s.v.* לְעֵט (no connection is here established between לְעֵט and לְהֵט).

17 Three may be adduced. (1) Genesis xlvii. 19 f., 'Wherefore shall we die... both we and our land? buy us and our land for bread....And Joseph bought all the land of Egypt for Pharaoh; for the Egyptians sold (מָכְרוּ) every man his field, because the famine prevailed over them.' (2) Amos ii. 6, 'For three transgressions of Israel, and for four, I will not turn away the punishment thereof; because they sold (עַל מִכְרָם) the righteous for silver, and the poor for a pair of shoes.' (3) Joel iv. (iii.) 2 f., 'I will also gather all nations...and will plead with them for my people...whom they have scattered among the nations, and parted my land. And they have cast lots for my people; and have given a boy for an harlot, and sold (מָכְרוּ) a girl for wine, that they might drink.'

18 Cicero, *De Officiis* 3. 14. 58 f.

19 The last few words, 'and Esau despised his birthright', may indeed be a gloss added by someone who no longer understood or approved of the original point of the story, and who wished to indicate that Esau lost his birthright of his own will, that he did not mind. But it is by no means impossible that the words belong to the original form of the story. For one thing, even in the original form as I have tried to interpret it, the idea is present that Esau preferred his wild joys (though not lentil soup) to his birthright, which means a 'despising' of the latter. For another thing, 'to despise' might here be used in the sense of 'not to heed': Esau let himself be tricked out of, he was not careful about, his birthright.

20 I Samuel xxviii. 25.

21 See Genesis xxvii. 4, 7, 19, 25, 27, 31, 33.   22 Par. 37.

23 P. Huvelin, *Études sur le Furtum*, 1915, p. 304. Cp. H. F. Jolowicz, *Historical Introduction to Roman Law*, 1932, p. 171, and P. Jörs, *Römisches Privatrecht*, 2nd ed., by W. Kunkel, 1935, p. 253 f.

24 See, *e.g.*, C. v. Schwerin, *Die Formen der Haussuchung in indogermanischen Rechten, Rechtsgeschichtliche Studien*, I, 1924.

25 See pp. 89 ff.   26 See pp. 284 ff., 292 ff.

27 Genesis xxxi. 17 ff.   28 Genesis xliv.

29 Judges xviii. 13 ff.   30 Joshua vii.

31 See, *e.g.*, Code of Hammurabi 6, 8.

32 See pp. 205 f.; cp. Joseph's procedure, p. 235, and the history of the search at Rome, pp. 284 f.

33 Joshua viii. 16, Judges vi. 34 f., I Samuel xiv. 20. The Hiphil of the verb, הִזְעִיק, signifies 'to summon' to battle a military force in Judges iv. 10, 13, II Samuel xx. 4 f. See Gesenius's *Handwörterbuch* and the *Lexicon, s.v.* זָעַק. It would be beyond the scope of this study to compare the use of the root זָעַק with that of the allied root צָעַק, though the result might be interesting.

34 See Gesenius's *Handwörterbuch* and the *Lexicon*.

35 Genesis xxxi. 24, 29.   36 Genesis xxxi. 32.

37 See above, pp. 5 ff.   38 Genesis xxxi. 37.

39 Genesis xxxi. 30 ff.   40 See above, p. 94.

41 See pp. 235 ff.   42 See pp. 236 f.

43 'Thou shalt not suffer a witch to live.' The form of the verb here used is the causative, Piel, לֹא תְחַיֶּה. It is worth mentioning that by keeping the same consonants but pointing the verb as Kal, we should arrive at 'A witch shall not live', quite parallel to Jacob's 'he shall not live'.

20-2

44 Exodus xxii. 7 f., 10 (8 f., 11). Cp. also Leviticus v. 1 and Judges xvii. 2.
45 See pp. 224 ff.
46 See P. Huvelin, *op. cit.*, p. 162, n. 5.
47 See pp. 236 f.
48 There are traces of this notion in the ritual preceding a medieval execution, though the dress is Christian.
49 See p. 237.
50 II Samuel xii. 5. See above, p. 101 n. 30, and pp. 163 ff.
51 I Kings xx. 35 ff. See above, pp. 116 f.
52 Another example of the idea under discussion is Numbers v. 22. The woman accused by her husband of intercourse with another man is given a drink that will prove her guilty or innocent; and to the formula uttered by the priest she has to reply 'Amen, Amen'. Even cases affecting not one specified person but the people at large could be adduced. Deuteronomy xxvii. 15 ff. ordains that curses are to be pronounced against those committing certain crimes. The assembled community is to accept them with 'Amen'. It may be added that the idea survives throughout the Talmudic age. (I should perhaps remark that confessing a crime and self-damnation are not quite the same, though they may often be combined. Achan, according to Joshua vii. 19 ff., was induced to admit his offence, but there is no reference in this pericope to the notion, here discussed, of the accused man's pronouncing his own sentence.)
53 See p. 219.   **54** Genesis xxxi. 30.
55 Genesis xxxi. 36 f.   **56** Genesis xxxi. 37.
57 See pp. 237 ff.
58 See, *e.g.*, H. F. Jolowicz, *Historical Introduction to Roman Law*, 1932, p. 176, and P. Jörs, *Römisches Privatrecht*, 2nd ed., by W. Kunkel, 1935, p. 269.
59 It is from this age that the rule of *noxa caput sequitur* comes down into classical law; the rule, namely, that if before a 'noxal' action is brought the guilty child or slave passes into another family, it is the new *paterfamilias* against whom the action must be brought.
60 See H. F. Jolowicz, *loc. cit.*, and P. Jörs (W. Kunkel), *loc. cit.*
61 See pp. 191 ff.
62 See pp. 193 ff., the first part of this study.
63 See above, pp. 192 f.
64 Genesis xxxi. 33 ff.
65 She was also one of the greatest tragic figures of Biblical times: see Genesis xxxv. 16 ff. and Jeremiah xxxi. 14 (15). This combination is possible only in literature of the very highest rank.
66 See p. 236.
67 Cicero, *De Officiis* 1. 10. 33. See above, p. 190.
68 See above, pp. 206 ff.   **69** Genesis Rabba on xxxi. 32.
70 Genesis xxxv. 16 ff.   **71** See above, p. 200.
72 Genesis xxxi. 44 ff. Verse 52, for example, says: 'This heap be witness, and this pillar be witness, that I will not pass over this heap to thee, and that thou shalt not pass over this heap and this pillar unto me, for harm.'
73 See p. 210.   **74** Genesis xxxi. 32.
75 I am not implying that the Biblical story in its present form is untrue. I am here concerned only with the growth of the narrative as a literary phenomenon, not with the events behind it. My thesis therefore is not meant as an attack on orthodox Jewish teaching.
76 Genesis xxxi. 32.   **77** 1. 6. 30.

78 Cp., *e.g.*, *Digest* 33. 7. 15. 2, 50. 4. 18. 10, 34. 1. 15. 1.

79 See p. 220.   **80** See above, pp. 195 and 197.

81 15. 739 ff. This pun is indeed a good deal subtler than Scropha's, though also more indecent (but Aristophanes could not help it): χοῖρος, like the Latin *porcus*, may be used in the sense of *pudendum muliebre*.

82 *Institutes* 3. 183 ff. See, for a detailed discussion, pp. 259 ff.

83 He discusses the case of Scropha in *Études sur le Furtum*, 1915, pp. 300 ff.

84 3. 4. 736. See P. Huvelin, *op. cit.*, p. 162.

85 8. 263. See P. Huvelin, *op. cit.*, pp. 314 f.

86 Cp. the example given by P. Huvelin, *op. cit.*, p. 162, n. 5. G. Jachmann, however, makes it probable (in *Plautinisches und Attisches*, *Problemata*, III, 1931, pp. 203 ff.) that the whole section 3. 4. 721 ff. is invented by Plautus himself and not taken from his Greek source.

87 This point must not be pressed. In 5. 6. 1351, the offence is treated as merely *nec manifestum*. Agorastocles there says to the pander: *Duplum pro furto mi opus est* (twofold penalty only). The matter is irrelevant to my argument: the pimp is ruined and at the mercy of Agorastocles whether his theft is *manifestum* or *nec manifestum*.

88 3. 4. 723 ff.

89 The few lines where the witnesses seem to take an interest, 732–5, *i.e.* from *Cum auri ducentis* to *Scilicet*, are spurious according to Leo's edition, vol. II, 1896, p. 210. The question is not of essential importance for my argument.

90 3. 5. 761 ff.   **91** 1. 1. 165 ff.

92 5. 7. 1393 ff. According to Leo, *op. cit.*, p. 241, these lines belong to a spurious section of the play. This does not, however, affect my argument, which is that no far-reaching conclusions as to the state of law should be drawn from an exclamation 'I'll swear' or 'He'll swear' in a comedy.

93 3. 2. 591–3. 6. 800.   **94** 8. 262 ff.

95 *Op. cit.*, p. 314.

96 It seems to be the usual interpretation. See J. Conington and H. Nettleship, *The Works of Virgil*, III, 1871, p. 106: '*abiuratae* refers to a disclaimer of Cacus not mentioned, but easily understood, after Virgil's manner'. But neither Ovid, *Fasti* 1. 543 ff., nor Propertius 4. 9. 1 ff., who depend on Virgil, have an oath. Dionysius of Halicarnassus 1. 39. 3 mentions a denial (οὔτ' ἰδεῖν φάσκειν); but it is not an oath, it is introduced in the course of a major alteration of the plot designed to represent Hercules as discovering the bulls by intelligent scheming instead of by accident, and in any case it hardly counts for Roman law. Significantly, Livy 1. 7. 7, otherwise nearer to Dionysius than to Virgil, makes no reference to a denial.

97 8. 222 ff.

98 The only meaning listed by them is 'to deny any thing on oath'.

99 *Codex Theodosianus* 10. 8. 2, *Imp. Constantinus A. ad Priscum Rationalem.*

100 *Novellae Maioriani* 5 *pr.*, *Impp. Leo et Maiorianus AA. Ennodio Comiti Rerum Privatarum.*

101 *Codex Theodosianus* 10. 21. 3 = *Codex Justinianus* 11. 9. 4, *Imp. Theodosius A. Maximino Comiti Sacrarum Largitionum.*

102 It is true that, from the point of view of those who might complain, it is a wrongful withholding. But even so there is no reference to an oath.

103 How deep-rooted the prejudice is that *abiurare* must mean 'to abjure falsely' may be seen from the fact that the standard dictionary of Roman law, Heumann's *Handlexikon*, 9th ed., by E. Seckel, 1907, renders the word by *abschwören, ableugnen,* 'to forswear, to deny falsely', giving as reference the very text here explained, *Codex Justinianus* 11. 9. 4, and no other. But it is simply impossible for me to find an oath in this decree, not to mention a false one.

104 *Op. cit.,* pp. 300 ff.   **105** 2. 4. 1 f.

106 This view is taken by Lewis and Short. Curiously, they refer to *De Re Rustica* 2. 4. 1 in support, though, as will presently be seen, Varro mentions the derivation from swine-breeding only to have it refuted by the agronomist Scropha's account of the origin of his surname.

107 *Sed quis e portu...prodit ac de suillo pecore expedit? Tametsi Scropham potissimum de ea re dicere oportere cognomen eius significat. Cui Tremellius, Ignorare, inquit, videre cur appeller Scropha....Cognosce meam gentem suillum cognomen non habere, nec me esse ab Eumaeo ortum. Avus meus primum appellatus est Scropha*—there follows the story cited above in the text.

108 See pp. 195 ff.

109 In *Truculentus* 2. 2. 268, Truculentus, decided not to let his master be caught by a certain lady or himself by her maid, tells the latter: *iam hercle ego hic te, mulier, quasi sus catulos pedibus proteram.*

110 See J. Leveen, *The Hebrew Bible in Art,* The Schweich Lectures 1939, 1944, pp. 60 ff.

111 Genesis xliv. There exist many similar stories, some of them no doubt influenced by the Biblical tale; one of these latter seems to be Carducha's trick in *La Gitanilla* by Cervantes.

112 Genesis xliv. 4.

113 Genesis xlii. 6, xliii. 26, xliv. 14.

114 Genesis xliv. 14.

115 Genesis xliv. 9.   **116** See above, pp. 206 ff.

117 See, *e.g.,* Deuteronomy xix. 12, 'Then the elders of his city shall...deliver him (the murderer) into the hand of the avenger of blood, that he may die (ומת)'; Deuteronomy xxi. 21, 'And all the men of his city shall stone him (the rebellious son) with stones, that he die (ומת)'; Exodus x. 28, 'And Pharaoh said unto him (Moses), Get thee from me...see my face no more, for in that day thou seest my face, thou shalt die (תמות)'.

118 See above, pp. 209 f.   **119** Genesis xliv. 10.

120 Genesis xxiii.   **121** Genesis xliv. 16 f.

122 Genesis xxxvii. 18 ff. (see above, pp. 3 ff., especially pp. 8 ff.). In addition, Joseph himself had forced them to leave Simeon behind in Egypt on the occasion of their first visit: Genesis xlii. 18 ff.

123 Genesis xliii. 1 ff. See above, pp. 8 ff.

124 Genesis xlii. 14 ff.   **125** See above, pp. 206 f.

126 Against the theory, playing havoc with the sources, that this is a late development, see Daube, *Journal of Roman Studies,* XXXIII, 1943, p. 88.

127 See above, p. 94.

128 See Mishnah Baba Kamma vii, Mishnah Sanhedrin viii. 6, and Mekhiltha on Exodus xxi. 37 (xxii. 1) ff.

129 See Tab. VIII. 14.

130 The question of the relationship between civil and criminal liability is most complicated; probably it was constantly varying. See H. F. Jolowicz, *Digest XLVII.* 2, *De Furtis,* 1940, pp. xii ff.

131 See above, pp. 211.

132 See above pp. 1   **133** Genesis xliv. 17.

134 See Daube, *Theology*, xlvi, 1943, p. 108.

135 Cp. above, pp. 154 and 213.   **136** Genesis xliii. 32.

137 See, for example, Daube, *Essays Presented to J. H. Hertz*, 1942, pp. 126 f.

138 Genesis xliv. 16.   **139** See above, pp. 3 ff.

140 Genesis xxxvii. 21 f.   **141** See above, p. 111.

142 See above, pp. 191 f.   **143** Genesis xliv. 10.

144 See above, pp. 91 f. and 200.

145 Genesis xlii. 21.   **146** Genesis xliv. 16.

147 Genesis xliv. 15.

148 See the first of these studies, pp. 1 ff.

149 See pp. 203 ff.

150 I have referred above (pp. 6 and 206) to the interesting case of Mishnah Baba Kamma x. 3, laying down that he who discovers articles stolen from him with a third party not the thief may claim them back, if he pays the price which the other man swears that he paid for them.

151 P. Huvelin, *op. cit.*, p. 304, quoted above, p. 201.

152 Elaborate reasoning is to be found in P. Huvelin, *op. cit.*, *passim*. The opinion is shared by P. Jörs (W. Kunkel), *op. cit.*, p. 254. Mommsen, *Römisches Strafrecht*, 1899, p. 748, was the first to formulate it, but at p. 747 he inclines to a different explanation, probably nearer the truth: see below, p. 312 n. 165.

153 *E.g.* H. F. Jolowicz, *Historical Introduction to Roman Law*, 1932, p. 171; see, however, below, this page, n. 161.

154 For some remarks on De Visscher's view, see pp. 278 ff.

155 See above, pp. 213 ff.

156 For details, see the following note.

157 The only passage, as far as I can see, where reference is made to the connection between the name *actio furti concepti* and *concipere*, 'to seize the stolen article in the house of the defendant', is Paul, *Sententiae* 2. 31. 5 (= *Collatio* 7. 5. 6). In some texts where one would expect a similar reference, Gaius 3. 186, or *Sententiae* 2. 31. 3 (= *Collatio* 7. 5. 4), its absence strikes one as odd. But the connection was probably so firmly established that it was not necessary to stress it. In any case, *concipere* is employed in the discussion of *furtum conceptum* as denoting 'to seize the stolen article in the house of the defendant' in most relevant texts, Gaius 3. 187, *Sententiae* 2. 31. 5 (= *Collatio* 7. 5. 6), and Gellius, *Noctes Atticae* 11. 18. 9. It is the use of the verb in the latter passage which seems to me to justify the view that the traditional explanation of *furtum conceptum* goes back to the late Republic or early Principate. Gellius has much of his material on *furtum conceptum* from Sabinus's *De Furtis* (see *Noctes Atticae* 11. 18. 12), and Sabinus himself draws freely on his precursors.

158 On the portion of this sentence that I am here omitting, see p. 299.

159 The same seems to be true of the *Epitome* of Gaius: see pp. 303 f.

160 *Études de Droit Romain*, 1931, pp. 215 ff. (= *Tijdschrift Voor Rechtsgeschiedenis*, vi, 1925, pp. 249 ff.).

161 H. F. Jolowicz, *Digest XLVII*. 2, *De Furtis*, 1940, p. lxxvii; cp. this page, n. 153.

162 See this page, n. 152.   **163** See p. 202.

164 De Visscher, *loc. cit.*, also attaches fundamental importance to the distinction between the case of *vestigii minatio*, immediate pursuit, and the case of search after some time has elapsed. He does not succeed, however, in working out his idea in a way agreeing with the sources. On a probable time-limit in Hebrew *vestigii minatio*, see above, pp. 204 ff., 235.

165 The distinction between the case where the owner of the house is treated as the actual thief and that where he is treated as having only received the object in question is stressed by E. Rabel, *Zeitschrift der Savigny-Stiftung für Rechtsgeschichte, Romanistische Abteilung*, LII, 1932, p. 480, and H. F. Jolowicz, *Digest XLVII*. 2, *De Furtis*, 1940, pp. lxxviii f. Indeed, already Mommsen, in one passage of his *Römisches Strafrecht*, 1899, says (p. 747) that the XII Tables made a separate delict of receiving stolen things, namely, the delict of *furtum conceptum*, of stolen things found in the house of the receiver. None of these authorities, however, succeeds in so working out the idea that it fits the sources.

166 *E.g.* H. F. Jolowicz, *Digest XLVII*. 2, *De Furtis*, 1940, p. lxxvi.

167 See O. Temkin, *Kyklos*, III, 1930, pp. 90 ff., on medical style, and now Daube, *Proceedings of the Oxford Society of Historical Theology*, 1944–5, pp. 39 ff., on legislation (the conclusions advanced in this paper were reached too late to be used for the present book).

168 The terms 'sister-in-law' and the like reflect a comparable situation.

169 It recurs in Gellius: see p. 301.

170 There is one exception. Gaius in 3. 188 says, *Est etiam prohibiti furti actio adversus eum qui furtum quaerere volentem prohibuerit*. Justinian inserts the words *testibus praesentibus* between *quaerere* and *volentem*. The most probable reason for this is that Justinian finds it necessary again to remind his readers that the *quaestio* was still of some special significance in those classical times and that, if it was to lead to *furtum conceptum* or *furtum prohibitum*, it had to be conducted in the presence of witnesses. By his time, the *quaestio* had gone: see pp. 274 ff., 299 and 303 ff.

171 The argument is far from conclusive. Two points may be mentioned showing how careful we have to be. First, in Gaius's account of *furtum conceptum* and *furtum oblatum*, in 3. 186 f., the term *res furtiva* is used: yet this section is evidently old, at least as old as the one dealing with *furtum prohibitum*, 3. 188, with the term *furtum* for the 'stolen article'. (It is true that the portions of 3. 186 f. using *res furtiva* do not seem to be taken from a statute or the edict, whereas the definition using *furtum* in 3. 188 may well be based on the edict.) Secondly, in Paul, *Sententiae* 2. 31. 3 (= *Collatio* 7. 5. 4), we find *furtum* used in the definition of *furtum conceptum* and *res furtiva* in that of *furtum oblatum*: yet the two definitions certainly go back to the same source.

172 See above, pp. 274 f.

173 Note the rather skilful abbreviation of the account to be found in Gaius 3. 183. Justinian does not mention the earlier view and, consequently, also omits the names of the authors of the two views. He further omits the phrase *quod sane verius videtur*, by which Gaius expresses his preference for the later view. On the other hand, he ought to have known better than borrow a classification that, for him, was no longer true: for him, both *furtum conceptum* and *furtum oblatum* required *dolus* and were proper cases of theft.

174 See pp. 272 and 274 f., and this page, n. 173.

175 This quotation seems to be in greater part from the *Sententiae*, not from Gaius. The only word coming from Gaius is *autem* (and even this does not occur in all manuscripts of the *Epitome*).

176 *Lance et licio dicebatur apud antiquos, quia qui furtum ibat quaerere in domo aliena licio cinctus intrabat. . . .*

177 See the next paragraph.   **178** See p. 288.

179 See Lenel, *Palingenesia Iuris Civilis*, II, 1889, p. 678, n. 2.

180 See p. 296.

181 But he (or is it again his source?) got fond of the idea. He applied it to a senatusconsult that gave effect to a legacy of a usufruct over perishables. See *Digest* 7. 5. 2. 1, from his commentary on the provincial edict: *Quo senatus consulto non id effectum est ut pecuniae usus fructus proprie esset (nec enim naturalis ratio auctoritate senatus commutari potuit), sed remedio introducto coepit quasi usus fructus haberi.* It is no doubt from here that the view came into Justinian's *Institutes* 2. 4. 2: *Ergo senatus non fecit quidem earum rerum usum fructum (nec enim poterat), sed per cautionem quasi usum fructum constituit.*

182 *Statim autem ab initio pluris quam simpli actio est velut furti manifesti quadrupli, nec manifesti dupli, concepti et oblati tripli.* Here as in 3. 183 one is struck by the absence of *furtum prohibitum*; though here, in contradistinction to 3. 183, there is no need to refer to it, since Gaius is giving illustrations of a certain category of actions only, not a classification that ought to be complete.

183 *Furti concepti, item oblati, tripli poena est.* Again, there is entire agreement with Gaius.

184 *Furti concepti actio adversus eum qui obtulit tripli est poena, et ipsius rei repetitio.* Whether or not the words *et ipsius rei repetitio* come from the hand of Paul, I think they are correct for all stages of Roman law.

185 Most differences between the two texts are merely formal. There is only one that seems material, *est inventum* in *Collatio* instead of *quaesitum et inventum est* in *Sententiae*. This will be commented upon in the text.

186 See above, pp. 260 ff.

187 It might perhaps be argued that we must not take the text so literally and that the word *alterum* is without any significance. But there is a point strongly speaking in favour of attaching real importance to this word. As I observed above (pp. 275 f.), Justinian also seems to interpret *furtum conceptum* as signifying just that case where the object is found in the house of a man who is not the actual thief, but has committed only a *suscipere et celare*.

188 See p. 300.

I. INDEX OF TEXTS

OLD TESTAMENT

References in brackets are to the A.V. where its numbering differs
from that of the Hebrew text.

322 *Index of Texts*

ROMAN LITERARY SOURCES

LATER SOURCES

II. INDEX OF TERMS DISCUSSED

3 5282 00022 1039